D1593084

The
Democratic
Left
in Exile

Charles D. Ameringer

THE
DEMOCRATIC
LEFT
IN EXILE

*The Antidictatorial Struggle
in the Caribbean,
1945-1959*

University of Miami Press
CORAL GABLES, FLORIDA

Designed by Bernard Lipsky

Manufactured in the United States of America

Library of Congress Cataloging in Publication Data

Ameringer, Charles D   1926-
    The democratic left in exile.

    Bibliography: p.
    1. Caribbean area—Politics and government.
I. Title.
F2183.A43   320.9'729'05   73-77477
ISBN 0-87024-238-5

For Jean

Contents

Maps

Maps by Cynthia D. Thaxton

Acknowledgments

I am indebted to The Pennsylvania State University for assisting me financially in this project through the Liberal Arts Research Office and the Latin American Development Studies group (LADS), with a grant from the Ford Foundation.

I wish also to thank Ricardo Montilla, Raúl Nass, and Enrique Tejera París of Venezuela and Benjamín Núñez of Costa Rica for providing me with useful information, for arranging interviews, and for making it possible to gain access to documents and private archives.

Lastly, as every author knows, there are those without whose help and understanding the work would not get done. My coauthors are my wife, Jean, my sons, Carl and Bill, and a little cocker spaniel, Buff, who didn't quite make it.

CHARLES D. AMERINGER

State College, Pennsylvania

The
Democratic
Left
in Exile

Introduction

THIS IS the story of the Democratic Left in exile and of its struggle between 1945 and 1959 to bring democratic government, economic progress, and social justice to the nations of the Caribbean. Comprised of a number of political groups and parties from various countries, the movement was democratic because it embraced the ideals that all men should enjoy equal rights and receive equal treatment and that governments should be representative of the people under a system of free elections; it belonged to the Left because it sought far-reaching economic and social change, including national planning for economic diversification and industrialization, a more equitable distribution of national wealth, the liberation of the economy from foreign control, a program of agrarian reform, and improved housing, education, and health. The Democratic Left desired, in essence, to overthrow repressive dictatorships and to inaugurate democratic regimes which would secure general economic well-being and social justice.

Located primarily in the Spanish-speaking Caribbean, a number of political parties shared these aspirations. The leading parties were the Democratic Action party, AD (Acción Democrática), of Venezuela; the Cuban Revolutionary party, PRC (Partido Revolucionario Cubano), commonly known as the Auténtico party (party of the Authentic Revolution); the National Liberation party, PLN (Partido Liberación Nacional), of Costa Rica; and the Dominican Revolutionary party, PRD (Partido Revolucionario Dominicano). Not as well developed ideologically and structurally but significantly involved in the movement were the Liberal party (Partido Liberal) of Honduras, the Revolutionary party (Partido Revolucionario) of Guatemala, and the Nicaraguan Revolution-

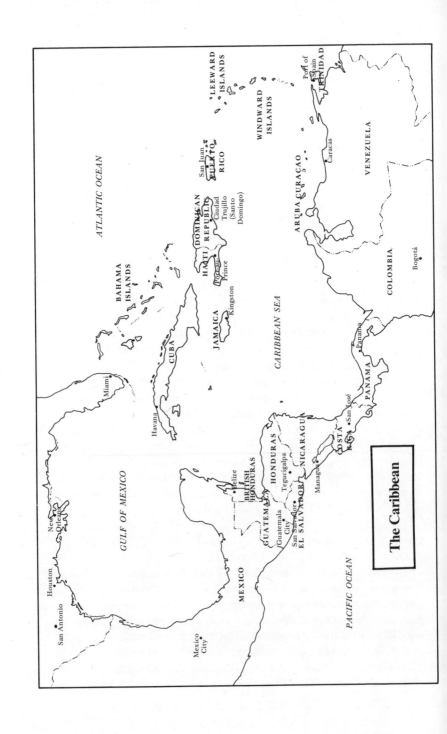

The Caribbean

ary Movement (Movimiento Revolucionario Nicaragüense). The latter was organized in exile in 1959 as a coalition of two traditional Nicaraguan groups, the Conservative party (Partido Conservador) and the Independent Liberal party (Partido Liberal Independiente). Finally, the Popular Democratic party, PPD (Partido Popular Democrático), of Puerto Rico served as a staunch friend and advocate of the parties of the Democratic Left. These parties, either in power or in exile, helped one another to survive and collaborated to overcome the dictatorial regimes of the Caribbean.

The dictators, of course, were not easily deposed. Despite the powerful indictment of World War II against totalitarianism, dictatorial rule prevailed in the Caribbean. Governments of force resisted popular rule and expected their peoples to play a passive role in the development of the economy. These governments maintained a monopoly of military power and made a mockery of the democratic process, rigging elections and silencing political opposition or driving it into exile. In the few cases where the Democratic Left achieved power, particularly in the immediate postwar period, its inability to fulfill overly ambitious promises and its inexperience rendered it vulnerable to counterrevolution. The Democratic Left, therefore, spent much of the time in exile, where it provided opposition to the dictatorships and kept alive the dream of democratic revolution.

The Democratic Left perfected the techniques of politics in exile. Action was taken on every possible front. The more adventurous and desperate elements attempted armed invasions of their captive homelands; these attempts were usually unsuccessful and counterproductive. The better organized groups undertook to arouse international public opinion in order to keep the dictators off-balance, deny legitimacy to their regimes, and force them to make concessions. In order to maintain a constant pressure upon the dictators and to stir the international community to action, the Democratic Left collaborated with various organizations and groups to promote human rights, freedom of the press, and the organization of labor. With the cooperation of friendly governments, it often goaded into action the Organization of American States, the United Nations, or one of their specialized agencies. Some of the parties of the Democratic Left in exile also maintained underground resistance movements at home, which required the establishment of effective communications between the two groups in order to coordinate activities and to render mutual assistance. The struggle of the Democratic Left assumed heroic proportions, even though the in-conveniences endured by its leaders were frequently humiliating.

Life in exile was difficult, both corporately and individually. It was essential to find a place of refuge where continued political activity would be tolerated, yet it was also necessary to act carefully so as not to compromise an ally or to embarrass a sympathetic host. Unless the host government was itself involved in the movement, exile leaders were subject to deportation or, in the case of the United States, to fine and imprisonment for conspiratorial activity. In all situations, moreover, the question of finances was urgent. The political organizations needed money to carry out their operations, and their partisans needed to find some means of livelihood to care for themselves and their families. In addition, no haven was fully safe. The Democratic Left in exile was harassed by agents of the dictators, who tried by one means or another to destroy its organization. Although the Democratic Left generally refused to cooperate with Communist groups, local situations and expe-diency sometimes resulted in strange coalitions and alliances. It was revealed much later that even the U.S. Central Intelligence Agency had channeled funds indirectly to support some of the activities of the Democratic Left. Despite the hazards, hardships, and misunderstand-ings, the Democratic Left persevered and came to be an integral part of the political dynamics of the Caribbean, its multifaceted struggle con-tributing to the decline of the dictatorships.

The Democratic Left had not won final victory, however, before a new crisis arose. By 1959, as some of its parties achieved power and prepared to assist their comrades against the remaining dictatorial regimes, the emergence of Fidel Castro presented a new challenge. For fifteen years the Democratic Left had worked to undermine the Carib-bean's dictators, but suddenly there was no certainty that its ideals would prevail once the tyrants fell. Because of the course of the Cuban Revolution, the United States became concerned about "unrest in the Caribbean." The Democratic Left abandoned its former intrigue and filibustering, because, in the words of one of its leaders, such methods were "too dangerous and too misunderstood."[1] This did not mean a reprieve for the dictators of the Caribbean, but it did require new tactics and restraint on the part of the Democratic Left. In entering upon a new phase, the trials of the past became significant; as a result of those experiences the movement had matured. Such parties as Acción Democrática of Venezuela and Liberación Nacional of Costa

Rica had learned much about the essence of power and had become more pragmatic, tolerant, and adaptive. The future of the Democratic Left was uncertain in 1959; but, standing between the extremes of military dictatorship and Castroism, it was a movement with deep historical roots and one which had already proven its resolve under the severest tests.

The study of the Democratic Left between the end of World War II and Castro's take-over in Cuba provides an excellent means for tracing the general development of Caribbean political affairs. It must be borne in mind, however, that the movement was made up of a number of political parties, each representing a specific national situation. There was no supreme high command. The leaders frequently lamented that the dictators and the Communists were organized internationally but that there was no "Democratic International." Therefore, while common historical roots, similarity of purpose, and cooperative action provided the unity of the Democratic Left, its story is incomplete without reference to the activities of the individual parties and to specific episodes. Only by examining the uniqueness of the members, can one understand the nature of the whole.

Rapidly changing conditions in Latin America, touched off by World War I and continuing through the next two decades, produced the parties of the Democratic Left. "World War I," observed a University of New Mexico study, "marked the beginning of the end of the old system under which Latin America's well-established economic and social organization was firmly tied to a stable Old World order."[2] The war stimulated in Latin America a process of industrialization and urbanization that profoundly affected its social structure. Cut off during the war years from its traditional sources of manufactured goods, Latin America built factories and sought economic independence. This promoted the growth of the middle and working classes, which increasingly challenged the primacy and values of the landowning oligarchy.[3] The emerging groups also acclaimed the triumph of nationalism in Europe and took note of the social changes there in the postwar period.

Contemporaneously, the Mexican and Russian revolutions provided additional examples of the breakdown of traditional authority. Latin American intellectuals idealized the nationalistic aspects of the Mexican Revolution and were inspired by its attacks upon the church, the landed aristocracy, and foreign economic interests. The Russian Revolu-

tion reinforced these antifeudal, anti-imperialist attitudes and helped
stimulate and support the establishment of Communist parties in Latin
America. Before discovering an "American revolutionary doctrine,"
many leaders of the Democratic Left turned to communism, because
the "Bolshevik message" seemed to provide answers for those disgusted
with the prevailing political, economic, and social orders of Latin America.[4] One of these wrote: ". . . some were affected more, others less,
but almost none was immune to the contagion of the moment—we
looked intently in the direction of the Kremlin, almost as if we expected to see a new Star of Bethlehem shining above its high walls."[5]
Many of those young men were able to explore Marxist and other
doctrines, as one of the first institutions to be affected by the changing
times was the Latin American university.

Students of the University of Córdoba, Argentina, initiated the
movement known as the University Reform in 1918. Seemingly, it was
an effort to modernize university administration and curriculum and to
give students a voice in university affairs. In reality, it sought to convert
the university from an institution of privilege and orthodoxy into a
sanctuary for free inquiry and a vehicle for social action. The tasks of
the new university were to diagnose society's ills and to prescribe reme-
dies and administer the dosage. The movement spread to other universities in other countries, and soon students were trying to transform the
ideas of their mentors, such as José Ingenieros and Manuel González
Prada, into practice. Some of the earliest skirmishes occurred in Peru,
where students of the University of San Marcos and young intellectuals
went into the streets to battle strongman Augusto B. Leguía. Among
the leaders was Víctor Raúl Haya de la Torre, who tried to unite the
student reformers with the new urban proletariat; but the dictator prevailed. Haya was exiled in 1923 and went to Mexico, where the following year he founded the American Popular Revolutionary Alliance,
APRA (Alianza Popular Revolucionaria Americana).

The APRA movement of Haya de la Torre was the precursor of the
parties of the Democratic Left. These parties owe a great deal to Haya
intellectually and have sometimes been classified as *Aprista* (from
APRA) parties. Haya was himself influenced by European ideologies,
but his ideal was an authentically American revolutionary doctrine that
would reflect the ethos and conditions of Latin America. In 1924 he
witnessed an important phase of the Mexican Revolution as the private
secretary of Minister of Education José Vasconcelos, who was one of

the outstanding philosophers of the movement and the patron of mural-
ists José Clemente Orozco and Diego Rivera. Haya also made the pil-
grimage to Moscow but was disappointed at the "abysmal ignorance" of
Soviet leaders concerning Latin America.[6] He considered Latin America's colonial-style economy as basic to its ills and proposed the "anti-
imperialist state"—a completely planned economy designed to thwart
imperialism and overcome the "collaborationist" landed aristocracy.
Under a comprehensive national plan, the state would be responsible
for the development and regulation of the economy. The program included land reform, popular education, public works, and a full list of
social services. This program, Haya affirmed, was not inspired by Marx
but by the "welfare state" of the ancient Incas.[7]

Referring to his program as "Indo-Americanism," for the regenera-
tion of the Indian was its critical aspect, Haya pointed out other dis-
tinctions from Marxism. It was not as "exclusive," since it was a multi-
class movement (*policlasista*) which embraced all classes that had a
stake in the elimination of the imperialists and oligarchs, namely, the
proletariat, the peasants, and the petty bourgeoisie. At the same time, a
substantial portion of the private sector of the economy was unaf-
fected; only certain key industries were to be state-owned. Furthermore, foreign capital, properly "conditioned" and subordinate to the
national plan, was still welcome. It was simply a question of who was
the master. Haya affirmed his faith in political democracy, with the full
enjoyment of civil liberties and human rights, and rejected violence as a
political tactic. He believed that APRA could achieve power in a free
election—if the people were educated and if APRA were able to present
its program.[8] Finally, he advocated the political, economic, and cultural integration of Latin America in order to promote progress and as a
defense against imperialism. While Haya de la Torre plotted the trajectory of the Latin American revolution, new student generations in
Venezuela and Cuba began the slow process of establishing the first
parties of the Democratic Left of the Caribbean.

1 | *The Caribbean Cockpit*

The Rise of the Caribbean's Democratic Left

IN VENEZUELA the development of the Democratic Action party, AD (Acción Democrática), originated with the activities of the Generation of '28 (1928). Venezuela in the late 1920s seemed ill-suited for producing apt political leadership, since it was under the rule of one of Latin America's most absolute dictators, Juan Vicente Gómez. The "tyrant of the Andes" had seized power in 1908, when many of the Generation of 1928, such as Rómulo Betancourt, were born. By the time they were students at the Central University in Caracas, they had yet to witness a free election or hear a countryman speak freely about political matters. The Gómez regime was narrow and corrupt and maintained itself in high style from its share of the oil production, which was mainly in the hands of foreign concessionaires. The masses were impoverished and inert. With grim humor, the Generation of '28 mocked the dictator's slogan, "Union, Peace, and Work," with "Union in the jails, Peace in the cemetery, and Work with the road gangs."[1] Nonetheless, within the university, through teachers such as novelist Rómulo Gallegos, they examined the current revolutionary doctrines and concluded that the attacks upon feudalism and imperialism were particularly applicable to conditions in Venezuela.

The events which gave identity to the Generation of '28 began innocently. Raúl Leoni, president of the Venezuelan Students' Federation, FEV (Federación de Estudiantes de Venezuela), had arranged with authorities to set aside 6-12 February 1928 as Students' Week. The activities included oratory, poetry reading, and other forms of cultural and creative expression. But the students of the Central University decided to use the opportunity to show their disapproval of the Gómez regime. Jóvito Villalba, a young law student, inaugurated the week's program with an emotional speech at the National Pantheon. Before the sarcophagus of Bolívar, he appealed to the Liberator to rally the university, because it was the refuge of the fatherland and it alone would heed his call to arms.[2]   In the evening of the sixth, the students selected their queen in ceremonies at the Teatro Municipal, and Pío Tamayo dedicated a poem to her, which, in fact, was a bitter denunciation of the regime. Two days later, Rómulo Betancourt spoke in the Cine Rívoli and lamented that the Venezuelan people were "forsaken by God and tormented by unfulfilled ideals." Less artistically, but no less expressively, Guillermo Prince Lara destroyed a commemorative stone bearing the name of the tyrant.[3]

The governor of the Federal District summoned Leoni to warn him that he would be accountable for further actions and statements, but already Students' Week had merged with the pre-Lenten carnival. The youthful laughter, merriment, and tomfoolery all seemed to ridicule the regime. The distraught government hesitated a moment; then on 14 February, just before Ash Wednesday, it arrested Betancourt, Villalba, Prince Lara, and Tamayo on charges of subversion. Betancourt was still in jail a week later, when he celebrated his twentieth birthday. In the meantime, the university students protested the detention of their comrades. They demonstrated and petitioned and sent delegations to speak to public officials. Finally, 210 students appeared before the Caracas police barracks and, "in a show of protest and solidarity," demanded that they, too, be arrested. The dictatorship obliged, but the public reaction was "spontaneous." In Caracas, Valencia, Maracaibo, and other cities strikes were staged in sympathy with the students. When more students came to demand imprisonment, the regime suddenly gave in and in early March released all but a few of the demonstrators. Pío Tamayo was kept in prison, because, the government affirmed, "he was not a student but a Communist."[4]   The Generation of '28 had not intended to start a revolutionary movement, but the events of February had gained momentum, and Gómez had seemed to falter.

Some of the more serious rivals of the old dictator, now a septuagenarian, sensed that the time might be ripe for overthrowing him. General Ramón Delgado Chalbaud and other exiles living in Paris sent a representative to Caracas, who contacted a number of young, dissident army officers. A conspiracy developed, first within the army, and then among certain civilian sectors, including employees of the Ministry of Development and leaders of the Venezuelan Students' Federation. On 7 April 1928 an armed uprising took place, but, although the rebels seized the presidential palace (Gómez was absent from Caracas in Maracay), the dictatorship rallied sufficient forces to crush it. Gómez showed that he was still in command, and he took steps to eliminate all forms of opposition. The action of the Generation of '28 could no longer be dismissed as youthful exuberance. Those student leaders who could do so fled the country.[5] For almost eight years—Gómez ruled without interruption until his death in December 1935—Betancourt, Leoni, Valmore Rodríguez, Ricardo Montilla, Gonzalo Barrios, Juan José Palacios, and other future leaders of the Venezuelan nation were forced to live in exile.

In exile, the Generation of '28 saw the need to find a strategy and a framework for what had been a rather vague set of ideals and list of grievances. Some of the *veintiocheros* (Generation of '28) organized filibustering expeditions, but failure had a sobering effect and they soon realized that armed action and protests were not enough. The struggle was not against Gómez alone, Ricardo Montilla observed, but against the system and the conditions which permitted Gómez to exist.[6] A number of the exiles settled in Barranquilla, Colombia, but others were scattered elsewhere. They all entered into "a continuing dialogue" by discussion and letter "in search of an ideology."[7] Their quest, from the start, involved the idea of a program "adapted to the needs of Venezuela," and for this reason "they devoted much of their time to the study of the history of Venezuela and to the examination of the political, economic, social, racial, and cultural problems which confronted their people."[8] In March 1931 they synthesized many of their ideas into the so-called Plan of Barranquilla and organized the Leftist Revolutionary Group, ARDI (Agrupación Revolucionaria de Izquierda), which was the embryonic organization of Acción Democrática (AD) founded a decade later.[9]

The plan had Marxist overtones—for Betancourt at the time was involved in the organization of the Communist party of Costa Rica—but its outlook was specifically Venezuelan. Despite its attack upon the penetration by foreign capital, which, it declared, "had deformed the Venezuelan economy and was exercising a powerful influence over its social and political organization,"[10] it did not advocate the nationalization of petroleum resources but only "the revision of the petroleum contracts granted by the dictatorship."[11] The plan also pledged to eradicate latifundia, graft and corruption, and illiteracy; to establish direct, universal, and secret suffrage for presidential, congressional, and other elections; and to replace the "army of the dictator" with "an apolitical depersonalized institution for the defense of the Constitution, the existing laws, and the national sovereignty."[12]

The association with the Communists, particularly on the part of Betancourt, was a source of future embarrassment, but, as in the case of Haya de la Torre and others of the Democratic Left, it was part of a process of study and experimentation. It subsequently gave way to the sentiments of democracy and nationalism. Betancourt explained that his Communist experience stemmed from "desperation" over the failure to overthrow Gómez as well as from "ignorance of the socioeconomic realities of the [Latin] American people, [which] . . . provided fertile terrain for the messianic hope of a revolution 'a la rusa.' "[13] But Betancourt did not make his confession "with a contrite heart." He asserted that the general effect had been beneficial, for "it began the active incorporation of our peoples into the social struggle."[14] He added that of those who became Communists in this era, some remained naïve, some entered the "enemy trenches," and some, "because of mental sterility or political cowardice," continued in blind obedience to the Communist line. Others, he stated, "remained faithful to their earlier convictions and . . . continued the painstaking search for an American revolutionary doctrine, but always sentimentally bound to those who had helped to set the course of the maiden voyage."[15]

Before he returned to Venezuela in 1936, Betancourt had broken with the Communists. On numerous occasions he reiterated his position and, at the same time, revealed his political orientation: "I reject the Communist party with all the force of my intransigent Venezuelan nationality, because its dependence upon Moscow converts it into a mere bureaucratic appendage of the Soviet state."[16] He also said that "the experience of Costa Rica, much study, and serious thought led me to the conviction that neither the communist thesis nor the Communist party were appropriate for reaching my revolutionary goals: the achievement of national liberation, of effective political democracy, and of social justice for my Venezuelan homeland."[17] Raúl Roa (the future foreign minister of Cuba under Fidel Castro) described Betancourt's "rupture" with Marxism as "violent." The "principal cause,"

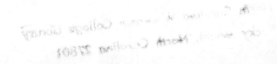

Roa related, "was Betancourt's repudiation of the stereotyped formulas of the Third International and the autocratic dictates of the Caribbean Bureau."[18] By the end of the first exile, Betancourt and his comrades of the Generation of '28 had evolved the broad outlines of a revolutionary nationalism, democratic in character, anti-imperialist, and *policlasista*. But the achievement of a national political organization was still distant.

Despite the death of Gómez, his political heirs remained in control of the government, whose repressive apparatus continued intact. A few notorious *gomecistas* were victims of reprisals, while others fled the country or were stripped of their illicit fortunes, but essentially the presidential succession was achieved smoothly. The successor of Gómez, General Eleazar López Contreras, proved more moderate than the old dictator but no less intolerant toward political opposition. "López Contreras had a strategy all his own of alternately tightening and relaxing the noose," one writer observed. "If he arrested a man, he immediately offered him every legal recourse. If he set him free, he imposed a number of restrictive conditions."[19] Under the circumstances, the government of López Contreras regained the initiative before any serious challenge to its authority developed.

The anti-*gomecista* forces had little more than the year 1936 to effect a political organization. This was too short a time, particularly in view of the ideological differences among the opposition groups. Certain of them thought in terms of political liberalism and limited their goals to the restoration of constitutional guarantees, such as the protection of life, the right to vote, the right of petition, and freedom of assembly. The Generation of '28, returning from exile, went farther and wished to mobilize the masses and raise economic and social issues, including the creation of a labor code and the recognition of the right to strike.[20] A small Communist party appeared, the Progressive Republican party, PRP (Partido Republicano Progresista), which also stressed economic demands and showed a desire to join other groups in "the united struggle against absolutism."[21] In March 1936 an attempt was made to organize an antidictatorial front through the Movement of Venezuelan Organization, ORVE (Movimiento de Organización Venezolana), which, in the words of one founder, Mariano Picón Salas, was designed "to look for what unites us and to avoid what divides us" and was dedicated to the preparation of position papers concerning Venezuelan problems.[22] Although claiming to be nonpartisan, ORVE was, in fact, another step toward the formation of Acción Democrática, since it was dominated by Betancourt, Leoni, Barrios, Carlos D'Ascoli, Andrés Eloy Blanco, and other future leaders of AD. During the next few months, political coalitions proliferated, usually involving ORVE, the Communists, middle-class liberals, the students' federation, and trade union (oil workers') organizations. They demanded electoral reform, presidential and congressional elections, and the revocation of the repressive Law of Public Order. When these petitions were ignored, the opposition groups called a twenty-four hour general strike for 9 June in Caracas. The strike succeeded initially but lost its momentum when the leaders tried to prolong it and extend it to other cities.[23]

In July, however, ORVE began to issue its position papers. These papers revealed much about the future course of the Venezuelan Democratic Left, particularly with reference to the critical issue of petroleum exploitation. Concerning this matter, ORVE criticized strongly the existing contractual relationship between the Venezuelan government and the foreign oil companies. It demanded higher fees for the granting of concessions for exploration and exploitation and a larger share of the profits from oil production. It advocated, moreover, higher wages for petroleum workers, increased benefits (including a number of social services), and the extension of collective bargaining and the right to strike.[24] These demands were more pragmatic than doctrinaire and foretold the future position of Acción Democrática with reference to the conservation of petroleum resources, the placement of more Venezuelans in technical and managerial positions, the establishment of refining facilities, and a virtual alliance with the oil workers' unions. In fact, ORVE had already attracted to its ranks future trade union officials Augusto Malavé Villalba and P. B. Pérez Salinas.

This orientation alarmed the López Contreras regime. The government grew increasingly reactionary and began to assert that the opposition was Communist-inspired. In October 1936, ORVE, along with the Communist PRP and other groups, formed the National Democratic party, PDN (Partido Democrático Nacional).[25] The government refused to register it as a legal party on the grounds that it was Communistic. In mid-December, the workers in the western oil fields went on strike demanding better wages and improved working conditions, but López Contreras personally intervened to end the strike and charged that it had been started by political agitators and Communists. Simultaneously, Venezuela held elections for municipal and state legislative bodies. These elections were important, since the resultant assemblies elected the deputies and senators who sat in the National Congress, which in turn elected the president. The government attempted to smear the opposition by publishing a *Red Book* of alleged Communistic activity. The *Red Book* was based upon uncorroborated material taken from dossiers of the *gomecista* secret police and included sinister-appearing "mug" photographs, excerpts from the Plan of Barranquilla, and letters exchanged by the Generation of '28 in exile, which in many cases were doctored or were plain forgeries.[26] Despite this action and serious limitations upon the suffrage, several opposition candidates were elected, including Leoni, Barrios, Eloy Blanco, Gallegos, Jóvito Villalba, and Luis B. Prieto.

This proved to be the last straw for López Contreras. A number of opposition leaders were arrested, ORVE and other groups associated with the attempt to organize the National Democratic party (PDN) were ordered to stop all political activity, and the elections of Leoni and Barrios, among others, were voided. A month later, López Contreras decreed the expulsion of forty-seven politicians "for a term of one year for being affiliated with communist doctrine and for being considered prejudicial to public order."[27] The list included a few Communists, Gustavo Machado, Rodolfo Quintero, and Juan Bautista Fuenmayor, but most were of the non-Communist Left, including Betancourt, Leoni, Barrios, D'Ascoli, Montilla, Villalba, and Valmore Rodríguez. Betancourt, however, managed to avoid arrest, and, while his comrades were sent into exile, he went underground and organized the PDN as a clandestine party.

For almost three years Betancourt remained a fugitive, becoming in that time something of a legendary figure. The fact that he escaped the police for so long stemmed more from moderation on the part of López Contreras than from inefficiency, but the prestige of Betancourt grew. Although he traveled about the country, visiting with workers, peasants, and students and organizing clandestine cells, he spent much of his time thinking and writing.[28] Between June 1937 and October 1939, Betancourt wrote articles which appeared almost daily in the Caracas newspaper *Ahora*. When the police finally captured him and sent him into exile in 1940, he reprinted the articles in Chile—almost six hundred of them—in a single volume entitled *Problemas Venezolanos*. By then, the political creed of Venezuela's Democratic Left was almost complete.

The essential doctrine was nationalistic and revolutionary, fit to the realities of Venezuela. Betancourt wrote: "I am and I shall always be in the trenches of the people. I fight and I shall always fight in the forward ranks of the Left. However, I shall continue to advocate for Venezuela the solution of national problems in accordance with the structure of the country and the existing historical epoch. These solutions are as distinct from the mediocre panaceas of liberalism, already inoperative and exhausted, as they are from the Soviet formulas."[29] The political orientation remained democratic and *policlasista.* No one man alone could achieve the transformation of Venezuela, affirmed Betancourt. "It requires the unanimous effort of the people, led in the historic undertaking by a disciplined party organization." An organization, he added, which included "all the popular classes of the nation" and which was "doctrinaire, internally democratic, and anti-imperialist." [30]

In the economic and social fields, which constitute the bulk of Betancourt's writings, the approach was still pragmatic. It contained a firm commitment to agrarian reform, but "upon the most just and humane bases." The *latifundio* was to be liquidated, for it was unjust and unproductive, but the landowner was "not to be violently dispossessed of his lands." The agrarian reform would be carried out "under appropriate legal standards and in accordance with the national Constitution." Betancourt advocated also the clearing and colonization of new lands, with assistance from the state through cheap credit, secure markets, and technical direction.[31] Concerning petroleum, Betancourt reiterated the anti-imperialist position and the need "to progressively break the bonds which tie and subordinate us, as a nation and as a state, to international high finance," but he avoided any reference to nationalization.[32] It was clear that Betancourt, while seeking a greater share of the profits and complete control over the nature and rate of exploitation, recognized an existing need for foreign capital, technical know-how, and marketing facilities for Venezuelan oil production. Petroleum was the key to the development and diversification of the rest of the Venezuelan economy and would finance an ambitious social program. Finally, the gains would be protected by a powerful trade-union movement.[33] Even as *Problemas Venezolanos* was debated, the events of World War II facilitated the return of Betancourt from exile and added a final aspect to the program of the Venezuelan Democratic Left.

Betancourt and his comrades had consistently opposed dictatorship within Venezuela, but World War II converted antitotalitarianism into an international cause and led to the adoption of an interventionist foreign policy for the eradication of dictatorships. In Chile in 1940 Betancourt attacked vehemently "the Nazi barbarities" and condemned those Americans who remained indifferent to "the fascist advance." He declared, "The triumph of fascist totalitarianism would mean for our America, weak but rich in essential raw materials, the imminent danger of being converted into a vast Abyssinia."[34] For this reason, Betancourt advocated cooperation with the United States for the continental defense, not through arms but through the flow of its resources, and announced that the opposition groups of Venezuela "had offered their loyal cooperation to President López in this crucial emergency." He was cautious, however; critical of the weakness of the Western democracies at Munich and in Spain and ever wary of the alleged imperialist danger, he recommended that "America unite and prepare the way completely for the defense of its primary products, of its sovereignty, and of its relative political freedom, and that, once united, in a solid, multilateral pact, it undertake to coordinate with the United States the defense of the hemisphere."[35] He repeated his message in Argentina and Brazil and began to earn a reputation as a "man of America," which fortified his belief in "the destiny of the American Left" and his conviction that "the Venezuelan movement must be the spearhead for the movement of America."[36]

When Betancourt returned to Venezuela in February 1941, he told a welcoming crowd: "We support the thesis that the social currents of the Latin American Left ought to take up the ideal of continental unity . . . but without renouncing for a minute the essential principle that each country is free to resolve democratically its own problems."[37] This statement contained the germ of two ideas which Betancourt developed more fully later. First, an interventionist doctrine, which he outlined in a press conference in 1946: "We support the collective intervention of democratically governed countries to prevent the existence of despotic or dictatorial governments in America."[38] Second, a rejection of the use of the label "Aprista" for describing Acción Democrática and other parties of the Democratic Left. While recognizing that there was a kinship among these parties, Betancourt felt that each was indigenous and responded to local realities. If any general term was to be used, Betancourt preferred the classification "national revolutionary."[39]

After the long search for a doctrine, Betancourt, Leoni, Barrios,

Montilla, and their comrades founded Acción Democrática and secured its recognition as a legal party on 13 September 1941. World War II and changing times had facilitated these steps. López Contreras, wisely sensing the prevailing political mood, had not sought reelection in April 1941 but had instead supported the candidacy of General Isaías Medina Angarita, who was not as strongly identified with the *gomecista* faction. Venezuelan presidents were still elected indirectly, and Medina's victory over the "symbolic" opposition of Rómulo Gallegos was a mere formality. Nonetheless, once in office, Medina disdained the puppet's role, and his tenure was marked by significant liberalization. Acción Democrática was relatively free to operate as an opposition party and to concentrate on the task of coming to power. This occurred sooner than anticipated.

Contrary to its convictions, Acción Democrática joined with a group of young officers to overthrow Medina in October 1945. The party deplored this course but believed that it had no alternative other than to participate or to lose influence among reform elements in the army and possibly the nation. The junior officers were determined to act with or without the cooperation of civilian leaders. What appeared to provoke the officers was Medina's intention to impose his successor in the 1945 elections; but even more determining was their disappointment at Medina's failure to reform the army. The young officers considered conditions in the army intolerable. They had expected Medina, who was a professional soldier with formal training, to remove the old *gomecista* generals, who were not academy graduates and who in most cases were corrupt and in some instances illiterate. By going along, AD was able to preserve the principle of civilian government, and Betancourt himself was named provisional president.

Acción Democrática had achieved power, but it was not alone. The 1930 Generation in Cuba had run a course similar to that of the Generation of '28 in Venezuela and had also evolved a party of the Democratic Left. The Cubans caught the political currents of the day and set out to make a revolution. Until 1930, the Cuban political atmosphere had been shoddy rather than repressive. Politics were venal, elections were fraudulent, social and economic problems were ignored, and all political groups had the same poor record. Even when an armed uprising in the name of reform managed to cast out one group of plunderers, the new administration succumbed almost inevitably to immorality and corruption. These circumstances gravely concerned Cuban students and intellectuals during the late 1920s. Cuban authors Fernando Ortiz and Nicolás Guillén were strong critics of conditions on the island, particularly with reference to the Negro poor. Conditions grew worse during the last years of the presidency of Gerardo Machado.

Machado, who was elected president first in 1924, added tyranny to the existing evils of Cuban politics. Machado's first administration had shown some promise. Although dishonesty remained endemic within his government, he undertook important public works, paid more attention to education, and studied means for rescuing Cuba from its extreme dependence upon sugar production. Enjoying a degree of popularity and asserting that he needed another term to finish his public works program, Machado had himself reelected in 1928. Even before this, he forced a subservient Congress to amend the Constitution extending the presidential term to six years. Havana University students reacted quickly to these high-handed actions, but Machado moved to quell any demonstrations and allegedly arranged the murder in Mexico of exiled student leader and Communist Julio Antonio Mella. Whether or not Machado was guilty, the murder of Mella set the tone for the remainder of his rule, which grew increasingly oppressive as economic depression in the United States affected disastrously the economy of Cuba. In Cuba there was a direct relation between political conditions and the price of sugar.[40]

The Generation of 1930 was activated by the tyranny of Machado and the misery of the Great Depression, and for the next three years it excited the sympathy and the imagination of much of Latin America. The struggle, in which Cuban students and young professionals resorted to terrorism and violence while Machado carried out cruel reprisals, was immortalized in journalistic copy, in novels and stories, and even in motion pictures. The question of who started the violence was lost in a vicious circle of terrorism and reprisal. Among those who became public figures during this period were Dr. Ramón Grau San Martín, a physician and professor of physiology at the University of Havana and later president of the republic; Juan Marinello, a law professor and later one of the Communist party leaders; Antonio Guiteras, student activist and leader of the Young Cuba movement; and Aureliano Sánchez Arango, student and one of the future leaders of Cuba's Democratic Left. Organized revolutionary groups assassinated key figures of the Machado regime, set off bombs in the streets of Havana, and engaged in various feats of derring-do. Machado declared martial law, closed the University of Havana, and threw hundreds of students and suspected agitators into jail. Between 1930 and Machado's fall in August 1933, suspected opponents of the regime almost nightly were taken for gangster-style rides by Machado's special squad of toughs, the *porristas,* often to be beaten or murdered and thrown to the pavement from speeding automobiles. In the jails, students were set upon and beaten by their jailers or "other convicts," and the *Ley de Fuga,* in which activists were killed "trying to escape,"[41] became a frequent occurrence.

With the suspension of individual guarantees, the opponents of Machado organized a number of secret revolutionary groups, the most important of which was the ABC. The ABC derived its name from the manner. in which it was organized into cells, that is, the top eight leaders of the movement made up the A cell, they in turn each commanded a B cell of eight persons, who themselves each directed a C cell, and so on presumably to form a vast "chain-letter" network.[42] Comprised mainly of students and professionals (the organization reached also into the army, where Sergeant Fulgencio Batista was a member), the ABC kept the island in turmoil and forced Machado to travel in a bulletproof car accompanied by armed patrols fore and aft. The ABC was primarily an action group, but it also issued statements of general purpose and, as in the case of the Venezuelan revolutionaries, declared that it sought not merely to destroy Machado but "to remove" the causes of the dictatorship.[43]

Many of the more prominent opposition leaders, representing both older political parties and the new generation, had to go into exile, where they engaged in propaganda and examined the problems of Cuba. Among the Generation of 1930 in exile were Grau San Martín and Raúl Roa. They studied the solutions of the far Left and stressed the economic and social content of the opposition to Machado. They, among others, were also anti-imperialist, focusing upon the powerful influence of the United States over Cuban political and economic affairs.

The influence of the United States was one of the realities of the Cuban situation; this was demonstrated clearly in the anti-Machado movement. The Platt Amendment of 1901 gave the United States the right to intervene in Cuba for "the maintenance of a government adequate for the protection of life, property and individual liberty." Although American presidents after 1910 avoided direct intervention, the United States was frequently the final arbiter of Cuban political affairs.

In addition, American economic interests in Cuba were enormous and exercised a great deal of leverage over Cuban domestic affairs and Cuban-American relations. The inability of Machado to maintain order and the worsening economic crisis led to efforts on the part of the United States to mediate between Machado and the revolutionary groups. During the summer of 1933, Sumner Welles, the ambassador of the new administration of Franklin Roosevelt, worked for a settlement calling for the resignation of Machado and the establishment of an interim government acceptable to all parties, pending new elections. Machado's efforts to avoid the inevitable resulted in an army coup d'etat on 12 August and in the installation of Carlos Manuel de Céspedes as president. Céspedes was the son of a Cuban patriot and was generally respected, but he could not control the swirl of events and lasted little more than three weeks. He was overthrown in the famous "sergeants' revolt" led by Sergeant Batista. The noncommissioned officers moved then to purge the army of Machado influences, particularly officers allegedly associated with the crimes of the dictator. A five-member commission of government was quickly established, comprised of representatives of the new army, the ABC, and Young Cuba. One of its members was Grau San Martín. A few days later, on 10 September, Grau was given sole leadership as provisional president.

Power came to Grau before he had a chance to develop his program fully, but its main outlines were nationalistic and socialistic. Grau clearly intended the economic and social transformation of the island, even though at the time the only political organization he could count on was the Student Directorate of the University of Havana. Grau issued decrees designed to improve working conditions and to guarantee the rights of labor, he also pledged opportunity and social betterment for Negroes. He criticized alleged interference by the U.S. embassy and promised to scale down the foreign component of the Cuban economy. Grau, however, also had difficulty in overcoming the turbulent conditions in Cuba. Personal vendettas were being carried out under the pretense that the victims were collaborators of Machado, and workers and peasants were seizing a number of properties and sugar mills. Grau was accused of being a communist, even though the Communists denounced him as the leader of a "bourgeois-landlord government . . . which defended the interests of the bourgeoisie, the landlords, and the imperialists."[44] Ambassador Welles did not see the situation in this light. He regarded Grau as an opportunist and as incompetent and held him responsible for the "seriously anarchic condition" of the country.[45] The refusal of Welles and his successor Jefferson Caffery to recommend U.S. recognition of Grau contributed to the disorder and ultimately led to the decision of Batista to remove Grau on 15 January 1934. The meaning of these events for the future of Cuba is analyzed succinctly by Professor Federico G. Gil, as follows:

> The refusal of the United States to recognize Grau San Martín was an important factor in the fall of his government. Concerned with the dangers inherent in social revolution and its impact on U.S. vested interests in the island, American policy was aimed at the preservation of the *status quo*. Sumner Welles and later Jefferson Caffery, as personal representatives of President Roosevelt, played a major role in bringing the revolution to a halt. From then on, the revolution became chiefly political, not social and economic. One cannot help but wonder whether or not events in Cuba would have taken a different course, if the United States at that time had favored needed social and economic changes in Latin America as it is doing now. It is valid to pose such a question, for in some respects, the Cuban phenomenon of the 1950s was simply the reincarnation of the revolutionary process interrupted in the 1930s.[46]

It may be asserted, however, that the 1933 revolution was not completely lost as a result of the fall of Grau. Although ex-Sergeant, now Colonel Batista dominated Cuban affairs in an autocratic fashion for the next decade, he tolerated political activity within limits and sympathized with the general need for the reform of all aspects of Cuban life. Most of the pre-1930 politicians were eased from public life, and they took many of their ways with them. The United States, in the spirit of the "good neighbor" and reacting to criticism of its role in the Grau affair, abrogated the Platt Amendment in May 1934. American economic interests also tended to decline, as some enterprises folded after the 1929 stock market crash and as Batista carried out a program to secure Cuban ownership of the sugar industry.

It was a situation of contrasts and contradictions. Batista ruled through puppets during the 1930s, often harshly. Thousands of opponents were jailed or exiled. Yet in 1934 the Cuban Revolutionary party (PRC), or Auténtico (party of the Authentic Revolution), was formed by Grau, Guiteras, Eduardo Chibás, Carlos Prío Socarras, Carlos Hevia, and others. In May 1935, during a series of strikes and outbreaks, Guiteras was shot and killed. The Auténticos refrained from active political campaigning and concentrated on perfecting their program and on strengthening their organization. If they got into trouble with Batista, it usually stemmed from their association with the numerous terrorist groups (*pistoleros*) that continued to operate after the fall of Machado. The major rivals of the Auténticos were the Communists, particularly in the struggle for control over organized labor. By 1939, when Batista decided to hold elections for a constituent assembly in order to restore constitutional government to Cuba, the patient labor of the Auténticos paid off with a substantial number of seats. The result was that, despite nearly a decade of strong man rule, the Constitution of 1940 embodied the ideals of the Generation of 1930 and was, for its time, an extremely progressive instrument.

The Constitution of 1940 was, in essence, the program of the Auténtico party, especially with reference to its economic and social aspects. The commitment to representative democracy was, of course, strong, as demonstrated in provisions for broad suffrage and in measures for curbing the powers of the executive. Civil liberties and human rights were enumerated and fully guaranteed. But what was really new and significant about the Constitution of 1940 was its attention to economic and social issues. Although influenced by the Mexican Constitution of 1917, the Cubans were also guided by a newer experience (one which generally affected the development of Latin American parties of the Democratic Left), namely, the New Deal legislation and programs of the Roosevelt administration in the United States.

The Cuban Constitution was decidedly prolabor. It recognized labor's right to organize and bargain collectively, established a minimum wage and fixed maximum hours, set up special boards of conciliation for labor disputes, and prescribed specific conditions for the employment of women and children. A full program of social security was provided, including accident and sickness benefits, old-age insurance, and unemployment compensation. The Constitution called for free, compulsory, public education and declared that "culture in all its manifestations is a primordial interest of the nation." It did not go as far in its economic measures as the Auténticos desired, particularly with reference to agrarian reform and control over the sugar industry, but the principle of the state as the regulator and director of the economy was established. Nationalistic features included special priorities for Cuban nationals in obtaining employment and the regulation of the economy in accordance with the national interest; but the Auténticos stood for even greater limitations upon foreign enterprises and for Grau's so-called *Cubanidad* program, which required that the personnel or labor force of any business or firm be at least fifty percent Cuban. Finally, also quite significant were the procedures for holding the government and its officials to strict accountability in the handling of public funds.[47] The Auténticos had reason for optimism over the acceptance of the Constitution of 1940, but, ironically, the first president elected under it was Fulgencio Batista.

Batista presided during the years of World War II, 1940-44. His rule was generally moderate, but the image of the strong man prevailed, which was increasingly difficult to reconcile with the democratic ideals of the times. In addition, Batista and his followers were unable to resist the temptations for personal enrichment and for profiteering provided by the booming, wartime economy. By 1944 the Cuban population had grown restive, and when Batista made the crucial gesture of permitting free elections, Grau San Martín easily won the presidency. Once in power, the Auténticos, very much like their Venezuelan brethren, felt the need to continue the fight against all dictatorships. While still president-elect, Grau visited New York in September 1944 and declared that the dictators of the Western Hemisphere "had to go" in order to assure unity in the Americas.[48] Obviously the Auténticos and Acción Democrática were disposed to cooperate in this task. The result was the spread of the struggle throughout the Caribbean. New parties of the Democratic Left emerged, and a revolution took place in Guatemala to challenge the entrenched position of the Caribbean's dictators. It is pertinent, therefore, to consider the political backgrounds of the other important participants in the Caribbean conflict, namely Costa Rica, Puerto Rico, Guatemala, the Dominican Republic, Honduras, and Nicaragua.

Democrats and Dictators

The National Liberation party, PLN (Partido Liberación Nacional), of Costa Rica came to be one of the most important parties of the Democratic Left, but its development before 1948 was slow and it was not founded officially until 1951. Before its rise, Costa Rican politics, though reputedly democratic, were, in fact, dominated by the large landowners. One observer referred to Costa Rica as "an oligarchical democracy";[49] it leaned dangerously toward authoritarianism in the

1940s. There was a kind of noblesse oblige about the Costa Rican oligarchy since it was neither oppressive nor venal and spent more money on education than on armaments. Facilitating this attitude was a friendly and hard-working population. Most of the land was concentrated into the hands of a few proprietors, but as many as two-thirds of the rural population possessed a small plot of land,[50] which provided some means of livelihood and independence. The land, however, was poor, and the small farmer survived only by hard work and perseverance. If possible, he supplemented his income by employment on a large estate or in some trade or by marketing a surplus. The population—described as homogeneous, specifically as white, which was probably exaggerated—was egalitarian; at least the conqueror-conquered relationship which created deep schisms and tensions in other countries of Latin America was lacking in Costa Rica.

The oligarchy was content to conserve this tranquil scene. If it extended the suffrage, it also controlled the electoral machinery and furnished the candidates. It resisted change that might undermine its authority, and its view of government was narrow, that is, it provided only the essential services and preferred to operate within a modest budget. Under its control, the country plodded along in rural isolation and failed to unite to solve broader economic and social problems. Some significant improvements were made by foreign capital, principally by fruit companies, which grew bananas on large plantations on both coasts. Because these companies were recipients of generous concessions from the ruling group and were unchallenged in their labor policies, they supported the status quo. An already deflated economy was therefore hit hard by the economic depression of the 1930s.

The thirties witnessed efforts to break the circle of poverty by building up new economic groups but ended with rule by a strong man. In 1929 the Communist party was founded by Manuel Mora Valverde, who tried to stimulate organized labor and advocated better working conditions and wages and a social security system. President Ricardo Jiménez Oreamuno (1932-36) sponsored a minimum wage, and the Communists, employing "popular front" tactics, obtained additional gains for urban and farm workers during the administration of León Cortés Castro (1936-40). A Center for the Study of National Problems was organized by university students and professionals, and a civic action group founded the Democratic Action (Acción Demócrata, not affiliated with the Venezuelan party). Both of these organizations con-

cluded that Costa Rica needed to modernize through increased governmental initiative in economic and social affairs and through industrialization, but they distrusted Manuel Mora.[51] In the presidential elections
of 1940 they had no strong candidate to offer, and Dr. Rafael Angel
Calderón Guardia, a highly respected physician and obstetrician who
had delivered a substantial number of the electorate's babies, won on a
program which promised social reform. Once in power, he founded the
right-wing National Republican party, PRN (Partido Republicano
Nacional).

Calderón Guardia was essentially an authoritarian, but he also desired a popular base, so he formed a working alliance with Mora's
Communist party. During the war years the Communists acquired respectability; in 1943 they renamed their party Vanguardia Popular.
Under the odd *caldero-comunista* alliance, Costa Rica instituted important social and welfare programs, including a strong labor code, a full
program of social security, and the restoration of the National University, but at the cost of its democratic institutions. Although Calderón
was not an oppressive tyrant, he used intimidation and fraud to domi-
nate elections between 1940 and 1948. Individual rights were violated,
and due process was frequently ignored.[52]

It was within this situation that José Figueres, the future leader of
Costa Rica's Democratic Left, suddenly appeared. Until July 1942 he
was an obscure grower of *cabuya* (sisal) in the mountains south of San
José. Born in 1906, the son of a physician, Figueres studied at the
Massachusetts Institute of Technology, but upon returning to his country in 1928 he took little part in national politics. He was a family
friend and admirer of the aged President Jiménez, but he devoted himself to developing a *finca* he had purchased, which he named "La Lucha
Sin Fin." There, in the solitary mountains, Figueres read and worked,
married and became a father. Only by the manner in which he handled
his workers did he give any indication of the social democratic programs which would characterize his later political leadership. He experi-
mented with socialist theories and built a small factory for manufacturing rope and sackcloth from the locally grown cabuya. He also studied
the policies of the Republican government of Spain, his father's homeland, and of the New Deal in the United States.[53]

A seemingly unrelated event abruptly ended this private life of José
Figueres. On 2 July 1942 a German submarine torpedoed the United
Fruit Company vessel *San Pablo,* docked in Puerto Limón harbor, and

caused several deaths. Two days later, demonstrations were organized in San José to mourn the dead and protest the sinking, and a crowd marched to the president's house. Calderón addressed the gathering, but Mora denounced the attack in inflammatory language. This transformed the crowd into a mob, which retraced its steps to the downtown district and began to smash and loot the stores and shops of German and Italian residents of the city. Figueres was shocked by these events and in collaboration with a few friends purchased radio time on 8 July in order to denounce Calderón generally and to charge specifically that the president had been the dupe of Mora and the Communists and had failed in his responsibility to maintain public order. Before Figueres finished his address, he was arrested; four days later he was banished from Costa Rica.[54]

Figueres went into exile in Mexico, where he decided it was necessary to participate more actively in his country's political affairs. He undertook to perfect his political education. He was able to observe firsthand the continuing fruits of the Mexican Revolution, particularly its progress in achieving the goals of labor and the campaigns against illiteracy.[55] This experience was later enriched by examination of Aprista doctrine and of the programs of Acción Democrática of Venezuela.[56] He also found time to write in exile and in 1943 published a lengthy essay entitled "Palabras gastadas"—the "wasted words" being liberty, democracy, and socialism—in which he revealed his basic belief in political democracy, his pragmatism and interest in socialism, and his deep respect for technology. The young men of the Center for the Study of National Problems now regarded Figueres as a champion, and a lively correspondence took place in which Figueres reiterated his political ideas and expressed the need to restore the liberty of Costa Rica.[57] In Mexico Figueres also entered into conspiratorial talks with exiles from other countries and became committed to the idea of overthrowing the dictators of Central America and the Caribbean. In the meantime, Calderón Guardia had imposed Teodoro Picado Michalski as his successor in February 1944, and Costa Rica remained under authoritarian rule. Shortly after Picado's election, Figueres returned to his homeland, where he continued preparations for the inevitable showdown with the Calderón-Picado-Mora regime. Thus, while AD held power in Venezuela and the Auténticos governed in Cuba, Figueres studied those movements and prepared for the day when he would join them in the antidictatorial struggle. At the same time, at the other extreme of the Caribbean, in Puerto Rico, Luis Muñoz Marín emerged as a political leader and collaborator of the Democratic Left.

Puerto Rico became important to the Democratic Left as a sympathetic friend and a place of refuge. Because of its ties to the United States, it could go no farther; but Luis Muñoz Marín, the island's most important political leader, shared the ideals of the Democratic Left and became the personal friend of its leaders. Muñoz Marín founded the Popular Democratic party (PPD) in 1938 in order to attack the problem of poverty in Puerto Rico, and in that he exhibited the influences of both Aprismo and the New Deal. Although Puerto Rico's status presented a peculiar problem, the enjoyment of political freedom was guaranteed, and Muñoz was able to concentrate upon economic and social issues. He had been a socialist as a young man, but he was not doctrinaire and his approach was experimental and even personalist. In seeking such goals as agrarian reform, mass education, and industrial development, his policy seemed to be, "if it works, use it."[58] One observer described him as "that rare combination of an idealist and a tremendously successful practical politician."[59] Muñoz himself had declared that "the old concept of economic democracy to the effect that a great many people have an equal opportunity to convert themselves into a few millionaires no longer satisfies or appeals."[60] Nevertheless, he welcomed and encouraged private capital, if he felt it could get the job done, just as he advocated government ownership of certain essential services or created autonomous public agencies to develop the economy and attract investment. Muñoz Marín was about ten years older than most leaders of the Democratic Left. He had been educated mainly in the United States, but he was effective in the Caribbean struggle because he moved with equal facility in the "two worlds" of North and Latin America.[61] With reference to conspiratorial activity, however, Muñoz had neither the freedom of action nor the inclination of the leaders of Guatemala.

Guatemala played an important role in the antidictatorial struggle after World War II, even though it lacked a party of the Democratic Left. In 1944, after fourteen years of arbitrary rule by Jorge Ubico, a combination of students, professional people, and young army officers acted to make a revolution. The movement, however, represented a mood (people were simply tired of being pushed around) rather than a climax of years of political activism or organization. Guatemala's small middle class was certainly aware of the changes taking place in Latin

America, particularly in neighboring revolutionary Mexico and as a result of the antitotalitarianism of World War II. What it lacked was an organization capable of arousing support and identifying national problems.[62] Moreover, economically and socially Guatemala was one of the most backward countries in the New World; its Indian majority was landless, illiterate, and exploited. Jorge Ubico (1931-44) was only the latest of a string of tyrants accustomed to ruling in behalf of the privileged and keeping the masses powerless and ignorant.

General Ubico, apparently an egotistical brute, gave the country stability and some material progress at the high cost of freedom and dignity. He has been described as "an impulsive, arbitrary, stubborn, opinionated, dominating, energetic and inflexible individual who was a policeman at heart."[63] Assuredly, the student generations of the twenties and thirties of the National University of San Carlos discussed current trends in social and economic thought, but their talks were safe only within the walls of the university and they did not dare venture outside to engage in overt political activity. Opponents of Ubico, real or fancied, were visited with jail, exile, or death, and they were all labeled Communists. Ubico permitted no criticism of his regime; there was no free press, labor unions were banned, and even private charitable and cultural organizations were watched closely to prevent any possible political tendencies.[64] The Indians supposedly called Ubico "Tata" (grandfather), but it is difficult to understand why. He instituted a law requiring them to work at least 150 days on the coffee fincas at piteously low wages, and those who failed to do so were declared vagrants and were put to work building roads. The landowner was virtually the law on his estate, even to the extent of being empowered to shoot trespassers or "poachers."[65] Ubico was overly solicitous about the welfare of foreign companies and granted generous concessions to such enterprises as the United Fruit Company. As small groups of literate Guatemalans pondered the meaning of such World War II documents as the Atlantic Charter, the Ubico regime became intolerable.

The overthrow of Ubico was relatively easy considering the unchallenged authority he had exercised for almost a decade and a half. The movement began in late May 1944 with a group of lawyers who demanded that Ubico replace an allegedly arbitrary judge. Students of the University of San Carlos quickly joined the lawyers and seized the opportunity to seek the ouster of certain administrators and professors. When Ubico seemed to hesitate, the students returned with a tougher

petition, which included demands for university autonomy, self-government, and "the incorporation of the Indian in the life of the country,"
and they gave Ubico twenty-four hours to answer. Ubico responded by
suspending individual guarantees and, ironically, noting Guatemala's
place at the side of the democracies in a war against totalitarianism,
declared that the university had been infiltrated by "Nazi-fascist
agents." Fearful of imminent repression, the student leaders sought
asylum in foreign embassies. But the movement now had momentum,
and the lawyers, joined by other professionals, circulated yet another
petition defending the students and demanding the restoration of constitutional rights. Ubico had once said that he would resign if three
hundred leading citizens requested it, so the petitioners managed to
collect the signatures of 311 prominent Guatemalans. While Ubico studied the "Memorial de los 311," a once obsequious population began to
march and demonstrate, demanding political freedom and progressive
reforms. The inevitable clash came on 25 June, when police and soldiers
suddenly charged a group of women demonstrators, one of whom,
María Chinchilla Recinos, a schoolteacher, was killed. Her martyrdom
provoked a general strike that paralyzed Guatemala City and brought
forth angry calls for the resignation of Ubico. The dictator held out
until 1 July and then stepped aside for a triumvirate of generals, who in
turn were replaced by General Federico Ponce Vaides as provisional
president.[66]

Ubico's resignation was a diversionary maneuver, but the revolution
was unfulfilled and the tactic did not work. Ponce represented only a
change in personnel at the top, and even here Ubico apparently continued to run the government from his private residence. But the promise
of change and the possibility of elections stimulated a burst of popular
activity, with the founding of numerous political parties and the return
of exiles. Among the latter was Juan José Arévalo, a teacher and writer
who had spent nearly a decade in exile in Argentina. Arévalo's modest
fame as a writer, and the general belief that he had left Guatemala in
disgust over Ubico's educational policies, made him the choice of such
newborn groups as the National Renovation party, RN (Renovación
Nacional), and the Popular Liberation Front, FPL (Frente Popular
Libertador). Very likely his greatest asset was the fact that, owing to his
relative isolation in far-off Argentina, he was untainted by any connection with the Ubico regime. As an idealist-scholar he seemed to stand
above it all.

The popular reception given Arévalo upon his return on 3 September greatly disturbed Ponce, who wanted to perpetuate the dictatorship, and soon the government began to break up meetings and to harass opposition leaders. In early October a newspaper editor critical of Ponce was beaten and killed, and Arévalo himself was forced to take asylum in the Mexican embassy. The political situation deteriorated into a series of strikes and government reprisals against student and professional leaders. The missing ingredient in the revolution had been the army; but the actions of Ponce alienated many junior officers, and some of them, including Captain Jacobo Arbenz and Major Francisco Javier Arana, concluded that only an armed insurrection could overcome the dictatorship. Together with a civilian, Jorge Toriello, they plotted a military coup and on 20 October successfully seized or subverted key garrisons and forced Ponce and Ubico to flee the country. Arana, Arbenz, and Toriello immediately constituted a junta of government and made preparations for the drafting of a new constitution and the holding of presidential elections.[67]

Arévalo was the choice of a coalition of revolutionary groups and he won a stunning victory in the presidential elections of December 1944. Although not a profound thinker—Arévalo described himself as a "spiritual socialist"—he shared the ideals of the Democratic Left. Born in 1904, he was of their generation, but he was inexperienced in practical politics, and was unable to transform his ideas into a revolutionary program for Guatemala. The Constitution of 1945 (drafted in January and promulgated in March, just two days before the inauguration of Arévalo) was essentially the work of Jorge García Granados, a man attuned to the times who borrowed heavily from the U.S. Constitution, the Mexican Constitution of 1917, and the Soviet Constitution of 1935.[68] Owing to the parallel between conditions in Guatemala and those in pre-1910 Mexico, there was much talk of a "Little Mexican Revolution."

The revolution lacked political organization, however. Because Guatemala had for so long been characterized as a "banana republic," and because of the real and mythical power of the United Fruit Company, the revolution exhibited strong antiforeign sentiments. In 1935, in an essay entitled "Istmania," Arévalo had advocated the ideal of Central American federation in order to create a strong state to defend the peoples' political and economic independence against despotism and imperialism.[69] It was obvious that Arévalo's foreign policy would concur with that of the Democratic Left—especially since he viewed dictatorship as an obstacle to Central American union—and that he would take part in the postwar antidictatorial struggle. But a problem arose because, owing to the lack of experienced political leadership, a small group of talented young Communists, sustained by Mexican, Cuban, and Central American comrades, became very influential within the Guatemalan Revolution. The resulting ambiguous situation confused and embarrassed the Democratic Left and compounded the difficulties of the antidictatorial struggle. Nonetheless, for a few years after 1945, Guatemala, Cuba, and Venezuela (and Costa Rica after 1948) were generally aligned against those Caribbean states where dictatorships prevailed, namely, the Dominican Republic, Honduras, and Nicaragua.

The changes which gave birth to the parties of the Democratic Left were virtually unfelt in the Dominican Republic. This small country, occupying the eastern two-thirds of the island of Hispaniola, had been ruled since 1930 by Rafael Leónidas Trujillo Molina. To many, especially foreign observers, Trujillo's regime was a definite improvement over the political and economic bankruptcy which had confounded the nation before he took over, but he was also one of the most complete dictators ever to rule anywhere. All that has been said about dictators may be repeated about Trujillo. He permitted no political opposition or criticism of his personal decisions or his regime's actions. There was only one legal political party, the Dominican party, which was the personal tool of the dictator and was supported fully by the machinery of the state. On rare occasions Trujillo permitted an opposition party to organize and participate in an election, but in any instance (the Communists operated legally during 1945-47) the situation was carefully controlled and was contrived to impress international opinion. As will be seen, the only real opposition parties were organized in exile. The labor unions which existed were a façade, and the right to strike was expressly forbidden. The press and other mass media, including radio and later television, served the exclusive interests of the "Generalissimo." They extolled the virtues of the regime or attacked with unbelievable vitriol anyone who displeased Trujillo. The internal security forces were large and efficient; Trujillo spied upon his people, and, although there was a court structure and supposedly a system of due process, those unfortunate enough to get into trouble were taken care

of in numerous extralegal ways, including arbitrary arrest and detention, extraction of confessions through torture, and even murder. Enemies of the regime frequently ended up as victims of automobile accidents. All this was characteristic of many dictatorships, but Trujillo
went farther.

Trujillo's passion for absolute control embraced a megalomania
which fed upon outward signs of acceptance and loyalty and resulted in
the virtual emasculation of the Dominican people. Merely being passive
or refraining from criticism of Trujillo was not enough; in order to
avoid suspicion of disloyalty, one had to profess his appreciation of and
devotion to "The Benefactor." Even private gatherings, such as
birthday celebrations, were opened with a toast in honor of Trujillo.
Public officials, civilian and military, elected or appointed, were suscep-
tible to the whims of Trujillo, not to mention the fact that each had
given him an undated, signed resignation. One read the newspapers
daily to see if his resignation had been published or if he had been
denounced in one of the columns appearing under Trujillo's pseudonym. But the Trujillo name was everywhere. Streets, towns, the capital
city, political subdivisions, and geographic features were named for him
or some member of his family. Citizenship, scholarship, feats of
bravery, or athletic achievement were rewarded in the name of Trujillo,
while Trujillo himself collected scores of decorations, honors, and titles.
"Dios y Trujillo," or "Trujillo y Dios," were emblazoned in neon lights
above the rooftops of the capital, Ciudad Trujillo (Santo Domingo).
For all this, petty caudillos and thieves were eliminated, the peasants
ate better, and the foreign debt was liquidated.

Trujillo developed the economy of the Dominican Republic because
he was interested in money. Except for women, he was not concerned
about personal indulgence, but he recognized what money could do.
With tremendous energy, Trujillo ran the island as if it were his personal
property. He operated much as a tycoon, but he was in the enviable
position of having absolute political power to guarantee the success of
his ventures. He used the army and publicly owned equipment to
harvest sugarcane on his plantations and to transport cattle to and from
his ranches, and there was no clear delineation between public monies
and Trujillo's personal fortune. Trujillo modernized many aspects of
the economy, especially through the mechanization of agriculture and
improved stock breeding, but the ambiguity between public and private
resources also concealed a great deal of waste and inefficiency. Trujillo,

or some member of his family (nepotism was rampant), possessed numerous monopolies, including the production, processing, and sale of milk, meat, cement, salt, etc., and even foreign investors agreed to payoffs or kickbacks for the privilege of doing business in the Dominican Republic. The workers and peasants were not ignored, and Trujillo was personally popular among them, but the paternalistic nature of his benevolence was unmistakable. Trujillo built roads and schools and paid much attention to sanitation and health. He also engaged in pyramid building and maintained a high military budget. Trujillo's armed forces were formidable for a tiny Caribbean state, and they were unquestionably loyal. Trujillo's enemies, most of whom were outside the country, had little prospect for success through any armed venture against him. On the other hand, they, and those who assisted them, had real cause to fear a retaliatory attack by Trujillo.

An important aspect of Trujillo's power was the care he took to maintain good relations with the United States. He was himself indirectly a creature of the U.S. military occupation of the Dominican Republic in 1916-24. The United States had tried to create an apolitical constabulary force to assure the stability of any civilian administration, but the result was a praetorian guard, which Trujillo used to bully his way to power. Trujillo never forgot that he once wore the uniform of a U.S. Marine. At the time of Pearl Harbor, Trujillo anticipated the United States by declaring war upon Germany and Japan first. He later made a fetish of his anticommunism. He cultivated friendships with influential North Americans, especially members of the U.S. Congress, whom he treated regally when they visited his island, and he spent substantial sums of money for propaganda in the United States proclaiming the virtues of his regime. When the Democratic Left and other revolutionary groups of the Caribbean began to attack Trujillo after 1945, reactions in the United States were mixed but generally worked to the Generalissimo's advantage. He proved to be the most redoubtable of the Caribbean's dictators.[70]

In Honduras, another long-term dictator resisted the growth of the Democratic Left as well as other forms of change. Tiburcio Carías Andino was elected president in 1932 and for the next sixteen years did not bother to refer again to the electorate. He continued in office first by rewriting the Constitution and later by amending it. This practice of *continuismo* was possible because of his control over the army; it also reflected Carías' rigid conservativism, which served the interests of a feudalistic society. Both man and land were underdeveloped in Honduras, as demonstrated by a high rate of illiteracy, primitive agricultural methods, lack of roads, and general low productivity. Carías overcame the turbulent political history of Honduras and virtually wiped out lawlessness, but the peace which he imposed was stifling. He also sought, as Ubico, to isolate his country from modernizing trends. The only positive effect of such stability was the encouragement it gave to previously cautious foreign investors, who undertook to develop an important banana industry on the north coast. Carías opposed any attempt at labor organization and cooperated with the fruit companies in union-busting activities. This policy contributed to violent strikes in the banana regions in the mid-1950s.[71]

Although the dictatorship of Carías seemed firm in 1945 and figured prominently in postwar events in the Caribbean, it was abruptly terminated three years later. Honduras then tended to move to the periphery of the Caribbean struggle. Carías ruled through the National party, which he had reorganized under his leadership in 1919. The only significant opposition, the tradition-bound Liberal party, was ineffective. Many of its leaders had gone into exile in 1936, when they failed to prevent Carías' first extension of power. During the 1950s, however, the Liberal party was converted into a party of the Democratic Left under the leadership of Dr. Ramón Villeda Morales. Villeda Morales, a pediatrician, managed to survive under Carías by concentrating upon his medical practice and by avoiding provocative political activity. He held moderately socialistic views and was politically idealistic but remained generally powerless until Carías stepped aside. In 1948, Carías, bowing to old age (he was then 72) and recognizing growing pressure for reform, decided to run his vice president, Juan Manuel Gálvez, for the presidency. Duly elected, Gálvez turned out to be no puppet, and his administration was notable for its political liberalization and energetic economic development. He instituted programs in education and economic diversification and followed the advice of foreign technical missions.[72] With reference to Caribbean affairs, he endeavored to remain aloof.

Under these conditions, Villeda Morales began to reshape the Liberal party and sought to win a popular base by stressing the need to solve economic and social problems. He won the presidential election of 1954, but conservative elements prevented him from taking office, and

Julio Lozano Díaz, the vice president of Gálvez, usurped the executive power. Lozano Díaz restored the dictatorship, which led in turn to his overthrow in October 1956 by a group of dissident army officers. After winning yet another election, Villeda Morales was finally permitted to become president in 1957. Villeda Morales sympathized with the Democratic Left, but, owing to the tenuousness of his position, he exercised caution and restraint in the antidictatorial struggle.

These events anticipate our main narrative, but a review of them was necessary at this point in order to provide a context for the shifting role of Honduras in Caribbean affairs—a role which was not at all predictable in 1945, when Carías was a dedicated member of the dictators' club. At that time, he was referred to as one of the "Three Ts"—Rafael Trujillo, Tiburcio Carías, and "Tacho" Somoza.[73]

The latter was Anastasio Somoza of Nicaragua, who presented no problem with reference to consistency. Somoza, who had exercised dictatorial rule over Nicaragua since the mid-1930s, with just one false step weathered the liberalizing trends of World War II and the postwar years. Like Trujillo, Somoza rose to power through his domination over the National Guard, which had also been created and trained by the U.S. Marines to serve as a nonpartisan constabulary force. Also like Trujillo, Somoza administered his country in the manner of a private business or personal estate. The Somoza enterprises included farming, stock raising, and numerous commercial ventures, which, without question, improved the Nicaraguan economy generally and won for Somoza many foreign admirers. Somoza was reputed to be one of the world's richest men, but his business acumen was probably exaggerated. Before he became commander of the National Guard and a dictator, he had failed in an automobile dealership set up for him by his father-in-law.[74]

Both Somoza and Trujillo were born before 1900 (Somoza in 1896, and Trujillo in 1891), which made them ten to fifteen years older than their rivals of the Democratic Left. Both were from rural, middle-class backgrounds. They did not go directly to the barracks, but neither did they go to the university. Somoza, however, had studied business at the Peirce School in Philadelphia, Pennsylvania, and had married into one of the first families of Nicaragua. He, therefore, was not as hostile toward the old oligarchy as was Trujillo.

Somoza tended to rule within the framework of traditional Nicaraguan politics. Ever since the early nineteenth century and the time of the Central American federation (1823-39), Nicaraguan affairs were dominated by the Conservative or Liberal parties, neither of which was a popular party, each representing only a few old families. Somoza ruled through the Liberal party, but he permitted the Conservatives a few seats in the National Congress and some freedom of expression and press. Within this context, Somoza rarely applied to the Conservative opposition anything harder than exile, but he was energetic in ferreting out conspiracies and there was never any doubt about the outcome of elections. He dealt severely with "labor agitators," "communists," and other "radicals." The mechanism of the dictatorship could be cruel, even though Somoza was described as good-natured and as fond of storytelling and dancing. Somoza's rule was assisted by the loyal collaboration of his two sons: Luis, the elder, who took charge of the family businesses, and Anastasio, Jr. ("Tachito"), who studied at the U.S. Military Academy and eventually commanded the National Guard. The only flaw in Somoza's tight reign was that an assassination had brought him to power, and it seemed likely that one day that crime would be avenged.

Somoza became Nicaragua's strong man following the murder of the guerrilla chieftain Augusto C. Sandino. On the evening of 21 February 1934, after dining with President Juan Bautista Sacasa, Sandino was apprehended by a detachment of National Guardsmen and taken to the Managua airfield, where he was executed by machine gun fire. Somoza, the guard commander, refused to allow an inquiry of the crime, which added credibility to charges that he had participated in the decision to eliminate Sandino.[75] The death of Sandino ended the career of the man who had defied the U.S. Marines in Nicaragua from 1927 to 1933 and who had thereby become a hero in many parts of Latin America. Sandino's revolution was weak ideologically, but it satisfied the anti-imperialist sentiments of many Latins. Haya de la Torre came to Nicaragua to work in behalf of Sandino, and the Communist-sponsored Anti-Imperialist League was active in several American countries raising funds for Sandino and eliciting sympathy for his cause. Although Sandino was not a Communist, in 1928 the Sixth World Congress of the Comintern sent from Moscow "fraternal greetings to the workers and peasants of Nicaragua, and the heroic army of national emancipation of General Sandino."[76] When the marines were withdrawn in 1933, Sandino and President Sacasa worked out a peace, but the National Guard, which had fought alongside the marines, deeply resented Sandino, and Somoza considered him a threat to his future and to that of the guard.

Whatever might have been the case, the future of Sandino was ended on the Managua airfield.[77] Since then, however, Somoza had to live with the fact that his enemies, including the Conservatives, who played the game, did not shrink from the idea of assassinating him.

The desire to eliminate Somoza fit into the general context of post-war politics in the Caribbean. By 1945 two mutually hostile groups faced each other. The Democratic Left, its allies and associates, and various refugees from totalitarian rule made up one side; the dictators of the Caribbean comprised the other. World War II constituted the final element of the rise of the Democratic Left and provided it with the essential justification for undertaking the destruction of all dictatorships.

The Impact of World War II

The invoking of democratic ideals during World War II undermined the rule of Latin American strong men and encouraged the emergence of democratic leadership. Rómulo Betancourt affirmed that the Four Freedoms of Franklin Roosevelt "gave hope to the oppressed peoples of Latin America."[78] Luis Muñoz Marín declared that the war "was releasing the forces of social revolution throughout the world," and added, "I assume that on the day of victory, the victory will be the same for Puerto Rico as for all the sectors which comprise the corps fighting for democracy in this world."[79] Such optimism also existed in Central America, where opinion was strong that an Allied triumph would produce important changes.[80] From his exile in Mexico City, José Figueres wrote to his friends in San José that man's desire for freedom could not be overcome, even though it might have to be demonstrated with blood, "as was being done now in Europe, with eloquent 8,000-pound bombs."[81] In Guatemala, Guillermo Toriello read the Atlantic Charter on 24 June 1944 to a crowd demonstrating for the resignation of Jorge Ubico. The "Memorial de los 311" concluded with the following assertion: "Guatemala cannot remove itself from the democratic imperatives of the era. It is impossible to frustrate with coercive measures the uncontainable impulses of that generous ideology which is being reaffirmed in the world's conscience by means of the bloodiest of struggles between oppression and liberty."[82]

At the war's end these same leaders felt that liberty was still unredeemed in the Caribbean. At first they searched for some peaceful procedure for eradicating dictatorship, hoping that the existing enthusiasm for democracy would prove irresistible. But they were soon disappointed. At the Inter-American Conference on the Problems of War and Peace—the Chapultepec conference, in February-March 1945—the Guatemalan government proposed unsuccessfully the withholding of recognition from those regimes "that may originate from coup d'etat against governments of a legally established democratic structure."[83] A bolder proposal was made by Eduardo Rodríguez Larreta, the Foreign Minister of Uruguay, who in November 1945 sent to the American governments identical notes in which he advocated collective intervention for the maintenance of democracy. There is a "parallelism between democracy and peace," he declared. He insisted that those governments which violate human rights violate the principles of democratic government and thereby constitute threats to the peace. He asserted that it was the responsibility of American governments to act collectively in defense of democracy and human rights. Although Rodríguez Larreta recognized the essential contradiction of such collective action with the principle of nonintervention, he stated that "nonintervention cannot be converted into a right to invoke one principle in order to be able to violate all other principles with impunity."[84]

The response of the Betancourt government, which had been in power in Venezuela for only a month, was spontaneous and warm. "Victorious democracy," Foreign Minister Carlos Morales replied, "will no longer allow the human factor, one of the most important ingredients of the state, to suffer violations, or even restrictions, of its inherent rights. To admit otherwise would be a contradiction and would exhibit as sterile the still latent and incalculable sacrifices of the United Nations. For these reasons, the government of Venezuela is favorably disposed to the thesis of the Uruguayan Foreign Ministry and welcomes it with the greatest sympathy."[85] The United States government also supported enthusiastically the proposal of Rodríguez Larreta, and Secretary of State James F. Byrnes declared: "Violations of the elementary rights of man by a government of force and the nonfulfillment of obligations by such a government is a matter of common concern to all republics. As such, it justifies collective multilateral action after full consultation among the republics in accordance with established procedures."[86] The endorsement of the United States recalled the long struggle in behalf of the principle of nonintervention and tended to frighten

some governments, and these, in combination with the existing dictatorships, rebuffed the Uruguayan *démarche*. As will be seen, in the
United States the administration of President Harry S. Truman wa
sympathetic toward the goals of the Democratic Left, but its policy was
modified by the outbreak of the Cold War. Despite this rejection,
Betancourt continued to work for the acceptance of the principle outlined in the Rodríguez Larreta proposal.

Betancourt's government recalled its diplomatic missions from Nicaragua and the Dominican Republic and severed relations with the Franco government of Spain. In July 1946 Betancourt made a swing around
the Caribbean, visiting Cuba, Mexico, Central America, and Colombia,
where he tried to rally support for the interventionist thesis. On 22
July, in Havana, Betancourt told newsmen that "no American country,
which practices and respects democracy, should maintain diplomatic
relations with governments which oppress or humiliate their
people.... When a criminal is carrying out a crime," he noted, "the
police will break down the door of the house where the crime is taking
place in order to stop it." In the same way, Betancourt continued, he
supported the collective intervention of democratic countries "in order
to prevent the existence in America of dictatorial or despotic governments."[87]   Just four days later, he shared the speakers' platform in
Guatemala City with Juan José Arévalo.

Both presidents reaffirmed their faith in the ideals of Franklin
Roosevelt as embodied in the Four Freedoms and the Atlantic Charter.
In his address Betancourt "declared war" upon the New World dictatorships and stated that it was a "perversion" they should continue to
exist. He announced that at the forthcoming inter-American conference
in Rio de Janeiro (scheduled for August 1947) he would seek the
establishment of a *cordon sanitaire* against the antidemocratic governments of the hemisphere.[88]   Betancourt repeated this intention in
Panama a few days later and explained, "As long as there exists in
America a single government which does not guarantee the free participation of all political parties; which does not guarantee the freedom
of the press, or the free expression of all ideological currents; as long as
there exists a single government which does not guarantee the Four
Freedoms of Franklin Roosevelt, the freedom of the entire hemisphere
will be threatened."[89]   The nature of governmental response to Betancourt's efforts was demonstrated in the case of Nicaragua.

In February 1947 Dr. Leonardo Argüello was elected president of

Nicaragua. There was nothing surprising about this event, because Argüello was the candidate of Somoza's Liberal party and it was widely held that he had been handpicked as a figurehead president. During the months preceding the election, opposition groups despaired that it would be honest and appealed to Spruille Braden, the U.S. assistant secretary of state for inter-American affairs, to act in behalf of democracy in Nicaragua.[90] Notwithstanding the admonitions of Braden against dictatorships in the Americas, the election went off without a hitch and Argüello, a man in his seventies, was subsequently inaugurated on 1 May. Then, in the same month, on the twenty-sixth, Somoza removed Argüello as "unfit" and replaced him with a provisional president, Benjamín Lacayo Sacasa. Apparently, the old man had a will of his own and had tried to remove a number of pro-Somoza officers from the National Guard—a possible first step to getting rid of Somoza himself as the guard's commander. The Somoza coup was swift and bloodless; but it was too brazen, even for those governments which opposed the interventionist doctrine of Rodríguez Larreta.

A majority of the American governments, including Mexico and United States, decided to withhold recognition from the Lacayo Sacasa regime. This action followed an informal consultation in Washington among the United States and Latin American governments.[91] The old Governing Board of the Pan American Union even refused to invite Nicaragua to attend the Inter-American Conference for the Maintenance of Continental Peace and Security set for Rio de Janeiro in August. However, there was no disposition to go farther. Nonrecognition alone could not dislodge a dictatorship such as that of Somoza. All that was needed, then, was a little time to legalize the situation. On 3 August, 1947 Somoza held elections for a constituent assembly. This body drafted a new constitution and, under its terms, named Somoza's uncle, Víctor Manuel Román y Reyes, as president of Nicaragua. By the end of the year, Nicaragua's relations with its sister republics were restored, and Nicaragua was invited to attend the Ninth International Conference of American States scheduled for Bogotá, Colombia, in March 1948. Only the Democratic Left clung to the nonrecognition policy. Betancourt, Arévalo, and Grau's successor, Carlos Prío Socarrás, continued refusing to maintain diplomatic relations with Nicaragua and the Dominican Republic. In the United States, Braden had resigned as assistant secretary of state in June 1947, and, according to Professor J. Lloyd Mecham, Latin America "hailed" Braden's resignation "as a return to the policy of nonintervention, and failure by the United States to impose its type of democracy on Latin America."[92]

Braden's departure from the State Department probably did mark an important shift in U.S. policy toward Latin America. Clearly, the Braden policy had been the subject of controversy within the Truman administration. Braden's famous campaign, when he was Ambassador to Argentina in 1945, against the Argentine strong man, Juan Perón, and his effort, when in the position of assistant secretary, to influence the Argentine elections of February 1946, demonstrated the ineffectiveness of interference in the internal affairs of Latin American states, no matter how well-intentioned. As has been observed, Braden continued to condemn dictatorships in 1946 and 1947, which then set him up as a target for Trujillo's propaganda mill. In 1947 Trujillo sponsored the publication of a slanderous book written by a Venezuelan emigré, José Vicente Pepper. Pepper's book, entitled *I Accuse Braden,* described Braden as a "perfect Communist" who had sacrificed "American fraternity before the greedy altar of the Red Moloch." The book was also laced with invective against Arévalo, Grau, and Betancourt, referring to the latter as "the most reliable agent of the Kremlin in America," but charged that it was Braden, because of his "hasty" recognition of the Betancourt government, who enabled the Soviet Union to establish a "bridgehead" in America. Finally, said Pepper, Braden's "scandal mongering" had pinned "the fascist tag" on the Dominican and "other democratic governments" in the Americas.[93] It may be assumed that Trujillo's vituperation alone did not force Braden from the State Department, but, on the other hand, Braden had little to show for the ill will which he had incurred, and the Cold War had reduced the alternatives. Although Braden was not a partisan of the Democratic Left, his resignation diminished its hopes for finding a diplomatic solution to the problem of dictatorships.[94]

The Democratic Left, in fact, had little chance of securing formal diplomatic support for its policies, because, despite the postwar rhetoric about democracy, it was in a minority position. The overwhelming rejection of the interventionist thesis of Rodríguez Larreta had demonstrated this. Although the withholding of recognition from unconstitutional regimes had proven harmless, when Betancourt, as a delegate to the Bogotá conference in 1948, tried to win its acceptance as a general principle of hemispheric conduct, he failed. This so-called Betancourt Doctrine remained little more than the policy of Acción Democrática and its closest allies. But the Democratic Left did not despair; it felt that its position was morally right, and it had on its side thousands of refugees from tyranny, plus the sympathy of influential liberal leaders throughout the hemisphere. Unable to overcome dictatorship by peaceful methods, it gave its support to revolutionary activity.

The interventionist policy of the Democratic Left went thus beyond that of Rodríguez Larreta and included collaboration with friendly exiles and governments for the forceful overthrow of despotic regimes. The chances of a successful internal revolt against the entrenched Caribbean dictatorships were poor, but the exiled political leaders from these lands were prepared to lead armed invasions and, in combination with internal sabotage and resistance, to rally their countrymen in uprisings against the tyrants. Many of these leaders were committed to the ideals of political democracy, and some of them had already formed parties of the Democratic Left in exile; but they all agreed that only by force could they liberate their homelands.[95] Betancourt, Grau, and Arévalo (and later Prío and Figueres) shared the impatience and frustration of these exiles; they, too, had experienced exile and had also felt the necessity to engage in armed uprisings. As responsible national leaders, they had to proceed cautiously, but they all supported these movements in some way by providing either money, or arms, or manpower, or training sites. During the fifteen years following World War II, the Democratic Left was generally involved in this kind of activity, but it was in the immediate postwar period that conspiratorial movements dominated Caribbean affairs. The activity was so intense that it seemed only one grand army of exiles was responsible.

2 | *The Caribbean Legion*

The Muster, 1945-1946

THE CARIBBEAN LEGION was allegedly an army of exiles dedicated to the overthrow of dictatorial regimes in the Caribbean, especially during the period 1947-50. Actually, the Caribbean Legion never existed as a "specific military organization";[1] rather the term was applied indiscriminately to a series of exile military operations and plots. These movements occurred with frequency following World War II because of the implicit anachronism of dictatorship in the post-war era, but there was no permanent central command. The leadership and political sponsors varied in accordance with the specific objectives of the movement, even though some individuals served in more than one operation and part of the same equipment turned up over and over again. The term was first used in connection with the Costa Rican civil war in 1948 and persisted because it appealed to newsmen[2] and because the dictators used it repeatedly in their propaganda. The Caribbean dictators reasoned that they could discredit the exile movement by treating it as a group of mercenaries, adventurers, and arms traffickers.[3] Thus, to speak about "The Caribbean Legion" may only contribute to perpetuate the myth; but the intent is to describe this period of intense militancy and to sort out the various movements and motivating factors.

The movements were symptomatic of the unrest in the Caribbean after 1945. Parties of the Democratic Left were already in power in Cuba and in Venezuela, and a revolutionary government had taken over in Guatemala; but elsewhere in the Caribbean despotic governments

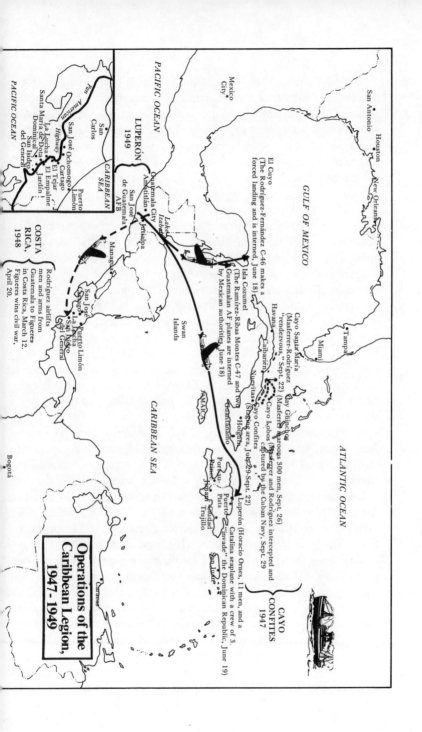

Operations of the Caribbean Legion, 1947-1949

PACIFIC OCEAN

San Antonio

Houston

New Orleans

Tampa

Miami

Mexico City

GULF OF MEXICO

ATLANTIC OCEAN

El Cayo
(The Rodríguez-Fernández C-46 makes a forced landing and is interned, June 18)

Cayo Santa María

Cayo Güinchos

Cayo Barcos

Havana

Caibarién

Isla Cozumel
(The Ramírez-Ribas Montes C-47 and two Guatemalan AF planes are interned by Mexican authorities, June 18)

Nuevitas

Cayo Confites

Cayo Lobos
(Masferrer and Rodríguez intercepted and captured by the Cuban Navy, Sept. 29

Cayo Santa María (Masferrer-Rodríguez "rendezvous," Sept. 22) (Masferrer harvests 300 men, Sept. 26)

(Swan area, July 29-Sept. 22)

Holguín

Guantánamo

Luperón (Horacio Ornes, 11 men, and a Catalina seaplane with a crew of 3, "invade" the Dominican Republic, June 19)

Port-au-Prince

Puerto Plata

Ciudad Trujillo

San Juan

Swan Islands

JAMAICA

CARIBBEAN SEA

Bogotá

Caracas

PACIFIC OCEAN

LUPERÓN
1949

Guatemala City
Aguacatán

San José
de Guatemala
AFB

Jutiapa

Lake Izabal

Managua

San José
Chinago

Puerto Limón
La Lucha
San Nicolás
del General

CARIBBEAN SEA

COSTA RICA,
1948
Rodríguez airlifts men and arms from Guatemala to Figueres in Costa Rica, March 12. Figures wins civil war, April 20.

PACIFIC OCEAN

San Carlos

San José
de Guatemala
AFB

LUPERÓN
1949

Pan American Highway

San Carlos

San José Ochomogo
Cartago
El Tejar
El Empalme
La Lucha
Santa María de Doña Jardín
Dominical
San Isidro
del General
Puerto Limón

CARIBBEAN SEA

CAYO CONFITES
1947

CAYO CONFITES 1947

continued to reign. From the Dominican Republic, Honduras, Nicaragua, and Costa Rica, refugees from tyranny flocked to the newly liberated lands, where they sought sympathy and assistance. The exiles were anxious to imitate the success of their hosts and saw the opportunity to ride the crest of a revolutionary wave. They were convinced that, with the connivance of friendly governments, they would be able to liberate their respective homelands by means of armed invasions. Ramón Grau San Martín of Cuba, Rómulo Betancourt of Venezuela, and Juan José Arévalo of Guatemala were disposed to aid such enterprises both as a matter of principle and as a matter of self-preservation. These leaders embraced the interventionist thesis in behalf of representative democracy and human rights. They also feared the possibility of counterrevolution because of the existence of dictatorships in neighboring states. There were also other factors. Close bonds, originating with the service of the Dominican Máximo Gómez in the cause of Cuban independence from Spain,[4] existed between Cubans and Dominicans. Arévalo was deeply interested in promoting Central American union. Betancourt detested Rafael Trujillo and suspected him of conspiring with former President Eleazar López Contreras.[5] Later, José Figueres of Costa Rica would try to repay a debt to Nicaraguan leaders in exile. Under these circumstances, the exile organizations took shape and a number of military movements emerged.

The Dominican exiles set up their main base in Cuba. The writer Juan Bosch, who had been in exile since 1937, took the initiative to form an anti-Trujillo coalition in 1945.[6] As secretary-general of the Dominican Revolutionary party (PRD), Bosch helped organize the Central Revolutionary Junta and its military arm, the Liberation Army of America (Ejército de Liberación de América). The junta was presided over by Angel Morales, a former vice-president of the League of Nations, whose exile began in 1930. The membership included Bosch, General Juan Rodríguez García, a Dominican millionaire who had fled the Dominican Republic in 1945 in order to join the movement against Trujillo, and Doctors Leovigildo Cuello and Juan Isidro Jiménez Grullón.[7] The latter was the grandson of a former president of the Dominican Republic and was, of course, a *"Jimenista,"* one of the two pre-Trujillo controlling factions. General Rodríguez was the commander in chief of the Liberation Army, largely because he was prepared to use his personal fortune to overthrow Trujillo. His chief of staff was Miguel Angel Ramírez Alcántara. Ramírez was not a professional soldier. He had been in exile since 1930, mainly in New York, where he had been a teacher of mathematics and Spanish and a commission merchant dealing in tropical fruit.[8] He claimed, however, that he was descended from four generations of professional soldiers, and during his exile years in New York he gained a great deal of experience organizing exile revolutionary cells and clubs. In the early thirties Ramírez had joined with Cuban exiles in plotting against the regime of Gerardo Machado.[9] Cubans now returned the favor.

Prominent Cubans played an important part in the formation of the Liberation Army. President Grau not only made it possible for the Dominicans to live in Cuba but said he "encouraged them in the task of restoring to the Dominican Republic its lost freedom."[10] Manolo Castro Campos, a Havana University student leader, helped organize the Liberation Army,[11] and Eufemio Fernández Ortega, chief of the Cuban Secret Police, was the army's chief of operations. Fernández had fought with the Loyalists in the Spanish Civil War and was the leader in Cuba of Acción Revolucionaria Guiteras.[12] The latter group was one of the many paramilitary organizations in Cuba left over from the days of the anti-Machado resistance movement. During the administrations of Grau and his successor Carlos Prío Socarrás, these bands of *"pistoleros"* were a serious national problem. In 1945-46, however, these groups were able to dissipate some of their energies in the exile military preparations.

Another very important Cuban (who was really a Spanish refugee) was Cruz Alonso, the owner of the Hotel San Luis in Havana. José Figueres described Cruz Alonso as the "godfather of all democratic causes,"[13] and someone else observed that he was the "innkeeper for every conspiracy in the Caribbean."[14] The general headquarters of the Liberation Army was located in the Hotel San Luis,[15] and it may be affirmed that virtually every important Caribbean exile leader stopped over at one time or another in that Havana hotel. The Dominicans were definitely in the best position for a strike against their homeland; exiles of other nationalities were in a less favorable situation.

The Hondurans as a group were neither numerous nor well-organized, but, paradoxically, they provided key personnel for the exile operations. This was because many of them were young army officers. General Tiburcio Carías Andino had retarded political and intellectual development in Honduras, and only an occasional barracks revolt disturbed his oppressive rule. One such futile attempt was led by Jorge

Ribas Montes in November 1943. Ribas, a twenty-three-year-old commander of the Presidential Guard and a graduate of the Military School
in Guatemala, was condemned to death but was spared after serving
two-and-half years in prison. He fled to Guatemala and then to Cuba,
where he joined the Liberation Army.[16] Eventually, other Honduran
officers followed him, either to Cuba or later to Costa Rica, to serve as
the captains, majors, and colonels of the Liberation Army. Among these
officers were Miguel Francisco Morazán, a descendant of one of the
great figures of Central American history, Francisco Sánchez Reyes (*"el
Indio"* Sánchez), Alfredo Mejía Lara, and Mario Sosa Navarro. These
were the most dedicated legionnaires. They were willing to fight even
though the chances for an early return to their homeland were remote.
The assault upon Carías would have to wait for those upon Trujillo and
Anastasio Somoza of Nicaragua.

In terms of time in exile and of numbers the Nicaraguans rivaled the
Dominicans, but they were troubled by factionalism. The largest colony
was in Mexico City, congregated around such figures as the septuagenarian General Emiliano Chamorro, an ex-president and wealthy leader of
the dynastic Conservative party, and General Carlos Pasos, another man
of wealth, who led a dissident wing of Somoza's own Liberal party.[17]
These leaders cooperated occasionally and were prospective financial
backers for revolutionary schemes, but the Chamorros tended to be
clannish and their concept of politics was personalist. Many of the
Nicaraguan intellectuals, such as Juan José Meza, Enoc Aguado, and
Pedro José Zepeda, advocated the ideal of a Central American federation. They had joined the Costa Rican writer Vicente Sáenz in founding
the Central American Democratic Union (Unión Democrática Centro-
americana) in Mexico in the early 1940s.[18] On the other hand, a group
of former National Guard officers preferred to go to Cuba and join the
Liberation Army. These included Manuel Gómez Flores, Adolfo Báez
Bone, and José María Tercero.[19]

Among the Nicaraguan exiles in Mexico also was a young physician,
Dr. Rosendo Argüello, Jr. Argüello was a member of a prominent
family generally associated with the Liberal party, but his father had
split with Somoza and gone into exile in Mexico between 1936 and
1942.[20] After his father's return to Nicaragua, young Argüello remained in Mexico and established a clinic. He enjoyed friendly relations
with most Nicaraguan exiles, although he disapproved of the "stodgy,
middle-aged attitude" of General Chamorro.[21]

In 1943 Argüello became acquainted with a Costa Rican exile in Mexico City, José Figueres. The two men discussed the situations in their respective homelands and concluded that Central America was suffering from a common malady which could be cured by a "common remedy."[22] They, therefore, sought means for promoting their common cause. Argüello suggested that they join the Central American Democratic Union, but Figueres apparently felt that the organization engaged in too much talk and not enough action.[23] Figueres' plan was for Argüello to assist him in the overthrow of Rafael Angel Calderón Guardia, with him in turn pledging to aid the Nicaraguans against Anastasio Somoza.[24] Figueres argued that Calderón was the "weakest link" in the dictatorial chain, which, once broken, would facilitate the destruction of the remaining dictatorships. Moreover, Figueres believed that the Costa Ricans would form a citizens' army in the same way that the people of the United States, whom he did not regard as militaristic, had raised armies to defend their democracy in two world wars.[25] Figueres and Argüello traveled together to Costa Rica in May 1944, and the following year Argüello returned to Mexico to secure support for their plan from the Nicaraguan exile groups.[26]

Argüello undertook to collect money and arms in preparation for Figueres' call to Costa Rica. General Chamorro was not interested in the plan, but General Pasos contributed $12,000, matching an identical amount raised by Figueres, and Dr. Zepeda permitted the use of his ranch, about fifty miles from Mexico City, as an arsenal and testing range.[27] Argüello also managed to persuade a fellow countryman, Edelberto Torres, to leave his university teaching in Guatemala and come to Mexico to assist in the plot. Torres shared the ambition for "federation and democracy" in Central America, and the frail professor personally helped crate Argüello's arms for shipment to Costa Rica.[28] Figueres, meanwhile, collected arms and buried them on his *finca* "La Lucha Sin Fin" and made trips to Managua and Guatemala in search of support. He also traveled to San Antonio, Texas, for a rendezvous with Argüello in the hope of acquiring more military equipment.[29] The Mexican police, however, discovered the activities of the conspirators and arrested Argüello and Torres on 11 February 1947, seizing thirty crates of arms which had been accumulated.[30] It was a hard blow to the movement of Figueres and Argüello, but, although the exile groups experienced such disappointments frequently, the plotting continued and the dream persisted.

Drawn also to the exile cause were a number of Spanish Republicans and North Americans. The Spanish Republicans, such as Alberto Bayo, Antonio Román Durán, Jacobo Fernández Alverdi, Daniel Martín Lambradeiros, and the Osuna brothers, were scattered throughout the Caribbean. Trujillo accused them of bringing communism to the Caribbean,[31] which made them objects of suspicion, but the Spanish Republicans contributed useful military skills and a romantic spirit to the exile movements. Concerning the U.S. citizens, many of them, like the Spaniards, were mercenaries. This was true particularly about the pilots—World War II veterans—who were attracted by the promise of adventure and money. But some were idealists, such as Hollis B. Smith, a munitions expert from New Jersey, who said he joined the Liberation Army because he did not feel "any people should be treated as Trujillo [was] treating the Dominicans."[32] And there was John W. Chewning of Miami, who died for the cause.[33]

Such, then, were the forces which kept the Caribbean in turmoil for the next few years.

Cayo Confites, 1947

One of the most ambitious buildups in the Caribbean for an exile military expedition took place in Cuba in 1947. The Liberation Army of America managed to recruit and train more than a thousand men and to acquire arms and military equipment valued at approximately two million dollars.[34] German-made weapons were obtained in Argentina,[35] and U.S. war-surplus equipment was collected from various sources. The North American Hollis B. Smith illegally airlifted over two tons of military cargo from Baltimore,[36] and twelve aircraft of various types were brought to Cuba for the invasion force.[37] The expeditionaries possessed a fleet of two landing craft, the *Aurora* and the *Berta,* and a Dominican motorship, the *Angelita* (renamed the *Maceo*), which they had seized on the high seas.[38] In all these operations the Liberation Army had the use of Cuban ports, airfields, and certain public buildings, and the police and army were alerted not to interfere.[39]

José Manuel Alemán, the Cuban minister of education, was chosen "expressly" by President Grau to coordinate the efforts of the Cuban government with those of the Liberation Army.[40] Alemán was an important leader in Grau's Auténtico party; he had presidential ambitions and was described as a "Cuban Rasputin"[41] (he later fled Cuba after allegedly stealing millions of dollars). Public school buildings were used as recruiting and reception centers for the revolutionaries, and public parks, such as the José Martí Children's Park (Parque Juvenil José Martí) in Havana, were used for drill and parade grounds. Alemán himself permitted the use of his ranch ten miles outside of Havana for the storage of a huge arsenal of arms.[42] Later, in August, the revolutionaries were moved, either in ministry trucks or by train, to the polytechnical schools in Matanzas and Holguín.[43] Funds were channeled to the Liberation Army from the budget of the Ministry of Education, and many of the Liberation Army leaders were placed on Alemán's payroll, including Manolo Castro, who was appointed national director of sports.[44] Castro used the ministry's funds to purchase arms in the United States; but he was caught and, along with Miguel Angel Ramírez and Hollis Smith, was indicted in Florida on charges of conspiracy to violate the export control act.[45] Other highly placed Cubans involved were Eufemio Fernández, the chief of the Secret Police, as mentioned; Rolando Masferrer, who later was also chief of the Secret Police but under Fulgencio Batista; and Enrique C. Henríquez, a senator and the brother-in-law of Carlos Prío Socarrás.[46] This assistance by Cuba is well documented. Such is not the case, however, regarding the involvement of Venezuela and Guatemala.

The nature of the support given this movement by Betancourt and Arévalo may be determined only in more general terms. Figueres has said that Arévalo supplied the expedition with arms;[47] in fact, Arévalo was the likely source of German-made arms from Perón's Argentina.[48] One of the Dominican exile leaders, Horacio Julio Ornes, about whom there will be more later, declared that the "true democrats" of Cuba, Venezuela, and Guatemala supported their project "materially and spiritually."[49] On 27 July and 24 August 1947, it was reported that the Dominican government had charged Venezuela and Guatemala with contributing "planes and large sums of money" to the anti-Trujillo forces based in Cuba.[50] In a formal note, which the Dominican Republic delivered to the Inter-American Peace Committee (IAPC) on 15 August 1949, these charges against the Guatemalan and Venezuelan governments were reaffirmed. The note specifically named Luis Augusto Dubuc, secretary of organization of Acción Democrática of Venezuela, as Betancourt's representative before the revolutionary junta in Cuba.[51] The IAPC made no formal investigation of these charges at the time; but later, with reference to them, the Argentine representative on the committee, Enrique V. Corominas, wrote that it had been "shown that the Democratic Action leaders had contributed all the elements they could muster in support of the subversive action."[52] Despite the fact that Trujillo's charges were phrased with abusive language and that he often falsified information, he usually had the essential facts owing to an effective espionage system and a "superbly efficient monitor service" of international radio and telephonic communications.[53] The general collaboration of Betancourt and Arévalo in this affair may therefore be assumed. But no intelligence service was necessary in order to know that an invasion of the Dominican Republic was being prepared in Cuba in the summer of 1947.

In fact, the fanfare given the activities of the Liberation Army of America, and its lack of security, had the effect of undermining the operation. Already in June the recruiting and training of the expeditionary force was general knowledge in Havana,[54] and by 27 July the *New York Times* reported specifically concerning the movement.[55] Mrs. Ruby Hart Phillips, the *Times*' correspondent in Havana, became aware of the preparations when she started receiving telephone calls for Generals Rodríguez and Ramírez—it happened that her telephone number was only one digit different from that of the José Martí Children's Park, where the revolutionaries were training.[56] At the end of July, *Alerta* of Havana reported that a revolutionary force was training in Holguín for the invasion of the Dominican Republic. *El Heraldo* of Holguín published a proclamation signed by two members of the Central Revolutionary Junta, Juan Bosch and Juan Isidro Jiménez Grullón.[57] As the number of these reports grew, it developed that not all Cubans approved of what was going on. The publicity led to controversy. Many opposition leaders attacked Grau's interventionist policy and criticized the use of public buildings and facilities by the exile groups. A scandal threatened over the suspected diversion of public funds to the movement.[58] Moreover, rumors circulated that Grau, Alemán, and other Auténticos were building up the exile army as a personal force to maintain themselves in power in Cuba.[59] Public concern deepened when Alfonso Luis Fors, a private detective allegedly in Trujillo's employ, was shot down in a Havana street by unknown assassins.[60] As adverse publicity and internal politics placed Grau's continued support of the movement in jeopardy, Trujillo exerted pressure in the international sphere.

On 23 July 1947 the Dominican government sent its first note of protest to the Cuban government concerning the exiles' activities, and for the next several weeks it continued the diplomatic offensive.[61] The Dominican Republic presented to Cuba the information it possessed relative to the conspiracy. It reminded Cuba of its treaty obligations to prevent subversive activities within its territory against a sister republic. According to the Dominicans, however, Cuba promised only to investigate the matter.[62] When this investigation failed to materialize, Trujillo, on 18 August issued a public statement charging that Cuban territory was being used as "a base for training an armed force which might be called an international brigade composed of noted Communists."[63] He called for the good offices or mediation of "some American governments" and warned that the situation "could possibly give rise to a war of great and serious proportions between Cuba and the Dominican Republic."[64] Two days later, Trujillo cabled Grau personally to request him "to intervene to stop the revolutionary preparations." He added the ill-concealed threat that he would regret the failure of his government's "sincere efforts made by diplomatic means" to find a solution.[65] Grau's reply to this was considered "evasive" by the Dominicans,[66] who then decided to seek a meeting of consultation of ministers of foreign affairs. The Dominican Foreign Ministry acted under procedures established at the Second Meeting of Consultation at Havana in 1940. On 30 August it sent a circular note to the foreign ministries of the American states in which it informed them of "everything it then knew about the progress of the plot in Cuba."[67] The Cuban government was outraged by this step. On 6 September it informed the Dominican government that it would not cooperate in this maneuver and threatened to terminate all communications relative to the matter if the Dominican Republic persisted in its course.[68] Although the situation seemed to be at an impasse, the actions of the Dominican Republic had been effective. The United States issued a statement on 2 August reaffirming its obligations concerning revolutionary movements in the Americas and took measures to prevent any violation of the neutrality of its territory.[69] Specifically, it revoked a license granted to Cruz Alonso for the export of the LCI *Patria,* because it had learned that the vessel was intended for use by revolutionaries.[70] The international and internal pressures were great upon Grau, but as yet he had neither decided nor been forced to stop the invasion. By mid-August the movement was being conducted with greater secrecy,[71] and the Liberation Army had moved to Cayo Confites, a small, deserted key off the Cuban coast, about fifty miles from the port of Nuevitas. [72]

Cayo Confites was to be the staging area for the invasion of the Dominican Republic, but it was a poor choice. Described as one of the most miserable keys off Cuba, Cayo Confites was hot, sandy, and swarming with flies and mosquitoes; there were no trees and there were only three buildings, which were occupied by the principal leaders. [73] The invasion army was made up of four so-called battalions averaging 260 men each: Sandino, Guiteras, Luperón, and Máximo Gómez, under the command respectively of Rolando Masferrer, Eufemio Fernández, Jorge Ribas Montes, and Diego Bordas (a Dominican who was a political ally of Bosch).[74] The total force was approximately 1,150—although, as John Bartlow Martin has observed, "If everyone who later claimed he was at Cayo Confites had actually been there, the invaders could have overwhelmed Trujillo by sheer numbers."[75] Nevertheless, even a casual look at the roll revealed the presence of the Caribbean's principal activists. Besides the battalion commanders, there were the Dominicans Juan Rodríguez García, Miguel Angel Ramírez, Horacio Julio Ornes, Juan Bosch, and José Horacio Rodríguez (the son of General Rodríguez); the Cubans Manolo Castro, Enrique C. Henríquez, and Fidel Castro Ruz (then a Havana University student leader); the Hondurans Alfredo Mejía Lara and Francisco (*"el Indio"*) Sánchez Reyes; the Nicaraguans José María Tercero and Adolfo Báez Bone (who were killed in April 1954 while trying to assassinate Somoza); Mario Climaco Alférez (one of the few Salvadorans involved); Jacobo Fernández Alverdi (a Spanish Republican); Nicolás Silfa (a Dominican exile residing in New York, who had served in the U.S. Army in World War II and had become a U.S. citizen); and the North Americans Hollis B. Smith, Thomas Sawyer, and Rupert Irwin Waddell (who supposedly had served as a flying officer in the Royal Air Force). The expeditionaries, however, awaited their D-day in vain.

The invasion force began to collect on Cayo Confites on 29 July and remained there until 22 September, when the plans went awry. Delay, discomfort, disorganization, and a lack of food and water demoralized the group.[76] Dissension and desertion had been problems throughout the operation,[77] but at Cayo Confites ill feelings apparently increased. For example, according to a story told by Ramírez, when Juan Bosch arrived on the islet without the arms and supplies he allegedly had promised, the other leaders "decided to court-martial and shoot him."[78] Ramírez claimed he saved Bosch's life by placing him in a hole in the sand and remaining guard over him throughout the night.[79] Then word came from the mainland on 21 September that in a surprise move the Cuban army had raided Alemán's ranch, where it confiscated thirteen truckloads of weapons.[80] At the same time, it seized "eleven bombers," which the expeditionaries had waiting on various airfields in Cuba.[81] Rodríguez hastened to Havana, but the army and navy were already moving against the invasion force, and Rodríguez was told to abandon the key in twenty-four hours.[82]

The expedition was collapsing, but Masferrer took command on 22 September and decided to sail anyway.[83] He went north to Cayo Santa María, off Caibarién, where Rodríguez rejoined him and upbraided him for his insubordination. Nonetheless, after a violent argument, the expedition sailed to Cay Güinchos in the Bahamas in an effort to elude the Cuban navy. There, on 26 September, Masferrer, tired of hearing complaints, asked those unwilling to proceed to say so. When three hundred men stepped forward, Masferrer became violent. He threatened to shoot them, but Diego Bordas intervened. Instead, in a scene not uncommon in the Old Bahama Channel, Masferrer stripped them of their arms, possessions, and even clothing, and left them on the key without food or water.[84] However, risking detection, the expeditionaries notified the Cuban navy about their marooned comrades (one of whom was Masferrer's nephew).[85] This group was the first to be returned to Havana, and its appearance led to the conclusion that the action of the Cuban navy was one of mercy rather than villainy. Two days later, Cuban warships caught up with Masferrer on the *Berta* near Cayo Lobo. Without explaining his need, Masferrer radioed to Rodríguez on the *Aurora* for help, and when the latter turned back to answer the distress call, much to his chagrin he was captured also.[86] The Cayo Confites operation was over, and all the revolutionaries were taken to Havana, where they were interned for a short time at Camp Columbia.[87] Only the question remained, why had Cuba, which had given so much assistance to the Liberation Army, reversed its policy and stopped the invasion?

The easiest answer was to blame President Grau. The excitable Senator Eduardo ("Eddy") Chibás accused Grau "of having betrayed the cause of Dominican freedom."[88] Mrs. Phillips reported that Grau disbanded the expedition at the "urging" of the United States.[89] The Dominican Republic claimed that Grau acted in the face of "domestic opinion" and the "clamor of the continent."[90] All of these factors undoubtedly influenced Grau, but there is some evidence that the

Cuban army may have taken the initiative without the president's consent.

A number of the revolutionaries charged that the chief of staff of the Cuban army, General Genovevo Pérez Dámera, was directly responsible. Rolando Masferrer called him a traitor.[91] Horacio Ornes added that Pérez Dámera had been bribed by Trujillo's "corrupting gold," [92] which, according to an unsubstantiated report in *Bohemia* of Havana, reached a sum "of seven figures."[93] It was further alleged that the betrayal was arranged in an interview in Washington between Pérez Dámera and Arturo Despradel, the Dominican foreign minister. [94] Eufemio Fernández published an open letter in *Bohemia* on 8 January 1950, in which he confessed that before Cayo Confites he had committed the "stupidity" of going to Pérez Dámera for assistance—a "stupidity," because, as he explained, Pérez Dámera was actually Trujillo's "friend," for whom he performed "relevant services."[95] No one could document that Trujillo used bribery in this instance, but it was his general practice to reach into other states and exert influence where he could. In Cuba, the mutual distrust between civilian and military leaders was exploitable.

During the invasion preparations, the rumor persisted that Grau intended to use the Liberation Army to perpetuate himself in power. When the army seized the arms cache at Alemán's ranch, the news reports made no mention of an international movement but referred to an attempt to overthrow the Cuban government. Pérez Dámera was quoted at the time as saying that it was "only the beginning" of the disarming of civilians.[96] Also, when the navy moved against the expedition at Cayo Confites, it was repeated that the revolutionary group was opposed to the Cuban government as well as to the Dominican Republic.[97] And at that moment one-half of the Cuban government was Pérez Dámera. A subsequent event illustrated this as well as Pérez Dámera's ties to Trujillo.

On 23 August 1949, Grau's successor, Carlos Prío Socarrás, fired General Genovevo Pérez Dámera as chief of the Army General Staff. It would be better to say, however, that Prío deposed Pérez Dámera, because the president literally swooped down upon the army headquarters at Camp Columbia and took Pérez Dámera by surprise. Prío carefully planned his action; he lined up the support of loyal officers, who accompanied him to Camp Columbia. Among the officers was General Ruperto Cabrera, who was installed on the spot as the new chief of staff.[98] It was, in effect, a *golpe,* but this time, instead of the army moving in from Camp Columbia to remove the occupant of the Presidential Palace, the president had gone to the barracks to throw out the general. Prío acted, he said, because he had information from the Dominican underground that Pérez Dámera was engaged in secret negotiations with Trujillo.[99] Such negotiations started on 19 July 1949, when Dominican radio broadcasts warned Pérez Dámera of a plot to kill him; the general was understandably alarmed because Trujillo had broadcast similar warnings to Colonel Francisco Javier Arana of Guatemala, who, indeed, was assassinated on 18 July. Prío advised Pérez Dámera to ignore the warning, but the army chief sent "two trusted men" to interview Trujillo. These interviews were followed by others, which led to a trip to Ciudad Trujillo by Colonel Camilo González Chávez, the chief of aviation. These actions convinced Prío that Pérez Dámera's anxieties had escalated to disloyalty, and Prío acted. [100] While these events were *ex post facto* with reference to Cayo Confites, they indicated the complexities of Caribbean politics and provided insights into the riddle of the failure of Cayo Confites.

Twenty years later, in an interview with the author, Pérez Dámera insisted that he stopped the invasion in order to protect the honor of Cuba. He affirmed that the United States had given President Grau thirty days to disband the invasion force, or else it would move against the rebels. Faced with the threat of direct intervention, Pérez Dámera claimed that Grau ordered him to break up the expedition.[101]

Despite the quashing of the expedition, all of the revolutionaries were given their freedom and none was punished. All of the men were released almost immediately upon their return to Havana, and the leaders were freed shortly thereafter.[102] The Cuban Senate censured Alemán, and he resigned as minister of education, but President Grau immediately restored him to the cabinet as minister without portfolio.[103] Finally, General Rodríguez was permitted to depart for Guatemala and to take with him a large portion of the arms he had collected for the invasion.[104]

Trujillo was, of course, irate over the leniency shown the expeditionaries and especially over the fact that they retained their equipment intact, "available for new adventures."[105] The Dominican government renewed the diplomatic offensive, not only to prevent the future use of Cuban territory as a base for exile revolutionary activity but, in accordance with the 1928 Havana Convention on the Rights and Duties of

States in the Event of Civil Strife, to force Cuba to turn over the Cayo Confites arms to the Dominican Republic. The Dominican government engaged the Cuban government in a lively diplomatic exchange throughout the following year. It sought "moral and material" reparations, suggested the submission of the matter to arbitration or to the International Court of Justice, and finally forced the revival of the Inter-American Committee on the Pacific Settlement of Disputes.[106] The latter body, revived and renamed the Inter-American Peace Committee (IAPC), persuaded Cuba and the Dominican Republic to agree in September 1948 to settle their differences by direct negotiations. The committee seemed satisfied that there had been a successful issue out of the conflict.[107] By this time, however, the activities of the exiles and their allies in another quarter of the Caribbean rendered this particular settlement inconsequential.

Costa Rica, 1948

Following Cayo Confites, most exile groups shifted their conspiratorial base to Guatemala. President Juan José Arévalo was willing to assume the role formerly played by Grau San Martín, and General Juan Rodríguez García was there with his arms. Rodríguez enjoyed the popularity of the only boy in the neighborhood with a football. Exile leaders wooed him and engaged in a vigorous rivalry for the use of his equipment. On the other hand, Rodríguez was still commander in chief of the Liberation Army of America, and he and Miguel Angel Ramírez were looking for allies in order to renew their fight.[108] Besides the Dominicans, the groups in Guatemala included the various Nicaraguan factions of Emiliano Chamorro, Carlos Pasos, and Toribio Tijerino; a number of Honduran elements of which the Cayo Confites veterans under Jorge Ribas Montes and Miguel Francisco Morazán were the most important; and the Costa Rican-Nicaraguan group of José Figueres and Rosendo Argüello, Jr.

Figueres and Argüello were particularly anxious to secure Rodríguez' arms. Their movement had suffered a setback when they lost their weapons in Mexico in February 1947, but Figueres had not abandoned his belief that force was the only way to unseat the *calderonistas* in Costa Rica. The election of 1944, by which Teodoro Picado Michalski had succeeded Rafael Angel Calderón Guardia as president, and the congressional elections of 1946, in which Calderón's National Republican party (Partido Republicano Nacional) scored large gains, were viewed as frauds by Figueres.[109] He expected little better in the upcoming 1948 elections. Even though he helped form a coalition of opposition groups in February 1947, which selected Otilio Ulate, editor of the *Diario de Costa Rica,* to oppose Calderón in 1948, Figueres was convinced that the so-called *"caldero-comunistas"* would make a mockery of the democratic process. As if to vindicate these misgivings, bands of toughs using "bullets, blackjacks, and tear gas" regularly attacked the political rallies of the national opposition.[110] To protest these outrages, the opposition staged a "sit-down" strike or work stoppage in San José at the end of July, but the authorities intervened and, after over a week of demonstrations, five persons had been killed and fifty-nine injured.[111] Under the circumstances, although Figueres did not openly disavow Ulate's efforts to get elected, he was convinced that the "First Republic" was dead and that he needed arms to establish the "Second Republic."[112]

In Guatemala Argüello worked hard to win over Rodríguez to Figueres' cause. The Figueres view remained that Calderón would be the easiest dictator to overcome, so that the plan was still Costa Rica first, then Nicaragua, and still later Honduras and El Salvador. The fight would continue until every tyrant in the Caribbean was eliminated. [113] According to Argüello, however, the struggle for the weapons was marked by so much bitterness and intrigue that Arévalo threatened to withdraw his support unless the various factions came to a unified agreement and settled their personal differences.[114] Argüello related that as a result of this "ultimatum" on the part of Arévalo, the leaders of the revolutionary groups of Costa Rica, the Dominican Republic, and Nicaragua undertook in December 1947 to coordinate their efforts by negotiating a Caribbean Pact.[115]

By the terms of the Caribbean Pact, as described by Argüello, the exiles agreed to form "a single revolutionary team." This team was to be presided over by a Supreme Revolutionary Committee comprised of Juan Rodríguez García and José Horacio Rodríguez Vásquez for the Dominican Republic; Rosendo Argüello, Sr., and Toribio Tijerino for Nicaragua; and José Figueres and Rosendo Argüello, Jr., for Costa Rica. The signatories of the pact were Juan Rodríguez for the Dominican Republic; Emiliano Chamorro, Gustavo Manzanares, Pedro José Zepeda, and Rosendo Argüello, Sr., for Nicaragua; and José Figueres for Costa Rica. The signatories agreed that the Supreme Committee would coordinate the efforts and determine the contributions of the participating groups and that Juan Rodríguez would be the permanent president of the committee as well as the "commander in chief of the allied armies." The pact stipulated that once a country was liberated the respective national group would form a junta of government which would have exclusive jurisdiction in internal matters, but in "general affairs" it would follow the "instructions" of the Supreme Committee until the last dictatorship was eliminated. The liberated countries would furthermore form a "democratic Caribbean alliance," the purpose of which included the "consolidation and purification" of democratic life within the member countries. The countries of the alliance committed themselves to the "recovery" of European possessions still existing in the Caribbean, the "strict adherence" to inter-American conventions, and a "permanent alliance in military affairs" with Mexico and the United States "for the common defense." The signatories also agreed that the "reconstruction" of the Republic of Central America was "a fundamental necessity" and to this end pledged that each liberated country would "incorporate this principle" within its new constitution. Finally, the signatories named Arévalo as the final arbiter in any difference which might arise over the interpretation or implementation of the Caribbean Pact.[116]

In view of Argüello's later falling-out with Figueres and the use which Figueres' political opponents made of the revelations by Argüello,[117] one might be skeptical about the validity of the document. However, the pact as described by Argüello was quite idealistic in tone and it certainly gave no support to Trujillo's charges that the Caribbean exile movement was an international brigade of Communists. Figueres confirmed the existence and essential terms of an antidictatorial agreement, which he called the "Pact of Guatemala."[118] Miguel Angel Ramírez stated simply that the Figueres group approached the Liberation Army for assistance and that the conditions of such aid were specified in a "pact of mutual cooperation."[119] On the other hand, the Trujillo regime asserted that Juan Bosch was the principal agent for the elaboration of a pact in 1947, which created the "Caribbean Liberation Committee," and that Bosch traveled about the Caribbean to secure the signatures of Arévalo and Juan Rodríguez, along with those of Rómulo Betancourt and Rómulo Gallegos of Venezuela and Aureliano Sánchez Arango of Cuba.[120]

It was evident that the Caribbean revolutionaries had regrouped their forces within a few months after Cayo Confites and that they were ready for "new adventures." They did not have to wait long for this new action; events in Costa Rica soon called for the fulfillment of their agreements.

In the Costa Rican elections on 8 February 1948 Otilio Ulate was the apparent victor, but as had been predicted the calderonistas moved to annul the vote. The Picado government first charged that there was evidence of fraud and then insisted that the election had to be submitted to Congress, because only two of the three judges of the Electoral Tribunal had certified the results. On 1 March, Congress, in which the government enjoyed a majority, annulled the elections. On the same day, the police attempted to arrest Ulate, and, although he escaped, a friend of his was shot and killed.[121] The following day Ulate was captured, but he was released through the mediation of the U.S. ambassador and other members of the diplomatic corps. The situation became tense; San José was at a virtual standstill. Calderón and the Communists brought in groups of banana workers from the coastal regions, the so-called *"mariachis,"* while Ulate threatened a general strike and some of his followers talked of civil war.[122] The archbishop of Costa Rica, Monsignor Víctor Manuel Sanabria, arranged a truce and hoped to use the time to find a peaceful solution. Although the truce held for about a week, in the end Calderón rejected the archbishop's efforts at mediation.[123] Meanwhile, Figueres had gone to his finca "La Lucha," in the mountains about thirty-five miles south of the capital, and prepared to take up arms.

Although there appeared to be a cause-and-effect relation between the nullification of Ulate's election and the initiation of military action by Figueres, the war was no spur-of-the-moment act—there had been, as Figueres had said, a six-year period of "gestation."[124] During those years of preparation, Figueres developed a relatively simple strategy.[125] Operating from the mountain fastness of his ranch south of the main centers of population of San José and Cartago, he would establish a defensive line across the Pan American Highway and seal off the southern portion of Costa Rica behind the rugged Cordillera de Talamanca. Farther south on the highway he would seize the town of San Isidro del General and occupy its airfield, so that his Caribbean allies could then fly in with reenforcements and arms. As soon as this zone was secured and his forces were equipped and ready, Figueres would initiate the "Plan Magnolia," which called for the concentration of all forces on the northern front, the penetration of the government lines, and an attack upon Cartago.[126] With the efforts at a peaceful solution unsuccessful, "Don Pepe," as all Costa Rica soon knew Figueres, set his plan in motion.

On 11 March Figueres began the forty-five-day War of National Liberation. At "La Luçha" he had gathered around him about two dozen men, such as Alberto Martén, a boyhood friend and close comrade; Frank Marshall, a quick-tempered, man-of-action type, who had been born in Costa Rica of a German father; and Father Benjamín Núñez, a fighting priest who was a leader of the Costa Rican labor movement. This group was quickly augmented by lawyers, doctors, businessmen, farmers, and farm laborers.[127] These troops seized San Isidro del General as planned and at the airfield captured three commercial DC-3s. Two of the aircraft were immediately flown to Guatemala, where Rodríguez awaited. On 12 March the DC-3s returned loaded with six hundred rifles, ammunition, and some machine guns and carrying seven Dominican and Honduran officers: Ramírez, Ribas Montes, Morazán, "el Indio" Sánchez, Horacio Ornes, Mario Sosa Navarro, and Alfredo Mejía Lara.[128] They landed at San Isidro del General and after commandeering transportation raced the some fifty-seven miles northward to Figueres' ranch. There they distributed the arms and began to train Figueres' citizen army, which eventually numbered seven hundred men.[129]

As commander in chief of the Army of National Liberation, Figueres pressed forward with his strategic plan. Attacked by government troops, however, he retreated deeper into the sierra and established his general headquarters in the picturesque village of Santa María de Dota. Ten miles to the north and several thousand feet higher, Martén, Ribas Montes, and Marshall established the defensive line, the "Northern Front," at El Empalme on the Pan American Highway. Ramírez, who had been named chief of staff, returned to San Isidro del General with 120 men to secure the supply base and the "Southern Front." [130] When Ramírez reached the airfield, another flight of planes arrived from Guatemala carrying Argüello and a group of Nicaraguan exiles, including Octavio Caldera, Generals Julián Salaverry and Antonio Velásquez, Adolfo Báez Bone, and José María Tercero.[131] Argüello went immediately to Santa María de Dota to join Figueres, who was obviously happy over the way the first phase of the operation had gone.

For the next month, Figueres maintained his defensive position while he received help from abroad and called upon the Costa Rican people to aid the National Liberation. In addition to the arms flown in from Guatemala, some of the Cayo Confites arms still in Cuban arsenals were now shipped to Costa Rica,[132] and Eufemio Fernández reportedly raised 114,000 pesos for the cause.[133] At Santa María de Dota, Don Pepe set up a radio transmitter and initiated a campaign of psychological warfare. In his broadcasts, which began with the opening notes of Beethoven's Fifth Symphony, the familiar dot-dot-dot-dash of the "V" for victory used by the Allied forces in World War II, Figueres exhorted the people to engage in acts of sabotage by placing barriers on roads and highways and by cutting communication lines.[134] During this time, the government assaulted the line at El Empalme repeatedly, but Ribas Montes and Marshall had dug in and managed to hold. Government forces did manage to raid "La Lucha" and to burn Figueres' small factory. On the southern front, the government, aided by Nicaraguan troops, made an amphibious landing at the port of Dominical and advanced against San Isidro del General, where Ramírez turned them back in a battle on 22 March.[135] Ramírez noted the irony of the fact that one of the government columns had been led by a Nicaraguan lieutenant, Abelardo Cuadra, who almost a year earlier had been with him at Cayo Confites.[136]

This was not the only irony of the little war. Picado received aid from both the rightist Somoza and the Communist Manuel Mora. As noted, Nicaraguan troops fought at San Isidro del General, while Mora's Vanguardia Popular, the Communist party, concentrated about five hundred armed men in San José for the capital's defense.[137] There were reports, however, that Mora and the Communists were merely waiting for Figueres and the government to exhaust themselves before "taking over" and that Picado had created a "Frankenstein's monster" in accepting the Communists' aid.[138] At any rate, the government was supplied with a planeload of arms and ammunition from Mexico through the "good offices" of Communist leader Vicente Lombardo Toledano.[139] The ambiguous position of the Picado regime also resulted in some confusion concerning the motives of Figueres. On the one hand, as the opponent of dictators, Figueres was placed on the Left and identified with Arévalo; it was even reported, though incorrectly, that he had fought on the Republican side in the Spanish Civil War.[140] On the other hand, in view of the reputation of the calderonistas for progressive legislation and their alliance with the Communists, there were reports that the Figueres movement was "capitalistic and reactionary."[141] Despite these conflicting stories, the American governments exerted constant pressure upon Somoza in order to force him to withdraw.[142] The United States, particularly, adopted a policy of "strict nonintervention" and sought to "localize" the fighting by "discouraging outside participation."[143] It made appeals to both Guatemala and Nicaragua to stop their meddling, and the most important result of its action was the decision by Somoza to pull out on 31 March.[144] Picado had been isolated diplomatically, and Figueres was ready to launch Plan Magnolia.

The war entered its final stage when the Army of National Liberation started its offensive on 10 April. In accordance with Plan Magnolia, most of the army was concentrated on the northern front, with only a platoon of soldiers left behind to protect the supply base in the south. Figueres collected his men in a woods outside Jardín, a crossroads just below the ridge at El Empalme, and traveling along backcountry cart roads under the cover of darkness infiltrated the government lines in order to reach Cartago.[145] Cartago, the former capital, less than fifteen miles southeast of San José, was surprised by the "phantom march" (*"la marcha fantasma"*) and fell with virtually no resistance. Only the military barracks held, but it was quickly besieged by a company of troops commanded by Sosa Navarro. Two companies under Báez Bone were sent to Ochomogo, a high point on the highway between San José and Cartago, and another company was deployed on the same highway at the entrance of Cartago in case Báez Bone failed to hold.[146]

A fifth company, with Ribas Montes in command, was sent to El Tejar, a village a few miles south of Cartago, to stand by against the forces which had opposed Figueres on the northern front but were now at his rear. The remaining company was divided into platoons, one of which was under Argüello, and received the task of patrolling the streets, of Cartago and engaging in mop-up action.[147] On 12 April almost simultaneously with the movements in Cartago, Horacio Ornes carried out an airborne attack against Puerto Limón. This was "Operation Caribbean Legion" ("Operación Legión del Caribe"), an added feature to Plan Magnolia by which Ornes with sixty men in two DC-3s captured the Caribbean port. Figueres considered this necessary in order to receive arms from Cuba.[148] It was also the first use of the name "Caribbean Legion," which was to be applied so loosely in future discussions of exile military movements in the Caribbean. By the time the government forces recovered from these bold thrusts and made their final fight in the battle of El Tejar on 14 April, Figueres was already engaged in negotiations preliminary to Picado's surrender.

Archbishop Sanabria again acted as mediator between the two sides. He was assisted by the diplomatic corps, principally by the U.S. ambassador, Nathaniel P. Davis. Figueres appointed Padre Benjamín Núñez to represent the National Liberation in the peace talks, and the flags of five countries protected him as he passed back and forth through the enemy lines. Núñez had to find a way to reconcile Figueres' demand for unconditional surrender with the desire of the *picadistas* and *calderonistas* for some form of guarantee of their personal safety and property. But his most difficult problem was the Communists. According to Padre Núñez, although the government resistance had virtually ceased, the Communists had been the most active in the fighting, and some of their leaders wanted to make a Madrid-style defense of the capital. [149] In order to avert this disaster, Núñez arranged a midnight meeting between Figueres and Manuel Mora alone in the "no-man's land" at Ochomogo, where Figueres tried to persuade the Communist leader that he sought only the overthrow of the dictatorship and had no intention of undoing the social legislation of the last eight years. [150] According to Núñez, the meeting was inconclusive, but subsequently, on his own authority, Núñez assured Mora in writing that the social legislation would be maintained and that the Communists would not be persecuted.[151]

When it appeared that the last obstacle to surrender had been overcome, Nicaragua's Somoza suddenly sent five hundred men across the Costa Rican frontier at San Carlos. Somoza was understandably apprehensive over a victory by a revolutionary army containing many of his enemies. The United States protested vigorously this new invervention, and Rómulo Betancourt, in riot-torn Bogotá at the Ninth Inter-American Conference, called Somoza's action an "invasion" and sought inter-American action.[152] On 20 April Somoza recalled his troops. A day earlier, Picado had surrendered, and on the twentieth, he, Calderón, and Mora went into exile. Santos León Herrera, an *ulatista* and third designate to the presidency, was named provisional president for a transitory period of eighteen days. Costa Rica's "longest and bloodiest civil war"[153] was over, and in the early morning of 24 April, Don Pepe entered San José.

Once in the capital, Figueres gave assurances that he had no intention of establishing a military dictatorship, but for the next eighteen months he was the dominant force in Costa Rica. On 8 May 1948, when León Herrera's interim presidency expired, Figueres was sworn in as the president of the Founding Junta of the Second Republic (Junta Fundadora de la Segunda República). Figueres had signed a pact with Otilio Ulate on 1 May under which Ulate's election of 8 February was recognized, but Figueres was to preside over a junta for eighteen months while elections for a constituent assembly were held and a new constitution was drafted.[154] It was a perfect arrangement whereby Figueres and the junta would undertake a task of "administrative and institutional reorganization" and counteract the "subversion of the fallen government," while legitimacy was preserved in the person of President-elect Ulate.[155] Although the junta enjoyed wide powers, individual guarantees remained in effect and it was affirmed that there would be no tyranny.[156] On the other hand, Ulate was able to dissociate himself from any unpopular acts of the interim government. For this very reason he had declined an offer from Figueres to become president of the junta.[157] The Caribbean exiles were, of course, delighted to see Figueres as junta president. In fact, one of Figueres' first acts in the international sphere was to sever diplomatic relations with the Dominican Republic.[158]

In the victory parade down San José's Avenida Central on 28 April, the prominent places occupied by the Caribbean exiles gave notice of Figueres' indebtedness to them. Even without a formal pact, he owed them much morally and financially. Juan Rodríguez was put up in a "very elegant villa,"[159] and Horacio Ornes and his "Caribbean Legion" were quartered in the Artillery Barracks in San José.[160] Actually, most of the Dominican, Honduran, and Nicaraguan Cayo Confites veterans— the Liberation Army of America—were under Ornes and, as *Time* correspondent Jerry Hannifin suggested, continued to use the name "Caribbean Legion."[161] The exile political leaders in Cuba, Juan Bosch, Eufemio Fernández, Jiménez Grullón, and Angel Morales, objected strongly to the use of the term; they felt it unnecessarily aroused the Caribbean dictators and the U.S. State Department.[162] But the term persisted in both its specific and general applications. Within a few weeks, Miguel Angel Ramírez resigned as chief of staff of the Costa Rican army and resumed command of the Liberation Army or Caribbean Legion.[163] However, even though the Supreme Revolutionary Committee continued to function under Rodríguez,[164] the old general was not the spokesman for all exile groups. Regardless of the wording of any pact, Figueres was in no respect subordinate to Rodríguez and, in fact, insisted on carrying out his original plan of helping Argüello to overthrow Somoza.

With Figueres' blessing, Argüello quickly organized, on paper at least, the Army of National Liberation of Nicaragua (Ejército de Liberación Nacional de Nicaragua). The choice of Argüello was not popular among the exile groups, but for the moment no one wished to challenge Figueres, and the decision to overthrow Somoza made good sense to all. Costa Rica was an ideal base for such an undertaking, and Somoza's fall would also undoubtedly bring down the remaining "tyrants" in Honduras and El Salvador. Only Trujillo would be left to face a "united and democratic" Central America–plus Cuba and Venezuela. The Nicaraguan government itself sensed the danger and on 23 May issued an invitation to Nicaraguans "in voluntary exile" to return to their homeland and "work for its progress."[165] The offer was, of course, spurned, and Argüello undertook to convert his paper command into a fighting force. For this he needed experienced soldiers. Juan José Meza, the secretary of the Revolutionary Junta of the Nicaraguan Liberation Army, was sent to Mexico to recruit some of the Spanish Republican officers there.

One of these Spanish refugees was Alberto Bayo, whom Meza contacted on 27 May and induced to join Argüello's forces.[166] Bayo was an aviation officer who had fled Spain when the Republic fell in 1939. He had spent years of exile in France, Cuba, and finally Mexico. When Meza visited him, he was on the staff of the Mexican Military Aviation School at Guadalajara. Bayo's life in exile had not been easy; he had done a variety of jobs to feed his wife and two sons, and whenever he was fired from one he complained that it was either because of the "black hand" of the Jesuits or the result of narrow, nationalistic laws which discriminated against foreigners.[167] Regardless of these experiences, Bayo did not appear bitter. He was an idealistic, even quixotic, soldier of fortune, who claimed he sought only a "friendly homeland" and the satisfaction of liberating it from an "oppressive dictator." [168] Although his wife warned him that he still would be regarded as a *gachupín* (a derogatory term applied to Spaniards by Latin Americans) and, even if successful, would be rewarded with "Nicaragua for the Nicaraguans,"[169] Bayo agreed to take charge of training the revolutionary aviation. He secured a two-month leave of absence from the Guadalajara school and managed to convince three additional Spanish officers to accompany him: Fernando Sousa, Esteban Rovira, and Daniel Lado.[170] Bayo stated that the only ones willing to come with him "without conditions" were Communists but that he had been instructed not to enlist them because the junta did not want to do anything that "would look bad" in the eyes of the United States.[171] On 5 June Bayo departed for Guatemala, where he joined other exiles, and then proceeded to Costa Rica. He related that as his plane flew over Nicaragua he thought about the "enslaved people below."[172]

Bayo traveled to Costa Rica with the belief that action against Somoza was imminent. But he was mistaken; the exile movement fell victim to indecision, division, and inertia. No one seemed able to make it go. At the end of June, Figueres turned over to Argüello a finca at Río Conejo for use as a training camp, but Argüello complained that Figueres did not give him enough money or arms for the undertaking.[173] Bayo asserted that Figueres supported Argüello fully but that the latter wasted the funds he was given and spent his time drinking wine.[174] Bayo became thoroughly disgusted with Argüello and with the way he ran his camp—not only because of the alleged revelry, extravagance, and lack of discipline but because of the failure to maintain security. According to Bayo, Somoza placed among their ranks "as many spies as he wished," who spread dissension and undermined the operations at Río Conejo.[175] For his part, Argüello accused Figueres of withholding funds and of playing off one exile faction against the other in order to take over the entire movement himself.[176] Ironically, while Argüello charged Figueres with betrayal, the truth was that Don Pepe's support alone maintained him.

This was made clear by Bayo, who revealed a conspiracy to get rid of Argüello once the invasion of Nicaragua was begun. Bayo claimed that a group of Nicaraguan generals, Carlos Pasos, Carlos Rivera Delgadillo, Antonio Velásquez, and Adán Vélez, deeply resented the choice of Argüello as commander in chief, because the latter was a civilian and "not fit to lead."[177] One night, according to Bayo, the generals invited him to dinner and told him that they were going along with Figueres because it was the only way to secure his help but that as soon as they crossed the frontier into Nicaragua they planned to remove Argüello and replace him with a "professional." They asked Bayo if he would at that moment place his aviation under the command of the new chief. Bayo in effect became a party to the conspiracy by stating that as a foreigner he would not presume to oppose "the decision of the forces."[178] Argüello was aware generally of the opposition against him on the part of Pasos and Gustavo Manzanares, the representative in Costa Rica of Emiliano Chamorro, but the Nicaraguans were not his only problem.

The leaders of the Caribbean Legion and of Figueres' own National Liberation also plotted against Argüello. According to Bayo, the Caribbean Legion chiefs, Ramírez, Ribas Montes, Sosa Navarro, Báez Bone, and Tercero, were all involved in the conspiracy to "dump" Argüello.[179] Frank Marshall, too, the quick-tempered Costa Rican chief of staff, hated Argüello intensely. Allegedly Marshall was bitter because of the amount of money Figueres was giving Argüello without any results in return. One night in a San José cabaret, Marshall struck Argüello during an argument over the delay in the invasion of Nicaragua.[180] Following that night, Marshall actually made several attempts to assassinate Argüello.[181] Argüello related that he had denounced Marshall before Figueres for allegedly committing atrocities during the civil war, which he claimed was the real reason for Marshall's aggressions against him.[182] With reference to the Caribbean Legion, Argüello said they made a "brave show" of parading in San José but "never made an efficient military unit"; all they did, he said, was "annoy the girls, get drunk, and raise hell."[183] From all this, it was apparent that the prospects which looked so bright in May had faded in September.

The position of Figueres during this period of intrigue and procrastination was somewhat ambiguous. He remained true in spirit to his interventionist policy, but his responsibilities to Costa Rica placed certain restraints upon him. He told his closest followers that, while he supported revolutionary movements in Latin America similar to that of the National Liberation, he would never place the nation in danger.[184] Bayo believed that Figueres was "afraid of Somoza" and that, although genuinely wishing to repay Argüello for his help, he did not want any trouble. "It did not bother him to give money, but he was unwilling to provide military facilities," wrote Bayo.[185] For this reason, Bayo complained, Figueres would not permit him to train pilots in Costa Rica and had suggested that he train them in Guatemala. The situation there was almost identical, according to Bayo, with the additional consideration that the powerful Colonel Arana was opposed to the exile cause.[186] Bayo added, however, that Don Pepe gave the "greatest help possible" to the movement against Somoza, despite the fact that his "entire cabinet" opposed him in that policy.[187] Figueres also visited the Río Conejo camp several times, and one time supposedly made a stirring speech, concluding with the cry, "On to Managua!"[188]

But the cry was rhetorical–too many factors were working against the plan to invade Nicaragua. First of all, the conduct of the exiles in Costa Rica was something of a national scandal. Aside from the general acts of rowdyism, which even Argüello did not deny,[189] a number of incidents occurred to embarrass Figueres, particularly those involving Nicaraguan visitors in San José.[190] Also, the movement enjoyed no secrecy and was, in fact, seriously compromised in July, when Nicaraguan guardsmen forcibly removed Edelberto Torres from an international flight during a stopover in Managua. Torres was traveling from Guatemala to San José and had in his possession a letter from Arévalo to the exile leaders in Costa Rica.[191] In October Somoza announced that he had detailed information about a plot against the governments of Nicaragua, El Salvador, and Honduras by the "Communist" governments of Prío Socarrás, Arévalo, Betancourt, and Figueres. The information had been supplied by an alleged defector, Octavio Arana Jiménez, who, according to the announcement, "had been working as an instructor of the Legion of Bandits with his salary paid by the government of Costa Rica."[192] Aware that Somoza was fully alerted, and in view of the fact that the Nicaraguan exiles were hopelessly divided, the Rodríguez-Ramirez group decided in October to shift its base of operations to Guatemala.[193] Figueres himself announced this step and asserted that the Caribbean Legion was being disbanded.[194]

Despite the fact that Figueres had, as reported, "cool[ed] off toward the idea of real assistance to the legion,"[195] he never completely abandoned Argüello. Argüello was not forced to give up his base at Río Conejo. One may even speculate that the announced disbandment of the Caribbean Legion was a maneuver to deceive Somoza and that Rodríguez had gone to Guatemala to open a "second front."[196] Early in September Cuban President-elect Prío Socarrás had visited Figueres. According to Argüello, Prío discussed with him and Figueres the plan to invade Nicaragua and promised to supply the arms needed for the undertaking. Figueres allegedly told Prío that Argüello could continue to count on his protection and the use of Costa Rica as a base of operations.[197] In November Argüello and Bayo flew to Cuba to arrange the arms shipment, but each gave a radically different version of what happened. Argüello claimed that Prío supplied him with "fourteen" planeloads of arms but that Figueres seized them when they arrived in San José.[198] Bayo asserted that Argüello failed in his mission and that he, Bayo, made a second trip to Cuba on 13 December. This time, with Juan Bosch supposedly supervising the operation, Bayo claimed he returned with "fifteen planeloads of excellent war material."[199] Thus, both Argüello and Bayo affirmed that Prío sent a large shipment of arms to Costa Rica, but each fixed a different date for the delivery, and this had significance in view of the action taken by Somoza in December 1948.

On 10 December an armed group proceeding from Nicaragua crossed the frontier into Costa Rica. This force, organized under Calderón-Guardia, had trained on Nicaraguan soil, and Somoza rendered it technical and logistical support.[200] In this light, one would conclude that Bayo traveled to Cuba to obtain arms for the defense of Costa Rica. But according to Argüello the arms were sent before the invasion,[201] which would lead to another conclusion, that is, that Somoza had grown tired waiting for Figueres to drop the other shoe and had attacked before there could be a new exile buildup. In any event, Figueres did not rely upon Prío's weapons for the defense of Costa Rica, nor did he permit any of the exile groups to become involved in the fighting, even though he had no army. Figueres had just disbanded the army on 1 December, so he appealed to the Organization of American States for assistance.

The Costa Rican government invoked the Inter-American Treaty of Reciprocal Assistance (the Rio Treaty), then in effect only a few days, and called upon the OAS Council to convoke a meeting of consultation. After receiving Costa Rica's complaint and listening to the explanation of Nicaragua, the council notified both parties that it had decided to take whatever measures were necessary to maintain the peace and security of the hemisphere and expressed confidence that the parties would cooperate with such measures.[202] Although this step in effect, halted the invasion, the council decided on 14 December to convoke a meeting of consultation. Pending the fixing of a time and place for the meeting, the council constituted itself as the Provisional Organ of Consultation and created a Commission of Inquiry to conduct an on-the-spot investigation of Costa Rica's charges. As moved by Nicaragua, the commission was also instructed to look into the "antecedents" of the affair.[203] The commission visited San José and Managua between 17 and 22 December and during this time conducted interviews with officials and interested parties, including exile leaders Ramírez and Ribas Montes in San José and Somoza's prisoner Edelberto Torres in Managua.[204] On Christmas Eve, the Commission of Inquiry reported to the OAS Council that Somoza had indeed aided the calderonistas but that the anxieties of Nicaragua were justified owing to the sympathy and support rendered the "so-called" Caribbean Legion by Costa Rica.[205]

At the same meeting, the council, acting provisionally as the Organ of Consultation, passed a resolution based upon the findings of the Commission of Inquiry. It called upon Costa Rica and Nicaragua to refrain from any hostile acts and to observe the principles of nonintervention and solidarity as contained in the inter-American treaties to which they were parties. Specifically, Nicaragua was admonished for facilitating on its territory the organization of a revolutionary movement against Costa Rica, whereas the Figueres regime was advised to take steps to prevent the existence in Costa Rica of conspiratorial military organizations.[206] In order to implement this resolution, the council appointed an Inter-American Committee of Military Experts to maintain a surveillance of the Costa Rica-Nicaragua frontier, to report on the steps taken by Nicaragua in fulfillment of its obligations, and to report the measures taken by Costa Rica to disband the exile military groups.

During the next two months this task was carried out. Nicaragua closed its frontier and prevented the departure of revolutionary elements destined for Costa Rica. In San José, Figueres personally suggested to Argüello that he take a "vacation" in Cuba or Mexico,[207] and on 11 February the Costa Rican government announced the departure from San José of "prominent Nicaraguan émigrés," including Argüello. It added that they would be followed in "the next two or three days" by Ramírez and other officers "who [had] participated valiantly in the revolution which led to the victory of Figueres."[208] In its report to the OAS Council on 17 February, the Committee of Military Experts expressed its complete satisfaction with the measures taken by Costa Rica to disband the "so-called 'Caribbean Legion' and other groups."[209] In the meantime, the council sponsored the drafting of a Pact of Amity, which Costa Rica and Nicaragua signed on 21 February 1949. Under the terms of the pact, the two governments agreed to take adequate internal measures to control revolutionary elements, to maintain border patrols, and to seek a pacific settlement in any future dispute.[210] Satisfied with its work, the council on the same day revoked its call for a meeting of consultation and terminated its action as the Provisional Organ of Consultation. This had been the first application of the Rio Treaty, and it was generally held that the OAS had successfully defended a peaceful and democratic state from the aggressive designs of an authoritarian neighbor.

This view did not tell the whole story. Somoza could find some satisfaction in the outcome. Although receiving a mild reprimand for his part in the affair, he was compensated by the fact that the Caribbean Legion had been ordered to disband. It was observed, in fact, that Somoza had "smoked out" the Caribbean Legion[211] and that, by invoking the Río Treaty, Figueres had fallen into Somoza's trap. Somoza's plan, it seemed, was to provoke Figueres into using the exile forces at the front, which would serve as a pretext for a full-scale intervention by Nicaragua on behalf of Calderon's meager forces. [212] Figueres' somewhat surprising appeal to the OAS, then, turned out to be a Pyrrhic victory. Bayo, too, was critical of Figueres for bringing in the OAS, because, he asserted, if Don Pepe had "remained silent, resisted, and then counterattacked," with the exiles' help he could have chased Somoza to the "North Pole."[213] Instead, the exile forces had to move on. But they were not finished yet. The movement, as noted, had not been faring well in Costa Rica even before Somoza's action, and Figueres' term in office was nearing completion. Bayo, among those who had remained to the end, was happy to answer the call of Juan Rodríguez in Guatemala, where already plans for "new adventures" were underway.[214]

Luperón, 1949

For obvious reasons the exiles did not abandon their fight. The Organization of American States had settled the immediate dispute between Costa Rica and Nicaragua but had not dealt with the question of dictatorship, which was basic to the tensions in the Caribbean. As long as there were dictators, there would be exiles. And as long as these exiles had a base of operations and possessed the resources for acquiring arms and organizing men, they would use military action to solve their problems.

Admittedly, this solution was now more risky. Not only was Costa Rica neutralized for the moment but Venezuela was lost to the democratic camp. In November 1948 Rómulo Gallegos had been ousted in a military coup, and he and Betancourt had gone into exile. Moreover, the Cold War was intensifying, and the dictators exploited the situation with a firm anti-Communist stand. Early in 1949, when Trujillo perceived that the most important exile leaders were moving to Guatemala, he launched a powerful radio campaign of abuse over "La Voz Dominicana." On 9 February a broadcast declared that the Caribbean Legion was a "core of Marxism" and that it had been given refuge by the "Communist degenerate" and "Quisling" Arévalo.[215] A few days later the Ciudad Trujillo transmitter beamed the charge that Cuba's Prío was supplying "no less than 100,000 pesos monthly for the support of the mercenaries and filibusters of Cayo Confites."[216] Toward the end of the same month Betancourt's name was added. He was accused of stealing $142,000,000 from Venezuela, which he allegedly was using to aid the "Marxist leaders" Figueres and Arévalo and to purchase arms in the United States for the Caribbean Legion.[217] In mid-March the Trujillo radio refuted the OAS claim that the Caribbean Legion had been disbanded and asserted that the legion "really existed" and was training in Guatemala under three Paraguayan (!) officers.[218] The following month this point was reiterated; "La Voz Dominicana" declared that the Caribbean Legion was neither an "invention" nor a myth but was "an instrument of Red expansion," and the broadcast named the Guatemalan town of Las Pacayas, near Jutiapa, as one of the training centers of the Caribbean Legion.[219] Much of what Trujillo broadcast was calculated propaganda; yet he was correct in affirming that the Caribbean exiles were actively plotting again and that they had the support of Arévalo, Prío, and even Figueres.

After the Costa Rican misadventure, Juan Rodríguez reasserted leadership over the exile movement. Whether his group was called the Liberation Army of America, which he and Ramírez preferred, or the Caribbean Legion, which Trujillo preferred, the principal leaders were Dominican, Cuban, and Honduran. The Nicaraguans had missed their chance, and Argüello in particular was finished. Arévalo gave the Rodríguez group extensive support, including the use of the air force base at San José de Guatemala, with the direct collaboration of the chief of the Guatemalan Air Force, Colonel Francisco Cosenza, and the use of Lake Izabal as a sea plane base.[220] Prío, by his own admission, supplied arms to Rodríguez in Guatemala,[221] and Eufemio Fernández and Juan Bosch were the intermediaries for these shipments.[222] Figueres facilitated, and even helped pay for, the transfer from Costa Rica to Guatemala of the arms belonging to Rodríguez.[223] According to Horacio Ornes, Figueres also supplied weapons of his own.[224]

As might be expected, the objective of the new expedition was the Dominican Republic. There was some effort to keep alive the idea that Nicaragua was still the target, but this was a decoy.[225] The decision to invade the Dominican Republic rather than Nicaragua stemmed from the frustrating events in Costa Rica during the preceding months. There also was evidence that members of a Dominican underground had contacted Bosch, Fernández, and Cruz Alonso in Havana with plans for a coordinated invasion and insurrection.[226] These three leaders then reportedly took charge and, after further negotiations with the leaders of the clandestine movement, traveled to Guatemala where they worked out an integrated plan with Rodríguez.[227] Also in connection with this plan, Prío's brother-in-law, Enrique C. Henríquez, traveled to Port-au-Prince in December 1948 to seek the cooperation of Haitian officials.[228] But he was unsuccessful; Haiti apparently tried to steer clear of such activities. The plan which eventually evolved was one which resembled that of Costa Rica rather than that of Cayo Confites.

The new strategy called for a relatively small expeditionary force comprised of experienced military leaders who would assume command of a revolutionary army recruited inside the Dominican Republic. The officers would come in by air and would bring with them enough arms to equip one thousand, two hundred men.[229] Friendly observers reported, however, that a larger force was actually training in Guatemala and that the plan called for numerous successive waves of invaders, both airborne and amphibious, once certain strategic points were secured.[230] The command structure for the invasion and uprising was worked out in cooperation with the clandestine leaders. General Juan José Rodríguez was named commander in chief; General Miguel Angel Ramírez was chief of staff; and Colonels Jorge Ribas Montes, Eufemio Fernández, and Horacio Ornes were chiefs of operations in the three zones respectively: south (San Juan de la Maguana), center (La Vega), and north (Luperón).[231] In addition, Juan Bosch was to serve as the "delegate" for the revolution in Cuba, and José Antonio Atiles, the former vice rector of the University of Santo Domingo, was to act in the same capacity in Mexico. Important political and diplomatic tasks were also entrusted to Dr. Antonio Román Durán, a Spanish Republican exile and "distinguished psychiatrist."[232] The essential ingredient in this operation was, of course, aircraft, and Alberto Bayo was initially given the task of procurement.

Bayo first went to Mexico on 4 March 1949. There he collaborated with José Horacio Rodríguez, the general's son. Acting on the assumption that Cuba would provide a fueling stop, they purchased a Lockheed Hudson and an Avro Anson V, both short-range aircraft.[233] When it turned out that they had been misinformed, they had to begin again and search for planes with longer range. After over a month of vain effort in Mexico, the two men traveled to Houston, Texas, where they sought the assistance of Marion R. Finley, a U.S. citizen and flyer known to be *"simpático."* [234] Together they traveled to New Orleans and Tampa and then to Miami, where they arranged the purchase of a PBY Catalina (U.S. registry N-1096-M) for $10,000. [235] Bayo left Finley behind to secure an export license for the seaplane and to make the delivery, although subsequently Jesse A. Vickers, a Miami airplane parts dealer, claimed he had only leased this aircraft and that it was exported illegally. [236] Bayo returned to Guatemala on 6 May amid criticism for taking too long. The job of purchasing aircraft, as well as the procurement of pilots and crews, had already been turned over to another and younger Spanish Republican, Jacobo Fernández Alverdi. [237]

Jacobo Fernández and José Horacio Rodríguez moved quickly to make up for lost time, while Bayo stayed behind in Guatemala as an advisor. During the month of May a number of planes were secured, including two Douglas C-47s, a Curtiss C-46, and another Catalina of questionable airworthiness. [238] In the purchase of the C-46 (with Mexican registry XB-HUB) the crew of the plane was also hired for the expedition. [239] The pilots and crews eventually recruited for the mission, as the aircraft, were either Mexican or North American. However, two additional C-47 aircraft, which took part in the operation, were Guatemalan Air Force planes. [240] These planes, concerning which there were contradictory reports, will be discussed in connection with the invasion itself. Bayo, as one might expect, was critical of his successor's activities, particularly the practice in certain of the cases of leasing planes and hiring pilots. Bayo asserted, with some truth (although after the fact), that leased planes would not fly and mercenary pilots would not fight. He argued that the revolutionary forces should consist of dedicated men, who placed the overthrow of the tyrant before monetary considerations. [241] Bayo also charged that Jacobo Fernández talked too much and that his indiscretions made the planned expedition an "open secret." For good measure, he was critical of Juan Rodríguez, who he felt was narrow-minded and impractical. [242] Nonetheless, by the end of May the airplanes with their pilots and crews were in Guatemala, and the preparations for the invasion entered the final stage.

The take-off date was set for 18 June; the men, arms, and planes were in readiness. A manifesto, drafted in large part by Antonio Román Durán and signed by the leaders of the Army of Liberation, Rodríguez, Ramírez, and Ornes, proclaimed to the Dominican people that the hour of liberation was at hand. The declaration expressed the ideal of democratic government and individual freedom and pledged agrarian reform, a labor code, social security, and a war on illiteracy, at the same time guaranteeing to respect private property.[243] There was nothing Marxian nor even very revolutionary about the document. There were seven aircraft, possibly eight (including the two Guatemalan Air Force transports) in the invasion squadron, and the expeditionary force which actually departed from Guatemala was comprised of seventy men. Most of the force was assembled at the San José de Guatemala Air Force Base, except for Horacio Ornes, who was at Lake Izabal with eleven men and the crew of three of a Catalina seaplane.[244] As Ramírez noted, the expeditionaries were a varied group with wide-ranging military experience.[245] Some, such as Ribas Montes, "el Indio" Sánchez, Alfredo Mejía Lara, José María Tercero, and Horacio Ornes, had fought in Costa Rica. Others, such as Daniel Martín and Ignacio González, though listed as Cubans, were veterans of the Spanish Republican Army. Still others, according to exile sources, were experienced soldiers from World War II, including the Osuna brothers, Gregorio, Antonio, and Santiago, Spanish Republican refugees who had been in the French underground; Carlos Gutiérrez, of possible Cuban nationality, who was twenty-six and supposedly had fought in North Africa against Rommel, had participated in the D-Day Normandy landings, and had served in General George Patton's Third Army; and the Dominican Federico Horacio Henríquez Vásquez ("Gugú" Henríquez), who had seen service in the South Pacific with the United States Marines.[246] Among the revolutionaries also were Manuel Gómez Flores, a highly respected Nicaraguan officer; José Horacio Rodríguez; and the North American Finley. With everything ready, the first of a series of disasters struck.

Just three hours before the time set for launching the invasion, two of the aircraft took off without authorization and fled toward Mexico. One plane, a C-47 piloted by "Yankee mercenaries" Ralph Wells and Bob Hosford, was pursued by Eufemio Fernández, but he ran short of fuel and had to give up the chase. The other craft was a Catalina leased from a Mexican, Angel Trechuelo, whose crew complained that they had been misled concerning the mission.[247] The pilot of the other C-47, the Mexican captain José López Henríquez, was prevented from joining the mutiny by Ribas Montes, who threatened him with a machine gun.[248] According to Bayo, Captain López had balked because he had not received a payment of $5,000 as promised. Only the crew of the C-46 "Curtiss Commando" apparently offered no resistance.[249] The Guatemalan Air Force transports were also prepared to take off, but they were loaded with arms and could carry no personnel. The size of the expedition was therefore cut to the capacities of the C-46 and C-47, plus the Catalina with Ornes at Lake Izabal. Bayo declared that a decision was made to leave behind many of the Spanish Republicans in order to avoid the charge of domination by "Red" Spaniards. He added, however, that the Osuna brothers carried a small Spanish Republican flag to show "there [would] always be Spaniards in these undertakings."[250] Although Eufemio Fernández recommended postponing the departure, Juan Rodríguez insisted that they should proceed, and the diminished invasion armada took off at 4 P.M. on Saturday, 18 June.

The planes followed a flight plan northeastward over Guatemala and then along the east coast of the Yucatán Peninsula, where they were to make a landing on Mexican territory at Cozumel. En route they passed over Lake Izabal and circled it twice as a signal for Ornes to begin his flight.[251] Ornes' Catalina, however, was overloaded and was unable to take off until the following morning. The stop at Cozumel had supposedly been arranged by Bonilla Atiles through "friends influential in Mexican politics but not officially," and he had sent special instructions for this delicate part of the operation.[252] The permission to land allegedly was for "commercial type" aircraft, but they were not to carry Mexican registry, nor to have Mexican crews, nor to display arms of any kind.[253] Cozumel was obviously a refueling stop and rendezvous point; Colonel Cosenza, the Guatemalan Air Force chief, had instructed his transports to fly there and deliver the arms they carried.[254] The Guatemalan C-47s bore official markings and were flown by regular air force pilots, Gustavo Girón C. and René Valenzuela C., so it was unlikely that they intended to go all the way to the Dominican Republic. Moreover, Bayo, in his criticism concerning leased planes, alluded to planes that "did not show up."[255] During the flight, the squadron encountered bad weather, and the rudder of the C-47 occupied by Ramírez and Ribas Montes was damaged, but it reached Cozumel. The Guatemalan Air Force transports followed it in. Juan Rodríguez and Eufemio Fernández in the C-46 were driven off course by the storm and forced to make an emergency landing at El Cuyo.[256] All four aircraft were quickly interned by Mexican authorities. Some of the exiles held Bonilla Atiles responsible for this unexpected action, but Horacio Ornes asserted that Ramírez' "irresponsible" disregard of every one of Bonilla's instructions caused the failure of the operation.[257] Bayo also defended Bonilla Atiles but would not give his reasons, because, he said, they were "part of the secret archive of the diplomacy of the Caribbean."[258] The invasion was, of course, stillborn; the expeditionaries interned in Yucatán were the lucky ones.

At Lake Izabal the third disaster and real tragedy was taking shape. As noted, Ornes had been unable to take off on 18 June. He had tried three times, and, after lightening his load, it was too dark to try again. The next morning at daybreak, unaware of what had happened in Yucatán, the Catalina finally managed to take off after jettisoning more equipment.[259] The seaplane followed a course over the open sea, past the Swan Islands, Jamaica, the Haitian peninsulas, and finally to Luperón on the north coast of the Dominican Republic. Because of the delay in its departure, the Catalina did not encounter the storms of the previous evening, and the flight was uneventful. The group was disturbed only by the thought that they had lost the element of surprise, for, they assumed, the other forces would already be fighting in the Dominican Republic. During the flight, however, their anxiety grew. They listened to the radio, particularly "La Voz Dominicana," and received no indication that an invasion had occurred.[260] They did not know it, but they alone were invading the Dominican Republic.

The group under the command of Ornes was a microcosm of the Liberation Army. In addition to Ornes, there were six Dominicans: José Rolando Martínez Bonilla, who had been at Cayo Confites; "Gugú" Henríquez, the U.S. Marine Corps veteran; Hugo Kundhardt, allegedly a Harvard graduate, who had also served in the Pacific (Guam) during World War II; Manuel Calderón Salcedo, a University of Havana medical student; Dr. Tulio Hostilio Arvelo Delgado, a lawyer, who had resigned as Dominican vice-consul in San Juan, Puerto Rico, and had joined the Cayo Confites expedition; and Miguel Feliú Arzenso, another Cayo Confites veteran. The group also included three former officers of the Nicaraguan National Guard, Alejandro Selva, Alberto Ramírez, and José Félix Córdoba Boniche; plus a Costa Rican, Alfonso Leitón, who had been with Ornes at Puerto Limón in 1948; and Salvador Reyes Váldez, a U.S. citizen of Dominican birth, who was also a medical student. The crew of the Catalina were all U.S. citizens from Miami, Florida: John W. Chewning, pilot; Habet Joseph Maroot (or Marcot), copilot; and George Raymond Scruggs, mechanic-engineer.[261] After eleven hours in the air, these fifteen men saw the lights of the small, coastal town of Luperón. They sang the Dominican National Hymn, and the Catalina descended onto the Bay of Luperón to begin the liberation of the people of the Dominican Republic.

As it turned out, the Luperón invaders enjoyed the element of surprise, but that was all. The "Frente Interno" (underground) failed to materialize. There was no uprising, nor any revolutionary army to lead. Ornes quickly concluded that the other groups had failed to reach Dominican soil.[262] The rebels seized the only local police official and cut the village's communications and electric power, but the only course open to them under the circumstances was to withdraw.

The movement was now beyond redemption. First, in the darkness and confusion, Kundhardt and Alberto Ramírez blundered upon one another and exchanged shots. The former was wounded, and the latter was killed.[263] Next, Leitón was wounded by a sniper's bullet. Finally, in the attempt to take off, the Catalina became lodged on a sandbar. A Dominican Coast Guard vessel entered the bay, and the expeditionaries fled to the shore fifty yards away. The two wounded men were left on the seaplane in the care of the medical student, Reyes Váldez, but, according to Ornes, the Dominican cutter fired upon the Catalina without provocation. The amphibian exploded, and the three men perished in the flames.[264] The survivors decided to flee to the west in an effort to reach Haiti, but the North Americans, apparently in the belief that their nationality would protect them, lagged behind. The Nicaraguan Selva remained with them, perhaps in order to act as an interpreter. [265] Once captured, these four were not spared, and, in fact, it was asserted that Trujillo had them shot in cold blood as an example for other U.S. nationals.[266] In the manhunt, led by Antonio Imbert Barreras, then the governor of the province of Puerto Plata (and later one of the assassins of Rafael Trujillo), "Gugú" Henríquez and Calderón Salcedo were also killed. The remaining five survivors were captured less than forty-eight hours after their landing.

The captives were not treated badly by the Trujillo regime, despite the latter's reputation for brutality in dealing with opponents. Ornes expected that he would be tortured in order to force him to give information about the underground, but the subject hardly came up, and, although the interrogations were unpleasant, there was no physical violence.[267] Rafael Trujillo, himself, conducted the first interview of Horacio Ornes and, in a calm, "almost friendly" manner, he sought mainly information about Arévalo, Prío, Figueres, Eufemio Fernández, and Bosch.[268] Ornes insisted that he revealed little about the activities of these leaders which was not already known. However, statements attributed to Ornes were broadcast over "La Voz Dominicana" on 24 June, which described the essential features of the invasion plan, including the bases used in Guatemala and the arms supplied by Figueres.[269] The only unusual feature in this alleged confession was the substitution of Cuba for Cozumel as the intermediate base. Later, Ornes signed a statement declaring that the governments of Cuba, Costa Rica, and Guatemala "had a marked Communist tendency," but he did so, he explained, in the hope of obtaining a pardon for himself and his comrades, and he felt it was a small price to pay.[270] Apparently, there was no resentment in exile circles concerning the behavior of Ornes following his capture, because several years later Arévalo wrote a flattering prologue to Ornes' book describing Luperón.

The most difficult part of the questioning of Ornes came in the interviews with General Federico Fiallo. The general was insistent upon the point that there was yet another aircraft involved in the invasion attempt. He charged that a Grumman seaplane, which belonged to Guatemala and which served as a presidential plane for Arévalo, had escorted Ornes to Luperón.[271] Ornes denied the assertion at the time, but later stated that a plane under orders of the U.S. embassy in Haiti had flown over Luperón on 19 June. He added that U.S. intelligence had long been interested in their movements, even as far back as Cayo Confites, when, he declared, a large amphibian based at Guantánamo had flown over the tiny key daily to take reconnaissance photographs.[272] The Dominican government was not dissuaded, however, and officially charged that the Grumman had been part of the invasion squadron and that it had been piloted by a U.S. citizen, Earl Adams.[273] This charge involving the name Earl Adams is interesting, because the same name may also be found on the list of those interned in Yucatán by the Mexican government.[274]

On 8 August 1949 the Luperón invaders were brought to trial by the Dominican Republic for crimes against the peace of the state. The following day they were found guilty and sentenced to thirty years at hard labor. However, owing to subsequent developments, and at the recommendation of the OAS, Ornes and his comrades were granted amnesty on 20 February 1950.[275] Five days later, they were freed, and on 30 May they were permitted to go into exile once again. The leniency shown the Luperón invaders was obviously a tactic to impress international opinion. As will be discussed, the Caribbean tensions became a matter for OAS action, and Trujillo found it useful to permit Ornes and his men to testify before an investigating committee of the OAS. It was also true that Horacio Ornes was the brother of Germán Ornes, then the editor of *El Caribe* of Ciudad Trujillo and a close collaborator of Trujillo. An additional factor may be that Trujillo, through his intelligence services, had all the information he needed, so that there was no need really to mistreat Ornes.

In Mexico City, on 30 June 1949, Joaquín Balaguer, then the Dominican ambassador there, asserted that his government "was aware of the conspiracy at least three months before."[276] A Trujillo agent, Antonio Jorge Estévez, had penetrated the exile movement and had supplied Trujillo with detailed information concerning the planned movement.[277] Specifically, according to Horacio Ornes, Estévez had furnished Trujillo with the names of two leaders of the Frente Interno, Fernando Spignolio and Nando Suárez, which, he affirmed, led to the liquidation of two hundred underground members in Puerto Plata province alone.[278] Estévez was himself subsequently assassinated in Cuba by the exiles whom he had betrayed.[279] It may also be that some of the motive for the slaying of Colonel Francisco Javier Arana in July 1949 was inspired by similar desires for revenge.

Arana, the chief of the Guatemalan armed forces, was very much opposed to Arévalo's support of exile military operations. Although Arana had been a leader of the Guatemalan revolution of 1944, he was more moderate than Arévalo. To the exiles, he was a reactionary and a traitor. According to one source, Arana had tried to prevent the departure of the expedition and had yielded only upon written orders from Arévalo.[280] The exile leaders, however, suspected that Arana's opposition went beyond mere obstructionism and that he had actually provided Trujillo with information about the invasion plans.[281]

In the wake of Luperón, the relations between Arévalo and Arana deteriorated further over the matter of the exiles' arms. The Guatemalan Air Force transports interned in Mexico were released and returned to San José de Guatemala with their cargo of exile arms intact. These weapons were then moved to a residence on the shores of Lake Amatit-

lán.[282] Arana feared that Arévalo planned to use the arms to strength-
en his hand domestically, particularly in the forthcoming presidential
elections in which Arévalo favored Arana's chief rival, Colonel Jacobo
Arbenz Guzmán. Therefore, in a move similar to that of Cuban army
chief Genovevo Pérez Dámera in 1947, Arana undertook to restore the
army's monopoly over arms in the country and demanded that Arévalo
turn over the weapons to him.[283] This confrontation supposedly led to
a decision to get rid of Arana, which resulted in his assassination on 18
July. Trujillo learned of the plot and the previous day broadcast a
warning to Arana over "La Voz Dominicana."[284] Arbenz, who had the
most to gain from Arana's death, was generally considered the author
of the crime, but Arévalo was not completely innocent.[285] Implicated
in the plot also was exile chieftain Miguel Francisco Morazán, which
gave rise to the charge that the Caribbean Legion had avenged Luperón
with the killing of Arana.[286] In the events immediately following
Arana's assassination the position of the exile groups was shown more
clearly.

Arana supporters in the army rebelled in reaction to the murder, but
the uprising was quickly suppressed. Assisting Arévalo in putting down
the revolt were exile leaders Morazán, "el Indio" Sánchez, Alfredo
Mejía Lara, Mario Sosa Navarro, Manuel Nóver, and Adolfo Báez
Bone.[287] Several of these had only shortly before been released from
Mexican custody. Moreover, Eufemio Fernández arrived by a special
flight from Havana with military equipment to help quell the revolt.
After this was accomplished, he and Morazán took a number of the
rebellious officers to Havana and turned them over to Erundino Vilela
Peña, the interim chief of the Cuban Secret Police, who in turn took
them to the exile headquarters in the Hotel San Luis, "where they
remained under guard for some time."[288] These strange actions indicated the state of Caribbean affairs in mid-summer 1949.

The Liberation Army had failed in its attempt to invade the Dominican Republic in June, but there was no doubt that it was prepared to
try again. In fact, its leaders said so in various published interviews.[289]
Aside from the Luperón tragedy, the exile forces were intact and they
possessed a sizable arsenal. They enjoyed full freedom of movement in
Cuba and Guatemala, and the governments of these countries seemed
more willing than ever before to assist in the task of overthrowing
Trujillo. Moreover, the conspiracy and intrigue surrounding the assassination of Arana and the firing of Pérez Dámera enhanced the position

and influence of the exile groups. The things that had gone wrong with the invasion attempt were evident, and, although there was some bitterness and dissension within the movement, the exiles were generally philosophical and agreed with Ramírez that they had failed because of a combination of "bad luck and bad weather."[290] By this time also the term "Caribbean Legion" was common, and not even the exile leaders could resist the romantic aura of the name. This was counterproductive, however, because, while it gave an inflated importance to the exile leaders, it also aroused general apprehension about the exile movement and tended to detract from its professed idealism. The possibility of further disruption and even of armed conflict in the Caribbean evoked the concern of the nations of the hemisphere, particularly the United States. For a number of reasons, the United States was anxious to maintain the peace of the Caribbean and undertook to find ways of easing the tensions there.

Spiking the Guns, 1949-1950

At the initiative of the United States, the Inter-American Peace Committee (IAPC) met in Washington on 4 August 1949 to consider means for the reduction of tensions in the Caribbean. Following Luperón, the Dominican Republic had gone to the Council of the Organization of American States for possible action under the Rio Treaty, but the United States had argued that a foreign ministers' meeting was neither wise nor necessary. There was the danger that the overly frequent convoking of the Organ of Consultation might undermine its prestige, particularly if possible preliminary steps were overlooked. Furthermore, the convoking of a consultative meeting to consider specifically the question of alleged wrongs done the Dominican Republic could prove embarrassing to governments not friendly toward the Trujillo regime.[291] It was considered preferable to study the situation existing in the Caribbean generally. The United States felt this could be accomplished by the IAPC, but, since the committee could not act unless requested to do so by at least one of the parties to a dispute, the United States suggested sending identical notes to the American states inviting them to make comments and furnish information concerning "the situation prevailing in the Caribbean political areas."[292] Such dispatches were circulated on 4 August by the IAPC over the signature of its acting chairman, Enrique V. Corominas of Argentina. As was expected, the Dominican Republic was the first to reply.

On 15 August the Dominican government presented a fourteen-page brief giving its version of events in the Caribbean since 1945. Although the Dominican presentation exaggerated the role of the Caribbean Legion, it outlined with substantial accuracy the exile military operations and the assistance rendered them by the governments of Costa Rica, Cuba, and Guatemala. It also vigorously denounced the interventionist policy of Acción Democrática during the time it exercised power in Venezuela. Moreover, the Dominican government affirmed that new attempts against it were in preparation and cited statements to that effect made by Eufemio Fernández on 9 July as well as a report of 30 July that the Caribbean Legion was purchasing arms in Czechoslovakia. This elicited the only allusion to Communist activity, wherein the Dominicans affirmed "that the imperialistic interventionism that is troubling the peace in the Caribbean zone persists in its plans . . . and does not cease in its endeavor to impose by force the ideology inspiring all that revolutionary movement."[293] The Dominican Republic concluded with an expression of willingness to cooperate with the IAPC but added that it was not renouncing its right to seek a consultative meeting.[294]

The United States followed three days later with a carefully worded memorandum in which it noted the activities of exiles in the Caribbean and their efforts, with the connivance of certain citizens and governments of the area, to bring about political change by means of armed invasion. The United States statement did not impugn motives nor make direct accusations but suggested that these actions were in violation of existing international obligations. Most of the information provided by the United States dealt with cases in which either U.S. nationals had been involved or there had been an effort to export arms from the United States in violation of its laws. Where there was specific legal action, such as that against Manolo Castro, Miguel Angel Ramírez, and Hollis B. Smith at the time of Cayo Confites, or that against Earl Adams and Marion R. Finley after Luperón, the United States was able to furnish detailed information. The United States did not confine its report to the activities of the revolutionary exiles but cited cases in which U.S. citizens had been involved in counterrevolutionary movements. For example, in 1947 two American citizens, Edward Browder and Karl J. Eisenhardt, along with a Dominican consular officer, Librado Blanco, stole weapons belonging to the U.S. government, which they intended to use in a conspiratorial movement against the government of Rómulo Betancourt. The United States concluded with the suggestion that the IAPC consider the applicability to the Caribbean situation of existing inter-American agreements with reference to non-intervention. It recommended a study of the degree to which states were observing their obligations under the 1928 Convention on the Rights and Duties of States in the Event of Civil Strife, and suggested the possible need to bring the treaty up to date. It also called to the committee's attention the resolution approved on 24 December 1948 by the council of the OAS acting provisionally as the Organ of Consultation on the occasion of the Costa Rica-Nicaragua dispute.[295]

Among the "accused," Cuba was the only one to reply formally. Cuba preferred to concentrate on what it considered the illness of the Caribbean, that is, the lack of the effective exercise of democracy, rather than the symptoms, or the activities of the exile groups. Cuba advised that the function of the IAPC was not to sit in judgment of the events but rather to promote improved relations "on the basis of fundamental standards that determine [inter-American] unity." Cuba affirmed that inter-American solidarity was based upon two principles, non-intervention and the exercise of democracy, and it insisted that the adherence to one must not sacrifice the other. It proclaimed, moreover, that the effective exercise of democracy was the "only safe means" of peaceful coexistence. In a possible allusion to the Arana and Pérez Dámera cases, it criticized the committee for concerning itself only with the activities of groups of exiles and for ignoring the actions of governments to bring about military coups. Concerning specific charges made by the Dominican Republic, Cuba lectured on the point that in a functioning democracy certain individuals and groups in the exercise of their freedoms might engage in activities subversive to another state. Despite this, however, the Cuban government noted the action it had taken in the Cayo Confites affair in 1947. Hence, it affirmed, there was no harm done to the Dominican Republic and the episode was strictly an internal matter.[296]

There were additional replies and suggestions from other states, but those already noted were the most significant. Nicaragua submitted only a short note in which it complained about so-called "criminal acts and outrages" on the part of the Caribbean Legion and threatened that if they were not controlled there could be an armed conflict.[297] Costa

Rica did not send a formal report to the IAPC, but, after learning of the charges contained in the Dominican brief of 14 August, its ambassador, Mario A. Esquivel, engaged in a heated exchange with the committee chairman, Luis Quintanilla of Mexico. Aside from his indignation over the Dominican charges, Esquivel observed that the committee's request for information was vague, that is, it contained no reference as to the meaning of the phrase "the situation existing in the Caribbean." Basically, however, Esquivel challenged the jurisdiction of the IAPC and its right to act.[298] Esquivel's views were expanded upon in a letter to the editor of the *New York Times* dated 22 August. In this letter, Esquivel replied to a *Times'* editorial which scored "lawless intervention" in the Caribbean and opined that it was time for "the ghosts of the soldiers of fortune" to join those of the buccaneers of earlier times.[299] Esquivel regarded this as a slur on the exiles and defended them as "sincere patriots," who would return home when representative democracy was restored to their lands. He stated that what the American peoples needed to do was to insist upon the fulfillment of inter-American commitments which called for the free exercise of democracy.[300] In essence, the Costa Rican position paralleled that of Cuba.

The IAPC took under advisement the reports and suggestions it had received and on 14 September 1949 issued "Fourteen Conclusions" in which it summarized the standards and principles essential to inter-American peace and solidarity. The committee believed that these points, if adhered to, would allay the tensions in the Caribbean and prevent their repetition. The Conclusions were weighted heavily in favor of the principle of nonintervention and referred to the "Additional Protocol Relative to Nonintervention" signed in Buenos Aires in 1936 and to Article 15 of the OAS Charter. In line with this principle, standards of behavior were outlined: the duty of a state to prevent the use of its territory for the preparation of aggressive acts against a sister republic; the need for a state to take action to rid its territory of militarily organized groups of nationals or foreigners whose purpose was to overthrow governments of other states; the desirability to avoid "systematic and hostile" propaganda aimed at another republic; and the desirability of maintaining "close and cordial" diplomatic relations among American states. The conclusions also advised each American state to inform its people of the commitments undertaken by the American governments with reference to nonintervention and the rights and duties of states in the event of civil strife. In reference to these standards, the IAPC recommended the ratification by states which had not yet done so of the 1928 Convention on the Rights and Duties of States and of the Charter of the OAS.[301]

The Conclusions, however, did not overlook the principle of the exercise of representative democracy and, in fact, indicated that it was "a common denominator of American political life." Specific reference was made to the statement of this principle in Article 5 of the OAS Charter, and it was affirmed that the "effective application" of Resolution XXXII of the Bogotá Conference of 1948, "on the Preservation and Defense of Democracy in America," would strengthen democratic government in the hemisphere. The IAPC also encouraged the American states to make use of its facilities for the pacific settlement of disputes, as well as the numerous other avenues within the inter-American system for the "reasonable settlement of any conflict."[302]

The Conclusions were not greeted with enthusiasm by any of the disputants. The Dominican Republic had wanted an unequivocal order requiring the disarmament and disbandment of the Caribbean Legion but, failing that, had expected at least the convoking of the Organ of Consultation. The antidictatorial bloc, on the other hand, was on record for its criticism of the principle of nonintervention as the refuge of dictators and for its insistence upon positive action by the American community to strengthen democracy. The elements opposing dictatorship were, of course, seeking basic change in the governments of the Caribbean, hence they were unwilling to subscribe to a code of conduct that left to Trujillo's conscience the matter of how much democracy his people would get. Only the United States seemed satisfied with the work of the committee. Caught in the middle, and not convinced that the situation in the Caribbean was a clear case of good versus evil, the United States sought mainly to restore law and order, with the hope that in the long run justice, too, would be done. Paul C. Daniels, U.S. representative on the OAS Council and a member of the IAPC, declared upon signing the Fourteen Conclusions on 14 September that "only careful and scrupulous adherence to the rule of law" would achieve "that high measure of solidarity and mutual confidence" necessary for the "future economic, social, and cultural progress" of the American states.[303] Secretary of State Dean Acheson, a few days later, expressed his hope that "rigorous adherence" to the Conclusions would "assure peace." He added, however, that while the United States opposed "aggression," it did not oppose "change."[304] On 20 October 1949 President Harry Truman reiterated the adherence of the United States to the principle of nonintervention but added his firm belief that hemispheric "solidarity and high aims [were] fostered by the exercise of representative democracy in the American states."[305] Given the situation in the Caribbean, these pious expressions, and the Fourteen Conclusions themselves, were ineffective, and the plots and counterplots continued.

After Luperón a number of the principal exile leaders left Guatemala and shifted their base to Cuba. Among these were Juan Rodríguez, his son José Horacio, Miguel Angel Ramírez, and Jorge Ribas Montes. On 14 August *Bohemia* published an interview with Ramírez in the Hotel San Luis and affirmed that he had come with Ribas Montes to organize the "Cuban branch" of the Caribbean Legion. Ramírez himself declared that the exile movement was not through, nor would it be through until "Santo Domingo, Honduras, and Nicaragua were restored to their place among democratic nations." He added that owing to the conditions in their "enslaved homelands," armed action was still their only recourse.[306] By mid-October reports began to circulate, first in Cuban newspapers, then in Dominican press releases, concerning preparations for a new expedition to oust Trujillo.

This time it was charged, and with some justification, that the Cuban Red Cross was assisting the Caribbean exiles. The president of the Cuban Red Cross was Colonel Rodolfo Henríquez, a Cuban of Dominican birth who had close ties with the Caribbean revolutionary movements. His brother was Enrique C. Henríquez, whose role in these events has been described. Colonel Henríquez maintained absolute control over the organization and had appointed to Red Cross posts a number of individuals who had been involved in the Cayo Confites affair.[307] In November it was reported that the Cuban Red Cross was building several landing fields in Cuba. The Dominican government was particularly concerned about one at L'Amelie in the extreme eastern part of the island near Guantánamo. Actually the landing strip at L'Amelie was meant to be used to bring in emergency supplies to a region inaccessible by road during the rainy season and it had absolutely no military value.[308] However, in the tensions of the moment, it was difficult to separate the real from the imagined use of L'Amelie. Furthermore, it was known that the Cuban Red Cross had tried to purchase a Catalina seaplane, a light launch, and other equipment, which "would better satisfy the needs of a military organization than the specific requirements of the Red Cross."[309] The Red Cross had also leased the "Anacra" airport for training its pilots. This airfield had been used for the same purpose during the Cayo Confites episode.[310]

As a result of these events, a new crisis was welling up in the Caribbean at the end of 1949. The Cuban government denied the charges of the Dominican Republic and on 7 December invited the Inter-American Peace Committee to come to Cuba to determine "the truth or falsity" of such charges.[311] For its part, the Cuban Red Cross requested the International Red Cross at Geneva to undertake an investigation of the allegations.[312] Trujillo, however, would not wait and took an extraordinary step calculated to shift the responsibility for any exile action squarely upon Cuba or to force the convoking of the Organ of Consultation. On 12 December he appeared before the Dominican Congress and requested authorization "to declare war upon any country which deliberately tolerates or protects concentrations of forces militarily organized, equipped, and trained within its territory for the purpose of invading the [Dominican] Republic."[313] Trujillo was "granted" his war-making powers on 26 December, despite the fact that U.S. Secretary of State Dean Acheson deplored the suggestion of war in the Western Hemisphere and declared that there were adequate measures within the inter-American system for dealing with threats to the peace or for repelling aggression.[314] On 29 December the IAPC addressed a formal note to the Dominican Republic in which it pointed out that the American states had "formally condemned war" in their mutual relations.[315] In the meantime, Cuba had placed its armed forces on the alert, and even former army chief Pérez Dámera had offered his services to President Prío.[316] While all events seemed to be moving in one direction, suddenly Haiti invoked the Rio Treaty.

Haiti, under the presidency of Dumarsais Estimé, was not in the dictators' camp but was also avoiding the revolutionary activity in the Caribbean. Nevertheless, Trujillo did not approve of the relatively liberal Estimé regime and was determined to oust him, following a policy which reflected both the traditional hostility between the two states and the existing tensions in the Caribbean. The Dominican government had charged in December 1948 that Enrique C. Henríquez had visited Port-au-Prince in the hope of enlisting Haitian support for an invasion of the Dominican Republic.[317] Although nothing came of this mission, Trujillo was himself conspiring with an ambitious Haitian political leader, Colonel Astrel Roland, for the removal of Estimé. Allegedly this conspiracy included a plot to poison Estimé by Roland's mistress, Johanna Verbracken, the "Mata Hari of the Caribbean."[318] When Roland's treason was uncovered in January 1949, Roland took refuge in Ciudad Trujillo and on 8 February used the microphones of "La Voz Dominicana" to attack the Haitian president as a "foul beast" and to incite the Haitian people to rebellion.[319] Haiti took this matter to the Council of the OAS, which declined to convoke the Organ of Consultation, and Haiti then appealed to the IAPC. Under the auspices of the Peace Committee, Haiti and the Dominican Republic signed a Joint Declaration on 9 June 1949, in which they pledged not to tolerate the activities of individuals or groups whose purpose was to disturb the internal peace of either party.[320] This settlement, however, did not end the intrigue.

The Dominican conspiracy against the Estimé government next entered a particularly bizarre phase. Roland, in league with another Haitian, Alfred Viau, continued the offensive broadcasts—one in June and another in November. More serious, however, was Roland's plot with John Dupuy, a Port-au-Prince businessman. Their plan was for Dupuy to create panic within Haiti by assassinating a number of high officials and by setting several fires in the capital and for Roland to cross into Haiti from Jimaní with an armed band once these events had occurred.[321] The Dominican government was deeply involved in this scheme through Anselmo Paulino Alvarez, then Trujillo's closest aide, and through the Dominican embassy in Haiti. On 8 November an agent of Paulino arrived in Port-au-Prince and delivered $2,000 to the first secretary of the Dominican embassy, Rafael Oscar de Moya, who in turn handed over the money to Dupuy. Between 8 and 13 December Dupuy traveled secretly to Ciudad Trujillo, where he met with Roland and arranged to pick up arms and ammunition in Jimaní, including two submachine guns.[322] On 19 December these plans came undone when the Haitian police raided Dupuy's home and killed him in a gun battle. But the most sensational part of the affair was yet to come.

Around Christmastime, the two top officials of the Dominican embassy in Port-au-Prince, "clearly frightened," abandoned their mission and left for the United States.[323] Secretary De Moya departed on 25 December, and Chargé d'Affaires Sebastián Rodríguez Lora followed him two days later. Although he later denied it, before fleeing Rodríguez Lora held an interview with Haitian Foreign Minister Vilfort

Beauvoir and revealed the reason for his unusual behavior. He declared that as part of the Dupuy-Roland plot the Dominican embassy in Port-au-Prince was to be set afire and that he and De Moya and their families were to be killed.[324] As a result of these revelations, the Haitian government was convinced that Trujillo's request for war-making powers was a direct threat against Haiti. The Haitian government believed that the burning of the Dominican embassy and the assault upon the diplomats was to serve as a pretext for a full-scale Dominican invasion of Haiti, not merely for an armed incursion by Roland. For this reason, then, even though most attention was focused upon the Cuban-Dominican crisis in December 1949, Haiti directed a note to the OAS Council on 3 January 1950 calling for a meeting of consultation.

The council met on 6 January to acknowledge the Haitian request and to provide the Haitian and other representatives an opportunity to speak on the matter. After the Haitian ambassador, Joseph L. Dejean, had spoken, the Dominican representative, Joaquín E. Salazar, did indeed avail himself of the opportunity to address the council. He dismissed the Haitian charges as absurd and reiterated the adherence of the Dominican Republic to the principle of nonintervention. He then delivered a lengthy note from his own government which reviewed events in the Caribbean from Cayo Confites to the moment and requested the convoking of the Organ of Consultation "for the purpose of studying and remedying the abnormal conditions prevailing in the Caribbean."[325] In this way, the Haitian affair was expanded to cover the entire Caribbean situation. The council agreed to invoke the Rio Treaty as requested by Haiti and the Dominican Republic and, in accordance with Article 12, constituted itself as the Provisional Organ of Consultation. It resolved to appoint an investigating committee to conduct an on-the-spot study and to render a report. The Caribbean exiles now faced the scrutiny of the highest organ of the OAS.

The Investigating Committee was installed on 9 January and spent over two months conducting a thorough examination of the Caribbean situation. The committee was made up of Guillermo Gutiérrez, Bolivia; Eduardo Zuleta Angel, Colombia; Alfonso Moscoso, Ecuador; Paul C. Daniels, the United States; and José A. Mora, Uruguay, chairman. It set up its permanent headquarters in Washington, but during its labors the committee traveled to Haiti, the Dominican Republic, Cuba, Guatemala, and Mexico, where it interviewed chiefs of state, high governmental officials, knowledgeable private citizens, exile leaders, and just about every significant personality involved in the events under study.[326] On 13 March 1950 the committee submitted its report, which, in the view of a U.S. State Department official, "was no whitewash" nor "a surrender to diplomatic camouflage."[327]

For purposes of clarity the committee divided its report into Case A, findings with reference to the Haitian request, and Case B, findings with reference to the Dominican request. In Case A the study left no doubt concerning the guilt of the Dominican Republic in the Roland-Dupuy affair.[328] Case B was, of course, more complex. The Cayo Confites and Luperón affairs were described in detail and the involvement of Cuba and Guatemala in these episodes was stated frankly. Haiti, on the other hand, was cleared of any part in these or any other revolutionary activities.[329] In its findings and recommendations, however, the committee clearly condemned the military operations of exile groups.

The committee was especially concerned because it believed that the circumstances which produced Cayo Confites and Luperón continued to exist. The investigators found, for example, that the diverse exile groups were still prepared to use force to secure their aims and were seeking the assistance of friendly governments. Certain officials of some governments, the committee reported, were openly sympathetic to these exiles and were willing to give them official support. In fact, some of the active participants in the Caribbean revolutionary movements were themselves in influential governmental positions. Finally, said the committee, there was insufficient control over the movement of arms and war matériel in the Caribbean, and there existed in the region professional revolutionaries, some of whom had no other means of livelihood.[330] The committee concluded that if there was no "specific military organization" called the Caribbean Legion, there definitely was "a band of individuals which constituted a subversive force," which, "[though] less organized and systematic than the hypothetical Legion, [was] more dangerous and more prone to the creation of serious antagonistic situations."[331]

In describing the action of the exiles, the Investigating Committee did not overlook the basis for their grievance, but this was only mild consolation. The committee affirmed that, while there were adventurers and mercenaries in the revolutionary movements, most of the exiles were "sincere and idealistic persons," who, "having been deprived of democratic guarantees in their homelands were forced to fight to return to political life."[332] Also, the investigators declared that their condemnation of interventionism in no way closed the door to "legitimate evolution and change." In their recommendations, they balanced an insistence upon the more effective control over "illegitimate activities" of political exiles and "illegal traffic" in arms with a call for a study of the means for making more effective the exercise of representative democracy in the Americas. But, again, they advised the Organ of Consultation to state clearly that "the principle of representative democracy . . . does not authorize any state to violate its international commitments concerning nonintervention."[333] Finally, in order to give force to its procedures, the committee suggested that the Organ of Consultation establish a special committee charged with seeing to it that its will was respected.[334]

On 3 April the Council of the OAS acting provisionally as the Organ of Consultation met to consider the report of the Investigating Committee and, after five days of debate, passed eight resolutions. Resolutions I and II endorsed the findings of the committee, that is, the Dominican Republic was criticized for its actions against Haiti and for other conduct "contrary to the norms of American coexistence," and Cuba and Guatemala were chastised for their support of subversive movements against the Dominican Republic.[335] All parties were reminded of their obligations under existing treaties and conventions, and the Organ of Consultation recommended a number of procedures by which the conflicting parties might normalize their relations. Due note was also made of the action of the Dominican Congress in repealing Trujillo's war-making powers. However, under the threat of sanctions, Cuba and Guatemala were requested to take "adequate measures" to prevent "the existence, within their territory, of militarily organized groups of nationals or foreigners, whose deliberate purpose was to conspire against the security of other countries." Cuba, Guatemala, and the Dominican Republic were requested to respect absolutely the principle of nonintervention, and Cuba and Guatemala were asked to supervise any arms in the possession of revolutionary groups and to prevent the illegal traffic of arms. Cuba, Guatemala, Haiti, and the Dominican Republic were advised to refrain from propaganda attacks upon other American states.[336] In order to monitor these resolutions, the Organ of Consultation decided in Resolution III to create a special committee for the Caribbean, a "watchdog" committee, which was to render a report concerning the implementation of Resolutions I and II within three months and to make another upon the completion of its work.[337]

These three resolutions clearly sought the termination of exile military operations, or, as the popular press put it, the breakup of the Caribbean Legion.

Resolutions IV and V were concerned with the underlying problem of the Caribbean (the "illness," not the "symptoms," as the Cubans had said), but they lacked any compulsion or any sense of urgency and resorted to the stale legalisms of the past. Resolution IV affirmed the principle of representative democracy, but dutifully declared it did not authorize the violation of the principle of nonintervention. Resolution V called for three potentially important studies: one study to be made by the Juridical Department of the Pan American Union concerning the strengthening and perfecting of the 1928 Havana Convention, particularly with reference to the means "governments should employ to prevent, within their territory, the preparation of activities directed at fomenting civil war in other countries"; and two studies to be undertaken by either the Inter-American Council of Jurists or the Inter-American Juridical Committee, one on how to make more effective the principle of representative democracy, and the other to deal with the problems created by political refugees and exiles.[338]

The remaining resolutions treated miscellaneous matters, such as the call for the ratification by all states of the OAS Charter and the expression of appreciation for the labors of the Investigating Committee. The council also terminated its provisional status as the Organ of Consultation and cancelled the summons for a meeting of ministers of foreign affairs. The council had again acted under the Rio Treaty without the need to call in session the supreme organ.

These actions were the manifestation of the passage of a phase of Caribbean exile activity. Although it was officially recorded in the Final Report of the Special Committee for the Caribbean on 14 May 1951, which stated that the countries of the Caribbean were carrying out the resolutions of the Organ of Consultation, the change was more complete than obedience to the dicta of the OAS. In essence, the hopes expressed so confidently in 1945 had been dashed. The seemingly irrevocable trend in favor of the Democratic Left had in fact been reversed, and the balance had shifted to the side of the governments of force. More critical than the proscribing of exile military operations was the loss of bases from which to operate. During most of the decade of the 1950s, the only parties of the Democratic Left in power in the Caribbean were those of Costa Rica and Puerto Rico, neither of which was in a position to oppose militarily its dictatorial neighbors. It was not realistic for the Democratic Left to think about continuing the military offensive; its main task was now survival.

Despite the rather gloomy situation of the Democratic Left during the 1950s, there was no lack of resolve. Conspiratorial activity and even filibustering did not disappear completely, but the substantial activity concerned itself with the development of new techniques of opposition and with the utilization of new avenues and opportunities for dissent, all of which was facilitated by the prevailing internationalism and the growth of the mass media. The Democratic Left maintained its sense of history and embraced a set of ideals which earned for it wide sympathy. Even in a world polarized by communism and anticommunism, the Democratic Left could survive if it was able to identify itself with the fundamental urge for human rights, civil liberties, and social progress.

Among the parties of the Democratic Left in exile Acción Democrática of Venezuela was the most adaptable to the exigencies of the political struggle of the 1950s. Banished from Venezuela after three years in power, AD possessed an experienced political organization and leadership. However, because it was still the country's most popular party, with continuing influence upon many organizations and institutions within Venezuela, AD also organized an underground resistance movement. In fact, during at least the first four years of its exile, Acción Democrática devoted a great deal of its energies and resources to the clandestine movement. Out of necessity, the strategy of the party was to avoid conspiratorial activity and to keep alive its ideals as an alternative and hope for the people of Venezuela. To accomplish this it maintained both its internal and external organizations as vehicles for dissent and for exposing the repressive policies of the new regime. The existence of a resistance movement in Venezuela, therefore, added a new dimension to politics in exile and to the antidictatorial struggle in the Caribbean.

3 | *The Clandestine AD*

The New Exiles

ROMULO GALLEGOS was deposed as president of Venezuela in a military coup on 24 November 1948. The factors explaining his overthrow were rooted in Venezuelan history and in the nature of the three-year rule, 1945-48, of Acción Democrática. The military and traditionalist sectors of Venezuela mistrusted and feared the revolutionary doctrine of AD, which sought a broad, popular political base and committed the state to social and welfare programs and to economic planning. AD's programs in agrarian reform, economic development, educational advancement, and rigid control over natural resources affected one or another of the vested interests of Venezuela. Moreover, AD's militancy, partisanship, and intenseness in carrying out its programs alienated other civilian, even mildly reformist, parties. When the army leaders, lieutenant colonels Carlos Delgado Chalbaud, Marcos Pérez Jiménez, and Luis Felipe Llovera Páez, made their move, they were able to exploit the anxieties and resentments resulting from three years of revolutionary government.

The showdown came when the colonels demanded a greater voice in the Gallegos cabinet and insisted that AD party president, Rómulo Betancourt, be excluded from the government. Gallegos rejected these demands, and the army leaders, affirming that the president had subordinated his office to the dictates of the AD party, acted to remove him.[1] In the deepening crisis AD had tried unsuccessfully to call a general strike, and, although this step was a reaction to the situation, not its cause, the army leaders cited it as another reason for their

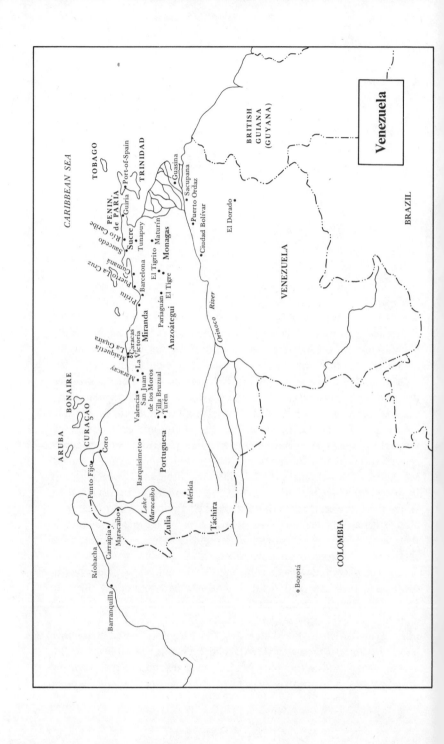

takeover.[2] In its explanations, the Military Junta also repeatedly asserted that the Gallegos government was hostile to the armed forces, that there had been periodic efforts to remove one or another of the colonels from his post, and that the AD sought systematically to divide the armed forces and even to create armed civilian militias.[3] Later came charges of peculation, corruption, and even communism, none of which had any relevance to the actual events.

The deposed leaders, of course, had other explanations for what had happened. Besides denying the validity of the military's charges, both Gallegos and Betancourt suspected some kind of foreign intrigue. Gallegos said that the U.S. oil companies were involved and noted that the U.S. army attaché, Colonel Edward F. Adams, had been in the Ministry of Defense at the time of the coup.[4] Although the oil companies were probably pleased over the ouster of Gallegos, there was no evidence that they had promoted the movement. The presence of Colonel Adams in the Ministry of Defense was inopportune, but it was not related to the coup.[5] More serious was the fact that the United States had shortly before recognized the *golpista* government of Manuel Odría in Peru, a fact which was looked upon as giving the "green light" to the Venezuelan colonels.[6] Betancourt, on the other hand, did not blame the United States and accused, instead, Juan Perón of Argentina and Francisco Franco of Spain. Betancourt charged that the "Franco-Perón Axis" was behind both the Peruvian and Venezuelan coups and that the Argentine leader, specifically, was the head of an *"Internacional de las Espadas."*[7]

Given the state of Caribbean affairs and the known enmity between Betancourt and Trujillo, one might wonder whether or not the Dominican dictator played any part. Trujillo was not mentioned in any of the post-golpe statements of Gallegos or Betancourt, but it was a fact that Pedro Estrada, an agent in the employ of Trujillo and a former police official under Eleazar López Contreras, had secretly entered Venezuela on 6 November.[8] There is no record of what he did, but his presence during this crisis raises some questions. Moreover, on 23 November, the day before Gallegos' ouster, "La Voz Dominicana" had already announced the event, along with a scathing attack on AD.[9] The postmortems continued for some time, but, essentially, democracy was weak in Venezuela and the military was still too close to the days of Juan Vicente Gómez, when the state had virtually existed to gratify its desires. Many of the same officers who had placed AD in power in

1945 had grown restive under the contention and seeming uncertainty of civilian rule and, despite the fact that Gallegos had been freely elected, decided to take back the power they had given and to exercise it themselves.

Gallegos and Betancourt were the first of the AD leaders to go into exile. Gallegos was permitted to depart peacefully for Havana on 5 December. Betancourt had a more difficult time. He had been the real force behind the Venezuelan revolution, and most of the complaints by the military leaders were directed against him. He went into hiding and contemplated leading the underground movement personally, but his life obviously was in danger and he himself admitted that his state of mind was so depressed that he could not give effective leadership. Moreover, he told his followers, his continued presence in Venezuela might give the impression that AD's return to power was imminent, whereas he believed the struggle would be long.[10] You cannot fight with barricades in the days of the armored tank and bombing plane, mused Betancourt.[11] On the night of 1 December Betancourt took asylum in the Colombian embassy, but, as if to vindicate his fears, he was unable to secure safe-conduct until 23 January. The remaining AD functionaries, including members of Gallegos' cabinet and parliamentary representatives, were detained in Venezuelan jails, and only slowly released, a few at a time, and sent into exile during the course of the next year.

The new exiles were quite distinct from those described in the preceding chapter. The AD regime was the first postwar, democratic government to fall. As such, its exiles had shortly before occupied high positions, had officially attended international conferences, and were on intimate terms with chiefs of state and high-ranking officials of other states. President Gallegos had visited the United States for twelve days in July 1948 as the guest of President Harry S. Truman, and the two presidents had traveled together to Bolivar, Missouri, for the unveiling of a statue of the town's Venezuelan namesake. During the same visit, Gallegos received an honorary degree from Columbia University presented to him by the university's president, General Dwight Eisenhower. The United States recognized the Military Junta in January 1949, but President Truman wrote to Gallegos on 13 February and stated, "I believe that the use of force to effect political changes is not only deplorable, but contrary to the ideals of the American people."[12] Like Gallegos, Betancourt was also a figure of hemispheric stature. He had been provisional president of Venezuela for over two years and in

April 1948 had been Venezuela's chief delegate at the Bogotá
conference. Similarly, Andrés Eloy Blanco, who had served as foreign
minister under Gallegos, was a poet of renown and just two months
before the ouster of Gallegos had addressed the United Nations General
Assembly. In exile, these leaders assumed the role of the opposition
which they were not permitted to perform within Venezuela.

Although dissolved by decree on 7 December, Acción Democrática
did not cease to exist. Eloy Blanco delcared, "We are not a party
created by decree. Therefore, we cannot be dissolved by decree."[13]
Betancourt affirmed, "We have been temporarily defeated, but we are
not conquered."[14] The tasks ahead for AD were outlined by the latter
during a radio broadcast from Havana on 4 February 1949, in which he
said Acción Democrática must, first, arouse hemispheric opinion against
the golpistas and, second, show faith in "the ability of the Venezuelan
people to recover their lost democracy" by serving as the "organized
vanguard" of the resistance.[15] The first task was a reassertion of the
antidictatorial policy followed by AD when in power, that is, the denunciation of military coups, the policy of nonrecognition, and the
marshalling of international opinion against the violations of human
rights by authoritarian regimes. This was a many-faceted struggle, taken
up mainly by the leaders in exile, and it will be described in more detail
in the following chapter. For the moment, two examples may be cited
which constituted important early actions.

The AD leaders in exile were immediately concerned with the question of diplomatic recognition of the Military Junta and with the plight
of their comrades imprisoned in Venezuela. For his first stop in exile,
Betancourt called upon President Carlos Prío Socarrás of Cuba, seeking
assurances that the *"cordón sanitario"* already established against Trujillo and Somoza would be extended to encompass the Military Junta of
Venezuela.[16] Prío, indignant over the crushing of democracy in Venezuela, responded by writing other democratic governments to "coordinate moral efforts in defense of the broken democratic unity of the
hemisphere."[17] This invitation was accepted by Chile, Costa Rica,
Guatemala, and Uruguay, which refused to recognize the junta. With
the first step taken toward the formation of an antidictatorial bloc,
Betancourt traveled to Lake Success, New York, where he addressed a
letter to UN Secretary General Trygve Lie on 28 March. In the note, he
charged the junta with "crimes against humanity" and declared specifically that there were two thousand political prisioners being held in

Venezuela without trial.[18] This move was supported by similar letters from Gallegos to UN delegates and to Uruguayan President Luis Batlle Berres. Gallegos and Eloy Blanco also wrote to Trygve Lie and pointed out the responsibilities of the signatories of the UN Charter to defend human rights in Venezuela.[19] These steps resulted in action by Uruguay on 7 April, supported later by Guatemala, by which the UN was asked to investigate the alleged violations of human rights by the Venezuelan regime. The United States, concerned that UN action might give the Soviet Union an opportunity to meddle, opposed the investigation. Instead, it preferred to work behind the scenes to secure a pledge from the Venezuelan regime to release the political prisoners.[20]

Slowly the doors of Venezuelan prisons opened, and many of the important AD leaders were released, a majority of whom were quickly sent into exile. Among those released after four to ten months imprisonment were Cabinet Ministers Raúl Leoni (labor), Ricardo Montilla (agriculture), Luis Beltrán Prieto (education), and Leonardo Ruiz Pineda (communications); and high-ranking officials and party officers Gonzalo Barrios (secretary of the presidency), José Angel Ciliberto (presidential press secretary), Luis Troconis Guerrero (editor of the party newspaper *El País* and president of the Municipal Council of the Federal District), Luis Lander (president of the Chamber of Deputies), Luis Augusto Dubuc (secretary general of AD), Alberto Carnevali (secretary of organization of AD and chief of the parliamentary wing of the party), and, finally, Valmore Rodríguez, the president of the National Congress and the highest-ranking AD leader to be imprisoned. Rodríguez unfortunately suffered two heart attacks during his ten months in the "Cárcel Modelo" of Caracas. It was an impressive array of talent. Most of them, as noted, were forced to join the struggle in exile, but some remained behind to organize the underground, and later a few returned clandestinely to serve as replacements for those who had fallen in the resistance.

The clandestine movement was the "organized vanguard" of the resistance. Its functions were to remind the Venezuelan people of the illegitimacy of the regime, to remain a center of agitation, and to exploit unrest or dissatisfaction within the country. It would not engage in terrorism, the clandestine AD affirmed, because such tactics did not correspond to its role as a democratic and popular party, nor would it repeat the error of October 1945, its leaders insisted, by taking part in any "putsch."[21] The policy of the clandestine organization seemed to promise only martyrdom to its leadership, but AD could not avoid the struggle within Venezuela if it were to remain a viable force. As far as Acción Democrática was concerned, the needs of the underground overrode most other considerations of the antidictatorial campaign. The leaders in exile did all that they could to support, guide, and protect their comrades inside Venezuela. Few expected that the fight would be easy, and, in many respects, it represented AD's "finest hour."

The Underground Organization

Resistance leader Leonardo Ruiz Pineda stated that the underground movement began only "days after" the coup–other leaders said the preparations were initiated "within hours" after the fall of Gallegos. [22] If so, all that could be done was to assess the extent of the wreckage and to elude the golpistas' dragnet. December 8, however, was the official date on which AD launched its clandestine struggle. On that date, Acción Democrática issued a manifesto in which it declared before the nation that it was going underground to lead the fight to restore the exercise of individual freedoms and the rule of popular sovereignty. It pledged to wage a nonviolent struggle: to organize public opinion, to mobilize all media of agitation and information, and to unleash "permanent action on all fronts." Its purpose was to bring about the "national crisis" which would topple the dictatorship from its "unstable base." AD affirmed that the struggle would be "cruel and brutal," because the adversary would use repressive means, but it swore not to be deterred nor diverted from its "sacred commitment" to Venezuela. [23] Time would test fully this resolve.

The aims of the clandestine struggle were described in more detail in a statement written in July 1952 by Leonardo Ruiz Pineda. He explained that the objectives of AD were, first, the internal organization of the party; second, the expansion of the areas of party influence; third, the continual agitation to deny stability to the regime; and fourth, "the creation of bases on which to build a powerful antigovernmental movement to bring down the junta." [24] AD's hope was to remain a popular party, despite the fact that it was outlawed, and to return to power at the head of a mass movement. This attitude reflected the old dispute between AD and the army, that is, whether democratic authority should control the military. Ruiz Pineda reiter-

ated that AD rejected the *"putchista"* tactic, and would rely instead
upon the daily work of wooing popular support and the constant struggle on the political front.[25] In this way, when the junta fell, AD would
operate from a democratic power base not reliant upon but superior to
the armed forces. Although the resistance had no timetable and it cau-
tioned its militants to be patient, Ruiz Pineda made it clear that the
movement was not passive. It would oppose the regime every step of
the way and be a dynamic political force even within a dictatorship. [26]

These public pronouncements were, of course, expressions of idealistic hopes. Many of the party militants were in fundamental disagree-
ment with the policy of nonviolence.[27] They favored direct action and
even terrorism. José Vicente Abreu, who fought in the AD underground
and later joined the Communist party, wrote a poignant novel based
upon his experiences in the resistance movement. One of his characters
was Ramón, a "man of action," who always carried a bomb in his car
and who "in the meetings was always talking about killing, . . . about
getting started right away with killing cops [and] officials."[28] At the
same time, it must be pointed out that contact with elements of the
armed forces was not absolutely ruled out. According to Ricardo Montilla, AD never lost touch with the military, particularly with its "liberal" elements. He asserted that the support of the armed forces was
essential for the overthrow of the junta.[29] He was not referring to a
golpe, however, but rather to the need to convince the members of the
armed forces that their true role was subordinate to the civil power and
the legitimate government. In order to accomplish this, the colonels of
the Military Junta were depicted as adventurers, who on the pretense of
defending the honor of the armed forces had disgraced them.[30] According to a document attributed to Betancourt, the contact with the
military was considered the most delicate aspect of the resistance movement, and it was to be made only by the highest officers of the
party.[31]

This same document, which AD denied to be authentic but which
contained good internal evidence, outlined other aspects of the resistance. Supposedly written by Betancourt in asylum in the Colombian
embassy, it instructed the party to organize groups of women to distribute in the markets and public places small leaflets bearing the insignia
of Acción Democrática. He wanted the women also to engage in a
systematic gossip campaign, complaining in shops and stores about the
cost of living and shortcomings of public services. Other groups were to

be formed to stir up discontent by "hammering away at" hard-to-solve administrative problems in water, road repairs, and housing. Still others, he advised, should begin a campaign of graffiti, scrawling the party initials and placing political posters on buildings and walls. Betancourt recommended that the party print its manifestos; he considered the mimeograph unsatisfactory for the political struggle. Finally, he made reference to organized labor, an area in which AD was particularly strong. Betancourt insisted that the unions at all costs maintain their legal status. For this, characteristic of the party strategy, he counseled against strikes and violent demonstrations. The unions would serve better as vehicles of propaganda and agitation, although he did recommend a campaign of subtle sabotage by means of planned accidents and general inefficiency.[32] Eventually, however, the fury of the repressive regime made the performance of even these tasks difficult.

While strategy and tactics were being worked out, the underground organization itself was taking shape. The movement was organized on geographic and functional lines. Before the fall of AD, the supreme organ of the party had been the National Directorate (Dirección Nacional), but since most of its members were in exile, the principal underground organ was the National Executive Committee, CEN (Comité Ejecutivo Nacional). Under it was a heirarchy of executive committees at various geographic levels: in descending order, sections (or regions), districts, zones, and sectors. The basic unit was the five-man cell, or *grupo de base.*[33] Running parallel to this geographic organization were cells and committees within particular professions or special groups: lawyers, doctors, professors and teachers, university students, and organized labor.[34] Since it was impossible to hold any kind of party assembly, the National Executive Committee (CEN) almost exclusively shaped party policy within Venezuela,[35] subject only to the will of the National Directorate in exile. The CEN was presided over by the secretary general of AD, who, as such, became the symbol of the resistance. Rómulo Betancourt remained the president of the party and the presiding officer of the National Directorate in exile (commonly referred to as the Dirección), so that it was necessary to maintain regular and systematic contact between the CEN and the exiled leader.

The AD leadership in exile also went through a period of reorganization. Since the AD leaders were scattered in a number of places, principally Havana, Mexico City, and San José, Costa Rica, the Dirección did not meet formally. Instead, the general direction of the work of the diaspora was achieved through a Coordinating Committee of the Exterior (Comité Coordinador del Exterior),[36] while the principal external guidance of the resistance movement was performed by Betancourt, acting with the authority of the Dirección.[37] In this way, Gallegos remained the constitutional president and the spokesman for all Venezuelans, while Betancourt performed the role of party chieftain. Betancourt established his first headquarters in Havana. When Prío was overthrown in March 1952, Betancourt moved to San José, and when the pressure became too serious for his friend José Figueres, he shifted his base to Puerto Rico in 1954.

Contact between the underground and the exterior was maintained by a secret network of communications and travel employing codes and ciphers, pseudonyms, and ordinary words with special meanings, or made-up words. Radio communications were maintained daily by means of short, five-minute transmissions in cipher. The exile radio, called *"el piloto,"* was first located in Cruz Alonso's Hotel San Luis in Havana but was moved in 1952 to Figueres' finca "La Lucha Sin Fin." The principal underground radio was located in Caracas, set up in various hideouts or, as the underground called them, *"conchas"* (literally, "shells"). Radio contact was also employed within Venezuela, with the CEN beaming instructions from Caracas to secret radios in the interior. Betancourt used the radio to send information and instructions, particularly concerning clandestine journeys to Venezuela by AD members or couriers. For this, they made up a verb, *"volandear,"* meaning, "to make a clandestine journey," and conjugated it in regular fashion. Two principal clandestine routes were employed: one, overland from Colombia by way of Ríohacha and Carraipia to Maracaibo; the other, from Trinidad in a dugout to the deserted south coast of the Peninsula of Paria. Both of these journeys were made in collaboration with smugglers, who had been carrying out these activities for generations. Once inside the country, travelers followed a Venezuelan version of the underground railroad.[38]

The radio transmissions also alerted the underground to letters or packages coming by post (*"estafeta"*), or via some other carrier, which contained instructions, special materials, and even money. On special occasions, when foreign dignitaries or international missions were scheduled to arrive in Venezuela, Betancourt informed the underground and recommended demonstrations or contact. For its part, the underground transmitted to Betancourt news from Venezuela, particularly about the arrest or mistreatment of comrades, so that the exiles could carry the protest to appropriate international agencies. In all contacts, the leaders used pseudonyms. Betancourt was known as "Roca" and "Alvarez," while among the resistance leaders there was Leonardo Ruiz Pineda, "Alfredo"; Alberto Carnevali, "Alí"; Antonio Pinto Salinas, "Luzardo" and "Peralta"; and Rigoberto Henríquez Vera, "Loyo." [39]

The Subterranean Struggle

The underground apparatus was not created overnight but evolved slowly. In fact, the countermeasures of the Military Junta kept the movement off balance for some time. Luis Augusto Dubuc, the first secretary general of the resistance,[40] was captured on 18 January 1949, and Octavio Lepage took over temporarily. Not until Leonardo Ruiz Pineda was released from the Cárcel Modelo on 19 April did the underground have a permanent chieftain. Ruiz Pineda was only twenty-nine years old when he became secretary general of the clandestine AD, but he had already served as governor of his native state of Táchira and as minister of communications under Gallegos. He was a lawyer by profession and, although for the next three and one-half years he was subjected to the life of the hunted, he was described by his comrades as a gentle man, well suited for the patient task of rebuilding the party and conducting the struggle on a responsible path.[41] Under his leadership things began to happen, so that by July reports came from Venezuela that the resistance was operating on the national level and down to the "most humble *barrio.*"[42] The National Executive Committee (CEN) had been organized with secretaries for finance, organization, and press and propaganda, but the outstanding success seemed to be the publication of a weekly newspaper, *Resistencia.* The paper consisted of only eight pages and, up to that point, was printed by mimeograph, but reportedly eight thousand copies were being distributed hand-to-hand, house-to-house by means of a laundry truck. One copy regularly turned up on the desk of the minister of the interior, whose responsibility was internal security.[43] *Resistencia* published lists of names of prisoners, as well as of "spies and traitors," but its most popular feature was a comic strip, "Los tres cochinitos" ("The Three Little Pigs"), which followed the "adventures" of the three colonels of the Military Junta.[44]

The editor of *Resistencia* was Luis Troconis Guerrero, who had been

editor of the AD daily *El País,* which had been outlawed the day after
the coup. Troconis was a member of the CEN from the beginning of the
struggle, but the junta was obviously unaware of it, because it arrested
him in December 1948 and then released him the following April, along
with Ruiz Pineda. He resumed his position as secretary of press and
propaganda, although he did not actually have to go into hiding until
January 1950. He was described as a man of indefatigable energy, who
wrote and edited every kind of party publication: manifestos, pamphlets, newspapers, and communiqués.[45] He even helped set up clandestine newspapers in the interior and managed to convert *Resistencia*
from mimeograph to typography. After sixteen months, however,
Troconis became "a casualty of the resistance."[46] The pressures of the
underground, coupled with the need to confine his great energy to the
limits of his "concha," apparently contributed to a heart attack. He
resisted for a while the orders of the Dirección to seek medical attention, but when he finally surfaced from the underground, he was immediately placed under police guard.[47] Despite his poor health, he and his
family were subjected to constant harassment by the regime. He was
finally sent into exile, going first to Cuba, then to Costa Rica, where he
died on 23 December 1951. He thus became one of the movement's
first martyrs.[48]

The first year of the junta rule, however, could be described as a
honeymoon period. There were several reasons why this was so. AD was
itself avoiding extremist tactics and was rebuilding. The regime, while
appearing to be secure, particularly with the armed forces' backing, was
split within. The junta president, Carlos Delgado Chalbaud, was the
most moderate member. He was well-educated, gentlemanly, and even
AD sources felt he took part in the coup reluctantly.[49] On the other
hand, the youngest member, Marcos Pérez Jiménez, was the ambitious
soldier who had come up through the ranks. Boorish, but popular with
the troops, he, as later events would show, aspired to dictatorial
power.[50] In between, as a tenuous balancer, was Luis Felipe Llovera
Páez, the playboy, who seemed interested only in keeping a good thing
going.[51] As a result of this situation, the junta was not anxious to
provoke serious incidents, and even the police were described as cour-
teous.[52] It probably explained why the regime yielded to international
opinion and freed so many of the imprisoned AD leaders during 1949.
In addition, a number of civilian parties continued to function legally.
These included the Democratic Republican Union, URD (Unión Repub-

licana Democrática), an amorphous party somewhat left-of-center, nationalistic, and dominated by the personality of Jóvito Villalba; the Christian Democrats (COPEI), a Catholic party, originally conservative, but tending toward moderate reform; and the Communist party (PCV). None of the aforementioned denounced the coup nor joined AD in the resistance. Only organized labor seemed to be a threat to the junta, so in this sector repressive action was taken.

The junta dissolved the Venezuelan Confederation of Workers, CTV (Confederación de Trabajadores de Venezuela), and its affiliates by decree on 25 February 1949. In explaining its action, the junta declared that the CTV had exceeded legitimate trade union activity and was, in fact, engaged in politics. Even before the decree went into effect, hundreds of labor and *campesino* union leaders had been imprisoned, scores of union locals had been sacked and closed, and the secretary general of the CTV, Augusto Malavé Villalba, had been forced into exile.[53] Although AD denied that it was exclusively a labor party, in power it had stimulated the development of the labor movement and had passed legislation designed to improve the condition of the working class. AD had obviously sought to build up organized labor as a base for challenging the power of the military. Correspondingly, most of the important labor leaders were members of Acción Democrática, and the Venezuelan labor movement was indeed politically oriented. Nonetheless, before the decree was announced the only action taken by AD labor had been a minor work stoppage in January by oil workers in Zulia.[54] With the national confederation and the state federations closed, local unions were permitted to operate, but only under the prescription of a subsequent decree of 9 March. This decree dissolved the existing governing boards of the locals and prohibited any incumbent from taking part in the reorganization of the union or to hold any office. Moreover, unions were not permitted to affiliate and all union meetings required the prior authorization of the inspector of labor for that jurisdiction.[55]

Despite these violations of trade union rights, the still unorganized resistance prudently followed the policy of refraining from violent demonstrations and strikes. Instead, action was taken by the exiles in the international sphere. Protests were lodged before the International Labor Organization (ILO) in Geneva by the workers' delegates, and in May exiled labor leader Malavé submitted a protest to the Fourth ILO Regional Conference of American States in Montevideo.[56] As a result of Malavé's protest and the strong backing given it by Serafino Ro-

mualdi of the American Federation of Labor, the Montevideo conference voted to instruct the director general of the ILO to seek an inquiry
of the alleged violations of workers' rights in Venezuela.[57] In order to
remove the sting from this action, the junta itself invited the ILO to
send a mission to Venezuela to observe trade union conditions.

At the end of July 1949 an ILO mission under Deputy Director
General Jef Rens arrived in Venezuela. Rens spent six weeks in Venezuela and made as thorough a study as possible, visiting all parts of the
country.[58] Apparently the junta expected a polite, perfunctory tour,
but Rens wanted to interview labor leaders, including those in jail. The
junta cooperated at first, but eventually relations cooled, and toward
the end of the stay the junta ignored Rens altogether. Rens was particularly disturbed by the fact that, even while the mission was on Venezuelan soil, some of the labor leaders whom he interviewed were then
imprisoned or forced to go into exile.[59]

Rens concluded his mission with a report entitled "Trade Union
Freedom and the Conditions of Labor in Venezuela," which was a
strong denunciation of the repression of labor in Venezuela, although it
was not issued publicly until August 1950. The report was especially
critical of the decrees dissolving the Venezuelan Confederation of
Workers (CTV) and the prohibition against holding union office by
members of dissolved governing boards.[60] This, the report explained,
deprived Venezuelan labor of experienced leadership and damaged its
effectiveness.[61] Although the Rens Report specifically found that the
trade unions of Venezuela "[did] not enjoy the freedom of action and
organization comparable to that of the trade unions of countries in
which workers' organizations [function] without administrative restrictions,"[62] it also addressed itself to the general question of the appropriate spheres of action of organized labor. The report conceded that
differences might arise between the state and organized labor concerning whether the latter was engaged in syndical activities or political
activities. However, it admonished the junta that in the event of such
differences it was essential to respect the fundamental guarantees of
human rights as provided for in the Universal Declaration of the Rights
of Man.[63] Thus, indirectly, the junta was censured for the jailing and
exiling of labor leaders, whether for labor or political activities. The
junta declared in rebuttal that until labor "followed a normal course
. . . independent of political parties," restrictions on trade unionism in
Venezuela would continue.[64] It denounced the references to human

rights in the report as outside the scope of the ILO inquiry and as an interference in the internal affairs of Venezuela. The Rens Report was the beginning of unhappy relations between the Venezuelan dictatorship and international labor.

The Rens mission did not force the junta to modify its repression of organized labor; in fact, following Rens' departure in September, the regime became more assertive. The junta adopted the policy of considering any strike or work stoppage as an act of sabotage or subversion and was noticeably harsher toward all political prisoners. The first group of AD prisoners, those arrested as part of the coup and its aftermath, were released and sent into exile, as has been seen. But as the resistance movement took shape, the regime showed a harder line and began to treat political prisoners quite differently. The principal repressive arm of the regime was the National Security police, SN (Seguridad Nacional), which gradually grew into one of the most dreaded instruments of political suppression in the hemisphere. The honeymoon period was over.

In October 1949 the SN began sending political prisoners to "El Dorado," a penal colony in the Venezuelan jungle previously used only for the most hardened criminals.[65] Even the timid Caracas press protested this action; but the junta replied that the first group of twenty-three prisoners, five of whom were students, had been convicted of "civil crimes," including the spreading of nails and tacks on highways and the defacing of public buildings.[66] Prominent Venezuelans, among them Rafael Pizani, the former rector of the Central University of Venezuela, and Vicente Emilio Sojo, the director of the Symphony Orchestra of Venezuela, wrote a public letter of protest.[67] Anticipating this move and showing perhaps some coordination, Rómulo Betancourt wrote to the American Committee for the Defense of Democracy (Junta Americana de Defensa de la Democracia), with headquarters in Montevideo, that it was necessary for the peoples of the hemisphere to support the "expected wave of public indignation in Venezuela" against the "Nazi-style concentration camp" of "El Dorado."[68] In response to this, *El Tiempo* of Bogotá editorialized against the "Green Hell of Venezuela," and the Mexican intellectuals, Alfonso Reyes and Jesús Silva Herzog, condemned "El Dorado" as a return to conditions which supposedly had disappeared "with the triumph of the democratic nations over the fascist systems in Europe."[69] Betancourt himself denounced the junta's new repression in a short speech in Freedom House in New York on 14 November 1949.[70] Shortly after these events the first open skirmish took place between the clandestine AD and the military regime.

Lieutenant Colonel Mario R. Vargas died in the Garfield Memorial Hospital in Washington on 23 December 1949. At his bedside at the time of his death were Betancourt, Raúl Leoni, and Gonzalo Barrios. [71] Vargas had been one of the principal military leaders in the October 1945 revolution and had served in the cabinet of Provisional President Betancourt. AD looked upon him as the leader of the liberal or loyal elements of the armed forces, but at the time of the ouster of Gallegos he was a tuberculosis patient at Lake Saranac, New York. Vargas hurried to Venezuela on 21 November 1948 but could not stop the movement.[72] Allegedly he tried to rally loyal elements to the defense of Gallegos, without success. On 23 December he returned to Saranac, presumably for more treatment but, in effect, an exile.[73] When Vargas died a year later, the junta supposedly rejoiced, but AD proclaimed national mourning and the National Executive Committee (CEN) issued a manifesto on 26 December. The manifesto declared that the death of Vargas constituted "a loss to the ranks of the resistance" and swore that "his memory" would inspire the final victory over the "usurpers." Boldly, the manifesto predicted a mass procession for the Vargas funeral.[74]

On 2 January 1950 Colonel Vargas was buried in Caracas. According to the resistance leaders, the junta tried to frighten off the crowds by threatening that the police would "empty their guns" if there were any demonstrations, but thousands attended anyway in an act of "profound civic mourning."[75] The underground also called upon one of its leaders to deliver a funeral oration. Just four days before his thirty-fifth birthday, Antonio Pinto Salinas, economist, writer, and poet, left his "concha," where he was serving on the staff of *Resistencia,* and made his way to the Cementerio General del Sur to pay homage to Vargas. [76] Pinto Salinas began his eulogy but was not permitted to finish it. Despite the fact that the resistance had planned a human wall to protect the orator, the police broke through and arrested him and hundreds more at the Vargas graveside.[77] Ten days later, Pinto Salinas was sent into exile, where he spent the next year in Guayaquil, Ecuador. The unfortunate Vargas was not forgiven even in death; guards were posted at his grave, and in 1952 his widow and five children were forced to go into exile.[78] The clash had been brief, but it had been a clear show of boldness.

As the resistance movement under Ruiz Pineda reached its first anniversary there were indications that it was preparing to enter a more militant phase. In March 1950 the National Security police (SN) claimed that it had discovered a cache of rifles in Caracas, along with AD publications and documents which allegedly proved the existence of a plot to assassinate several government leaders.[79] The SN made such "discoveries" periodically, which the underground affirmed were fraudulent, being trumped up by the regime in order to justify its repressive measures. But in April the SN apprehended two youthful AD activists, Luis Augusto Dubuc and Domingo Alberto Rangel, who had reentered Venezuela clandestinely from exile.[80] AD was reenforcing the underground, significantly with leaders who were men of action. Then came the first really serious challenges to the Military Junta. On the third of May forty thousand workers went out on strike in the oil fields of western Venezuela, and two days later some thirty armed men tried to storm the Boca del Río Air Force Base at Maracay. One cannot affirm conclusively that the two events were related, but AD leaders were involved in both, and the reaction of the junta in both cases was vigorous, as if its very existence was at stake.

The oil workers' strike was met with full, military force. According to the workers, the strike was in protest of the antiunion policy of the junta, meaning the jailing of labor leaders and the measures taken by the government to prevent the workers from securing the fulfillment of existing contracts with the oil companies.[81] AD took the line that the junta and the "imperialistic petroleum companies" were cooperating in union-busting and strike-breaking activities. For its part, the junta declared that the workers' rights were fully guaranteed and that laborers had adequate means for securing redress for legitimate grievances. The junta, therefore, denounced the strike as illegal and as having purely political ends. It treated the strike as a subversive movement and ordered the army into the area. When the workers remained in their homes, the junta shut off the water, electricity, and gas, and forcibly closed all shops, stores, and other sources of food. Allegedly the troops entered workers' homes, destroyed existing stocks of food, and forced some workers to return to their jobs. The workers' families were kept at home under the army's guns as hostages. The army's seige lasted ten days, and then the strike collapsed. Before that, on 6 May, the junta decreed the dissolution of forty-seven petroleum unions and seized their existing funds and assets.[82] The junta also outlawed the Communist party on grounds that it had cooperated with AD in the so-called subversive movement.[83] AD found it necessary not only to deny any link with the Communists but to refute the basic issue that the strike was illegal. AD persisted in the stand that the strike was not a movement to overthrow the government but had as its sole purpose the assertion of workers' rights in the face of violations by the junta and the oil companies. This stand was a reaffirmation of the AD policy against "adventurism." Several months later, in October, Betancourt addressed specifically the AD militants: ". . . we would not be loyal to ourselves or to what Venezuela expects of the party and of its members if we tried to apply simplistic and miraculous solutions to the complex political situation of Venezuela."[84] These words could also serve as a defense against charges that the resistance planned and carried out the attack on Boca del Río.

The raid on the air base at Maracay was much shorter in duration than the oil strike, but the junta's response was no less severe. At dawn on 5 May, a group of armed civilians made a surprise attack upon Boca del Río, the principal air base in Venezuela, and managed to seize and hold it for more than an hour. When the government forces counterattacked, one raider was killed, eighteen were captured, and the remaining few fled. The resistance leaders described the event as a "courageous feat," which demonstrated the spirit of the Venezuelan people, but did not themselves admit involvement in it.[85] The junta viewed the attack in the context of the oil strikes and charged that AD and the Communists had carried out the raid together in order to sabotage aircraft and equipment. None of the persons taken at the time of the Boca del Río assault were known AD leaders, but about a month later the junta announced the arrest of two AD militants, Carlos Behrens Quijada and Romero Córdoba, and charged them with participation in the affair. Both had also recently returned to Venezuela illegally from exile.[86] The unfortunate individuals taken prisoner in the action were subjected to the cruelest treatment. They were taken to the Cárcel Modelo in Caracas and virtually disappeared from sight; cut off from contact with relatives and, indeed, with other prisoners, their food and confinement were subhuman. It was as if the regime wanted to blot out from memory any record of the incident, and Pérez Jiménez was quoted as saying, "As long as I am in charge, not one of those men will go free."[87] According to resistance sources, news of the plight of the prisoners was scribbled on a scrap of paper, which, wrinkled and dirty, was passed from hand to hand and somehow reached the outside from the depths of the prison.[88] There was something to be said for the theory that the attack upon Boca del Río was intended to support the oil workers' strike. If the disorders had continued, the neutralizing or tying up of the country's major air base could have been crucial. On the other hand, it may have been the work of dissident groups impatient over the cautious policy of the CEN.

The violent outbreaks of May, however, demonstrated the need for caution. If their purpose was to create a national crisis, they obviously failed. Hence, the underground saw the need to continue to build, to make propaganda, to agitate, and to watch for weaknesses in the junta. In the meantime, the exiles kept up their pressure. In May, in Havana, the founding conference of the Inter-American Association for Democracy and Freedom (IADF) was held. This conference, attended by democrats of the American nations, pledged to fight against all forms of totalitarianism: fascism, nazism, communism, and falangism. It was the fruition of the dream of Betancourt, Prío, and others for a democratic bloc against dictators, and Betancourt closed the conference with the conviction that its first result "was to revitalize the badly shaken faith of Latin Americans in their democratic institutions."[89] Betancourt also spoke to Venezuela over Havana radio numerous times in an effort to keep alive the spirit of AD and to give encouragement to the resistance. In September, on the occasion of the ninth anniversary of Acción Democrática, Betancourt compared the accomplishments of the AD governments with those of the junta and claimed that more than ten thousand Venezuelans had passed through the junta's jails, that hundreds were still imprisoned, and that six hundred were then in exile. [90] In October, he commemorated the fifth anniversary of the October Revolution and, as already noted, directed himself to the party militants in a plea for discipline.[91] In November Betancourt wrote to Trygve Lie again and reminded him of the sad condition of political prisoners in Venezuela; he added that the violations of human rights in Venezuela were just as serious as those involved in the case of Cardinal Mindszenty, then pending before the UN.[92] While Betancourt spoke and wrote in the exterior, the resistance was given an important lift. In October the very able and popular Alberto Carnevali entered Venezuela clandestinely. This event was overshadowed for the moment, however, by another of grave consequence for the immediate future of Venezuela.

On 13 November Junta President Delgado Chalbaud was assassinated. The crime was bizarre in all its details and had no connection with the resistance, although it was to affect it greatly. The murder was carried out by Rafael Simón Urbina, a retired general with a long record of adventurism and revolutionary activity. He was an old-style *caudillo*, an opportunist, whose political connections, if any, were with reactionary circles. On the morning of 13 November Urbina, with over twenty confederates, abducted Delgado and an aide, Lieutenant Carlos Bacalao Lara, just outside the home of the junta chief. It may have been that Urbina merely intended to kidnap Delgado and to hold him for some political advantage; no one who knew ever told. But in the act of taking Delgado to the group's hideout, Urbina was accidentally shot in the ankle. Apparently, this event resulted in, or at least precipitated, the decision to kill Delgado and his aide, and both were shot and left for dead.[93] About an hour later, sometime after 10 A.M., Urbina and his family took asylum in the Nicaraguan embassy. That same afternoon, however, Urbina left the embassy in the company of SN agents, because a physician supposedly advised him that he needed to be hospitalized. By that time, Lieutenant Bacalao Lara, who had somehow survived three bullet wounds, had identified Urbina as the assassin. As Urbina was being taken to the infirmary of the Cárcel Modelo, he allegedly tried to escape (though he reportedly could not walk on his injured foot) and was shot dead.[94]

The AD leaders, of course, viewed this as a badly bungled plot. To them it was the culmination of the rivalry between Delgado Chalbaud and Pérez Jiménez. Betancourt declared that the two colonels had been "spinning webs," that neither had ethics nor scruples, and that it was inevitable one should seize the sole power "over the bones of the other."[95] Furthermore, according to resistance leaders, there was every indication that Pérez Jiménez intended to "frame" the clandestine AD for "Delgado's disappearance," but that the failure to kill Lieutenant Bacalao Lara and the almost immediate identification of Urbina frustrated this plan and instead sealed the fate of Urbina. AD asserted that there had to be collusion in the Urbina plot, because such an undertaking could not escape the attention of the National Security police, "that hydra of twenty thousand heads."[96] Lending substance to this suspicion was the fact that Urbina had sent a note to Pérez Jiménez from the Nicaraguan embassy requesting protection. AD speculated that Urbina left the sanctuary of the embassy convinced that he would not be harmed.[97] Instead, asserted Betancourt, he was shot by the SN agents because "he knew too much."[98] Certainly, Pérez Jiménez was the principal beneficiary of Delgado's death, but if he had conspired with Urbina, the latter had apparently kept the secret from his confederates. In August 1956 the members of the *urbinista* group, including Urbina's widow, were tried publicly and given sentences ranging from five to twenty years in prison. One can only speculate about the reasons why, but no one in that group of over twenty persons mentioned the name of Pérez Jiménez.

Although events made it unnecessary for AD to have to deny any part in the crime, Betancourt took the opportunity to reaffirm AD policy against political assassination. In a press release on 13 November, he stated AD's emphatic repudiation of the "personal attack as a method of political struggle."[99] At that point, moreover, Betancourt was obviously fearful of retaliation against AD leaders in prison, and in his letter to Trygve Lie on 15 November, already cited, he emphasized the risk to political prisoners in Venezuela, where "the political crime is the order of the day."[100] On grounds of practical politics, as well as principle, AD had to avoid the violent tactic, since their comrades, such as Dubuc, Lepage, and Rangel, were virtual hostages in the junta's jails.

Following the death of Delgado, the junta was reorganized, and Dr. Germán Suárez Flamerich, a civilian, was installed as president of the junta on 27 November. Pérez Jiménez was without question the most powerful figure in the government, but, as Betancourt remarked, "Macbeth does not always immediately occupy the bloody throne of Duncan."[101] Suárez Flamerich was to serve as Pérez Jiménez' puppet —a civilian frontman to allay suspicions that Pérez Jiménez planned a military dictatorship. In addition, the junta announced plans for the holding of presidential elections in 1952. None of these developments boded well for AD. With Delgado out of the way, the regime would act with less restraint in dealing with the underground, and AD no longer had a divided junta around which to maneuver. The possible restoration of a legal government, no matter how fraudulent its democratic trappings, would complicate AD's task of winning internal and international support. In essence, Pérez Jiménez was moving to stabilize his regime, and it is hard to argue with stability.

Already out of power two years, AD's voice was sometimes difficult to hear. Although the underground boasted fourteen clandestine newspapers in 1951, the Seguridad Nacional maintained rigid censorship over the Venezuelan press. At the same time, foreign press agencies, such as the Associated Press and United Press, were harassed in their operations, so that, according to Betancourt, they sent only a minimum of news from Venezuela, and what they sent generally coincided "with the wishes of the regime."[102] Those that did not were suppressed. Pérez Jiménez did not approve of the way *Time* magazine reported Delgado's assassination and, as a result, expelled two of its reporters, Henry Wallace and Philip Payne.[103] Generally, however, it was AD which complained of the foreign news coverage. The *New York Times,* in reporting Delgado's death, commented that opposition to the junta was slight, existing only in the "shadowy underground" and comprised of a "small band of die-hard fanatics."[104] On 31 January 1951 the *New York Times* correspondent C. H. Calhoun reported from Caracas that the junta was making progress in its plans for elections and added that the Venezuelan people seemed "generally apathetic."[105] Betancourt replied with a lengthy letter-to-the-editor in which he denied that the Venezuelan people had "accepted" the junta's rule. "They have endured it, which is something different. And they had resisted it, besides. . . . " Betancourt wrote. Betancourt objected to the paucity of news of Latin America in the U.S. press, particularly the lack of any mention of the resistance struggle in Venezuela. He then proceeded to describe the clandestine struggle: "They print newspapers, they publish and circulate manifestos, they organize and direct the resistance, and they make themselves felt in every sphere of the national life." He told about Leonardo Ruiz Pineda and advised the *New York Times* to keep an "up-to-date file" concerning him, because "one day he will make news."[106] Eventually, the *New York Times* increased its coverage of news of Latin America and became a principal champion of its democratic causes, but in the early 1950s Betancourt's complaint of neglect seemed justified.

In addition to the difficulty in getting its story told, AD was faced with distortion of the news and deception on the part of the junta. The junta maintained its own press and propaganda office, and writers such as Roldán Bermúdez and José Vicente Pepper turned out pamphlets and copy which were described as "obscene." The latter was the same person who had written *I Accuse Braden* for Trujillo in 1947. Often "pornographic" leaflets and "phony" newspapers were attributed to Acción Democrática and distributed in a clandestine manner in trucks belonging to the SN.[107] The Caracas Catholic daily *La Religión* became so upset over these activities that in an editorial of 27 April 1951 defied the censors and vigorously denounced such vulgarity.[108] Although this did not end the deceit, the regime occasionally displayed a clumsiness which defeated its own purpose.

Those who wrote about apathy among the Venezuelans, however, overlooked the activities of the university students. Betancourt commented that at the end of 1950 university students were a center of resistance to the junta. On 18 December, student leaders at the Central University (Caracas) and at the universities of Zulia (Maracaibo) and Los Andes (Mérida) addressed a public letter to Suárez Flamerich calling upon him to restore full constitutional guarantees to Venezuela, including the freeing of all political prisoners and the permission for all exiles to return.[109] Suárez Flamerich was a former professor and dean of the law school at Central, and the students hoped that in the light of his past distinguished career he would respond sympathetically. Heading the list of signers was Eduardo González, the president of the student federation at Central and secretly an AD militant, who was to suffer torture, imprisonment, and exile as a result of his activities during the course of the following year. In June 1951 the same group of student leaders addressed Suárez Flamerich again. By this time the junta had announced its intention to hold elections for a national constituent assembly and had set down the ground rules in an Electoral Statute. The students pointed out the need to restore civic guarantees if the elections were to be truly representative of the popular will. They expressed dismay that elections should be held without freedom of the press, without the right of assembly, without full freedom of political organization and discussion, and with hundreds of citizens in exile and in jail. They demanded the end of police persecution and the absolute neutrality of the agencies of the government in the electoral campaigns.[110]

The junta suspected that Acción Democrática had influenced these moves and decided to suppress the student activity. Central's rector, Julio de Armas and vice-rector, Ismael Puerta Flores, were removed on 30 August 1951 and replaced by Eloy Dávila Celis and Luis Eduardo Arocha, respectively. Dávila Celis was anathema to the students. He had been rector at Los Andes where in November 1949 he had permitted troops to enter the campus to put down a student strike. On that occasion, the student federation of Central, in an act of solidarity, declared him a "traitor to the university and an enemy of the student body."[111] Therefore, when Dávila Celis was appointed rector of Central, Eduardo González and his fellow students called a strike on 3 October 1951. They distributed handbills denouncing the new rector as an insult to the dignity of the university and demanded his resignation.[112] Three days later, according to news reports, students physically attacked the rector, who claimed that the agitation was obviously inspired by political motives and was "part of the conspiracy and acts of terrorism conceived and carried out by members of the outlawed Acción Democrática."[113] Betancourt retorted that the students did not attack the rector but merely blocked the entrance to his office. Nonetheless, the police were called in and tear gas was used to disperse the demonstrators.[114] From this point on, events began to occur rapidly, and the strike at the Central University tended to pull together much that had been happening in Venezuela during the preceding months.

During 1951 Pérez Jiménez had taken additional steps to consolidate his power and to legalize his regime. An Independent Electoral Front, FEI (Frente Electoral Independiente), was created as the vehicle for the election of Pérez Jiménez as president, and government funds and resources were channeled to it. The tempo of the harassment and persecution of all forms of political opposition was increased. In March, Luis Tovar, the president of the dissolved oil workers' federation, was arrested and charged with operating a clandestine radio transmitter. [115] The following month a macabre attempt was made upon the life of Betancourt in Havana. According to the official report of the Cuban police, the assailants had been hired by the Venezuelan Junta.[116] On 1 May the workers' May Day parade was broken up by the National Security police (SN), and several days later the regime announced the arrest of Alberto Carnevali. Carnevali's capture was an important achievement for the junta. He was an intelligent and energetic young man who, according to the SN, headed a Special Activities Committee, a kind of action squad which allegedly had planned the Boca del Río raid.[117] However, the junta's rejoicing was short-lived, for on 26 July Carnevali made a dramatic escape from his captors. Supposedly Carnevali had been injured in a fall and was taken to a hospital for treatment; there, four AD militants, posing as orderlies, freed him at gunpoint from his guards.[118]

According to Betancourt, this event fired the popular imagination and drove the junta to new repressions. Betancourt claimed that in Caracas alone two thousand homes were searched without a judicial warrant and that two hundred persons were imprisoned.[119] On 16 August, on the eve of the Fifteenth National Convention of the Venezuelan Federation of Teachers, FVM (Federación Venezolana de Maestros), the entire directorate was arrested. When the convention met anyway, the SN surrounded the hall and loaded 216 delegates into buses and hustled them off to prison.[120] The faculty of the Caracas Medical School reacted vigorously to these detentions and demanded the release of their colleagues.[121] Other protests and disorders occurred in all parts of Venezuela. In the midst of the mounting tension there was a shake-up in the Seguridad Nacional itself. The director, Jorge Maldonado Parilli, whom AD considered a "sadist," was replaced by Pedro Estrada on 31 August. Thus arrived on the scene the man whom one day AD would denounce as "the Heinrich Himmler of Latin America." If Pedro Estrada proved no less cruel than his predecessor, he clearly was more effective, as demonstrated during the first months of his tenure.

As noted, October 1951 was a climactic month. The student strike was the first in a series of disorders which by design or accident spread across Venezuela. On 11 October two men were gravely injured when an explosion ripped apart a house in Caracas. As the men lay dying in the emergency ward, Estrada interrogated them, despite the protests of the attending physicians. The next day, the security chief declared that the men were injured while manufacturing explosives in a "clandestine grenade factory" and that they were involved in a plot to assassinate government leaders during the upcoming Columbus Day celebrations in Caracas. Acción Democrática claimed that the SN then issued orders for the arrest of "all citizens suspected of antigovernmental sentiments" and affirmed that it had intercepted a message in which the National Guard chief, Major Oscar Tamayo Suárez, had instructed his men "to shoot the criminals, since they are not to be taken alive."[122] By 13 October Venezuela was aflame. Outbreaks occurred in a number of cities: Puerto La Cruz, El Tigrito, Río Caribe, Saucedo, Tunapuy, and Tunapuicito. In Caracas three hundred persons were arrested, and the government stated that it had located other centers of "terrorist organization" in such cities as Maracaibo, Coro, Maturín, Barcelona, Barquisimeto, La Victoria, and Valencia. According to the official version of the events, presented to the nation by Minister of the Interior and junta member Llovera Páez, the terrorist attacks were carried out by the outlawed AD and Communist parties. Llovera Páez asserted that AD had turned to terrorism and insurrection due to its failure to organize an effective clandestine political movement. Llovera Páez also declared that the events were directly tied to the disorders at Central University.[123]

AD's response was to deny emphatically any terrorist activity and to charge that the regime had "invented" the Columbus Day plot. It was Betancourt's contention that the junta, faced with general commotion in the nation and particularly with the student strike at the Central University, seized upon the 11 October accidental explosion as a pretext to prepare a "St. Bartholomew's massacre." However, he added, the AD militants, learning that they were about to be the victims of a new wave of arrests, vexations, and imprisonments, decided to strike first. They took "rusty revolvers, machetes, and hunting rifles" and made vain assaults on SN posts in "four or five towns" in Venezuela. He concluded by denying any collaboration with the Communists, saying that "even in the days of Yalta and Teheran, AD had remained separate from them."[124] Valmore Rodríguez concurred in this denial with even greater emphasis. Writing to the editor of the *New York Times,* he declared that, although conditions in Venezuela justified acts of rebellion, "as the vice-president of Acción Democrática, I can truthfully affirm and guarantee that our party neither favors terroristic plans or political assassinations, . . . nor has any documentary proof been uncovered calling for any uprising on the date indicated by the Junta."[125] The novel by José Vicente Abreu, however, describes just such a plot to kill the members of the junta in the Plaza Colón on 12 October 1951 and tells how Cástor Nieves Ríos, an actual member of AD's Special Activities Committee, planned personally to lead the assassination attempt.[126] Irrespective of who was responsible for the violent events of October, the junta effectively remained in control of the situation. In its repressive measures, the regime gave particular attention to the Central University, where the first disturbances had occurred. Many of the student leaders were arrested, and the junta undertook to eliminate the university as a center of opposition.

On 17 October the junta created by decree a five-member Reform Council for the Central University. It was to assume the functions of all administrative officials and governing bodies of Central while undertaking a technical and administrative reorganization of the university. In the meantime, all classes remained suspended, and the Reform Council was empowered to fix responsibility for the disturbances at Central and to suspend or expel the guilty parties for as long as three years.[127] Two days later, almost the entire faculty of the Central University signed a public letter protesting the decree and threatened to resign if the autonomy of the university was not restored.[128] But the junta responded with more oppression and sent into exile some of Venezuela's most distinguished educators, including former Rectors Rafael Pizani and Julio de Armas, and Professors Humberto García Arocha, José Antonio Mayobre, and Foción Febres Cordero.[129] One signatory, José M. Siso Martínez, who a decade later served as minister of education, was arrested and imprisoned in the Cárcel Modelo for seven months before he was expelled from the country.[130]

With the most outspoken leaders among the faculty and students in jail or in exile, the Reform Council announced on 30 January 1952 that it would reopen Central. Classes were to resume on 7 February, although the Reform Council would remain in control of the university pending the elaboration of a new organic statute. Stern conditions were enumerated for the provisional operation of the university. At the same time, the Reform Council suspended nine students for three years, including, of course, Eduardo González, the president of the student federation, and it denied one hundred, twenty-eight students the right to attend classes for one year.[131] These measures only provoked new resistance, because on 7 February the students, reenforced by faculty allies, sent a six-member delegation to protest before the minister of education, Simón Becerra. The minister listened to the students' appeal for the restoration of university autonomy and for the reinstatement of the expelled students but in the meantime put in a call to the National Security police (SN), which immediately came and arrested the group. Two other delegations, one of which was also dispatched to the Ministry of Education and the other to approach Suárez Flamerich, were alerted to the fate of their classmates. They took refuge in the cloister of San Francisco, but the police entered the church and at gunpoint marched the students, thirteen in number, to police headquarters. In entering a church to make arrests, the underground charged that "the junta did what Juan Vicente Gómez did not dare to do during his twenty-seven years of barbarism."[132] These events triggered new disorders, and the efforts to hold classes at Central after 7 February were unsuccessful. On 22 February the university situation reached its climax; the Reform Council, acting under the authority granted it on 17 October, closed the Central University. AD protested this blow to the cultural life of the nation, which affected the lives of six thousand

young Venezuelans and forced one thousand, five hundred of them to
go abroad to study. The junta, however, placed the blame upon a
minority of politically motivated students and faculty, and the doors
remained shut.[133]

In the wake of the October disturbances, notably in the handling of
the university problem, the junta showed itself ruthless and confident.
The Seguridad Nacional under Pedro Estrada made wholesale arrests in
which citizens, including women, were held for indefinite periods
without due process and were subjected to all kinds of hardships and
indignities, and homes were entered and searched without a judicial
warrant.[134] Strong evidence appeared of the growing use of physical
torture in interrogations conducted by the SN, in which handcuffed
victims were stripped and deprived of food and water and the opportunity to attend to bodily necessities. They were beaten and whipped,
struck with the flat of a sword or machete, garroted, probed with
electrical shocking devices, and burned with matches and cigarettes. In
some cases, the naked prisoners were seated upon blocks of ice or
forced to stand upon a steel tire ring during their torments. According
to the testimony of victims, Pedro Estrada personally attended many of
these tortures, although they were most often conducted by his "chief
torturer," Ulises Ortega, the chief of the Political Section of the SN. [135]
The clandestine struggle had definitely entered its most savage period.
Pérez Jiménez had managed to consolidate power in his hands and
wanted next to make it legitimate. For this, elections for a constituent
assembly needed to be held, and Pedro Estrada was expected to eliminate any threats to the regime. From the end of 1951 until well into
1953, the clandestine AD was hounded relentlessly.

"A Most Frightful and Terrible Time" [136]

Nothing symbolized more fully the new harshness of the regime than
the opening of a concentration camp on Guasina Island in the delta of
the Orinoco River. Guasina, was a low-lying jungle island, continually
flooded, hot, and ridden with insects and venomous species, which
made it inhospitable to man. López Contreras used the island as a penal
colony beginning in 1939, but four years later the Ministry of Health
recommended that it be closed. It was reopened briefly in 1948 and
1949 as a detention center for illegal immigrants but was abandoned

again and remained uninhabited until the junta sent the first group of political prisoners there on 8 November 1951.[137] In April, July, and November 1952 three additional groups were sent to Guasina, so that in all approximately nine hundred prisoners were assigned there.[138] The natural horrors of the place coupled with the regimen of the camp condemned the men to illness and to a variety of disorders, including malaria, dysentery, beriberi, tuberculosis, typhoid, and diseases of the skin. Disease took the lives of some of the prisoners, such as Santiago Díaz, José Lino González, and Cosme Damián Peña.[139] The prisoners were put to work building dikes, or engaged in logging operations, or fishing, and endured brutal treatment, poor food, and inadequate sanitary and medical facilities.[140] Among those sent to Guasina was Eduardo González, the youthful student leader, who arrived with the second group of prisoners in April 1952. Upon arrival at Guasina, the new prisoners were lined up, and González could see those who had preceded him, "half-naked, barefoot men, deformed by hunger and illness, were carrying wood logs upon their shoulders. Those were the political prisoners of Guasina, whose physical appearance we, ourselves, would soon resemble."[141] Most of those sent to Guasina were *acciondemocratistas*, many of whom were students or professionals who were not used to hard, manual labor even under ideal conditions. For example, Cosme Damián Peña was a registered pharmacist. AD, naturally, took the lead in protesting Guasina, out of compassion for its comrades and with the realization that the camp's existence was a serious deterrent to political action.

Within Venezuela, the clandestine AD exposed the terrors of what it called the "Nazi-style" concentration camp. In a major effort to force the immediate closing of Guasina and to secure the release of the prisoners, the underground collected information about the prison and compiled a list of those sent there. It used the clandestine press, special publications, and any other means of communication possible to describe conditions in the camp. It also sent up-to-date reports to the leaders in exile.[142] In June, when AD had reports of typhoid at Guasina, a group of women, whose fathers, husbands, sons, or brothers were imprisoned there, presented an anguished appeal in their behalf by means of an open letter to medical, health, cultural, and religious leaders, to editors of newspapers and periodicals, and to managers of radio stations.[143] Other political parties, too, protested the scandal of Guasina. On 20 June the Christian Democrats (COPEI) took action in a public letter, but the SN responded ten days later by brutally beating *copeyano* leader, Edecio La Riva.[144] The secretary general of COPEI, Rafael Caldera, renewed the protest on 4 August, and Jóvito Villalba, chief of the Republican Democratic Union (URD), also denounced the camp's existence. Most embarrassing to the junta was the action of its ambassador to the United States, Dr. Antonio Martín Araujo, who resigned in May in protest against the repressions of the regime and who declared that Guasina could "be compared only to Devil's Island." [145] There was little doubt that the campaign against Guasina was effective.

The AD leaders in exile also exerted their full energies in order to arouse international opinion in condemnation of Guasina. Rómulo Gallegos, interviewed in the Mexican press, charged the junta with "inhuman treatment" of political prisoners at Guasina and referred to the threat of typhoid there.[146] Valmore Rodríguez wrote a letter to the *New York Times* in which he described the penal colony in full detail and reiterated that typhoid had already taken the lives of two prisoners.[147] These denunciations led to the publication of a full-page article about Guasina in *Time* magazine on 18 August. Protests were also raised by the labor organizations of the hemisphere, including the Inter-American Regional Organization of Workers, ORIT (Organización Regional Interamericana de Trabajadores), Rerum Novarum of Costa Rica, and the Bolivian Workers' Union, COB (Central Obrera Boliviana). [148] The regime remained generally quiet about Guasina; among its rare comments was that of Dr. Raúl Soulés Baldó, the minister of health, who asserted that the prisoners were vaccinated against all diseases and were protected by officials of the Public Health Service.[149] However, the junta finally yielded to the outcry and closed Guasina on 18 December 1952. The prisoners were moved to Sacupana del Cerro, which was still in the Orinoco region, but was more healthful. Eventually, most captured AD militants and other political prisoners were assigned to the Cárcel Nueva of Ciudad Bolívar, which was remote but was no worse than any other prison. However, as will be seen, when Guasina was closed, it was no longer needed. By that time, AD had suffered a number of setbacks, which seriously affected its ability to oppose the regime. The first of these was the loss of Cuba as a base for exile operations.

On 10 March 1952 Fulgencio Batista overthrew President Prío Socarrás of Cuba. Betancourt and other Caribbean exiles, such as Juan Bosch, immediately took asylum in the Guatemalan embassy, which caused "La Voz Dominicana" to remark, "That is where the puppets of the Moscow master would necessarily have to go."[150] The coup not only deprived Betancourt of his Cuban base but cut further the ranks of democratic governments in the Caribbean. In fact, although there was no concrete evidence of foreign intrigue in Batista's take-over, Venezuela, the Dominican Republic, Nicaragua, and Spain were the first "to welcome and recognize" the Cuban strong man.[151] The Venezuelan junta was particularly pleased over the fall of Prío.[152]

In the months before Prío's fall, Cuban-Venezuelan relations had deteriorated badly. In November 1951 the Cuban House of Representatives passed a resolution to petition the Venezuelan government to release all political prisoners and to restore constitutional government.[153] Later the same month, Prío addressed the national convention of the Cuban Revolutionary party (Auténtico); on this occasion he called upon the party to denounce the Caribbean dictators before international organizations and recommended that Cuba stop trading with countries where tyrants were "enthroned."[154] As a result of Cuba's concern for the plight of imprisoned political and labor leaders in Venezuela, the Cuban chargé in Caracas was recalled in December, presaging a possible complete rupture of relations. The attitude of the Cuban government was linked directly to the "effective campaign" then being waged in Havana against the junta by Betancourt and other AD exiles.[155] Prío's fall was, therefore, a shock to the democratic camp, but all was not lost, for Betancourt was able to move his base of operations to Costa Rica and to maintain contact with the clandestine AD by means of a radio transmitter installed at Figueres' finca "La Lucha Sin Fin." But, while the exiles were making these adjustments, Pedro Estrada stepped up his campaign against the underground.

On 14 April 1952 Pedro Estrada announced the "discovery" of another plot to assassinate Pérez Jiménez. The opportune arrest of a number of AD militants coupled with two panics in crowded churches during Holy Week were the basis of a new effort by the National Security police to depict Acción Democrática as a terrorist organization. According to Pedro Estrada's communiqué and to SN records reproduced by José Vicente Abreu, fourteen members of the underground (eleven men and three women) were arrested on 6 and 7 April on charges of manufacturing bombs for use in terrorist attacks. [156] Estrada stated that, according to the confessions of the prisoners, the bombs were to be used in an attempt to assassinate Pérez Jiménez on 9

April (the Wednesday before Easter) and that they were manufactured under orders from Leonardo Ruiz Pineda and Alberto Carnevali. [157] Estrada declared that the assassination of Pérez Jiménez was the major aspect of an elaborate plot to sow "confusion and panic" in order to create the conditions for seizing power but lamented that, despite the foreknowledge of the terrorists' intentions, his men were unable to prevent the tragedies which occurred in the churches of Santa Teresa and San Francisco.[158] Estrada was referring to the fact that on 9 April there had been a panic in the church of Santa Teresa in Caracas caused by shouts of "fire," in which forty-seven persons were killed and one hundred were injured. Two days later, on Good Friday, a similar panic in the church of San Francisco resulted in injury to twenty persons. It was first reported that the panic at Santa Teresa was caused by false alarms shouted by pickpockets, "in order to facilitate their work," but on 13 April a priest claimed that the riot was "terrorist-inspired." [159]

The linking of AD to the Holy Week tragedies appeared contrived in view of the lapse of time between the arrest of the alleged terrorists and the announcement of the "discovery" of an antigovernmental plot. Moreover, according to SN records, Jesús Alberto Blanco, one of the individuals listed in Estrada's communiqué, actually had been arrested on 24 March.[160] The National Executive Committee (CEN) immediately issued a statement in which it denied any involvement in acts of violence or plots and charged that Estrada was trying to place "the accusation of common criminal on the leaders of our party."[161] Likewise, Robert J. Alexander of Rutgers University, a close friend of Betancourt in the United States, affirmed in a letter to the *New York Times* that the accusation was intended to justify "beforehand" the murder of AD leaders.[162] Pérez Jiménez, however, tried to treat the charges as proven fact and declared that elections would be held in 1952 "despite terrorists' efforts to retard the country's march to constitutionality."[163] Hence, "shoot-to-kill" orders were issued for Ruiz Pineda and Carnevali, while at the same time the junta made preparations to hold national elections.[164]

Because of its ability to breach the junta's security, the clandestine AD was aware that the regime was making steady progress in its electoral campaign. Unable to persuade either the Christian Democrats (COPEI) or Villalba's party (URD) to support its candidacy, the junta created the Independent Electoral Front, FEI (Frente Electoral Independiente). During the period March-August 1952, friendly telegraph employees furnished Acción Democrática with copies of confidential cipher messages passing between the minister of the interior, Llovera Páez, and the governors of states and other officials. These messages proved that the public power and treasury were being used to assure victory for the Independent Electoral Front (FEI). The governors were instructed to report monthly the number of FEI registrants and were given special funds in order to implement this order. They were instructed specifically to list registrants among public employees and to report those who resisted inscription and to give preferential treatment to cooperative contractors and newspapers. The public authorities were further instructed to harass and even persecute the remaining legal opposition parties.[165] In the face of these maneuvers, AD recognized the need to formulate a policy with reference to the elections.

With the conviction that the elections would not be free, Acción Democrática decided to abstain from any participation and, furthermore, to call upon all political, social, and economic forces to join in a unified movement to overthrow the junta. It pledged, if successful, to set up a coalition government and subsequently to hold free elections.[166] AD affirmed that it neither opposed nor feared the electoral process. If there were any chance for an honest election, AD declared, it would make the "supreme sacrifice" and instruct its partisans to vote for candidates of the "legal" opposition parties. It claimed, however, that the junta intended an "electoral farce" and that such action, therefore, would be futile and would, in fact, damage the democratic institutions.[167] AD's call for the overthrow of the regime and the pledge to form a coalition government represented important changes in its policy. AD did not specify how it intended to wrest power from the junta, but absolute electoral abstention was its essential first step. It was a policy with a new urgency; if the junta elected a "spurious" government, the only alternative would be insurrection.[168] In promising to form a coalition, AD was admitting that it could not defeat the junta alone.[169] In order to gain adherence to its policy, particularly on the part of Rafael Caldera of COPEI and Jóvito Villalba of URD, Acción Democrática undertook its most ambitious propaganda effort yet.

In September 1952 the National Executive Committee (CEN) published a book, *Venezuela bajo el signo del terror, 1948-1952. Libro negro de una dictadura.* Known commonly as *The Black Book,* it was basically a campaign document in which AD outlined its philosophy,

aims, and tactics and in which it depicted the history of the junta
government as a brutal tyranny. Ruiz Pineda wrote a lengthy prologue
dated July 1952. He proclaimed *The Black Book* "a living document,"
which, because of its exposé of the savage crimes of the junta, "will
tomorrow torment the spirit of our sons."[170] In an effort to attract
wide support, the resistance leader outlined in detail and "without
deception" the philosophy and programs of the party. He described AD
as a "multi-class party of the revolutionary Left, purged of demagogy
and dedicated to the fulfillment of the democratic and anti-imperialist
revolution, with the aid of all political, economic, and social forces
interested in the transformation of the nation."[171] Ruiz Pineda indicated also that AD had matured and mellowed in the four years of the
clandestine struggle. He claimed that the struggle had shown Acción
Democrática to be flexible and broadly based and not sectarian nor
arrogant as had been charged.[172] Ruiz Pineda reviewed the four years
of the resistance movement and affirmed that it had not been in vain,
because it had given the junta "no public peace" and had exposed its
violence and corruption.[173] Now, however, in "an hour of extreme
difficulty," AD was calling upon "all political forces, all social nuclei,
and all economic groups" to band together to overcome "the common
danger." Ruiz Pineda called for concurrent action in overthrowing the
regime and in establishing a coalition government and he announced
AD's decision to abstain from participation in the elections.[174] He
concluded by stating that those who had led the work of the resistance
were returning to the people the faith which had been entrusted to
them and that *The Black Book* was a weapon, among other things, in
"the fight without quarter between the usurpers and the national resistance."[175]

Following the prologue came a more specific statement concerning
the elections in a chapter entitled "La farsa electoral de la dictadura"
("The Electoral Farce of the Dictatorship"). The major section of this
chapter, with a summary of all its arguments and conclusions, consisted
of a manifesto, "Acción Democrática ante la farsa electoral" ("AD
Before the Electoral Farce"), which had already circulated separately
on 13 September.[176] The manifesto was signed on behalf of the CEN
by Betancourt and Ruiz Pineda, which indicated the close collaboration
of the exiled and underground leadership. It charged that the junta was
holding elections "to give the usurpation of power the aspect of legal-
ity" and to enable it "to carry out the irresponsible distribution of the

national oil reserves to foreign companies."[177] In order to achieve these goals, declared AD, the junta was leaving nothing to chance and was maneuvering to steal the election. As proof, it summarized the contents of eighty-seven confidential government telegrams, appending the complete texts to the discussion.[178] AD was careful to include those which demonstrated government harassment of the electoral activities of the Christian Democrats (COPEI) and the Republican Democratic Union (URD). For example, the authorities in Barcelona had reported preventing a meeting of the URD because at its headquarters resided a person who had the chicken pox, which "placed in danger the health of anyone attending the meeting."[179] In the light of the evidence, AD reiterated the wisdom of the policy of electoral abstention and repeated the call for a unity movement to overthrow the junta and to constitute a coalition government.[180] Acción Democrática concluded, however, that, should this "new stage in its political struggle" fail, it would not quit but would channel the same efforts to the overthrowing of the "outlaw" government.[181]

The remainder of *The Black Book* was a detailed history of the four years of the junta's rule. It was a massive collection of data and testimony which added up to a severe indictment against the regime. AD omitted no detail of its martyrdom and it denounced the dictatorship for its coercion of labor, the press, and the university. Although partisan in nature, *The Black Book* was a significant document which, as Ruiz Pineda stated, bore witness to a brave and tragic struggle. It did not, however, achieve its immediate goal.

Both COPEI and URD decided to present a slate of candidates in the elections for a national constituent assembly to be held on 30 November 1952. Despite the urging of AD and of some of their own partisans, Caldera and Villalba believed it would be "political suicide" to abstain from the elections.[182] Both, however, were cautious about their chances for success. On 14 September COPEI declared its intentions but complained that even the "minimum guarantees" were lacking for a proper electoral campaign.[183] The URD followed with a manifesto of 27 September in which it not only expressed doubts about the validity of the election but charged that "a gigantic fraud [was] on foot."[184] Villalba, however, one of the Generation of 1928, was hopeful of attracting large numbers of AD votes. He denounced the junta's proscription of Acción Democrática and presented a program similar to that of AD, particularly with reference to nationalistic issues.[185] AD was disappointed in the actions of these parties, but such disappointment was insignificant in comparison with the misfortunes which followed.

On 29 September and 1 October a number of uprisings occurred in scattered places in Venezuela. At the Boca del Río Air Force Base, two officers, .Captain Wilfrido Omaña and Lieutenant Héctor Navarro Torres, tried to seize the base and implored their fellow officers to join in the mutiny. When other officers refused to take part, Omaña fled and took refuge with the underground in Caracas, but Navarro Torres surrendered with his troops.[186] On the same day, 29 September, armed campesinos and workers attacked National Guard posts at Turén and Villa Bruzual in the state of Portuguesa. The assaults were quickly repelled, although the attackers were not finally rounded up until 15 October.[187] In Maturín, a group of soldiers and civilians seized the "José Gregorio Monagas" barracks in the early hours of 1 October. They also managed to take over the SN and police barracks for a short time, but within three hours the rebellion was suppressed. Captain Juan Bautista Rojas, the highest-ranking military conspirator, was killed in the action, and Dr. Jorge Yibirín, the chief of AD in the state of Monagas, fell gravely wounded.[188] There were thirty-six officers and men and forty civilians involved in the attempted golpe, which appeared to be a clear case of collaboration between AD and elements of the armed forces. These rebellions were an indication of the desperation of AD and were a departure from its avowed policy against military uprisings. Pedro Estrada, in response, was determined to smash the clandestine apparatus. Hundreds of persons were arrested, and in the dragnet the Security Police (SN) captured Cástor Nieves Ríos, whom the junta had accused of terrorism and on whose head it had placed a price.[189]

In the effort to force him to talk, Nieves Ríos probably suffered the cruelest martyrdom of all those of the resistance movement. Betancourt charged that Pedro Estrada personally shot Nieves Ríos on 6 October after subjecting him to two days and nights of the vilest tortures. [190] AD described these terrible tortures but declared that the underground leader remained silent until his death.[191] The junta affirmed, on the other hand, that Nieves Ríos was shot attempting to escape. He allegedly had agreed to take SN agents to a place where he had concealed some arms, but while he was leading the agents to the hiding place he suddenly seized a guard's gun and shot wildly, causing the agents to shoot him in "self-defense."[192] The SN account had the familiar ring of the *ley de fuga*. Moreover, the fact that the body of Nieves Ríos was not turned over to any authority outside the SN and that its place of burial was not revealed gave substance to the claim that he was mutilated and murdered within the walls of the SN headquarters.[193] The efforts of the Seguridad Nacional were producing results, however, because the trail led next to the leader of the clandestine AD.

In the early evening of 21 October, Leonardo Ruiz Pineda was killed in a fusillade of machine gun bullets as he drove along a street in the San Agustín del Sur section of Caracas. Traveling with approximately twelve comrades in three cars, he was shot from ambush by the SN. [194] He had managed to elude the security forces for three-and-a-half years, but the persecutions of the first weeks of October apparently flushed him from his "concha" and, possibly moving to another hideout, his luck finally ran out. Pedro Estrada denied that he had been ambushed and stated that Ruiz Pineda had caused his own death. Allegedly, Ruiz Pineda had shot at two SN agents from his moving car and was killed when they returned the fire.[195] Such action, however, did not fit the behavior of the slain leader.

Acción Democrática reacted to the murder of Ruiz Pineda with grief, outrage, and resolution. That very night, Alberto Carnevali, who succeeded Ruiz Pineda as secretary general, mourned him as a man, "who never used any weapon other than his idealistic and stirring pen, his rousing oratory, and his strong faith in the destiny of a people." Carnevali pledged to continue the struggle until the "barbarity" was destroyed, "smashed to pieces by the hands of the people."[196] Betancourt declared that the murder was "another example of fascism in Venezuela, which he had to denounce before the free conscience of America."[197] In Mexico City, Gallegos and Eloy Blanco eulogized the "poet of Táchira," and Gallegos reiterated that for months Ruiz Pineda had been the object of a "shoot-to-kill search."[198] In the future, 21 October would be dedicated to the memory of "Leonardo," and one day the Caracas street which had been stained with his blood would be renamed the Avenida Leonardo Ruiz Pineda. The death of Ruiz Pineda was mourned by the other political parties also; at the concluding campaign rally of URD on 26 November, AD's martyred leader was given a moment of silent tribute.[199] In fact, according to Betancourt, the public revulsion resulting from Ruiz Pineda's assassination affected greatly the outcome of the election.

AD's Black October had shattered its preelection strategy, but before

all the ballots were counted it salvaged at least a moral victory. Persecuted and in disarray, AD decided to spread the word quietly to its
adherents to vote for the Unión Repúblicana Democrática.[200] According to Octavio Lepage, in an interview recorded by Professor John
Martz, AD did not publicize its decision because it feared countermeasures by the regime.[201] A source close to AD exile circles asserted
that the decision was made only forty-eight hours before the balloting,
because the underground learned that an overly confident junta was
going to hold a free election.[202] One is unable to say precisely how
many were informed of this decision, but with or without instructions
it was evident that those who supported AD in past elections (and
would support it in the future) went to the polls in November 1952 and
voted for the URD.[203] The regime was obviously unaware of any such
maneuver; feeling assured that the way had been prepared for a victory,
it permitted the people to go to the polls and exercise their choice.[204]
When the Supreme Electoral Council announced the first returns on 1
December, with 547,458 voted counted, the URD had 294,593 votes to
147,528 for the government party, FEI.[205] That same evening, the
International News Service announced that the URD was losing in only
two states, which were identical to those Acción Democrática had lost
in 1946. This indicated, it reported, that AD was supporting Villalba's
group.[206] The junta had been repudiated by the people.

In order to reverse the defeat at the polls, Pérez Jiménez found it
necessary to carry out a coup against his own government. After the
release of the first returns, rigid censorship was applied. On 2 December
it was announced that the junta had resigned and had turned over the
government to the armed forces, which had then named Pérez Jiménez
provisional president. Partial election returns were also released, which
now placed the FEI in the lead. Two days later, the final tabulation was
given as follows: FEI, 788,086; URD, 638,336; and COPEI,
300,309.[207] Llovera Páez, upon whom fell the major responsibility for
the fiasco and who reportedly had been feuding with Pérez Jiménez
even before the election, was momentarily in disgrace, and he and
Suárez Flamerich took "vacation" trips.[208] Dr. Laureano Vallenilla
Lanz, the new minister of the interior, tried to persuade Villalba and
other urredistas to accept the situation and to occupy the seats which
they had "won" in the Constituent Assembly. When Villalba refused to
cooperate, he and six others were placed aboard a plane and flown to
Panama, "without extra clothes or money."[209] Vallenilla Lanz charged

that Villalba had tried to incite a rebellion by calling for a general strike and by engaging in "secret talks with members of dissolved parties." [210] In order to show a conciliatory tone, Pérez Jiménez at the same time ordered the closing of Guasina.

On 9 January 1953 the government managed to secure a quorum for the Constituent Assembly by filling the seats of the URD and the Christian Democrats (COPEI) with alternates and substitutes. COPEI had informed Pérez Jiménez that it would participate in the assembly if he would restore constitutional guarantees, release political prisoners, and permit the return of exiles. The regime responded by making additional arrests, so that no COPEI or URD delegate was present when the assembly convened. The Constituent Assembly first confirmed Pérez Jiménez as provisional president and then undertook the task of drafting a new constitution. However, in order to avoid a repetition of the November miscalculation Pérez Jiménez decided to make the Constituent Assembly the vehicle for "legalizing" his de facto government.[211] The Constitution, ratified by the Constituent Assembly in April, provided for the automatic confirmation of Pérez Jiménez as constitutional president for a five year term. In the same manner, it confirmed approximately twelve thousand persons in various offices, including senators and deputies of the National Congress, members of state legislative assemblies, and justices of the Supreme Court, all of whom were nominated by the very same Constituent Assembly. [212] Despite strong editorial opinion in the hemisphere against this cynical disregard of the popular will, Pérez Jiménez was de facto president of Venezuela and was more firmly in power than at any time since the overthrow of Gallegos in 1948. In the meantime, Pedro Estrada had been active and had not permitted the regime's embarrassment at the polls to interfere with his campaign to destroy the clandestine AD.

In quick succession the SN dealt serious blows to the underground apparatus and its leadership. On 5 January the Caracas police and the SN arrested twenty-five armed AD militants who had occupied the Dodge Automobile Agency at the Corner of Puente Soublette, not too far from the spot where Ruiz Pineda had been killed. The group had gained access to the agency the preceding evening at about 8:30 P.M. by overpowering two watchmen. Although the affair was completely hushed up, apparently the men had rendezvoused at the garage in order to take part in a military conspiracy organized in the nearby Bermúdez barracks.[213] However, since it was a Sunday, when the business was normally closed, a woman in the neighborhood became suspicious and called the police. Shortly after 1:15 A.M. radio patrol cars and SN agents arrived, and after a short skirmish the AD militants surrendered.[214]

Two weeks later, in a similar raid, Alberto Carnevali and a number of middle-rank AD leaders were captured by the SN. Carnevali had assembled about twenty underground activists, many of whom were chiefs of zones in Caracas, for an organizational meeting and planning session. They met above a dress shop in an old building in the Santa Teresa parish, where they had hidden, among other things, photographic equipment used for making false identification cards.[215] Such a meeting entailed great risk, but Carnevali had obviously opted for quick and vigorous action. In this desperate hour, the "miraculous solution" made sense. On the one hand, the clandestine structure was seriously compromised, whereas, on the other, the new Pérez Jiménez regime was still in something of a crisis. In a few months Pérez Jiménez would emerge all-powerful, but in the meantime he was beset with problems resulting from the December coup, the expulsion of the URD leaders, the temporary eclipse of Llovera Páez, and the transparent maneuvering of the Constituent Assembly. Unfortunately for Carnevali, Pedro Estrada had learned about the meeting, and the security police surrounded the building. The Sunday morning quiet of Caracas was broken on 18 January by the shots of an hour-long *"tiroteo,"* in which ten AD militants were seized and four fell wounded. Five others managed to escape over adjoining rooftops.[216] Pedro Estrada claimed that the clandestine group opened fire first, but Betancourt asserted that Estrada's "shoot-to-kill" order against Carnevali was still in effect and that only by resisting did the underground leaders prevent their massacre.[217]

Carnevali, however, was already a doomed man, and he soon died in prison. It developed that he was suffering from cancer of the colon. In view of his earlier dramatic escape, the regime imprisoned him in the maximum security penitentiary of San Juan de los Morros and refused to transfer him from there even after an exploratory operation in April revealed the nature of his illness. Betancourt considered Carnevali "one of the most brilliant political and intellectual figures of Venezuela"[218] and felt very close to him personally. Carnevali, who was thirty-six years old, was more the activist than the gentle Ruiz Pineda, but he could also rally men with words. On 24 December 1952 he had written a manifesto summoning the people to "civil rebellion" and calling for "coordinated and skillful action by the masses," which was not to cease until Pérez Jiménez was left with the dilemma of either "recognizing the popular will or of annihilating the Venezuelan people."[219] When the clandestine AD learned about Carnevali's illness, they informed the exile leaders, who then exerted every effort to have Carnevali sent abroad for treatment or at least transferred to a private hospital. International leaders were enlisted in Carnevali's behalf, but despite a plea from the president of Bolivia, Víctor Paz Estenssoro, and steps taken in the United States by Roger Baldwin of the International League for the Rights of Man and by Norman Thomas, the regime refused to move him. Carnevali died in his prison cell on 20 May 1953.[220] After his death, the government maintained that Carnevali had received every attention and had not been moved because he was too ill to travel.[221] Betancourt, while conceding that cancer had been the cause of death, was bitter and charged that the regime did not give him "adequate medical assistance."[222]

Even while the stricken Carnevali was in prison, another AD leader was shot down in a Caracas street. This time, Captain Wilfrido Omaña, who had led the abortive uprising at the Boca del Río Air Force Base the preceding September, was the victim of an SN ambush. Omaña emerged from his "concha" on the evening of 24 February for a street-corner meeting with another army officer in the Los Chaguaramos section of the city. When he arrived at the appointed site opposite the Central University, the officer was waiting, but so were a large number of security agents, who opened fire from their places of concealment when Omaña stepped from his automobile. The captain fell mortally wounded on the pavement, but his driver, José de los Santos Gómez, was taken alive.[223] The SN considered Gómez an important catch. He reportedly had served as a driver for Ruiz Pineda and Carnevali and was familiar with a number of "conchas" in Caracas. In fact, he had taken Carnevali to his last meeting but was one of those who had managed to flee.[224] Now, he was not so fortunate and was subjected to brutal tortures.[225] Four days later, two more clandestine leaders were seized. One was Rafael Antonio Sandoval Martínez, who was arrested in an apartment in the El Silencio section of Caracas. He had been sought since October 1952 as a suspected accomplice of Nieves Ríos. According to SN records, the apartment was an "estafeta" (clandestine mail address) for the correspondence of Ruiz Pineda, Carnevali, and other members of the National Executive Committee (CEN).[226] The SN also seized Gustavo Ramón Ramos Urbina and charged him with sheltering in his apartment Ruiz Pineda and Carnevali and the latest secretary general of AD, Dr. Eligio Anzola Anzola.[227]

Anzola had been appointed the clandestine leader shortly after Carnevali's arrest, but he inherited a rapidly deteriorating situation. A party veteran and former minister of the interior under Gallegos, Anzola apparently did not deviate from the desperate policy of trying to overthrow Pérez Jiménez before he consolidated his power. However, he was no more successful than his predecessors. An uprising was planned for 19 April, Venezuela's Independence Day and the day on which Pérez Jiménez was to be sworn in as president. The preparations for the movement were undertaken in the states east of Caracas: Miranda, Anzoátegui, Sucre, and Monagas, and coordinated with exiles in Trinidad. Proceeding from Trinidad on 13 April, José Angel Rodríguez Rojas (alias José Manuel Rivas), landed on the coast near Güiria and brought with him some small arms and other equipment.[228] His *volandeo* was in vain, however, because the plot had already been discovered. On 10 April the SN seized an arms cache in Píritu, a cluster of houses on the highway east of Caracas, and arrested José Angel Ciliberto, the secretary of organization of the clandestine AD, and Leoncio Dorta, a founder of AD and secretary of propaganda.[229] Two days later, the top clandestine leaders of eastern Venezuela, all of whom were also high-ranking labor leaders, were captured: Tomás Alberti, Máximo Reynaldo Acuña, David Nieves, Ramón Quijada, and Cruz Alberto Márquez. Before the roundup was completed, Anzola himself was captured on 24 April.[230] Five days later, Rodríguez Rojas was caught in Maturín. The clandestine AD was now on the run—only a handful of experienced leaders remained—but Pedro Estrada was determined to snuff out the organization completely, and not even Anzola was spared violent torture.[231]

In view of the desperate plight of the underground, the Dirección in Costa Rica decided to order Antonio Pinto Salinas to leave Venezuela. Pinto Salinas, who had been expelled after his oration at the Vargas funeral, had reentered Venezuela clandestinely in July 1951. He was another of the party's top young leaders and had served in a number of important jobs, including AD's contact with Wilfrido Omaña for the uprising in Boca del Río.[232] After the death of Ruiz Pineda, he returned to Caracas and, using the pseudonym, "Peralta," was the leader of a clandestine action squad. In April, he succeeded Ciliberto as secretary of organization and, as such, was the likely successor of Anzola. His position, however, was gravely compromised. Although Pinto Salinas had changed his pseudonym to "Luzardo," Pérez Jiménez and Pedro Estrada had learned that Luzardo, Peralta, and Pinto Salinas were the same man, and they ordered his liquidation.[233]

Pinto Salinas, therefore, reluctantly agreed to leave the country. On 9 June he left the house of Manuel Jiménez Castro, which he shared as a "concha" with his friend and comrade, Rigoberto Henríquez Vera, who had been appointed the new secretary general.[234] In the company of Manuel Acosta and another comrade, probably Hermán Contreras Marín, he left by automobile for Pariaguán in the interior, where another contact was to take him to the coast and thence to Trinidad.[235] Now, however, a traitor had penetrated the underground. His treachery enabled the SN to seize Henríquez Vera, Jiménez Castro, and Simón Alberto Consalvi, a young journalist, in the Caracas "concha" and to capture Pinto Salinas and his companions on the outskirts of Pariaguán.[236] The leaders in exile had learned of this possible treason, and, lacking radio contact, sent Enrique Tejera París, a future ambassador to the United States, to Venezuela clandestinely in order to warn the underground leaders. Despite the grave risk he took, his arrival was just a few hours too late.[237] Pinto Salinas was taken first to El Tigre, where he was questioned and tortured. Then, on the afternoon of 10 June, the SN agents placed the prisoners in two station wagons and started out for San Juan de los Morros. Pinto Salinas was in the second vehicle separated from his comrades. Very early the next morning, not too far from their supposed destination, the station wagon bearing Pinto Salinas stopped, and he was ordered out. A few feet down the road, the handcuffed Pinto Salinas turned and faced his captors, who shot him down in cold blood.[238] He was the third of AD's young leaders to die in less than eight months; such had been the terrible sacrifice of the underground.

Quiescence, 1953-1956

The clandestine AD was a shambles. Its experienced leadership was either dead or in jail and its apparatus was compromised, including "conchas," sources of funds, and "volandeo" routes. Thousands of AD militants were in prison, and the SN continued its relentless pursuit, almost routinely, in order to root out even the most humble underground cell. For example, over a dozen telegraph employees were arrested in April and May 1953 for having given copies of official telegrams and cipher keys to the clandestine AD.[239] The SN had not forgotten that one of the most devastating aspects of *The Black Book* was the reproduction of government messages revealing preelection maneuvering. But the underground was not completely disbanded. It entered into a stage of reorganization and rebuilding, not unlike that of the three and a half years following the November 1948 coup. It never recovered to the extent that it did under Ruiz Pineda, and on several occasions new beginnings were uncovered and destroyed by the SN. The underground returned to the policy of patient resistance and tried to maintain its security as tightly as possible. Even the name of the secretary general was kept secret, a post which was occupied during the next four years by Héctor Vargas Acosta, Manuel Vicente Ledezma, and Simón Sáez Mérida successively.[240] If the underground found anything to cheer about from the events of 1953, it was the fact that the political situation in Venezuela forced postponement of the Tenth International Conference of American States. However, it was rescheduled for Caracas for March 1954, which meant that neither AD nor Pedro Estrada could relax.

Even as the clandestine movement suffered its most severe repression, Betancourt traveled to a number of South American capitals—La Paz, Santiago, and Montevideo—to denounce this persecution and to call upon the American states to boycott the Caracas Conference. On 2 June 1953 Betancourt addressed a session of the Uruguayan Chamber of Deputies, where he described conditions in Venezuela and declared that the Tenth Inter-American Conference must not meet in a country "where systematically, day-by-day, the fundamental rights of man and of the citizen are violated."[241] He pointed out that the delegates were to assemble in the Great Hall of Central University, whose doors were then closed to Venezuelan students and professors. He warned that if the conference were held it would be an insult to "the free conscience of America," and it would "inflict one more wound on the already shaken faith of the peoples in international organizations, maybe a fatal one."[242] Betancourt's attacks upon Caracas as a "South American Budapest" were fruitful to the extent that the national congresses of Chile and Uruguay passed resolutions urging their governments not to attend the Caracas Conference, unless the Venezuelan government released political prisoners, permitted exiles to return, and prepared an "internal atmosphere" which would provide a "dignified setting" for the conference.[243] In obvious response to international pressure for some gesture, the Venezuelan government announced the release on New Year's Day 1954 of four hundred political prisoners, who, it asserted, represented sixty per cent of the total number of persons imprisoned for political reasons.[244] In the end, only Costa Rica refused to attend the conference; President José Figueres explained that he hoped his action would serve as an "eloquent cry, calling attention to the long abandoned problem of internal democracy in Latin America."[245]

On the other hand, Pedro Estrada was determined that there would be no repetition in Caracas of the bloody rioting which had marred the Ninth Inter-American Conference in Bogotá in 1948. He told Sydney Gruson of the *New York Times* in December 1953 that there would be no *"Bogotazo"* in Caracas, "even if we have to round up every suspicious character in the country and jail them throughout the conference."[246] Gruson observed that the AD underground was destroyed; it had been shorn of effective leadership and "knocked off balance." He said Estrada intended to keep it that way by constant harassment, that is, by frequent arrest of suspects, who would be held a short time, released, and then picked up again.[247] This was the technique of "control," a kind of probation, adopted by the SN by means of which former political prisoners and suspected *acciondemocratistas* were ordered to report twice weekly to the Seguridad Nacional and to notify it of any change in residence, occupation, or status.

Estrada's security measures turned out to be very effective during the Tenth Inter-American Conference. There were no incidents, which was remarkable in view of the dramatic nature of the conference involving the issue of Communist intervention in the Americas and the confrontation between U.S. Secretary of State John Foster Dulles and the Guatemalan Foreign Minister Guillermo Toriello. Prior to the conference five AD militants were arrested in February in Maturín on charges of distributing a clandestine newspaper, *Rebelión,* and of planning to disrupt the inter-American conference.[248] On the eighteenth of the same month, a student, José de Jesús Alvarez, was arrested and described as "one of the principal agitators at the [Central] University," where he allegedly planned to foment disorders during the assembly.[249] While the conference was in session, Narciso Herrera Arana, an

AD cell chief, was arrested on 23 March and charged with planning to
hold a demonstration on Avenida Sucre (a main thoroughfare connec-
ting with the superhighway between Caracas and the international airport at Maiquetía) in which Toriello himself was supposed to participate.[250] On 13 March AD labor leader Luis Hurtado was taken from
his apartment by SN agents, beaten to death, and buried in a hidden
grave.[251] Two months later, the SN picked up Simón Sáez Mérida and
imprisoned him for a year for his activities connected with efforts to
cause a boycott of the inter-American meeting.[252] Although the clandestine AD presented no serious threat at the time of the conference,
some observers regarded Estrada's "extreme precautionary measures" as
justified, in view of the fact that, as the delegates sat unmolested in
Caracas, a group of Puerto Rican nationalists invaded the United States
House of Representatives and shot several congressmen.[253] Estrada's
star was high and, much to the disgust of Betancourt, when the security
chief visited the United States in November 1954, the New York *Herald
Tribune* praised him "for smashing the Communist menace in the Caribbean" and for creating "a police net in the Caribbean . . . of extraordinary efficiency."[254]

The efficiency of the SN was demonstrated time and again during
those years. Not too long after the Caracas Conference, probably sometime in April, at a meeting held in the home of Carlos José Mujica in the
Jardines del Valle section of Caracas, the reorganization of the party
was undertaken.[255] Almost immediately, however, the work was un-
done, when during May and June the National Security police arrested
over a dozen AD militants, including three who had attended the Jardines del Valle meeting: Mujica, Silvestre Ortiz Bucarán, and Roberto
Hostos Poleo. The arrest of the latter in June and that of José Mercedes
Santeliz in May were particularly damaging, for both were members of
the new National Executive Committee (CEN) and of the clandestine
Coordinating Committee for eastern Venezuela.[256] On 19 October
1954 the SN announced that it had frustrated an attempt on the part of
Acción Democrática to dynamite a viaduct on the Caracas-La Guaira
autopista, but Betancourt claimed that this was an invention of the SN
and affirmed that one of the so-called "terrorists," Francisco Espejo,
allegedly shot in the act of trying to blow up the bridge, had been
arrested by the SN on 14 September.[257] During 1955 and for much of
1956 the clandestine AD was hardly heard from; it surfaced once on
the occasion of the death of Andrés Eloy Blanco in Mexico in order to

distribute a handbill paying tribute to the AD leader and calling upon Venezuelans to attend his funeral.[258] Nonetheless, although silent, the underground had continued to rebuild and it had even restored radio contact with the exiles in Costa Rica. But the SN also persisted, and in late summer 1956 it delivered virtually the coup de grâce.

On 9 August 1956 Pedro Estrada informed the press that the Seguridad Nacional had discovered a plot to assassinate Pérez Jiménez. He claimed that Betancourt directed the plot by "remote-control" from Puerto Rico and that arms for the attempt had been supplied by the Costa Rican government.[259] He announced that eighteen alleged conspirators had been arrested. Betancourt denied emphatically the existence of such a plot. He acknowledged that a few of those arrested were members of AD but affirmed that many of the accused had no record of political activism. Among the latter was Mario Pérez Pisanty, a wealthy industrialist, who, Betancourt declared, was arrested "because, in accordance with the technique of conspiracies prefabricated by dictatorial police, one must find a financial backer."[260] The unfortunate Pérez Pisanty died of undisclosed causes in the jail of Seguridad Nacional.[261] Betancourt contended that the affair was another of Estrada's "discoveries" designed to justify a new wave of terror in Venezuela and to force him to leave Puerto Rico.[262] Gallegos denounced the accusations and reiterated the party's repudiation of the personal attack as a method of political struggle. He declared that Venezuelan democracy would gain nothing through the assassination of Pérez Jiménez, since the fight was against a system not a man.[263] However, the later clandestine chief Sáez Mérida declared that Acción Democrática had actually planned to assassinate Pedro Estrada (not Pérez Jiménez) at that time.[264] It was possible, then, that the SN had uncovered a plot, especially since the underground membership was increasingly youthful and less in sympathy with the tactics of restraint. But more significant at the moment was the fact that the underground had suffered severely in its Sisyphean labor of reconstruction. The remnants of its leadership had been captured and its radio transmitter and receiver had been seized. Even as late as 1957, Sáez Mérida observed that the resistance was confined mainly to Caracas and that "its best leaders were either in exile, in jail, in the torture chamber, or in the cemetery."[265]

During these years also, Seguridad Nacional took measures to secure the borders of Venezuela. In October 1953 the SN seized in Puerto

Ordaz an English motor-launch, the *Spindle,* on which four accion-democratistas were working as crew members and serving as couriers between exiles in Trinidad and the AD underground. The Venezuelan dictatorship, therefore, undertook to halt the clandestine travel from Trinidad and Curaçao. In April 1954, the colonial governor of Trinidad, Major General Sir Hubert E. Rance, visited Caracas, and reports followed that authorities in Port-of-Spain were cooperating with the Venezuelan government by placing exiles under surveillance and even by deporting some when requested to do so.[266] At the same time, the Venezuelan government signed contracts with two French shipbuilders for the construction of twelve high-speed patrol boats.[267] On the western border, too, Pérez Jiménez enjoyed good relations with his fellow dictator, Gustavo Rojas Pinilla of Colombia. On 10 June 1954, in Barranquilla, an SN agent shot and killed Lieutenant León Droz Blanco, who had been accused of conspiring against Pérez Jiménez and had fled Venezuela with the assistance of the AD underground. The assassin was apprehended, and documents found on his person showed him to be a member of the SN. On 25 July, however, he "mysteriously" escaped and returned to Venezuela.[268]

Although the SN never abated its Gestapo-like techniques, there was a curious inconsistency in its actions in 1955 and 1956. The SN maintained the atmosphere of a dictatorship and, in order to remind Venezuelans of their situation, occasionally eliminated members of the resistance in a sensational fashion.[269] On the other hand, it freed a large number of political prisoners and permitted them to go into exile. Those who left the country in 1955 and 1956 comprised an impressive list, for example: Dubuc, Anzola, Henríquez Vera, Consalvi, Quijada, Alberti, Nieves, Dorta, Hostos Poleo, and Sáez Mérida. The action was obviously designed to impress international opinion, but it also resulted in a strengthening of the exile cadres. In addition, on 3 February 1956 Pérez Jiménez gave instructions to Venezuelan consuls to issue visas for the return of three hundred exiles, including Betancourt and Gallegos, and promised a general amnesty.[270] Acción Democrática rejected the offer on the grounds that it was insincere, that is, it was impossible to return while the jails were still filled with political prisoners and while Pedro Estrada still directed the SN and ignored the basic rights of citizens.[271] It was also noted that only selected exiles were being given the opportunity to return and that even these had to agree to restrict their political activity; on this point Gallegos declared simply that he could not return unless he could do what he had to do, that is, liberate the people.[272] Even the National Executive Committee (CEN) distributed a manifesto in Caracas in which it denounced the "masquerade" of Pérez Jiménez and asserted that the promise of amnesty was designed to confuse and deceive national and international opinion.[273]

These moves by the Venezuelan regime, while principally intended as propaganda, were also indications of confidence. A confidence which stemmed from the effectiveness of the SN and from the general prosperity which Venezuela was enjoying. Sam Pope Brewer of the *New York Times,* while admitting that his inquiry was superficial, remarked after a visit to Venezuela that ". . . partly through ruthless repression and partly through the effects of a boom prosperity, opposition to the government has almost disappeared."[274] Tad Szulc, a writer for the same newspaper, described the Pérez Jiménez regime as a "technocracy" which, while suppressing political opposition, was trying to achieve "generations" of material progress in less than a decade. He asserted it was a government dominated by technicians, who believed that "democratic politics" would impede the economic and social "thrust" forward. Moreover, he reported, opposition from Acción Democrática was "hardly noticeable."[275] In this epoch, then, the outlook for democratic government within Venezuela appeared dismal, and even Betancourt admitted that "despotism seemed firmly established in Venezuela."[276] However, the struggle had not ceased; it merely had changed its nature. In fact, it had been in a process of change for a number of years.

There was an inverse relationship between the decline of the clandestine AD and the significance of the political activity of Acción Democrática in exile. As long as the resistance movement remained viable, the activity of the exiles was subsidiary and was designed to render assistance to the underground. By their nature, these activities were conspiratorial and were oriented to the specific problems of the struggle taking place within Venezuela. When the resistance began to collapse toward the end of 1952, the leadership in exile assumed more of the burden of opposition to Pérez Jiménez and made more effective use of the forms of opposition peculiar to exile. These involved greater stress upon public opinion and greater reliance upon friends and allies, that is, upon groups outside Acción Democrática itself. This meant that the struggle became more international in scope and more concerned with general principles which tended to unite the various groups in a common cause.

The antidictatorial struggle in the Caribbean centered increasingly, therefore, upon the activities of exiles. Although the resistance within Venezuela had been more intense and prolonged than that within any other Caribbean country, the collapse of the clandestine AD was an indication of conditions generally in the Caribbean area. Internal opposition had been snuffed out in most of the states. If the dictators were to be restrained and if the ideals of the Democratic Left were to be preserved, it was up to the leaders in exile to accomplish it. The entire struggle to achieve change and make essential reforms within the framework of democratic government depended upon the ability of the Democratic Left in exile to survive and to defeat the dictatorships. The manner in which the dispossessed groups did this, overcoming formidable obstacles, constitutes one of the important chapters of Caribbean history.

4 | *The Diaspora*

Life in Exile

POLITICAL EXILE is usually a bitter experience. Despite its sometimes romantic or mysterious image, it is often a lonely, uncertain, and humiliating existence. Unlike the immigrant, who leaves behind the disappointments of his former land and seeks a fresh start in a new one, the exile looks homeward and regards his uprooting as transitory. He lives, Miss Frances Grant has observed, in a "political and social limbo," often without legal status and abandoned by friends of better days.[1] Rómulo Betancourt described exile as "a room in a cheap hotel,"[2] and as the feeling of helplessness when comrades suffer martyrdom at home.[3] Raúl Roa, who one day himself would drive many Cubans into exile, concurred with Euripides, who centuries earlier had said, "exile is an evil so grave that words cannot express it," and with the Ecuadoran Juan Montalvo, who had written, "add to the indignation caused by the injustice, the heartbreak of seeing tyranny triumph."[4] Venezuelan labor leader Augusto Malavé Villalba experienced in exile the anguish of not being able to go home to attend his mother's funeral.[5] And Jacobo Arbenz, upon going into exile in 1954, replied to inquiries about his plans that he had no plans. "The only thing a political exile can have," he mused, "is patience."[6] Yet, exile occupies a place of importance in Latin American history.

In many cases the most productive writing and thinking have been accomplished by political leaders during periods of exile. This is affirmed by a contemporary Colombian writer, Oscar Falchetti, who stated, "the best in America has often been born in exile."[7] He cited as proof the works of Juan Alberdi, Domingo Sarmiento, and Juan Montalvo, and he might have added those of Víctor Raúl Haya de la Torre, Rómulo Betancourt, Juan José Arévalo, and Juan Bosch. In exile these leaders were free to reflect and also to provide the political opposition that was outlawed at home. And as exile was broadening, it also served in the diffusion of ideas. José Figueres in exile in Mexico studied the revolutionary programs there with the idea of possible application to the problems of Costa Rica.[8] The Apristas during their long hegira from Peru influenced the thinking of numerous Latin American leaders, including Betancourt, Figueres, and Bosch.[9] What was true about the historical significance of exile in Latin America generally was particularly applicable to the situation in the Caribbean during the 1950s.

By 1952 virtually the entire Spanish Caribbean was dominated by tyrants, so that political opposition in the area came almost exclusively from exiles and their allies. The principal centers for Caribbean exiles were Mexico City, San José, San Juan, Miami, and New York. Guatemala also provided refuge for exiles, but, owing to particular circumstances, exile activities there will be treated separately. Acción Democrática in exile was heavily concentrated in Mexico, probably a thousand-strong and "closely knit" around the personality of Rómulo Gallegos,[10] but some of its elements also resided in San José and San Juan. Dominicans were found in all locations, but the largest numbers were in San Juan and New York. Haitians also tended to congregate in the latter city. Miami was the traditional stronghold for Cubans, but they were also active in Mexico City, San Juan, and New York. The Nicaraguans and Hondurans still preferred Mexico and, depending upon the circumstances, San José. The more militant exiles of all nationalities, including many of the veterans of Cayo Confites and Luperón, were in Arbenz' Guatemala.

The majority of exiles were, of course, involved in some kind of political activity, but almost all were presented with the problem of earning a living. They were engaged in a variety of occupations. Although employment was sometimes difficult to find owing to the lack of proper credentials, the existence of nationalistic laws, or even prejudice, the most important leaders managed to remain busy. Journalism and writing was particularly suitable for their talents. Rómulo Betancourt was a regular contributor to *Bohemia* and *Cuadernos Americanos,* as were Rómulo Gallegos and, while he lived, Andrés Eloy Blanco. Valmore Rodríguez, until he died of a heart attack in Chile in 1955, was an editor of *Selecciones,* the Latin American edition of *Readers' Digest.* The staff of *Humanismo,* a strongly liberal, Mexican monthly, included Ricardo Montilla, Simón Alberto Consalvi, and Ildegar Pérez-Segnini, all of Acción Democrática. Frequent contributors to the magazine included Gallegos, José M. Siso Martínez, Raúl Roa, Carlos Pellicer, and Vicente Sáenz.[11]

In April 1956, a group of AD exiles in Mexico, Carlos Canache Mata, Lucilia Velázquez, and P. B. Pérez Salinas, began publication of *Impetu,* "a cultural magazine at the service of liberty."[12] Such journalistic and intellectual activity also embraced an impressive production of books. Too numerous to list them all, they included: Valmore Rodríguez, *Bayonetas sobre Venezuela* (Mexico, 1950); Domingo Alberto Rangel, *Venezuela, país ocupado* (La Paz, 1955); Rómulo Betancourt, *Venezuela: política y petróleo* (Mexico, 1956); Horacio Ornes, *Desembarco en Luperón* (Mexico, 1956); Luis B. Prieto Figueroa, *El concepto del líder; el maestro como líder* (Mexico,1956); Jesús de Galíndez, *La Era de Trujillo* (Santiago, 1956); Analuisa Llovera, *Entre dos fuegos* (Mexico, 1957); Germán Ornes, *Trujillo: Little Caesar of the Caribbean* (New York, 1958); Juan Bosch, *Trujillo: causas de una tiranía sin ejemplo* (Caracas, 1959); and Pedro Joaquín Chamorro, *Estirpe sangrienta: los somoza* (Buenos Aires, 1959).

Teaching was another important endeavor of a number of exiles. For ten years before he became president of Guatemala in 1945, Juan José Arévalo was a professor of history at the University of Tucumán, Argentina.[13] In 1956, Siso Martínez conducted a course in U.S.-Latin American diplomatic history at the National University of Mexico.[14] The Nicaraguan Edelberto Torres was a member of the faculty at San Carlos in Guatemala, and Jesús de Galíndez, the Basque-Dominican exile, was an instructor at Columbia University in New York. Juan Bosch taught at the Inter-American Institute of Political Education (later renamed the Inter-American School of Democratic Education), which had been organized in Costa Rica in November 1959 by the democratic parties of the Caribbean area.[15]

Lecturing and public speaking was another source of income, as well as a forum, for the exiles of the Caribbean. Rómulo Gallegos was a popular speaker and he addressed numerous intellectual and cultural events in Mexico, where his reputation gave prestige to the exile cause. In September 1956 he spoke before the conference of the Congress for Freedom of Culture and advocated "intervention through ideas" to an audience of influential American thinkers (including Alfonso Reyes, Norman Thomas, and John dos Passos).[16] Several months later, on 10 January 1957, Gallegos delivered a eulogy of the Chilean winner of the Nobel Prize for Literature, Gabriela Mistral, during the celebration of the fifteenth anniversary of *Cuadernos Americanos.*[17] The following May, he spoke at a banquet honoring Vicente Sáenz, and in August 1957 he gave a public lecture at *Bellas Artes,* where he read passages from a novel he was then writing, *La brasa en el pico del cuervo.*[18] Betancourt's activities as party chieftain restricted his public appearances, but in January 1957 he spoke at a luncheon in his honor in New York sponsored by the Inter-American Association for Democracy and Freedom (IADF),[19] and the following July he presented a lecture at Stanford University.[20] The IADF also sponsored a series of press conferences and meetings for the Honduran leader, Ramón Villeda Morales, who left his exile in Costa Rica to come to New York for two weeks in September 1956.[21] When Acción Democrática returned to power in Venezuela in 1959, the Central University sponsored an address by Juan Bosch on 27 February. Numerous exiles, especially labor union leaders, were often delegates and main speakers at international conferences. In November 1956 Venezuelan exile Roberto Hostos Poleo spoke in Mexico before the First Congress of the International Union of Postal, Telegraph, and Telephone Workers.[22]

Many exiles found employment with international organizations and specialized agencies. Collaborating in various United Nations technical assistance programs were Venezuelan economists Carlos D'Ascoli, José Antonio Mayorbe, and Enrique Tejera París. Another Venezuelan, Alejandro Oropeza Castillo, served as the special representative of the UN secretary general and chief of the Technical Assistance Mission in Bolivia.[23] Luis B. Prieto was assigned to a UN educational mission in Honduras, and P. B. Pérez Salinas was a member of the Executive Board of the Inter-American Regional Organization of Workers (ORIT). He also served as assistant to the director of education of the ORIT. The rank and file of exiles, particularly those with a facility in two or more languages, could be found on the staffs or secretariats of numerous international agencies. Among the exiles also were a large number of professional men, such as Dominican physicians Drs. J. Edmundo Tavares and Félix García Carrasco, who had large practices in Puerto Rico.[24]

The emigrés also filled a variety of less glamorous jobs. In the large

U.S. cities, such as Miami and New York, the great number of the Cubans and Dominicans served in retail stores and hotels and restaurants, drove taxicabs, ran grocery stores, worked as construction workers and factory employees, and freelanced as translators and language tutors. The list of occupations was probably as long as the positions available. In addition, a large number of exiles were students.

Of course, not all students from the Caribbean area studying abroad were political exiles, but in 1955 AD affirmed that seven thousand Venezuelans were studying outside the country either because of political oppression or the high cost of education within Venezuela.[25] After four years of confinement in Venezuelan prisons, Eduardo González went into exile and continued his studies at the National University of Mexico, where he was the author's classmate in 1956 and 1957. González was still recognized as the president of the Central University Student Federation and he represented Venezuelan students at numerous gatherings and conferences in Mexico.[26] The students tended, of course, to be active politically, and for this reason they were not always welcome. In July 1956 the Honduran government was reported trying to persuade Guatemalan student exiles to depart for Costa Rica, because it did not want them to stir up the local student body.[27] The main problem for students, however, was money. Although some received funds from parents either at home or abroad, they, as well as many of the rank and file, were often dependent upon the exile community at large.

The exiles tended to look out for their own. The better organized exile parties, such as Acción Democrática, the Dominican Revolutionary party (PRD), and the Cuban Auténticos, contributed to the well-being of their militants. The AD exiles in Mexico City were particularly close. The party managed to raise funds for some of its activities through voluntary contributions and occasionally through such means as a raffle in which the prize might be a special edition of a book of poems by Eloy Blanco or Betancourt's *Venezuela: política y petróleo*.[28] The raffle was used particularly to help pay for the annual Christmas party, which included a *piñata* and gifts for the children, "the innocent hearts . . . who endured in Mexico the harshness of prolonged exile imposed upon their parents."[29] In October 1955, in the wake of violent storms in Mexico, the AD exiles collected 5,200 pesos from among themselves for disaster relief.[30] In spite of this picture of altruism, sharing, and even hard times in the ranks, Marcos Pérez

Jiménez and Rafael Trujillo charged that Betancourt had looted the public treasury before he fled Venezuela and that he had deposited large sums of money in Canadian banks, which enabled him and others to live in "princely fashion" in "golden exile."[31]

There was probably more substance to such charges with reference to the Auténticos. A number of Cubans indeed lived in "princely fashion" in Miami and Miami Beach. Carlos Prío Socarrás allegedly had become wealthy while in political office, but he was also generous in promoting the exile cause. In October 1952 Prío provided $248,000 for the purchase of arms to overthrow Batista, but his unfortunate agents, Manuel Fernández Madariaga and Cándido de la Torre, were held up for the entire amount in a Fort Worth, Texas, motel.[32] Two months later, police in Mamaroneck, New York, raided an abandoned garage and seized a large arms cache which had been purchased with funds also supplied by Prío.[33] For the next six years, Prío was a major patron of Cuban exile activities. Another benefactor was "millionaire" José Alemán, who gave refuge to many Cubans in his Trade Winds Apartment Hotel on Miami Beach.[34] Alemán was the son of José Manuel Alemán of the Cayo Confites affair, who before his death had invested heavily in Miami real estate. There were other wealthy backers among the exile groups, such as the Dominican Juan Rodríguez and the Nicaraguan Emiliano Chamorro.

The exiles also received financial support and aid from elements outside their ranks. The Inter-American Association for Democracy and Freedom (IADF) and the Inter-American Regional Organization of Workers (ORIT) provided some funds. Norman Thomas, Frances Grant (secretary-general of the IADF), Louise Crane (publisher of *Iberica*), and Roger Baldwin (president of the International League for the Rights of Man and a founder of the American Civil Liberties Union) often rendered assistance, particularly to the exile colony in New York.[35] At the end of 1956, when Pérez Jiménez expelled hundreds of trade unionists with only the clothing on their backs, the IADF and trade union organizations raised funds for their temporary relief.[36] The AFL-CIO alone, through Serafino Romualdi, its representative before the ORIT, contributed $2,000.[37] Really needy exiles in the United States secured help through various social and welfare agencies. And, toward the end of the decade, the U.S. government also helped finance the exile movement, although indirectly and covertly.

In February 1967 *Ramparts* magazine exposed the fact that the principal students organization in the United States, the National Students Association, had received funds for its international activities from the Central Intelligence Agency. Further disclosures revealed that by means of various funds and foundations, either directly or indirectly, the CIA had channelled money to "a wide spectrum of youth, student, academic, research, journalist, business, legal, and labor organizations" operating in the international field. These included the ORIT and its parent organization, the International Confederation of Free Trade Unions (ICFTU).[38] In most cases the ultimate recipient was unaware of the original source of the funds. Using the J. M. Kaplan Fund of New York as a "conduit," the CIA transferred substantial sums to the Institute for International Labor Research, of which Norman Thomas was chairman, and to the Institute of Political Education in Costa Rica.[39] As will be seen, the CIA funds had no bearing upon the work which these and similar organizations had been performing for years, which, in fact, was often quite antagonistic to official U.S. policy. Although the method employed would later raise grievous questions, the purposes for which the CIA money was used, in the Caribbean area at least, reflected a shift in U.S. policy, not a corruption of the groups aiding the Democratic Left. Their collaboration with the Democratic Left in exile was long-standing.

While the problem of financial need was serious, graver yet was the physical danger which many exiles faced. No exile, no matter where he resided, was fully beyond the reach of the dictators of the Caribbean. The Dominican exiles, particularly, were watched carefully by their home government.[40] Rafael Trujillo maintained an efficient espionage system and used the Dominican diplomatic and consular services to harass and even liquidate his enemies in the exile community.[41] Over the years, a number of Dominican emigrés were victims of violent crimes, which seemed linked to their political opposition to Trujillo. Although the first crime of this nature took place in 1935 (i.e., the murder of Sergio Bencosme in New York), Trujillo stalked the exiles especially during the 1950s.

In December 1950, Mauricio Báez, a Dominican labor leader in exile in Havana, disappeared from his home and was never seen again. Just before his disappearance, Báez had submitted a request to the International Labor Organization for an investigation of trade union conditions in the Dominican Republic.[42] Although concrete evidence was lacking, Horacio Ornes charged that Báez was "murdered by gangsters in the pay of Trujillo" and that the crime was directed by Félix W. Bernardino, who at that moment was the Dominican commercial attaché in Havana.[43] Four months later, José Figueres affirmed that the disappearance of Báez was part of a general plot to eliminate "Latin American democratic leaders in power or in exile."[44] He listed an "overt attack" against Juan Bosch in San José in March, an assassination plot of which he himself was the target in early April, and an attempted murder of Rómulo Betancourt in Havana on April 18.[45] In August 1951, Enrique C. Henríquez, the long-time foe of Trujillo in Cuba, mysteriously dropped out of sight for thirty-six hours and then reappeared before the Cuban House of Representatives to charge that Trujillo had tried to kill him. He declared that Trujillo had offered $30,000 for his murder and asserted that, with the help of Cuban military intelligence and "Trujillo's own agents," he had feigned his abduction and murder in order to trap the Dominican chargé d'affaires, Braulio Méndez, into paying off. Méndez was at that moment in Miami, Henríquez proclaimed, having fled Havana when the "agents" telephoned him to report that the "mission [had been] carried out."[46] If Henríquez had been an intended victim of Trujillo, he was one of the few to live to tell about it.

On 3 October 1952, shortly before midnight, Andrés Requena was shot to death in the hallway of a tenement in the lower East side of Manhattan. Requena was a Dominican exile who earned his living as a tailor. He had become a U.S. citizen after serving in the U.S. army from 1944 to 1946, but he remained an outspoken critic of Trujillo and expressed his views in a pamphlet, *De Patria,* which he published on an occasional basis. Why Requena had gone to the place where he was murdered is unknown, but according to the driver of his taxicab he was unfamiliar with the neighborhood and had asked the driver to wait for his return in five minutes.[47] When questioned by reporters about the crime, the consul general of the Dominican Republic in New York, Félix W. Bernardino, replied that "he had heard" Requena was a member of the "Caribbean Legion" and that Requena had sought to "besmirch" the reputation of Trujillo.[48] The following day, Bernardino changed his story and asserted that Requena had sought a reconciliation with the Dominican government and had, therefore, been assassinated by his own friends for deserting their ranks.[49] Although the slayer of Requena was not apprehended, at Requena's funeral Nicolás Silfa, the leader of the Dominican Revolutionary party (PRD) in New York, accused the Trujillo regime of the murder.[50] The presence in New York of Bernardino, whom Robert Crassweller described as "a connoisseur of wickedness . . . a man of animal passion and violence,"[51] seems more than coincidental, as likewise that of Emilio Sánchez Hinojosa, another Trujillo agent, who had also been in New York at the time of the murder of Bencosme and in Havana at the time of the disappearance of Báez.[52] Sánchez Hinojosa was in Havana again in September 1955, when Manuel de Jesús Hernández ("Pipi" Hernández) was murdered. [53]

The murder of Hernández started a feud between Batista and Trujillo, which confounded any overly pat interpretation of the Caribbean turmoil as "dictator versus democrat." Although many exiles had fled Cuba when Batista seized power, those who remained were not harassed, even those who continued to engage in anti-Trujillo activities. Apparently Batista wanted to preserve some semblance of democracy.[54] Hernández, a Dominican, had been in political exile in Cuba for twenty years. He was a political activist and at the time of his death had been campaigning against Cuban participation in the "World's Fair" scheduled to open in Ciudad Trujillo (Santo Domingo) in December. [55] Unlike earlier crimes, this one resulted in arrests; two Trujillo agents, Alejandro Robinson and Rafael Soler, were charged with the murder. [56] The Hernández affair demonstrated that Trujillo had taken matters into his own hands, and Cuban-Dominican relations deteriorated to their 1947 level. Trujillo's pique was so great that he entered into a conspiracy against Batista, reportedly aligning himself with Carlos Prío, Fidel Castro, and Policarpo Soler.[57] The latter was a notorious Cuban *pistolero,* who allegedly was in Trujillo's service as a "professional assassin."[58] Although Castro broke with Trujillo before his invasion of Cuba in December 1956, some of the money and arms used in that expedition had been supplied by Trujillo.[59] Meanwhile, Trujillo had also continued his attacks upon exiles residing in the United States and had become involved in one of the most sensational criminal mysteries of recent times.

Jesús de Galíndez, an instructor at Columbia University, disappeared on the evening of 12 March 1956. After finishing a class, he entered the subway but never made it back to his apartment. Officially, he is still a missing person. Investigations of the case, however, revealed the hand of Trujillo, as well as the deaths of two other men, who were killed in clumsy efforts to cover up the original crime.[60]

Galíndez was a Basque Spaniard who had gone to the Dominican

Republic as an exile in 1939. Five years later, he took up a second exile in New York. Here he was active among exile and intellectual circles; he attended the founding conference of the Inter-American Association for Democracy and Freedom (IADF) in Havana in 1950, was a member of the Requena Memorial Committee, and served as the treasurer of the Basque Government in Exile. His troubles started, however, when he undertook to write his doctoral dissertation describing "The Era of Trujillo." Dominican agents tried to purchase the manuscript for $25,000 and apparently silenced Galíndez when he refused to be bribed.[61] When Galíndez disappeared, the Dominican consul general in New York was again Bernardino, but working with him this time was an even more sinister figure, Arturo Espaillat. "The Yellow Cat," as Espaillat was called,[62] held the rank of brigadier general and had been Trujillo's intelligence chief. By his own admission he was also a spy, an intriguer, and a murderer.[63] The friends of Galíndez, including Roger Baldwin, Frances Grant, Norman Thomas, Serafino Romualdi, and Wenzell Brown, petitioned Attorney General Herbert Brownell to investigate the case.[64] And they aroused the public through the publication of letters and articles in leading newspapers and magazines. Nicolás Silfa charged that Galíndez had been disposed of in the boilers of a Dominican freighter, the *Fundación,* which had been in New York harbor on 13 March, but a four-hour search by the New York police yielded no clues.[65] In fact, the investigation by the police in general had no success. The U.S. government showed little willingness to become involved, and the Dominican principals, Bernardino and Espaillat, took refuge in their diplomatic immunity. Just as interest in the matter was fading, a seemingly unrelated event revived it.

On 4 December 1956 authorities in Ciudad Trujillo reported the disappearance of Gerald Murphy, a young pilot from Eugene, Oregon, under circumstances which suggested that he had fallen from a cliff into shark-infested waters. This explanation did not satisfy Murphy's parents, nor his fiancé, and they appealed to Oregon Congressman Charles O. Porter for help. The ensuing investigation forced the Dominican government to concoct a story that Murphy was killed by a fellow pilot, Captain Octavio de la Maza, who, authorities said, resented alleged homosexual advances on the part of Murphy. However, before De la Maza could be questioned by representatives of the U.S. Department of State, he supposedly committed suicide in his jail cell. It turned out that the suicide was badly contrived: the suicide note was proven a forgery and the water pipe from which De la Maza hanged himself was neither high enough nor strong enough to support a man of his size and stature.[66] These events, plus additional information about Murphy's activities as a pilot in the Dominican Republic and his extravagant spending in the months before his death, gave credence to a theory that Murphy had surreptitiously flown Galíndez to the Dominican Republic to die by Trujillo's hand. The news media next publicized the events.

In May 1957 Edward R. Murrow presented an hour-long television documentary, "The Galíndez-Murphy Case: A Chronicle of Terror," over the Columbia Broadcasting System network,[67] and a fictionalized version was dramatized on another major television program. Representative Porter took the issue before Congress, where not only the Galíndez-Murphy disappearances were debated but also U.S.-Dominican relations in general. In July a congressional investigation was ordered. The executive branch now entered the case, which resulted in the indictment of John Joseph Frank for failure to register as an agent of the Dominican Republic.[68] Frank, a U.S. citizen and former agent of the Federal Bureau of Investigation, had been retained by the Dominican government in various capacities, including the handling of security arrangements for Trujillo during visits to the United States and the conducting of private investigations.[69]

During the Frank trial in November 1957, the essential features of the Galíndez-Murphy affair were revealed, particularly through the testimony of Harold French, a U.S. Air Force sergeant and confederate of Murphy. Murphy had leased a twin-engine aircraft at an airfield in Linden, New Jersey, and, with the help of French, had added extra fuel tanks to extend its range. French testified that Frank, using the alias, "John Kane," had assumed the costs of this activity and that through him he had been introduced to Bernardino and Espaillat.[70] On the night of Galíndez' disappearance, Murphy took off from an airport outside of Amityville, New York, shortly after an ambulance had arrived and transferred a figure on a stretcher to his aircraft. Murphy flew to Miami, where he stopped for refueling. There, an airport attendant, Donald J. Jackson, saw an "unconscious body" in Murphy's plane.[71] This was as far as the flight was traced, but the U.S. Department of Justice was certain that Frank had withheld information about the case and it insisted that the court give him the maximum penalty.[72]

The Dominican Republic continued to refuse to waive diplomatic immunity for Bernardino and Espaillat, but in an effort to counteract the unfavorable publicity it retained Morris Ernst, a prominent New York attorney with a reputation as a liberal, to conduct an "impartial" investigation. On 1 June 1958, Ernst, in collaboration with William H. Munson, issued a lengthy report, which concluded that there was "not a scintilla of evidence" that Trujillo was connected with the disappearance of Galíndez.[73] Three weeks later, however, the findings of Ernst and Munson were challenged, when the Justice Department made public Murphy's notebook and flight logbook, in which the pilot had written the names of Galíndez and Germán Ornes and had outlined an itinerary similar to the alleged flight.[74] There was little doubt that Trujillo's reputation in the United States had been severely damaged. However, if these events exposed the "long arm" of Trujillo, they apparently did not restrain it, because even while the Galíndez-Murphy case was under investigation another attack under similar circumstances occurred.

Tancredo Martínez García, a Dominican lawyer living in exile in Mexico, was shot in the face at close range on 23 September 1957. Miraculously, he survived. Martínez was the representative in Mexico of the Dominican Revolutionary Vanguard, VRD (Vanguardia Revolucionaria Dominicana), an exile party founded earlier the same year in San Juan, Puerto Rico, under the leadership of Horacio Ornes.[75] Martínez was able to identify his assailant as Ricardo Bonachea León, a Cuban gunman allegedly in the pay of Trujillo, who, Mexican authorities believed, was under orders of Policarpo Soler.[76] Trujillo attributed the Martínez shooting to exile politics and asserted that Bonachea León was a member of Fidel Castro's 26 of July Movement and not a Dominican agent.[77] It will be recalled, however, that the preceding year Trujillo had been in liaison with Castro. Moreover, on 21 May 1957, three Cuban *pistoleros,* all linked to Policarpo Soler, were arrested in San José and charged with planning to assassinate President Figueres.[78] These men, Herminio Díaz García, Juan Manuel Delgado Chaves, and Jesús Fermín González Cartas. "El Extraño" ("The Stranger"), had also been involved in Trujillo's erstwhile conspiracy against Batista, but when Trujillo and Batista were reconciled, they accepted a new assignment, the assassination of Figueres for $200,000.[79] Exile politics were murky indeed, but Trujillo, although lacking finesse, intrigued almost compulsively. In March 1958 Tancredo Martínez visited the United States under the sponsorship of the IADF and described his near fatal shooting in Mexico. He charged that Policarpo Soler was the leader of a "troop of murderers" operating in Central America and Mexico and that all were directed by another of Trujillo's violent lieutenants, Johnny Abbes García.[80]

Abbes García was a man of base and cruel disposition who helped fashion the diabolical character of the Trujillo regime. His talents, as those of Bernardino and Espaillat, were obviously necessary in an authoritarian government. The Trujillo dictatorship at least avoided the charge of hypocrisy. These loyal henchmen occupied high positions and, although they worked in the shadows and performed contemptible deeds, were visible and moved freely in Dominican society, where they embraced even foreign dignitaries. Appointed chief of the Military Intelligence Service (SIM) in late 1957, Abbes García served as Trujillo's most influential collaborator. His career in subversion and intrigue began in Mexico in 1955, where he had been assigned to the Dominican embassy to keep watch over the Dominican exile community.[81] He advanced rapidly and by 1957, as Tancredo Martínez charged, was directing numerous intrigues in Central America. He was linked to the plot to assassinate Figueres in May 1957. In October of the same year, Abbes García, officially the military attaché of the Dominican embassy in Guatemala, was accused of planning and taking part in the murder of a Guatemalan truck driver, Narciso Escobar Carrillo.[82]

The Escobar murder had grave implications, because the so-called truck driver was apparently an agent (probably a double agent) involved in the assassination of Guatemalan President Carlos Castillo Armas on 27 July 1957. Certain members of the Guatemalan Congressional Commission in charge of the investigation of the assassination of Castillo Armas had expressed the view that Trujillo was somehow involved in the affair. The murder of Escobar, who supposedly possessed key information about the case, reenforced these suspicions, and by December 1957 Dominican-Guatemalan relations were near a rupture.[83] Although the role, if any, of Trujillo and his agents in the assassination of Castillo Armas remains speculative, Trujillo had complained that Castillo was ungrateful and uncooperative. For example, Castillo had refused to turn over to Dominican authorities legionnaire Miguel Angel Ramírez, who had been arrested after the fall of Arbenz.[84] This was hardly a motive for assassination; however, the charge persisted, and as late as August 1958 the Guatemalan attorney general continued to investigate possible Dominican involvement in Castillo's death, as well as in "eight other mysterious deaths that [appeared] to be related."[85] At the same time, the Guatemalan government complained that the Dominican embassy had aided the escape from Guatemala's Central Penitentiary of Cuban pistolero Gildardo Montifar Gutiérrez, who, it added, was really Ricardo Bonachea León, the assailant of Tancredo Martínez and a fugitive from Mexican justice.[86] Rómulo Betancourt had written that dictatorship was a "contagion" which could send its paid assassins anywhere in the world.[87] Judging by the activities of Bernardino, Espaillat, Policarpo Soler, and Abbes García, Betancourt was right.

Trujillo, however, did not use physical violence alone in his campaigns against the exile community. He also employed other forms of pressure or coercion with reference to the emigrés. In one case, Trujillo's "spies and bullies" allegedly caused a young Dominican woman residing in Puerto Rico to lose her job as an airline stewardess. Denounced as an enemy of the Trujillo regime, the girl was dismissed when the airline employing her was threatened with the suspension of its flights to the Dominican Republic.[88] In another instance, a group of exiles in New York, organized as the Dominican Democratic Workers' Committee, was forced to cancel plans for a solemn mass at St. Patrick's Cathedral because, they were informed, their planned activities were offensive to the Dominican government.[89] The group sought the mass in order "to ask God's protection for the workers in the Dominican Republic and in exile," but its money was returned with the notice that such requests had to be made through the Dominican consul general in New York.[90] The spokesman for the group, Nicolás Silfa, complained to Cardinal Spellman that this was equivalent to asking Hungarian "Freedom Fighters" to forward their requests through the Hungarian consulate in New York.[91]

Silfa was himself frequently the object of various forms of harassment by the Dominican government. In December 1956 he was arrested in New York on charges of practicing dentistry without a license. He claimed in his defense that a Dominican agent had "planted" dental instruments in his home,[92] and he was acquitted when a Dominican merchant seaman disclosed that Trujillo agents had asked him to give false testimony.[93] On another occasion, while Silfa was attending a conference of the International Confederation of Free Trade Unions (ICFTU), seeking a labor boycott of the Dominican Republic, the New York public school attended by his son had to be evacuated because of an anonymous bomb threat.[94] Silfa complained that once, when he traveled from the United States, customs officials subjected him to an unnecessarily thorough search and examination, and he implied that it was done because of his anti-Trujillo activities.[95] As noted, Trujillo had friends in the U.S. Congress, either because of his strong anti-Communist policy or because of the expensive lobby he maintained, and he was able to inspire close scrutiny of the activities of Silfa and other exiles. In August 1957 Congressman B. Carroll Reece of Tennessee denounced Silfa before the House of Representatives. He asserted that Silfa, a U.S. citizen, was actively plotting against Trujillo and affirmed that the United States should not permit its citizens to engage in such activities.[96] During the debates on the Galíndez affair, Reece, along with Representative George S. Long of Louisiana, presented a vigorous rebuttal to the assertions of Representative Porter. Senator Olin D. Johnston of South Carolina, described as the "Trujillo-admiring chairman of the U.S. Senate Internal Security Subcommittee," declared in November 1957 that U.S. policy was being influenced by " 'irresponsible revolutionary left-wing groups' of exiles in New York and Miami."[97] With such powerful friends, Trujillo checked quite successfully the activities of Dominican exiles residing in the United States.

The Dominican dictator also exploited fear for the safety of relatives still in the Dominican Republic as a lever against exiles. When Germán Ornes, the editor of *El Caribe* of Ciudad Trujillo, took asylum in the United States in December 1955, his aged father became a virtual prisoner.[98] Porfirio Ramírez, the brother of Miguel Angel, was murdered in 1950 in retaliation for Cayo Confites and Luperón.[99] On the other hand, Trujillo occasionally wooed his antagonists with bribes of money or amnesty. One Dominican exile, a veteran of Cayo Confites, who in 1953 operated a fruit stand at Park Avenue and 113th Street in New York, was reconciled publicly with Consul General Bernardino and rewarded with an $18,000-a-year post as Dominican consul in Los Angeles.[100] The Requena murder had just occurred, and Bernardino had placed a notice in the New York Spanish language press stating that Dominicans wishing to return home but lacking the funds to do so would receive assistance from the consulate.[101] In May 1955 the Dominican Congress passed an amnesty bill, and President Héctor Trujillo announced that the government would help exiles seeking repatriation.[102]

Such were the problems and difficulties confronting Dominican exiles, but their situation was not unique. Other dictators, such as Pérez

Jiménez of Venezuela, also reached out to deal with enemies, wherever they might be. The Venezuelan dictatorship seemed especially anxious to eliminate Rómulo Betancourt. In April 1951 a man attacked Betancourt on a street in Havana and, using a syringe, tried to inject cobra venom into his shoulder. Betancourt fought off the would-be assassin, who fled, but Cuban police reported subsequently that the attacker was Joe Cachatore, one of a group of gangsters from Tampa, Florida, who had been hired by the Venezuelan junta to kill the head of Acción Democrática.[103] In June 1954, when Betancourt had taken up residence in San José, Costa Rica, a Venezuelan aircraft overflew the city and dropped leaflets depicting Betancourt and José Figueres as homosexuals.[104] Betancourt observed that this obscene attack was merely a repetition of the tactics employed by the Seguridad Nacional within Venezuela, and he compared the incident with Venezuela's past, when its armies had fought proudly in foreign campaigns under the "captains of independence."[105] Nonetheless, because his presence placed the government of President Figueres in grave peril from both Venezuela and Nicaragua, Betancourt left Costa Rica in July to reside in Puerto Rico. But the SN continued to track him.

Betancourt made a trip to Mexico in June 1955 to attend the funeral of Andrés Eloy Blanco, who had died in an automobile accident. There, the Mexican secret police notified him of a plot against his life, but assured him that he would be protected and assigned two radio patrol cars to guard him during the remainder of his stay.[106] A year later, according to AD sources, a similar incident occurred in Puerto Rico. Following a meeting in Ciudad Trujillo between Pedro Estrada and Trujillo, three agents of the Seguridad Nacional arrived in Puerto Rico allegedly to carry out a plan to abduct and liquidate Betancourt. The mission was stillborn, because Governor Luis Muñoz Marín, learning about a possible plot, instructed police to watch Betancourt's residence day and night.[107]

When the plot to assassinate Betancourt failed, the Venezuelan regime tried to drive him from Puerto Rico in the same way that it had forced him to leave Costa Rica earlier.[108] Venezuelan authorities raised questions concerning the propriety of Betancourt's activities in Puerto Rico, hoping to influence North American leaders to demand his ouster. It was in this context, in early August 1956, that Pedro Estrada announced the "discovery" of the plot to assassinate Pérez Jiménez and accused Betancourt of directing it from Puerto Rico.[109] Despite Betancourt's denials, the campaign to discredit him continued on several fronts. On 16 August *El Caribe* of Ciudad Trujillo declared that the "close relationship" between Betancourt and Muñoz Marín was "creating a grave problem in inter-American relations" and called upon the U.S. Senate to investigate Betancourt's "subversive" activities. [110] Roldán Bermúdez, the notorious propagandist, was the Venezuelan consul in Puerto Rico. He decried Betancourt's "immunity for conspiracy" and charged that Betancourt was violating his asylum. He, too, observed that it was incumbent upon United States authorities "to investigate the conspiratorial activities of Rómulo Betancourt." [111] Some U.S. Congressmen actually called for the deportation of Betancourt; but Muñoz Marín, supported by liberal elements within the United States, resisted the pressure, and the AD leader remained in Puerto Rico. The vulnerability of Betancourt's position in this instance pointed out yet another problem of exile life, that is, the restrictions upon freedom of action encountered in most places of refuge.

The exiles who seemed to have the most difficulty adjusting to this situation were the Cubans. This may have been because there were so many of them, or because of their persistent activism. A more likely explanation, however, was that they tended to congregate in the two countries most sensitive to the issue of interventionism—Mexico and the United States.

Although Mexico respected the right of asylum, it sought to avoid embarrassment and watched the activities of political exiles carefully. In August 1953, for example, when it was discovered that Mexican arms had been used in Fidel Castro's 26 July assault upon the Moncada Barracks in eastern Cuba, Mexican authorities undertook to prevent arms smuggling to Cuba and expelled two Cuban exiles.[112] However, the Cuban government continued to find Mexican weapons among arms caches uncovered on the island, which caused Mexico to send a special envoy, Benito Coquet, to assure Batista that Cuban exiles would be watched more closely.[113] This surveillance resulted in the arrest in June 1956 of Fidel Castro, Alberto Bayo, Ernesto Guevara, and a score of others on charges of plotting a revolutionary action against Batista.[114] Two months later, authorities in Mérida, Yucatán, prevented another group of *Fidelistas* from shipping arms to Cuba clandestinely. Nevertheless, before the year ended, Castro had invaded Cuba, and Yucatán had served as his staging area. Probably as a result of this experience, during the second half of 1957, Mexico ousted approximately 550 "undesirable" aliens, many of whom were North Americans with criminal records, but also others who were engaged in "political activities considered dangerous or embarrassing to the Mexican government."[115] For this reason, and because Pérez Jiménez had been ousted in Venezuela, Cuban exiles began "flocking" to Caracas in 1958.[116] They also came from New York and Miami.

The situation of the Cuban exiles in the United States was almost identical to that in Mexico. The United States followed a similar if somewhat more energetic policy, in which it provided a haven but would not tolerate violations of its laws. This attitude was clearly stated on 8 September 1954 by Judge Edmund L. Palmieri, who presided over the trial of ex-Presidents Carlos Prío and Carlos Hevia, among others, on charges of conspiracy to send arms and war materials to Cuba in violation of the U.S. Neutrality Act. The trial resulted from the seizure of a huge arms stockpile in Mamaroneck, New York. In assessing only relatively light fines upon Prío and the others (the court had the authority to impose a five-year jail term), Judge Palmieri stated, "It is clear that the defendants are not criminals in the strict sense of the term. However, our laws have been infringed upon."[117] In August 1955 Prío returned to Cuba, but by the following May he was back again in Miami. This time U.S. immigration officials required him to sign a statement as condition for asylum that he would not engage in activities "which may be prejudicial to the public interest," nor violate any U.S. laws.[118] Of course, Prío and his followers continued to conspire, and in 1957 U.S. customs agents were kept "going night and day" trying to prevent arms smuggling to Cuba. One agent, Joseph A. Fortier, estimated that $250,000 in arms and ammunition were seized in South Florida in 1957, and that despite all efforts, "about fifty percent of all contraband shipments managed to slip through."[119] It was obvious, with the Cubans as with all exile groups, that despite hazards and difficulties—personal, financial, physical, and legal—political activity took precedence over everything else. Each group perfected techniques appropriate to its situation.

Politics in Exile

Acción Democrática was the largest of the exile parties and the best organized. As has been seen, AD had capable and articulate leaders, with clearly defined party organs to handle such matters as policy, finances, press and propaganda, and discipline. Rómulo Betancourt, residing in Havana, San José, and San Juan, respectively, was president and head of the National Directorate (Dirección), but after 1954 he was isolated from the rank and file. Rómulo Gallegos was the recognized spokesman in Mexico, and Luis Augusto Dubuc presided over affairs in Costa Rica. Liaison was maintained by the Coordinating Committee, actually something of a secretariat, which Dubuc also administered in Costa Rica. By far the largest number of AD exiles were found in Mexico, where party structure and activity most resembled its preexile form. Here, the Confederation of Workers of Venezuela in exile (CTV), under the direction of AD militants P. B. Pérez Salinas and Augusto Malavé Villalba attended to labor affairs and collaborated closely with the international free trade union movement. Special focus was given to youth and student affairs by the Juventud (Youth) of AD under the leadership of Eduardo González, César Rondón Lovera, Régulo Briceño, and Gilberto Morillo. The most important exile newspaper, *Venezuela Democrática,* was edited in Mexico by Ricardo Montilla and Gonzalo Barrios; fifteen issues were published at irregular intervals between January 1955 and September 1957.

In order to set basic policy and to maintain solidarity and morale, periodic public meetings were held, principally in Mexico and Costa Rica. They were held particularly on the Venezuelan independence days, 19 April (Venezuelan national independence) and 5 July (declaration of independence from Spain), and on the anniversary of the founding of Acción Democrática, 13 September. Party leaders Gallegos, Betancourt, Eloy Blanco, Barrios, and Dubuc normally addressed these assemblies, or sent messages to be read to the party faithful. Eloy Blanco's death in an automobile accident in Mexico on 21 May 1955 occurred just after he had addressed a meeting to mark the second anniversary of the death of Alberto Carnevali. But these meetings were not confined to AD speakers. On the occasion of AD's sixteenth anniversary in 1957, Cuban Mario Llerena addressed the group in Mexico on behalf of the 26 of July Movement, and in San José, Benjamín Núñez and Fernando Fournier of the Costa Rican Liberación Nacional were speakers.[120] Up to 1952, Betancourt's remarks were broadcast to Venezuela from Havana over radio stations CMQ and RHC, and after 1955, the declarations of the leadership were reproduced in *Venezuela Democrática.*

Beginning in 1955, Acción Democrática set aside 21 October as a special day for gatherings and public statements. The anniversary of the death of Leonardo Ruiz Pineda became "The Day of the Heroes" and commemorated not only the martyrdom of Leonardo, but of Alberto Carnevali, Antonio Pinto Salinas, and Cástor Nieves Ríos in the underground and of Andrés Eloy Blanco, Valmore Rodríguez, and Luis Troconis in exile.[121] AD proclaimed these fallen leaders "national heroes," and affirmed that their sacrifice was not partisan but on behalf of the people's struggle against tyranny.[122] The death of Venezuelans in exile inspired AD to recall the campaigns of Bolívar in Colombia, Ecuador, and Peru, when, in the wars of independence, "Venezuelan bones lined the highways of America."[123]

During the first four and a half years of exile, AD leaders were much preoccupied with the activities of the underground. The need to aid and direct the clandestine struggle, as well as the necessity to coordinate actions against the regime inside and outside of Venezuela, absorbed a great deal of the energies and resources of the exiles. The entire orientation of the emigré command was toward exploiting the prevailing political crisis within Venezuela.

In these efforts the exiles had a number of successes. They were able to establish a secure and reliable communications system. They definitely forced the regime to modify its repressive tactics. Betancourt declared that the release of Valmore Rodríguez and others from prison in 1949 did not stem from the "generosity" of Pérez Jiménez but rather from the appeals which Gallegos, Eloy Blanco, and he made before the United Nations for an investigation of the violation of human rights within Venezuela.[124] Likewise, exile agitation was instrumental in the closing of the El Dorado work camp in 1949 and of the Guasina penal colony in 1952. An important achievement was the publication of *The Black Book*—already referred to—which attested to the coordination and communication between the exiles and the underground. A year earlier, a group of exiles, among them Raúl Leoni, Rodríguez, Barrios, and Montilla, had edited a book, *Rómulo Betancourt: Pensamiento y Acción,* which contained the speeches, articles, letters to the editor, and press releases of Betancourt between January 1949 and October 1951. The party's decision not to participate in the elections of 1952 was obviously not followed, but by that time Security Chief Pedro Estrada had the underground on the run, and the tactics of the exiles were altered appreciably.

In its second four and a half years of exile, AD opposed Pérez Jiménez almost entirely from outside the country. It sought primarily to discredit the regime and to place in doubt the legitimacy of its actions. The first step in this regard was the effort to prevent the holding of the Tenth Inter-American Conference in Caracas, or at least to induce a number of countries to boycott it. Although only Costa Rica refused to attend, the national legislatures of Chile and Uruguay passed resolutions critical of the Pérez Jiménez government. The exiles were more successful in organizing a boycott of the Fifth Conference of the Petroleum Committee of the International Labor Organization (ILO) held in Caracas in April 1955. Through the collaboration of the Inter-American Regional Organization of Workers (ORIT), such important unions as the American Federation of Labor (AFL), the Congress of Industrial Organizations (CIO), and the International Federation of Petroleum Workers refused to send representatives.[125] Similarly, the ORIT and its parent organization, the International Confederation of Free Trade Unions (ICFTU), forced the postponement of a conference sponsored by the United Nations Educational, Scientific, and Cultural Organization (UNESCO) scheduled for Caracas in December 1955.[126] This alliance between exile groups and the international free trade union movement will be discussed more fully, but it may be noted here that, because of the activities of Acción Democrática, the Pérez Jiménez dictatorship usually faired badly in dealings with international labor. In cultural affairs, too, the AD exiles frequently embarrassed the dictatorship.

In mid-March 1956 the AD emigrés were incensed to learn that the Pan American Union intended to hold its first "Festival of Books of America" in Caracas that November. *Venezuela Democrática* wrote that it "vexed the mind" to think that such an event was to be held under the auspices of a regime which had committed every possible crime against culture,[127] and the Venezuelan Confederation of Workers (CTV) wired the ICFTU to request its cooperation in denouncing the "farce."[128] From Buenos Aires, a number of Argentine writers, including Jorge Luis Borges, and the Colombian author visiting there, Germán Arciniegas, stated that they would not permit the exhibition of their books in a "festival of hypocrisy."[129] Another group of authors took the same step, declaring in an open letter to the Organization of American States (OAS) that, in view of the anti-intellectual nature of the Venezuelan government and its outrages against freedom of expression, they would not submit their works to the festival. [130] Even across the Atlantic, the Paris newspaper *France Observateur* noted that it was incongruous to hold an inter-American book fair and bar the literary talents of Rómulo Gallegos, Juan Bosch, Eduardo Santos, and Miguel Asturias. [131] It may be questioned whether or not the interests of the Venezuelan dictatorship were served by its sponsorship of such events.

As to international conferences held elsewhere, Acción Democrática was usually present to denounce the dictatorship in Venezuela and to embarrass its representative at the meeting. In January 1956 a group of Venezuelan lawyers in exile, including Barrios, Siso Martínez, and Carlos D'Ascoli, delivered a memorandum to the Third Meeting of the Inter-American Council of Jurists in Mexico in which they raised the question of Venezuela's membership in the OAS. They challenged its right to belong, claiming that its government was illegal and that its "procedures and norms" violated the juridical and political principles of the organization. [132] At a Pan American conference on the aged in Mexico in September 1956, exiled physician Dr. Aníbal Mestre Fuenmayor took the floor and charged that the data presented by the official delegate of Venezuela had been falsified. [133] One month later, the Twelfth Conference of the Inter-American Press Association (IAPA) convened in Havana. Exiled journalist and AD militant Simón Alberto Consalvi addressed the plenary session on 20 October and denounced press censorship and the lack of freedom of expression in Venezuela. He also declared that he was one of thirty-seven Venezuelan journalists in exile. [134] In La Plata, Argentina, in April 1957, in the absence of an official delegation, Venezuelan student exiles attended the Second Latin American Congress of Students and presented a detailed report on the "tragic conditions" of student life in Venezuela. [135] As a result, the congress passed a resolution condemning the suppression of university autonomy in Venezuela and demanding the release of students imprisoned in Caracas and Maracaibo. [136]

In addition to its attacks upon the totalitarian character of the Pérez Jiménez government, AD exposed any incident of inefficiency, immorality, or corruption on the part of the regime. Acción Democrática disputed, for instance, the generalized picture of Venezuela as a prosperous nation. The exiles affirmed that the petroleum resources of the nation were being wastefully exploited and were benefitting only corrupt politicians, the privileged few, and foreign companies. Every issue of *Venezuela Democrática* reiterated this charge. It reported, for example, that, while the people were hungry, Venezuela ranked fifth in 1955 among all nations of the world in the importation of champagne from France, [137] and it cited figures to show that 96.2 percent of public works expenditures were confined to Caracas and the Federal District. [138] Betancourt elaborated fully these themes in his book *Venezuela: Política y Petróleo,* published in 1956. Betancourt wrote that Pérez Jiménez, "like Hitler and Mussolini," engaged in "pyramid-building," which enabled "well-paid press agents" to extol the glories of the regime abroad and provided opportunities for peculators at home but neglected the needs of the people. [139] He observed that Pérez Jiménez had built the most luxurious officers' club in the world but had "put a brake upon" agricultural development [140] and, similarly, that, owing to graft and corruption, the celebrated Caracas-La Guaira *autopista* (superhighway) was the "costliest highway in the world." [141]

Betancourt noted that industrial development had been entrusted to Llovera Páez, whom he described as "the King Faruk of the tropics." [142] Concerning oil policy, he charged that Pérez Jiménez had granted overly generous concessions to the foreign companies and had reduced Venezuela to its former colonial status. [143] For this reason, Betancourt made reference to a warning issued by the clandestine AD in September 1952 that such contracts were made by an illegitimate government not backed by the people and were, therefore, illegal. [144] In an obvious effort to frighten foreign investors and keep Pérez Jiménez off-balance, this threat was repeated on a number of occasions. As late as January 1957, Betancourt reminded investors that there would be a day of reckoning, when all oil concessions would be "reviewed." [145] While pointing out the shortcomings of the Venezuelan government, AD also served as the "conscience" of the international community.

As it had done during the earlier period, Acción Democrática continued to rally international opinion in the area of human rights. In November 1955 student exiles in Mexico petitioned the United Nations and listed specific violations of the Universal Declaration of Human Rights on the part of the Pérez Jiménez regime. With reference to the treatment of students, they cited cases of imprisonment, torture, denial of due process and freedom of movement, and exile. [146] A year later, AD exiles in Mexico again wrote to the UN—this time to Secretary General Dag Hammarskjöld—and affirmed that "flagrant outrages" against human rights persisted in Venezuela. They noted that U.S. President Eisenhower had sympathized with Hungarian victims of barbarism but did not seem to show the same concern for Venezuelans, who were the victims not of a foreign occupying force but of "a dictatorial and despotic government which [had] stifled all liberties and ... shed Venezuelan blood." [147] In May 1957 *Venezuela Democrática* observed that in December the Fourteenth Session of the Human Rights Commission was to meet in Paris, where ten years earlier the nations had adopted the UN Declaration of Human Rights. The exile organ declared that the gathering should not be confined to empty ceremony. "What is there to prevent the regimes whose conduct conforms to the pact," it asked, "from demanding of the others the fulfillment of an obligation undertaken mutually?" [148] One has difficulty in determining the effectiveness of these measures, but it has been noted that AD itself believed such actions restrained the hand of the dictatorship.

There were occasions, however, when the political opposition of Acción Democrática was less statesmanlike. The foreign missions and external activities of the Pérez Jiménez regime were its exposed side, and it was often bruised by AD and its sympathizers. In 1955 the Venezuelan government undertook to exhibit a film abroad, *"Dinámica de un Ideal"* ("Dynamics of an Ideal"), which praised in technicolor the programs of Pérez Jiménez for economic development and public works under the so-called "Ideal Nacional." In mid-August the Venezuelan embassy in Colombia leased the finest theater in Bogotá and through newspaper notices invited the public to attend the showing of the film. On the evening of the performance, AD exiles gathered outside the theater and distributed a handbill denouncing "the tyrannical nature of the Venezuelan regime and [its] false policy of ostentatious works." During a reception following the showing, the Venezuelan military attaché spoke abusively about the conduct of the exiles, but a foreign diplomat at the affair read the handbill aloud in order to demonstrate its "civility." [149]

Later the same month, the Venezuelan embassy in Havana rented the Teatro Blanquita in order to show the film but this time avoided publicity and sent invitations only to the diplomatic corps and to high Cuban military and civil authorities. Nonetheless, the minute the lights were turned down and the projection started, "hundreds" of voices shouted, *"Viva Venezuela libre! Abajo las dictaduras de Pérez Jiménez y Batista!"* ("Long live free Venezuela! Down with the dictatorships of Pérez Jiménez and Batista!"), and "thousands" of leaflets rained down upon the audience. The presentation ended at that point; representatives of the exile community and of the Havana University Student Federation (FEU) had infiltrated the theater, and the gathering broke up in disorder. This time, even the reception planned for after the performance was canceled.[150] The Venezuelan government decided to try one more time. Proceeding almost clandestinely, Angarita Arvelo, the Venezuelan ambassador in Mexico, arranged a showing in Mexico City in the private screening room of a film laboratory. However, the ambassador's security measures were not totally successful; a critic of Pérez Jiménez penetrated the select audience and, following the showing, "dedicated a few lines" to the film on a wall in the men's room.[151]

Some months after these events, the Venezuelan embassy in Havana filed a complaint against Venezuelan exiles Simón A. Consalvi, César O. Hernández, Rubén Antonio Muñoz, and Gerardo Estaba, all prime suspects in the Teatro Blanquita affair, and charged them with pelting the embassy building with rocks, eggs, and tomatoes. Although the exiles denied the accusation, a demonstration had taken place before the embassy on 22 February 1956, resulting at the time in the arrest of a number of Havana University student leaders.[152] Much later, the harried Arvelo in Mexico clashed openly with Venezuelan student exiles. He had scheduled a ceremony for 5 July 1957 before the Bolívar statue in Mexico City to commemorate independence from Spain, but when he arrived, the Venezuelan students were already there. They had placed a floral wreath before the Liberator's statue and had begun a round of oratory. The ambassador reacted angrily and demanded that the authorities break up the student rally, which resulted in a shouting and shoving melée and in a few hours of detention for AD youth leader, Régulo Briceño.[153] Given the persecution that AD had suffered, it was surprising there were not more incidents as these, but, paradoxically, the long years in exile had something of a mellowing effect upon the party.

By 1957 AD was less partisan in its attitude, more willing to enter into a coalition with other Venezuelan political groups, and hopeful that Pérez Jiménez would permit an electoral solution to the nation's political problems. During the years of AD rule, 1945-48, its relations with other civilian parties were poor, and after it was ousted in 1948, it resented deeply the continued participation of these parties in national political life. However, following the election of 1952, Jóvito Villalba and other leaders of the Democratic Republican Union (URD) were forced into exile, and the Christian Democrats (COPEI), while still operating legally within Venezuela, were constantly harassed. Several attempts were made upon the life of *copeyano* leader Rafael Caldera. In the crucible of common adversity, with evidence that the tide was turning against the dictators, and with Pérez Jiménez' term of office due to expire at the end of 1957, AD's tactics underwent a change.

The earliest indication of this change was exhibited by Betancourt in a statement, "Reaffirmation of the Faith," on the occasion of the fourteenth anniversary of Acción Democrática, 13 September 1955. Acknowledging that the "despotism" appeared established and that the clandestine movement had been crushed in 1953, he insisted, nonetheless, that beneath the surface in Venezuela unrest and insurgency were "equal to other years." He said that he discerned "promising signs," which included economic difficulties internally and growing opposition to dictatorship internationally. Moreover, he observed, U.S.-Soviet relations had improved, which, he believed, might cause the United States to be less tolerant of regimes whose only virtues were stability and outspoken anticommunism. Under these circumstances, he invited the URD and COPEI to join AD in a "Front for Liberty."[154] This suggestion was followed up quickly by Acción Democrática in a "Conference of Exiles" held in Puerto Rico in January 1956. The conference was convened to plan a course of action with reference to the anticipated crisis of the election year, and the AD exiles adopted the so-called *"la nueva táctica"* (the New Tactic), which called for "a policy of full and active cooperation with all other political parties."[155] The New Tactic did not mature immediately into a coalition of AD, URD, and COPEI, but events during 1956 favored this development.

Toward the end of 1956, AD's exile Coordinating Committee completed a study which declared that important groups within Venezuela would not tolerate a repetition of the events of December 1952, when Pérez Jiménez usurped the presidency, and concluded that a political change was inevitable. The committee reported that one by one the dictators of Latin America were falling, and it listed specifically Juan Perón of Argentina, Manuel Odría of Peru, Julio Lozano Díaz of Honduras, and Paul Magloire of Haiti.[156] The committee was especially heartened by the example of Odría, the Peruvian dictator, who had voluntarily stepped down in June 1956 and had permitted honest elections for the choice of his successor. On this basis, the Coordinating Committee called for "a democratic and peaceful solution to the question of the presidential succession."[157] These sentiments were repeated by Betancourt in a luncheon address at the Carnegie International Center in New York on 12 January 1957. Betancourt stated: "We are not fomenting revolutions and we believe appropriate for Venezuela what has already occurred in Peru: the transition from a regime of force to one which is democratic by the normal way of the ballot box." [158] Agitation for free elections became the basis for unifying the Venezuelan opposition groups, and the New Tactic was set.

During 1957 the New Tactic developed into a formal coalition. Acción Democrática negotiated with the leadership of URD in exile and of COPEI within and without Venezuela. By mid-year, AD stated explicitly its repudiation of violence and subversion and pledged to seek "necessary changes" in a spirit of "patriotic harmony." It added that its agreement with URD and COPEI on this point was so firm that any one of them could speak for all of them.[159] The Venezuelan Confederation of Workers (CTV) in exile also endorsed this concept. On 10 June it called upon AD, COPEI, and URD to form a "Grand Front of National Salvation" in order to choose a presidential candidate and to work in "harmony and coexistence" for "economic reconstruction and institutional stability."[160] Following Pérez Jiménez' announcement on 26 July that elections would be held on 15 December, Betancourt met with news reporters in Washington and affirmed the decision of "the three, large democratic parties" to seek a "pacific and evolutionary solution." He expressed skepticism over the kind of guarantees Pérez Jiménez would make but gave assurances that if a free electoral process evolved, the three parties would have no difficulty in selecting a single candidate (*"un candidato único"*).[161] At the same time, *Venezuela Democrática* reproduced a cable from Villalba to Pérez Jiménez in which the URD leader advised Pérez Jiménez to reject the counsels of *continuismo,* to fulfill the Constitution which he had sworn to uphold, and to follow the example of his Peruvian "teacher" (Odría).[162]

By the time of AD's sixteenth anniversary, 13 September 1957, Betancourt was able to outline specifically the plan for unified action agreed upon by the democratic parties. He announced, first, that despite misgivings about the origin and background of the present government and constitution, the three parties would participate in elections sponsored by that government and under procedures established by that constitution, provided essential freedoms were restored and a general amnesty was declared; second, that AD, COPEI, and URD had agreed to support a single candidate for president; and, third, that the parties had resolved to enter into an agreement designed to avoid partisan strife in the future and to "eliminate forever" political extremism.[163] The terms of the agreement, according to Betancourt, were being circulated within Venezuela by the clandestine apparatus and abroad by the exiled leaders of AD, by Villalba of URD, and by Luis Herrera Campins of COPEI.[164] Implicit in the New Tactic was also the possibility of a golpe. AD's aversion to a military coup was long-standing, but its moderate position was calculated to woo the armed forces and provide the justification for them to act.

Whichever way the deepening political crisis might go, AD hoped to detach a significant sector of the military from Pérez Jiménez. In his message, Betancourt stated that the "electoralist thesis," along with AD's express pledge to refrain from conspiracy and violent revolution, had allayed the fears of "an important nucleus" of the military. He added that Pérez Jiménez was supported only by the Seguridad Nacional and the armed forces, but that of the latter merely a small minority had received favors from the regime; the majority had remained loyal, he explained, because it had been misled into believing that the democratic parties intended to get rid of the army and even "to annihilate physically" anyone wearing a military uniform. Betancourt repeated that the electoralist policy was breaking down this "wall of apprehension."[165] On the same occasion, Malavé Villalba, speaking on behalf of the CTV, declared that Venezuelan labor was disposed to find an "adequate and just solution" to Venezuela's political problem, without "vengeance or retaliation."[166] Betancourt noted, however, that after announcing elections, Pérez Jiménez had established a news blackout and on 23 August had arrested Caldera, who, it was generally assumed, was the likely "candidato único." For these reasons, Betancourt affirmed that the demand for free elections would continue until 15 December but that, if it was ignored, the way remained open "for other forms of struggle and other methods of action."[167]

Without being cynical or insincere, AD made provision for the early exploration of "other forms . . . and methods." It made contact with potential golpistas, but this step was top secret and done only at the highest level.[168] The underground began to stir and in February 1957 started to distribute again two of its newssheets, *Ofensiva* and *Resistencia*. However, the underground was expressly prohibited from engaging in conspiracies.[169] When Simón Sáez Mérida was ordered to enter Venezuela in October and to assume command of the clandestine movement, an antigovernment movement under the so-called Junta Patriótica had already been organized, but AD was not represented. [170] This junta, which led the popular uprising against Pérez Jiménez in January 1958, was directed by *urredista* Fabricio Ojeda, a young journalist, and was comprised mainly of young people and students. The Communist party was also active in the movement, which enabled it for a time following the fall of Pérez Jiménez to join the AD-COPEI-URD coalition.

The main tasks of Sáez Mérida were to organize AD's clandestine apparatus and to inform the party about developing conspiracies. Any negotiations, however, were to be conducted by AD's top level leadership. According to Sáez Mérida, "the civilian acciondemocratistas who conspired in December 1957 and January 1958 did so at their own risk, except in cases where they were authorized by the organization or where the party had made some commitment."[171] In this flux, Pérez Jiménez provided the ingredient for his own downfall when he tried to perpetuate himself in office by means of a plebiscite in which he was "el candidato único." Elements of the air force failed to bring down the dictator in a New Year's Day revolt; but after three weeks of crisis, in which even SN chief Pedro Estrada was fired, the Junta Patriótica led the people into the streets in bloody rioting, and Pérez Jiménez fled. Ironically, AD's role in the overthrow of Pérez Jiménez was in manpower rather than in leadership; yet, the regime was toppled by the kind of popular revolt envisioned by Leonardo Ruiz Pineda and the early strategy of the clandestine AD.

The leaders of Acción Democrática had lived through another exile. But survival was not the sole aspect of AD's exile. During nine years it effectively opposed the dictatorship and maintained a party structure, so that it quickly became an important element in the liberated country. As will be seen, AD eventually regained power and continued the struggle against the dictators of the Caribbean. Few parties of the Democratic Left in exile enjoyed the same dramatic success as Acción Democrática, probably because none of them was as well-organized. Yet, all of them contributed to the changes occurring in the Caribbean near the end of the decade of the 1950s, so that even their failures may not be ignored by history.

In this respect, the Cuban Auténticos in exile, while disappointed in the end, helped to bring down the Batista dictatorship. On the surface, the Auténticos were as strong as any party of the Democratic Left in exile. They possessed an organization with experience in national political office, they had substantial financial resources, and their leader in exile was the deposed constitutional president Carlos Prío Socarrás. Upon a closer look, one found serious problems. First of all, the Cubans were deeply divided. A number of rival parties existed, including the Cuban People's party, or Ortodoxo, and the Communist Popular Socialist party (PSP). The Auténticos were themselves rent by factionalism of the personalist variety, which revealed a fundamental weakness of the party. Second, the Auténticos had been discredited during their years in office. Under them, graft and corruption had been widespread, and gangsterism, or *pistolerismo*, had reached an alarming state. Cubans had been shocked and ashamed by Batista's coup, but they seemed disposed initially to give him a chance to correct these ills. Moreover, Batista (especially in the beginning) tolerated the press, organized labor, and even political parties, and left open the doors of Havana University. As already noted, he also permitted a number of Caribbean exiles to remain in Cuba, much to the chagrin of the Dominican dictator Trujillo.

Under these circumstances, the Auténticos found it difficult to arouse sympathy for their cause, particularly with many Cubans disillusioned by their previous leadership. They, therefore, as well as other Cuban exile groups, tended to rely upon conspiratorial activity. They made some efforts of a nonviolent nature, depicting Batista as a tyrant and rallying international opinion against his regime, particularly after 1956, but most of their energy and resources were spent in active and violent forms of opposition. Guerrilla and revolutionary activity already occupied a special place in Cuban history and politics. Even pistolerismo had strong political antecedents, so that the question of whether or not this phenomenon was political or criminal may be better resolved in specific cases than in general terms. Men such as Aureliano Sánchez Arango, Eufemio Fernández, Fidel Castro, Rolando Masferrer, and Policarpo Soler differed in their ideals and political scrupples, or lack of them, but their activism was in the Cuban political tradition. Not all Cuban political leaders, of course, were activists in the violent sense. Nonetheless, the most successful usually had a patron-client relationship with leaders of activist groups. In power and in exile, Prío, the Auténtico leader, filled the patrician's role.

Ideologically, Prío belonged to the democratic camp, even if the dishonesty which marked his administration was embarrassing. While

president, he gave refuge to Betancourt and Bosch, and his support of
the exile cause was vigorous and generous. In exile, his status among
these leaders remained intact. Less than five months following his overthrow, he was the guest of Governor Luis Muñoz Marín at the ceremonies proclaiming the new Constitution of the Commonwealth of
Puerto Rico.[172] Prío operated from both Mexico and the United
States, and, while the source of his fortune was questionable, he gave
extensive financial support to schemes for the overthrow of Batista. In
fact, if Batista himself was a reliable source, though he probably exaggerated, as of April 1957 Prío had spent five to six million dollars
buying arms and shipping them to Cuba for revolutionary purposes.[173]
Prío's difficulties with the United States for engaging in arms smuggling
have already been described, but these cases give some indication of the
amount of money which Prío contributed to the struggle against
Batista.

Prío's name figured prominently in virtually every revolutionary
action in Cuba from the time of his fall to that of Batista on 1 January
1959. Prío supplied arms to Fidel Castro for his famous attack upon
the Moncada barracks in Oriente Province on 26 July 1953. Later, in
1955, when Castro went into exile in Mexico and began training a
revolutionary band to invade Cuba, Prío again supplied the necessary
arms and funds. Still later, after Castro was in the Sierra Maestra waging
his guerrilla struggle, financial assistance, though perhaps in diminishing
amounts, continued to come from Prío. In the meantime, since Castro
had been an Ortodoxo, Aureliano Sánchez Arango formed an action
group, the so-called "Triple A" (Asociación Amigos de Aureliano), in
1954 in order to give the Auténticos a more direct role in the revolutionary activity.[174] On the surface, it appeared that he had broken
with Prío, but the split was more tactical than political, and Sánchez
Arango received Auténtico assistance in his activities.[175] Another
group of Auténticos under Calixto Sánchez formed the Organización
Auténtica, which made a landing on the north coast of Oriente in May
1957. Batista's forces captured the group, however, and executed a
number of them.[176] Later the same year, in September, Prío was involved in a revolt by elements of the navy at Cienfuegos. This time, one
of his top lieutenants, Antonio de Varona, acted as the principal contact man.[177] On a number of occasions during these years, "Tony"
Varona shuttled back and forth between Miami and Cuba as liaison
between Prío and insurgent elements inside Cuba.

Prío and the Auténticos also endeavored to unify the rival groups opposing Batista. One of the earliest efforts took place in June 1953 in Montreal, Canada. There, important Auténtico and Ortodoxo leaders, including Prío, Varona, Carlos Hevia, Emilio Ochoa, Eduardo Rivas, and José Pardo Llada, met and signed the "Montreal Pact," which demanded that Batista step down and called for the restoration of the Constitution of 1940 and the holding of elections under the auspices of a provisional government.[178] Probably at the same time Prío agreed to supply arms to the young Ortodoxo leader in Cuba, Fidel Castro. In August 1955 Prío returned to Cuba specifically for the purpose of organizing a united front against Batista, but factionalism persisted, and Prío found the task impossible. Nonetheless, Batista still considered him a threat and expelled him again in May 1956, just in time to enable him to render effective assistance to Castro.[179]

The period of Fidel Castro's exile in Mexico, 1955-56, was an interesting one. Most of the dictators of the Caribbean seemed to be at their apogee. Mexico, always an exile Mecca, was a last refuge. Many of the emigrés were frustrated and angry, and their mood was sharpened by a bitter and resentful group of exiles which had come from Guatemala after the overthrow of Jacobo Arbenz in 1954. Others had moved from Costa Rica, where Figueres had just survived another attack by Somoza, and from Puerto Rico, where Muñoz Marín was being pressured to expel Betancourt. The governor himself was being denounced by the more extreme elements, owing to the influence of the Puerto Rican Nationalists. Anti-United States sentiment was at its highest, and the Soviet embassy was in close touch. In this atmosphere, Castro secured a hacienda outside of Mexico City and began training forty to fifty men for an invasion of Cuba. Most of the men were Cubans, but the young Argentine "Che" Guevara and the old Spaniard Alberto Bayo, both of whom had fled Guatemala in 1954, instructed the group in guerrilla warfare. In June Mexican authorities raided the hacienda and arrested Castro and others and seized a quantity of arms and ammunition. Later, in August, the Mexican government threatened to expel Castro. However, this time he avoided arrest and, with arms and equipment supplied by Prío and Figueres, managed to sail from Yucatán for Cuba at the end of November 1956.

Once the fighting broke out in Cuba and Castro's movement showed signs of persevering, the Cuban political groups recognized the need for cooperation among them. In October 1957 the groups in opposition to

Batista met in Miami and formed the Council of Cuban Liberation (Junta de Liberación Cubana). The only real common denominator was their opposition to the Cuban dictator, but they managed to agree upon a statement calling for democratic government and for social and economic reforms under the Constitution of 1940. The signatories to the agreement were: Prío, Hevia, and Varona for the Auténticos; Manuel Bisbé and Roberto Agramonte for the Ortodoxos; Felipe Pazos for the 26 of July Movement; Carlos Maristany for the Organización Auténtica; Ramón Prendes for the University Students Federation (FEU); Fauré Chaumón for the Directorio Revolucionario (a revolutionary organization made up of students operating in Havana); and Angel Cofiño of the *Directorio Revolucionario de Trabajadores* (Cuban organized labor had not broken with the Batista regime).[180] Subsequently, Castro disavowed membership in the council and denounced the leaders in exile for "presuming" to speak for those who were making the sacrifices in the mountains.[181]

Castro's decision to go it alone proved costly. He lost the financial support of Prío and, lacking the support of the other groups, was unable to bring off a general strike in April 1958. After the fall of Pérez Jiménez, Caracas became the principal Cuban exile center, but, in an obvious effort to strengthen Prío's hand, Betancourt made Venezuelan support conditional upon political unity.[182] In July, Castro changed his mind and entered into the "Pact of Caracas," which was essentially the same as the Miami agreement. It called for a provisional government comprised of the various factions and for prompt general elections. Manuel Urrutia signed for Castro; Varona for the Auténticos; and Bisbé for the Ortodoxos.[183] The Communists were not represented.

Castro resented the need to make concessions to the exiled political leaders and, once Batista fell, made it difficult for them to collect their political debts. He succeeded because of a number of factors, which included the suddenness of Batista's flight, the disintegration of the Cuban army, his own charisma, and the unexpected military preponderance of the guerrilla forces. In addition, not even seven years had erased the disappointment of Cubans over the Auténtico administrations, nor the memory of Prío's meek surrender to Batista in March 1952. Nonetheless, the Auténticos contributed substantially to Castro's overthrow of Batista. They gave him more than logistical support; they gave his movement legitimacy. In the context of exile political activity during the 1950s, the antidictatorial struggle of the Democratic Left had won wide support, and Castro became identified with it through Prío and the Auténticos. Castro, however, soon repudiated this image, leaving the Auténticos and the Democratic Left to face an uncertain future not only in Cuba but in the entire Caribbean.

While this situation was developing with reference to Cuba, the exiles of the Dominican Republic were also trying to find the means for overcoming the Caribbean's most entrenched dictator, Rafael L. Trujillo. The Dominican exiles had been scattered the longest. Angel Morales and Miguel Angel Ramírez had gone into exile in 1930, and Juan Bosch, Angel Miolán, and Nicolás Silfa joined them in 1937. Not too long afterward, they were followed by Juan Isidro Jiménez-Grullón and Horacio Julio Ornes. Juan Rodríguez García and José Antonio Bonilla Atiles were relative newcomers in 1945 and 1946 respectively. By the time Germán Ornes went into exile in December 1955, he complained that he found an "aristocracy of exiledom," in which those who had been in exile the longest looked down upon the recent arrivals and regarded them with suspicion as collaborationists.[184]   Although the observation of Germán Ornes probably stemmed from his former close connection with Trujillo, the Dominican exiles were, indeed, divided into factions and cliques.

The political organizations of the exiled Dominicans were, themselves, creatures of exile. Before Trujillo, there were no true political parties; after he came to power, none were tolerated. The pre-Trujillo, personalist-oligarchical factions of former presidents Juan Isidro Jiménez and Horacio Vásquez, the "Jimenistas" and the "Horacistas," were represented in exile by Juan Isidro Jiménez·Grullón and Angel Morales, respectively, but they lacked any real organization. The closest that the Dominicans came to a political party in the modern sense was the Dominican Revolutionary party, PRD (Partido Revolucionario Dominicano), which was founded in Havana in 1939 by Bosch and Miolán. Other groups, all founded in exile, were at best splinter parties and at worst a handful of followers of a single leader. The latter remained independent possibly for ideological reasons but more likely to gratify a sense of self-importance fed by the need to include them in united front movements or coalitions.

The PRD almost alone had a program and an organization. It represented the ideals of liberal democracy and it had strong leanings toward socialist philosophy in the economic sphere. Despite the Batista dictatorship, it maintained headquarters in Cuba until 1958, when it moved to Caracas. Bosch was the president of the party and the head of its Political Committee, and Miolán was the secretary general. Among its branches, Ramón Castillo was the secretary of the section in Puerto Rico, and Silfa was the secretary in New York.[185] Other important leaders included Alexis Liz and Buenaventura Sánchez. The party had been involved in the movements of the Caribbean Legion, but in the 1950s it operated quite effectively in the nonviolent sphere. Owing to the contacts of Bosch with democratic leaders and organizations, it managed to elicit strong denunciations of the Trujillo regime internationally. The size of its membership was conjectural, and it apparently was short of funds. However, it persisted in exile for over two decades and it was the principal organizer of protests against Trujillo in the exile community.

The rival groups were a collage of political tendencies and personal ambitions. Aside from the Communists, only one of these organizations lasted beyond the exile years. It was the Dominican Revolutionary Vanguard, VRD (Vanguardia Revolucionaria Dominicana), founded in Puerto Rico in late 1956 by Horacio Julio Ornes and Miguel A. Pardo. It represented generally the ambitions of Horacio Ornes, who was supported by business and professional men in exile in Puerto Rico. Horacio Ornes and Pardo were the party's secretary general and president, respectively. The VRD had two branches, one in Mexico under Tancredo Martínez, and the other in New York directed by Ricardo Roques Martínez.[186] Another group in Puerto Rico was the Dominican Populist Party, PPD (Partido Populista Dominicana), which set up a picket line each week in front of the Dominican consulate general in San Juan.[187] Its leader was Francisco Javier Guilliani, who also made periodic radio broadcasts to the Dominican Republic (the author has searched in vain for any reference to him after Trujillo's death in 1961).

In 1956 a group known as the Dominican Popular Movement, MPD (Movimiento Popular Dominicano), published an exile newspaper, *Libertad,* in Havana. [188] This may have been the same MPD which Máximo López Molina organized in the Dominican Republic in 1960 and which later Ambassador John Bartlow Martin described as "Castro/ Communist" and as advocating terrorism in defiance of the "old Communists."[189] Of similar nebulous background was the Dominican Liberating Action (Acción Libertadora Dominicana), an exile organization in New York, which occasionally joined the Dominican Revolutionary party (PRD) in protest demonstrations. There was also the Dominicans in Exile, whose spokesman was Juan Díaz, a long time activist and the proprietor of a small *bodega* (grocery store) in New York.[190]   Bonilla Atiles, who had been the vice-rector of the University of Santo Domingo before he fled the Dominican Republic, headed a group in New York called the Dominican Revindication Association and edited its publication, *ARDE*. Bonilla Atiles was influential among the exiles and an essential member of any united front movement. [191] One such movement was the Requena Memorial Committee, which, while strongly influenced by PRD leader Silfa, was broadly based, be-cause the Requena murder served as a rallying point for the numerous Dominican exile factions.

Such loose coalitions, in fact, characterized the activities of the Dominican exiles in New York. They reacted together in the Requena and Galíndez affairs and, with the help of such groups as the Inter-American Association for Democracy and Freedom (IADF), contrib-uted to the disrepute of Trujillo in many sectors of U.S. opinion. They organized protests against Trujillo when he came to the United States for four months beginning in December 1952, as the Dominican repre-sentative before the United Nations. Even when Trujillo went to Washington in January, Silfa followed him there with a group of pickets. They demonstrated outside the Mayflower Hotel, where Tru-jillo was staying (the police would not permit them to get too close, for Trujillo had ambassadorial rank and there was a District of Columbia ordinance prohibiting demonstrations within five-hundred feet of an embassy). The pickets wore black mourning bands and carried a coffin, in memory of Requena, and distributed leaflets admonishing the United States for "dealing with ruthless dictatorships."[192]

When Trujillo returned to the UN the following month, the demon-strators turned up again, with their mourning bands and coffin. Trujillo reacted to such harassment, the press noted, by employing twice as many bodyguards as the Russian delegate, Andrei Vyshinsky.[193] Tru-jillo also organized a counter-demonstration—in February, he brought one thousand, three hundred "Dominicans" from New York to Wash-ington in a special train, in order to march in support of him.[194] At the same time, as previously noted, the Dominican consulate general in New York made an offer of amnesty and promised free passage home to "repentant Dominicans." Nonetheless, when Trujillo visited the United States again in August 1954 and was honored at a luncheon at Blair House, the PRD, Requena Memorial Committee, and Acción Libertadora Dominicana were close-by on the sidewalk on the other side of Pennsylvania Avenue. They circled before the White House and carried placards, one of which declared: "It is understandable that [the] tyrant Trujillo should have been welcomed in Madrid, but this should never happen in Washington."[195] The exiles encountered difficulties in holding these demonstrations, because there was a residue of nervousness in Washington as a result of the attempt by Puerto Rican Nationalists to assassinate President Truman in 1950. But neither hostile attitudes nor even the weather deterred the pickets; on 20 December 1955, in fourteen-degree weather, they demonstrated in New York against the opening of Trujillo's ill-starred "Fair of Peace and Fraternity of the Free World." How, they asked, could a fair dedicated to "brotherhood" be held under a "tyranny"? [196]

The disappearance of Galíndez, of course, spurred the anti-Trujillo activities of the Dominican exiles. As has been noted, they were assisted in this cause by liberal elements in New York. On 12 June 1956, after Galíndez had been missing for three months, a memorial service was held in the New York Community Church. The speakers included Norman Thomas, Frances Grant, Sabi Nehama (of the International Ladies' Garment Workers' Union) and Juan Díaz, and the assembly passed a resolution urging a Congressional investigation of the Galíndez case. [197] On the same day, homage was paid Galíndez in Puerto Rico by Angel Morales, Leovigildo Cuello, and Horacio Ornes, on behalf of the "United Dominican Front."[198] On the first anniversary of the Galíndez disappearance, "fifty American, Basque, Dominican and Spanish organizations" sponsored a memorial program in New York in the Casa de Galicia. Representative Charles O. Porter was the principal speaker; Juan Díaz and Nicolás Silfa also spoke.[199] In the meantime, as previously described, the Trujillo regime took steps to counteract the bad publicity of the Galíndez affair. One of these measures was a letter to the *New York Times* in praise of Trujillo from a number of prominent Dominicans. Because one of the signatories was The Most Reverend Ricardo Pittini, the Archbishop of Santo Domingo, Nicolás Silfa wrote to Pope Pius XII criticizing the archbishop's stand.[200] Two years later, Silfa wrote to the new pope, John XXIII, and, describing himself as "a devout Catholic," charged that representatives of the Catholic church in the Dominican Republic and the United States were supporting Trujillo. He requested a papal inquiry of these charges.[201] In August 1956, the "Dominican Cultural Society," a pro-Trujillo group, picketed the *New York Times* to protest "criticisms" of Trujillo; but the anti-Trujillo groups quickly appeared (Dominicans-in-Exile, Requena Memorial Committee, Spanish Republicans-in-Exile, and the PRD) to picket the pickets and to distribute leaflets attacking Trujillo as "a murderer and torturer."[202] The following year, in the context of the Galíndez-Murphy affair, Acción Libertadora Dominicana requested the State Department to demand that Trujillo and his family get out of the Dominican Republic. According to "secret sources" inside the Dominican Republic, the group insisted, "a firm and unequivocal request by the State Department" would force Trujillo to step down.[203]

The Dominican exiles, with their protests and demonstrations, seemed puny in comparison with the dictatorship of Trujillo, but their activities had important effects. They denied to Trujillo the complete submissiveness he demanded. They contributed to an atmosphere which facilitated a shift in U.S. policy when it became necessary to do so. Trujillo himself overreacted to the exile activities, which caused his regime additional scorn and ridicule. Despite the factional differences, the Dominican Revolutionary party developed an adequate machinery and acquired sufficient prestige, so that when the time came it could try to provide a democratic alternative for a people who had known only tyranny for thirty years. The PRD was free from any collaborationist taint, a claim not even the Communists could make.

The discussion of exile political activity to this point has stressed the role of the Democratic Left without reference to the issue of communism. The issue existed, of course, but, although the dictators constantly raised it as a smear tactic, it related specifically to the orientation of the Guatemalan government under Jacobo Arbenz. The Guatemalan case compounded the difficulties of the Democratic Left, for it provided a base for its rivals of the Communist Left and also tended to strengthen the hand of the dictatorial Right. The Guatemalan situation, moreover, had a direct bearing upon events in the rest of Central America. The rivalry between Costa Rica and Nicaragua and the hopes of Nicaraguan exile groups were especially affected. For these reasons, exile movements in Central America comprise a very special story during the 1950s.

Guatemala, Costa Rica, and Nicaragua

The struggle of the Democratic Left in exile against dictatorship was never clear-cut, but the problem of communism in Guatemala after

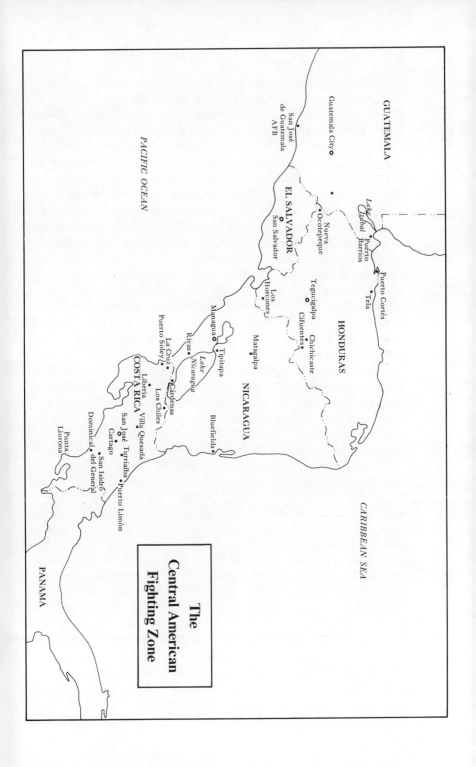

The
Central American
Fighting Zone

1950 complicated the situation still further. Evidence of growing Communist influence in the government of Jacobo Arbenz created a dilemma for the democratic exiles because of their avowed support of the ideals of the Guatemalan Revolution and their open collaboration with Juan José Arévalo, the predecessor of Arbenz. Although they regarded the Communists as political rivals, they looked upon the dictators of the Caribbean as more serious threats to the peace and well-being of the area. They were certain that if the dictators were defeated, the Communist threat would diminish. Under these circumstances, they deplored the anticommunism of the dictators as fraudulent and counterrevolutionary and even as enhancing the position of the Communists by identifying them with the achievement of legitimate revolutionary goals. The problem, however, was the attitude of the United States, which at best viewed the position of the Democratic Left as naïve and as minimizing the Communist infiltration in Guatemala and at worst as pro-Communist.

Undoubtedly, the fact that the leaders of the Democratic Left considered the Communists as mere political rivals caused them to appear soft on this issue. Strengthening this impression was the seeming similarity of goals of the Democratic Left and the Communists and the fact that they both appealed to the same constituency and employed the same revolutionary language. Nonetheless, although they did not fear the Communists, the Democratic Left generally refused to cooperate with them in the antidictatorial struggle, because they considered them insincere. They declared explicitly that the Communists were unreliable and that their purpose was to convert the campaign against the Caribbean's dictators into one against the United States.[204] They charged that the Communists subordinated their activities to the goals of Soviet foreign policy and that they were guided by expediency.[205] In addition, the Venezuelan Acción Democrática shunned the Communists in order to maintain the support of "liberal and democratic elements" in the United States.[206] Rómulo Betancourt referred to these elements as the "other side of Uncle Sam" and indicated that he valued their support so highly he avoided contact with the Communists.[207] But this was as far as the Democratic Left would go, lest its opposition to communism be construed as alignment with the United States. The democratic exiles exhibited contempt for official U.S. policy, which, they affirmed, "financed and decorated Latin American dictators."[208] These same factors determined the attitude of the Democratic Left with reference to the state of affairs in Guatemala.

Exiled Communist leaders were conspicuous in Guatemala. This fact alone was not unusual—during the same time, exiled Communists found refuge in Havana and Mexico—but the Communist exiles were also active in Guatemalan political affairs. The Cuban Communist leaders, Salvador Aguirre, Blas Roca, Juan Marinello, and Lázaro Peña, were frequent visitors to Guatemala. These were old hands, whose "advice, experience, and prestige," according to Ronald Schneider, "greatly aided the young Guatemalan Marxists in their rise to control of organized labor."[209]

Playing a similar role, though no exile, was the Mexican Communist Vicente Lombardo Toledano, whose Confederation of Latin American Workers, CTAL (Confederación de Trabajadores de América Latina), was a principal vehicle for organizing Guatemalan labor and for bringing it under Communist control.[210] The Venezuelan Communist leaders Gustavo Machado and Juan Bautista Fuenmayor were also frequent visitors to Guatemala.[211] However, among the most active of the foreign Communist leaders were the Salvadorans, Miguel Mármol Chicas, Abel and Max Cuenca Martínez, and Virgilio Guerra Méndez, who helped found the Confederation of Guatemalan Workers, CTG (Confederación de Trabajadores de Guatemala), in August 1945. They were also responsible for organizing the Escuela Claridad, a Communist indoctrination school, which Arévalo ordered closed in January 1946.[212]

A number of Nicaraguan Marxists, among them Alejandro Bermúdez Alegría, Armando Flores Amador, Edelberto Torres, Sr., and Edelberto Torres, Jr., took active part in Guatemalan political affairs. Both the older and younger Torres were members of the Guatemalan Labor party (PGT). Torres, Sr., concerning whom the author is reluctant to apply any label, taught at San Carlos University and was the chief of press of the Ministry of Education, which published the *Revista del Maestro*.[213] The young Torres was very active in the Communist youth movement. During 1952-54, he served as secretary general of the Alliance of Guatemalan Democratic Youth, AJDG (Alianza de la Juventud Democrática Guatemalteca), an affiliate of the Communist World Federation of Democratic Youth, and he traveled to Communist-sponsored youth festivals in Berlin (1951) and Bucharest (1953), with a trip to the Soviet Union and China after Bucharest.[214]

The Dominican Communists were young and inexperienced but deeply involved. The Ducoudray brothers, Juan and Félix, and Pericles Franco directed the Dominican Popular Socialist party, PSPD (Partido Socialista Popular Dominicano), in exile in Guatemala. This was the

Dominican Communist party, but they also belonged to the Guatemalan Labor party, PGT (Partido Guatemalteco del Trabajo). They published a monthly newspaper, *Orientación,* and conducted a regularly scheduled radio broadcast, "Solidarity with Santo Domingo," over TGWA, Guatemala City.[215] In early 1952 they undertook to organize all Dominican exiles under a Committee of Dominican Exiles (Comité de Exilados Dominicanos), and in June their "Solidarity" broadcast claimed a favorable response to this project from Dominicans everywhere.[216]

Other national groups in exile established similar "united front" organizations in Guatemala, purposely exploiting the ambiguity of the position of the Democratic Left. With a secure base, sufficient funds, and an antidictatorial and national revolutionary program, these movements attracted exile activists who represented a wide variety of political viewpoints. These organizations included the Salvadoran Democratic Association (Asociación Democrática Salvadoreña), the Movement of Nicaraguan Partisans of Democracy (Movimiento de Nicaragüenses Partidarios de la Democracia), and the Honduran Democratic Revolutionary party (Partido Democrático Revolucionario Hondureño).[217] The Spanish Republican exiles were also active and they joined with these groups to form the Democratic Front of Spanish and American Exiles (Frente Democrático de Exilados Americanos y Españoles).[218] Similarly, in a number of other countries, including Mexico, Cuba, and El Salvador, societies of "Friends of Guatemala" organized to refute the charges of communism in the Arbenz government. Outstanding political leaders and intellectuals, among them Lázaro Cárdenas and Jesús Silva Herzog, "asserted that Guatemala was not Communist but simply labeled such by the foreign monopolies and the other enemies of reform."[219] It may be noted, however, that the leadership of the Cuban Auténticos, the Dominican Revolutionary party (PRD), and the Venezuelan Acción Democrática avoided participation in any of these movements. Even the U.S. Department of State reported in its Guatemalan White Paper in May 1954 that "the local leftists have also cultivated the local exile branch of the Venezuelan *Partido Acción Democrática* but without apparent success as yet in subverting it to Communist uses."[220]

The new drift of exile activity in Guatemala was apparent. In the 1953 May Day parade, the exile groups marched with 70,000 partisans demonstrating loyalty to President Arbenz. The exiles carried posters and banners attacking their home governments, "charging some with being 'puppets of the Yankees.' "[221] The struggle between the Guatemalan government and the United Fruit Company provided a convenient example of "Yankee imperialism" and created the basis for preaching the broader implications of imperialism in the Marxist sense. Guatemalan and exile leaders regarded the Korean War as an example of the alleged warlike proclivities of the United States; they condemned the United States as an aggressor and accused it of engaging in bacteriological warfare. In 1952, the National Peace Committee, an affiliate of the World Congress of Peace and a virtual arm of the Guatemalan Labor party (the Communist PGT), sponsored the showing of a film, "Bacteriological Warfare in Korea," in the towns and villages of Guatemala. The following year, in response to the Budapest World Peace Council, Guatemalan leaders circulated a petition in the country calling upon the major powers to negotiate outstanding international questions and secured over 175,000 signatures.[222] At the same time, Guatemala campaigned actively against the Caribbean dictators.

There was a marked deterioration in relations between Guatemala and its neighbors after 1950. Both sides gave assistance and refuge to exile groups and both pursued interventionist foreign policies. But between 1951 and 1954 Guatemalan diplomats were declared *persona non grata* by a number of governments, among them Panama, Costa Rica, Nicaragua, and Honduras. The charge was usually the same, that is, distributing Communist literature and propaganda and engaging in conspiracies against the existing government. Guatemala's neighbors also accused it of seeking to disrupt hemispheric solidarity. They affirmed that this purpose accounted for Guatemala's withdrawal from the Organization of Central American States (ODECA) on 7 April 1953. Guatemala disclaimed any such motive and declared that it had withdrawn because of ODECA's intention to study Communist infiltration in Central America, which, it asserted, constituted intervention in its internal affairs. Guatemala also complained to the United Nations, bypassing both ODECA and the Organization of American States, that it was the intended victim of a "political-military pact" comprised of its Central American neighbors plus the Dominican Republic and Panama.[223] Guatemala made similar charges in January 1954, claiming that it possessed correspondence between Guatemalan exiles Colonel Carlos Castillo Armas and General Miguel Ydígoras Fuentes which implicated Nicaragua, El Salvador, the Dominican Republic, Venezuela, and the United States in a plot against the Arbenz regime.[224] In this context the famous confrontation between the United States and Guatemala occurred at the Tenth Inter-American Conference in Caracas in March 1954.[225]

A series of events, following the Caracas conference in rapid order, resulted in the overthrow of the Arbenz government. The first of these events was an attempt to assassinate Somoza early in April. Although the plotters entered Nicaragua from Costa Rica, a number of them were Caribbean Legionnaires who had been residing in Guatemala and did not transfer to Costa Rica until late December 1953.[226] As will be seen, Somoza became incensed at Figueres of Costa Rica for his alleged part in the scheme, but Somoza also severed relations with Guatemala and reportedly decided at that time to do all he could to overthrow Arbenz.[227] The second of these events began on 4 May in the form of a strike of banana workers in northern Honduras. Within two weeks, this strike involved fifty thousand workers and took on the dimensions of a general strike which threatened the government of Juan Manuel Gálvez.[228] Although the strike was not Communist-inspired and in the end was firmly in the hands of non-Communist labor leaders, there was evidence that Guatemala interferred in the strike and tried to exploit it for political advantage.[229] Three Guatemalan consuls in the area (at Tela, Puerto Cortés, and Nueva Ocotepeque) were expelled for alleged subversive activities, and the Guatemalan radio station, TGWA, exhorted the strikers to hold to their demands and not surrender.[230] Honduran-Guatemalan relations grew so bad that observers believed war to be imminent, and Gálvez apparently decided to turn his back on preparations by Castillo Armas for an invasion of Guatemala from Honduran soil.[231]

The third crisis was the arrival in Guatemala on 15 May of approximately two thousand tons of arms from Communist sources. A Swedish charter vessel, *Alfhem,* took the arms on board at Stettin, Poland, and sailed for Puerto Barrios on 18 April, although it initially pretended its destination was Dakar, then Curaçao, then Puerto Cortés before reaching Guatemala. The shipment aroused the entire Caribbean area but especially the United States. On 23 April the United States had already signed a mutual defense agreement with Nicaragua; on 20 May it signed a similar pact with Honduras, and on 24 May U.S. Air Force "Globemaster" transports airlifted shipments of "small arms" to Nicaragua and Honduras.[232] With these weapons and the support of the governments of Honduras, Nicaragua, and the United States, Castillo Armas crossed the Honduran frontier into Guatemala with his Liberation Army on 18 June.[233] There was little fighting, and the fate of Arbenz and his government was largely decided in the National Palace in Guatemala City. Although a hoped-for popular uprising in support of Castillo Armas did not materialize, neither did a Communist plan to arm the workers for the defense of the regime. The army was unwilling to arm civilians, and Lieutenant Colonel José Luis Cruz Salazar headed a conspiracy within the army to prevent it from taking action against Castillo Armas.[234] Lacking army support, Arbenz resigned on 27 June. The first Communist-dominated government in the Western Hemisphere had fallen with relative ease, which affected deeply Caribbean politics.

The dictators of the region were elated and sought to use the defeat of Arbenz to discredit or reduce their opposition still further. The exiles, of course, fled Guatemala, and after they had gone Castillo Armas placed their names on a list entitled "Communist Agents Forbidden to Return to Guatemala." The list included prominent non-Communists, such as the Venezuelan AD leaders, Carlos d'Ascoli, J. M. Siso Martínez, and Simón Alberto Consalvi, and the Dominican PRD leader, Juan Bosch.[235] Trujillo's propaganda writers depicted the events of early 1954 as a vast conspiracy on the part of José Figueres, Jacobo Arbenz, and Rómulo Betancourt for "control of the entire western perimeter of the Caribbean from Mexico to Panama."[236] The plot, according to Trujillo, called for "Communist agitators" to touch off a banana strike in Honduras in order to paralyze that nation's economy, while "trained assassins" entered Nicaragua from Costa Rica to murder Somoza. Following the death of Somoza, revolutions were to break out in Honduras and Nicaragua, with the help of "volunteers" from Costa Rica and Guatemala. Timed to coincide with these movements was the arrival at Puerto Cortés of a shipload of arms from Poland.[237] Supposedly, only the failure to assassinate Somoza dictated the abandonment of the plot and caused the rerouting of the *Alfhem* to Puerto Barrios, with disastrous consequences for Guatemala.[238] One trouble with this explanation was that the attempt against Somoza misfired almost two weeks before the *Alfhem* sailed from Stettin. Nonetheless, the part about the effort to kill Somoza was based upon fact, so that the most serious events following the Guatemala affair involved relations between Costa Rica and Nicaragua. José Figueres was certain that Somoza was out to get him and he suspected the CIA of helping in repayment for Nicaragua's part in ousting Arbenz.[239]

The Somoza assassination plot in April 1954 produced the gravest crisis of all those between Costa Rica and Nicaragua. Figueres and Somoza disliked one another intensely and were deeply divided ideologically, but the fact that they were neighbors and that Nicaraguan exiles enjoyed free movement in Costa Rica created almost intolerable tensions. More than any other exile group, the Nicaraguans operated on a personalist basis, which divided their ranks and limited their objective— or obsession—to Somoza. As previously noted, they did not shrink from the idea of assassination, for they regarded it as revenge for the slaying of the guerrilla chieftain, Augusto César Sandino in 1933. It is a moot question whether or not Figueres knew the full details of the revolutionary plot against Somoza, which included an attempt on his life, but it seems fairly clear that he cooperated with the conspirators and rendered them direct assistance in their preparations.

The plot was carried out by elements of the disbanded Caribbean Legion, who entered Nicaragua clandestinely on 1 April, and by prominent opposition leaders inside Nicaragua, who formed a "Frente Interno." Pablo Leal led the legionnaire group. He was a youthful Nicaraguan who used Costa Rica as a base and began in September or October 1953 to gather support for a revolutionary movement against Somoza. He traveled to Miami, where Prío Socarrás pledged to support him and instructed him to get in touch with Eufemio Fernández and Enrique Henríquez in Mexico City.[240] With their help, arms were shipped to Costa Rica, which eventually were smuggled into Nicaragua concealed in sacks of corn and beans.[241] Leal next went to Guatemala, where he recruited Nicaraguan revolutionaries Colonel Manuel Gómez Flores, Captain José María Tercero Lacayo, Luis F. Gabuardi, and Juan José Ruiz. Another Nicaraguan exile, Francisco Ibarra Mayorga, was apparently very influential in Leal's dealings in Guatemala.[242] Out of deference to Juan Bosch and José Figueres, Leal avoided contact with Miguel Angel Ramírez. Allegedly Bosch and Ramírez were now enemies,[243] and obviously it was not prudent to permit Ramírez to return to Costa Rica. However, the Honduran Jorge Ribas Montes was persuaded to join the group and he, in fact, became the operation's second-in-command.[244] Just after Christmas 1953, these elements departed Guatemala for Costa Rica.

Leal made the final preparations in Costa Rica, including the formation of a National Revolutionary party (Partido Nacional Revolucionario).[245]   According to Ribas Montes, Leal and Manuel Gómez met with Figueres, Bosch, and Rómulo Betancourt during the weeks of preparation, and Bosch, Pompeyo Alfaro (another Dominican), and the Cuban Sergio Pérez helped in the acquisition of weapons from various sources.[246]   In order to avoid suspicion, the arms were stored in a villa in San Isidro de Coronado, outside of San José.[247]   Toward the end of March 1954, Leal received a telegram from Managua that everything was ready there.[248]

With a force of twenty-one men, Leal loaded the arms he had collected into two trucks and departed San Isidro de Coronado for the Nicaraguan frontier on 30 March. According to subsequent "confessions" of the conspirators, the trucks were the property of President Figueres and the convoy was escorted to the frontier by Colonel Rodolfo Herrera Pinto, director of Costa Rica's Civil Guard, with the connivance of Colonel Humberto Pacheco Coto, the vice-minister of security.[249]   Of the twenty-one comrades who accompanied Leal, sixteen were Nicaraguans and five were of various nationalities.[250]   After making their way to the frontier, early in the morning of 1 April, they slipped into Nicaragua near the town of Cárdenas, where they rendezvoused with elements of the Frente Interno on the south shore of Lake Nicaragua.[251]   Ibarra Mayorga entered Nicaragua at the same time, but traveled alone by another route.

Leal's contact man inside of Nicaragua was Julián Salaverry, who had fought alongside of Figueres in the civil war of 1948. The Frente Interno included, among others, General Emiliano Chamorro, the aged Conservative party leader and ex-president, who had returned to Nicaragua and was then in the Senate; Ernesto Solórzano Thompson, the nephew of former President Adolfo Díaz; Humberto Chamorro; Enrique Lacayo Farfán, the leader of the Independent Liberal party (Partido Liberal Independiente); Dr. Fernando Agüero, a prominent physician and political leader; Captain Adolfo Alfaro, a National Guard officer; Hernán Robleto, the editor of *La Flecha* of Managua; Pedro Joaquín Chamorro, the editor of *La Prensa,* also of Managua; and Adolfo Báez Bone, a former legionnaire.[252]   Four National Guard officers on active duty were also implicated in the plot. Through General Chamorro, Salaverry obtained the use of Alberto Chamorro's launch, *La Nena,* to cross the *Gran Lago* with Don Alberto's son, Roberto, and fetch Leal, his men, and the arms. Returning across the lake, they disembarked at Río Tipitapa, just south of Managua, where they and the arms were placed in trucks belonging to General Chamorro. Concealed beneath a cover of cotton, they were transported through Managua and taken to the general's villa, "San Salvador."[253] There the group remained hidden until Saturday evening, 3 April, when they intended to ambush Somoza and his two sons, Luis and Anastasio, upon their return from a reception at the suburban Managua home of U.S. Ambassador Thomas Whelan.[254]

In the meantime, the Frente Interno held two councils of war with Leal, Gómez, and Amadeo Soler, a Dominican member of the group. They met on Friday evening at "Chula Vista," the villa of Solórzano Thompson, where, according to General Chamorro, they discussed a plan calling for Báez Bone to lead two-hundred men in an assault upon the "Loma de Tiscapa" (the presidential mansion and the National Guard headquarters are situated on this hill dominating Managua). The Conservative leader denied that there was any talk of assassinating the Somozas, although he remarked that "kidnapping" them would "serve the same purpose" as the taking of the "Loma de Tiscapa."[255] However, Pedro Joaquín Chamorro stated that a plan to assassinate Somoza was discussed at a meeting which he attended at the villa "La California" on Saturday afternoon, but added that he opposed the act on moral grounds.[256] The truth is that an ambush was prepared on Saturday evening but that it had to be abandoned, because after the men had taken their positions along the highway persons in the area became suspicious and summoned the National Guard to investigate. The conspirators tried to improvise another attempt on Sunday morning, but the National Guard was now on alert and had set up patrols. Under these circumstances, two guardsmen came upon Leal and his men and were killed in an exchange of gunfire. Just that fast the dream became a nightmare. The National Guard closed the frontier with Costa Rica and in the next few days hunted down Pablo Leal and his men.

Only a handful of those who came to Nicaragua on the launch *La Nena* were able to escape with their lives. The survivors were Manuel Gómez, Ribas Montes, Salaverry, and three others.[257] Of these, only Gómez escaped the National Guard altogether and reached safety in Honduras. Among those killed was Amadeo Soler, the Dominican, who was a close friend of Juan Bosch and to whom Bosch dedicated a book published in 1959, *Trujillo: causas de una tiranía sin ejemplo.* The brothers Adolfo and Luis Báez Bone of the Frente Interno also died in the manhunt.[258] It was charged that Leal and many of his men were actually captured alive but were tortured and then murdered.[259] This was plausible, given the high death rate and the fact that General Somoza released a statement on 9 April in which he was able to report the essential details of the plot, including names, dates, and places.[260] The younger son of Somoza, Anastasio Somoza Debayle, and the son of former Costa Rican President Teodoro Picado, both West Point graduates, were accused of personally torturing the prisoners.[261] Pedro Joaquín Chamorro declared that the younger Anastasio "hung Ribas Montes by his testicles" in order to extract a confession from him. [262] Ribas Montes was not permitted to leave Somoza's prison alive. On 20 March 1955 he was sentenced to nineteen years imprisonment, but on 5 June 1957, after rumors of his death reached his wife in Costa Rica and she petitioned for his body, Luis Somoza informed the Costa Rican ambassador that Ribas Montes "had been killed when he attempted to escape from prison."[263]

The Frente Interno, too, felt the wrath of the Somoza regime. Some of the men, such as Hernán Robleto, had time to reach asylum in foreign embassies, but a large number, including Pedro Joaquín Chamorro and Lacayo Farfán, were arrested on Sunday afternoon, 4 April, to begin a long calvary of interrogation, abuse, and imprisonment.[264] General Chamorro, enjoying immunity as a senator, was subjected to an inquiry by a special commission of the Chamber of Deputies. He admitted that he helped smuggle arms into Nicaragua but denied any intention to kill Somoza and his sons.[265] On 12 February 1955, he and another senator, Fernando Abel Gallard, and a deputy, Raúl Arana Montalván, were found guilty of the crime of rebellion, and all were banished to the town of Bluefields on the Caribbean coast.[266] In the meantime, as a result of its investigations, the Somoza regime had charged Costa Rican officials with complicity in the plot.

On 18 May 1954 the Nicaraguan government delivered a note to the government of Costa Rica in which it accused President Figueres and Colonels Pacheco Coto and Herrera Pinto of direct involvement in the plot to assassinate the Somozas and in which it demanded the expulsion of a number of persons from Costa Rica. Figueres was charged specifically with giving arms to the conspirators and with permitting them to use trucks belonging to him. Pacheco Coto and Herrera Pinto were accused of helping the rebels to hide the arms and then to transport them to the frontier. Nicaragua demanded their immediate dismissal. Rómulo Betancourt was depicted as the mastermind behind the plot and as the new leader of the Caribbean Legion. He was to be ordered from Costa Rican territory, along with the Dominicans Bosch and Pompeyo Alfaro, the Cuban Sergio Pérez, the Honduran Marcial Aguiluz, and a long list of Nicaraguan exiles.[267] Figueres responded to these charges with a statement on 21 May and by means of a diplomatic note a month later. Generally, he denied any involvement in the affair on the part of himself or any official of the Costa Rican government but observed that he was not responsible for Somoza's "domestic problems." He pointed out that Costa Rica's surveillance over Nicaraguan emigrés was apparently adequate in view of the fact that Somoza's complaint was limited to only twenty-two of the four thousand living in the country.[268] Somoza could not be humored; he had confessions (regardless of how he might have obtained them) and he indignantly recalled his ambassador from San José. For the moment, however, the United States managed to allay the crisis by arranging Betancourt's move from Costa Rica to Puerto Rico.

The expulsion of Betancourt from Costa Rica was a key issue in the crisis. He was anathema to all of the dictators of the Caribbean. Venezuela, particularly, resented the asylum granted Acción Democrática exiles in Costa Rica. In October 1953 Somoza was the "honored guest" of Marcos Pérez Jiménez in Caracas, and, according to Betancourt, the "Siamese twins" established close relations.[269] These soon took "unworthy forms," he asserted, particularly in view of Figueres' refusal to send a delegation to the 1954 Caracas Conference. Rafael Trujillo, likewise, disapproved of Betancourt's presence in Costa Rica. On 2 February 1954 the Dominican Military Intelligence Service affirmed that Betancourt was behind a transfer of "thirty Russian spies" from Guatemala to Costa Rica (it probably had a line on Leal) and that he was preparing an attack against the Dominican Republic.[270] Within hours after the discovery of the plot against him in April 1954, Somoza alleged that Betancourt had "directed" the entire operation from San José.[271] Even before Nicaragua made its formal demand for Betancourt's ouster from Costa Rican territory, Allan Stewart, first secretary of the U.S. embassy in Costa Rica, approached Betancourt with an offer of asylum in the United States.[272] By 20 April, the story was circulating that Betancourt would leave San José, although sources stressed that he was leaving of his "own free will" and that no official pressure had been brought against him.[273] Before Betancourt's departure, however, a Venezuelan aircraft, as noted, dropped obscene leaflets over San José attacking Betancourt and Figueres. By the time that Betancourt finally left Costa Rica on 26 July, the situation on the surface had improved.

The United States had also helped cool off the dispute by sending several planeloads of arms to Figueres, thereby redressing the balance of power in Central America. As noted, the United States had delivered weapons to Somoza in May during the Guatemalan crisis; this, of course, strengthened Nicaragua's military position in Central America generally. On 4 July Costa Rican Foreign Minister Mario A. Esquivel announced that under a military assistance agreement his country would receive a quantity of arms from the United States.[274] Ten days later, six U.S. Air Force C-47 cargo planes delivered fifteen tons of light arms to San José. The moral support of the United States in this instance was just as important to Costa Rica as the arms. But Somoza was not through.

Although Somoza abandoned any immediate plan he might have had for making war on Costa Rica, he and the Venezuelan dictator, Pérez Jiménez, entered into a conspiracy with Figueres' old enemy, Rafael Angel Calderón Guardia. They decided to undertake another filibustering expedition against Costa Rica. The Nicaraguan National Guard provided training sites, arms and equipment, technical personnel, and even "volunteers" for the preparation of a *calderonista* army against Figueres. The force was under the command of Teodoro Picado, Jr., who apparently was on close terms with the younger Anastasio. Reportedly, Calderón Guardia made four trips to Caracas during the second half of 1954, one of which took place just before the leaflet incident.[275] It was also rumored that Calderón had the support of Castillo Armas. Although Castillo assured Costa Rica that he would not permit the use of Guatemalan territory for the preparation of hostile action against it, the calderonistas had aided Castillo and were counting on him to return the favor.[276] Subsequently, after the invasion had taken place, a rebel prisoner confessed that he and three hundred others had been trained at Chiquimula, Guatemala.[277] Throughout the period, Somoza conducted a "war of nerves," climaxed in December with the purchase from Sweden of twenty-five vintage F-51 Mustang fighter planes.

Figueres, on the other hand, made some half-hearted attempts to pacify his rival. In mid-April he requested the Council of the Organization of American States to investigate Somoza's charges, but the council, in turn, advised him to try to settle the matter through direct negotiations. The recall of the Nicaraguan ambassador in July closed this channel, and an effort by El Salvador to mediate the dispute also failed. During the summer of 1954, the Figueres government quietly arranged the departure of a number of Nicaraguan exiles from San José. Somoza did not consider any of these steps as satisfying his demands; he stated that Nicaragua wanted "moral reparations" for the attempt on his life, that is, an apology, and he wanted a written statement that Betancourt would not be permitted to return to Costa Rica. [278] Figueres was unwilling to go that far; he also was stubborn. According to Serafino Romualdi, Betancourt made arrangements to leave Costa Rica "in strict confidence so as not to upset Figueres,"[279] and when the Costa Rican minister of security resigned his post in October, Figueres defiantly named Vice Minister Pacheco Coto to the position. This was the very man whom Somoza wanted fired.[280] By the end of 1954, a Figueres-Somoza clash seemed unavoidable.

The long-expected invasion of Costa Rica by forces proceeding from Nicaragua occurred on 11 January 1955. For all its preparation and buildup, this attack was no more effective than those sponsored by the democratic leadership. There were approximately five hundred men in the rebel forces comprised mainly of Costa Ricans, with a sprinkling of Nicaraguans, Hondurans, and other nationalities. The staging area was near Rivas, Nicaragua, from which the invaders entered the northwest corner of Costa Rica and occupied the town of La Cruz. Some troops also came in by water at nearby Puerto Soley, and there was an uprising at Villa Quesada, deeper inside Costa Rica. On the day of the invasion, unidentified aircraft made bombing and strafing attacks on a number of Costa Rican cities, including San José, Cartago, Liberia, and Turrialba.[281] A rebel radio came over the air and identified itself as the "Voice of the Authentic Anti-Communist Revolutionary Army" (Ejército Revolucionario Auténticamente Anti-Comunista). It called upon the people to throw out "Figueres and the Communists" and gave instructions for committing acts of sabotage. "The Figueres regime," declared the rebel announcer, "is similar to that in Guatemala under Arbenz."[282] Once across the frontier, young Picado was apparently on his own, although Nicaragua continued to truck supplies to him and made a number of air drops of equipment and war material. Picado, however, showed little ability or willingness to take the offensive and contented himself with propaganda broadcasts and air raids. In the meantime, the Costa Rican Civil Guard quelled the disturbance at Villa Quesada. Despite this success and Picado's inertia, Costa Rica appealed to the Organization of American States, which took quick and decisive action. The OAS reenforced Figueres militarily and restrained Nicaragua.

On 8 January, even before the attack took place, Costa Rica had requested the Council of the OAS to convoke a meeting of consultation. Costa Rica referred to its general anxieties over Nicaragua's behavior but particularly to its growing apprehension because of Nicaragua's acquisition of F-51 aircraft and because "another American government" (Venezuela) had just sent ten military transport planes to Nicaragua.[283] Nicaragua's purchase of the Mustang fighters was counterproductive, because they were not delivered before January and they served only to reenforce Nicaragua's warlike image. The arrival of Venezuelan military aircraft in Nicaragua gave the impression that the Caribbean dictators were combining against the region's remaining democracy. The OAS Council postponed action on Costa Rica's note until 12 January in order to give representatives an opportunity to receive instructions. However, when Costa Rican Ambassador Antonio Facio notified the council on 11 January that an attack had occurred, the council met the same day in extraordinary session. Without delay, the council resolved to convoke the Organ of Consultation and, pending the fixing of a place and date for the consultative meeting, constituted itself as the provisional Organ of Consultation. It created an Investigating Committee to make an on-the-spot study of the situation and to report.[284] The Investigating Committee left very early on 12 January, but the lack of facilities for night landings in San José delayed its arrival until the morning of 13 January.

The Council of the OAS acting provisionally as the Organ of Consultation and its Investigating Committee worked effectively to end hostilities in Costa Rica. While the Investigating Committee was en route, the council passed a second resolution which requested the committee to make a preliminary report as soon as it reached Costa Rica and asked member states to refrain from hostile acts and to make available observation aircraft for the committee's use. Accordingly, on the thirteenth the committee cabled its first report, which left no doubt that Costa Rica had been the victim of aggression. It stated that foreign-based aircraft had violated Costa Rican airspace and had strafed and bombed its territory. It added that there were "serious indications" that rebels operating inside Costa Rica had received arms and munitions from foreign sources.[285] After additional reconnaissance flights in planes supplied by the United States, the committee was more specific in its report of 14 January. It declared that rebel forces were continuing to receive supplies and reenforcements across Costa Rica's "northern frontier." For this reason, it advised the council "to direct immediately a formal appeal to the government of Nicaragua" and point out the growing seriousness of the situation, which threatened "the integrity, sovereignty, and political independence of Costa Rica."[286] The council condemned these acts.

Despite the council's appeal, however, Nicaragua persisted in its intervention. This next took the form of a World War II fighter plane, which brought the affair to a sudden and dramatic conclusion. Late in the afternoon of 15 January, the Investigating Committee cabled that an F-47 Thunderbolt (or "Jug") had been observed at La Cruz and that this aircraft had buzzed the committee's observer plane and had then bombed and strafed Liberia. The committee reported that Costa Rica lacked either aircraft or arms for defense against a plane of this type.[287]

Then, in the early hours of the sixteenth, the council received an urgent appeal from Costa Rican Foreign Minister Mario Esquivel, in which he referred to the attacks by the F-47 fighter plane and requested the provisional Organ of Consultation to invoke article 8 of the Rio Treaty, which would authorize the use of armed force to preserve the integrity, sovereignty, and political independence of Costa Rica. [288] Previously, Ambassador Facio had asked the council to establish control over the Costa Rican-Nicaraguan frontier and to furnish his country with arms and aircraft for defense against air attacks. In a hastily convened session at 2 A.M. on 16 January, the U.S. representative notified the council that if requested his government would sell aircraft to Costa Rica.[289] The council authorized the sale, and within hours U.S. Air Force pilots were ferrying four F-51 Mustangs to San José, sold to Costa Rica for one dollar apiece. Figueres claimed that he was able to secure this support through action by "liberals" in the United States, such as Senator Paul Douglas of Illinois, and by "career State Department people." At the same time, he was convinced that the U.S. Central Intelligence Agency had aided Somoza and the rebels by placing at their disposal the identical F-47 which had flown sorties for Castillo Armas in June 1954.[290] With the arrival of the Mustang fighter planes, the rebellion and intervention were over.

The danger remained, however, of a direct clash between Costa Rican and Nicaraguan forces. Throughout the crisis, Somoza had denied any part in the affair and had affirmed that the conflict was an internal matter.[291] When Figueres accused him of intervention, Somoza replied that Figueres was a "damned liar" and challenged him to a duel. "If he [Figueres] has so much personal hate for me," Somoza declared, "let's put it on a man-to-man basis. There is no reason for bloodshed between our two countries. If he hates me, as was evident when he tried to assassinate me, then why not settle it this way?"[292] The possibility existed, then, that an enraged Somoza might take advantage of some incident to commit his forces to battle, particularly as Costa Rican troops approached the border in pursuit of the rebels. Somoza obviously also felt some obligation for the safety of the rebels. Therefore, when the Nicaraguan government protested on 19 January that its territory had been violated by two F-51s engaged in bombing runs over La Cruz, the Investigating Committee moved quickly.[293] It not only established a surveillance over the frontier, but set up a "security zone," three miles on each side of the border, into which neither Nicaraguan nor Costa Rican ground or air forces were permitted to enter. This arrangement was made on 20 January and remained in effect through the twenty-fifth. During this time rebel forces were able to reach Nicaragua safely, where under the agreement they were interned.[294] By 28 January the situation had improved so greatly that the Investigating Committee was able to return to Washington, where it rendered its report the following month.

The report of the committee made it clear that the role of the Organization of American States had been to preserve Costa Rica but not to humiliate Nicaragua or Venezuela. The committee's report was a factual account of its activities and observations. It showed that Costa Rica had been the victim of aggression, but, although a thoughtful observer had sufficient information with which to draw a valid conclusion, it did not name the attacker or attackers. This situation displeased one member of the Investigating Committee. Ambassador José R. Chiriboga, the representative of Ecuador, submitted a reservation in which he protested the failure of the report "to identify the author or authors of the 'foreign intervention.' "[295] Despite Chiriboga's dissent, the council refused to fix sole responsibility and, still acting provisionally as the Organ of Consultation, met on 24 February in order to recommend procedures by which Costa Rica and Nicaragua might settle their differences bilaterally, with the inference that neither was blameless in the events of the preceding months. In order to facilitate these negotiations, the council created a Special Committee, comprised of nine members, which worked closely with the two parties during the course of the following year. Matters proceeded well; on 8 September 1955 the Special Committee recommended that the council cancel the call for a meeting of consultation, and four months later, almost a year after the invasion, Costa Rica and Nicaragua reached agreement on two pacts. The first, a Pact of Amity, outlined measures for avoiding disputes in the future, specifically pledges by each to prevent the preparation of assassination plots against the chief of state and the high functionaries of either party. The second, a Treaty of Conciliation, established a permanent Committee of Investigation and Conciliation with broad powers for settling any dispute which might nonetheless arise between the two parties.[296]

Costa Rica had been, in effect, neutralized in the antidictatorial struggle in the Caribbean. Thanks to the United States, Figueres had been rescued from possible disaster, but, according to Figueres, Henry F. Holland, the assistant secretary of state for inter-American affairs, looked upon him and his friends as "troublemakers."[297] This view was supported by Herbert Matthews, who wrote that, while the United States had a "primary role" in saving Figueres, "it is also noted that the State Department has pointedly indicated it desired peace in the Caribbean and had no intention of antagonizing dictators in Venezuela, Nicaragua, the Dominican Republic, and Cuba."[298] Moreover, the invasion had caused domestic political and economic strains for Figueres. The people had rallied around him during the invasion, but observers felt he might lose their support if he persisted in his "Quixotic crusade" against the dictators.[299] The dispute with Nicaragua had caused capital flight, along with a marked decline in business and in tax receipts. For these reasons, Costa Rica entered into the bilateral negotiations with Nicaragua under the auspices of the OAS and at the same time undertook to renew diplomatic relations with the Dominican Republic and Venezuela.

In March 1955 Figueres sent a representative to a UN-sponsored social security conference in Caracas, where he had refused to go the previous year for the Tenth Inter-American Conference.[300] Although Figueres did not fully abandon his policy of assistance to antidictatorial exiles, he exercised greater caution and restraint following the events of January 1955.

Nicaraguan politics, however, remained agitated, particularly after the slaying of Sandino was avenged. On the evening of 21 September 1956 Somoza attended a dance in León, where he was felled by four bullets. He was shot by Rigoberto López Pérez, a young poet without a political background, who apparently acted alone, although he reflected the general tendency of Nicaraguan exiles toward tyrannicide.[301] The young man had returned to Nicaragua from exile in El Salvador only a few weeks before the shooting and if he had any confederates he was unable to tell, because he was killed on the spot by Somoza's bodyguards. Somoza clung to life for over a week. President Dwight Eisenhower rushed his own surgeon to Somoza and then had the dictator flown to the Panama Canal Zone for further surgery, where he succumbed on 29 September. While Eisenhower called the assassination a "cowardly deed," democratic elements generally mourned López Pérez as a "soldier of liberty."[302] In Mexico a Nicaraguan exile publication printed a full-page picture of the new martyr, with a caption quoting Thomas Jefferson, "The tree of liberty must be watered periodically with the blood of tyrants." Even Acción Democrática, which reiterated its opposition to personal attacks on grounds of principle and on the basis that such acts did not change the conditions favoring dictatorship, declared that it could not grieve the death of Somoza nor evade paying homage to López Pérez, "an idealistic youth impassioned with liberty."[303] A year later, on the anniversary of the death of López Pérez, Guatemalans, Cubans, Puerto Ricans, Venezuelans, and Nicaraguans gathered in the Ateneo Español in Mexico City to honor him.[304] Still, AD was right; the assassination of Somoza did not result in any basic change within Nicaragua.

The sons of Somoza, Luis and Anastasio, continued in his place. Following the shooting, the foes of Somoza were arrested; some of those who had been imprisoned in April 1954 were taken again in the dragnet. According to one of them, Pedro Joaquín Chamorro, they and a dozen more were tortured cruelly in an effort to make them confess to an assassination plot which did not exist.[305] Even as Somoza lay dying, his presumptive heirs were concerned that the exiles might take advantage of the situation to prepare revolutionary movements. On 26 September Foreign Minister Oscar Sevilla Sacasa sent a circular dispatch to the American governments in which he asserted that "Nicaraguans and others living abroad" were plotting a revolution against Nicaragua and he requested the governments "to exercise effective and strict control . . . [over these] subversives."[306] Nicaragua was generally satisfied with the responses it received from other governments concerning exile activities, except in the case of El Salvador.

El Salvador normally played a conciliatory role in Central American affairs and followed a strict noninterventionist policy. This was evident by the fact that one of its nationals, José Guillermo Trabanino, had been elected secretary general of the Organization of Central American States (ODECA) in August 1955, when one was surprised that these countries could even agree to meet. However, because Somoza's slayer had been in exile in El Salvador and because Salvadorans had demonstrated in sympathy for the young poet, Nicaraguan-Salvadoran relations became tense.[307] The Nicaraguan government charged that a plot to assassinate Somoza had been elaborated in El Salvador and that the Salvadoran government had been overly hospitable to Nicaraguan exiles. It, therefore, made especially sharp demands upon tiny Salvador regarding the control of exiles. In fact, it requested the extradition of certain Nicaraguan exiles, among them Captain Adolfo Alfaro, who had fled Nicaragua after the events of April 1954.[308] El Salvador denied that there was sufficient evidence to establish the fact of a conspiracy in Somoza's assassination and refused to extradite exiles for what it considered were political reasons. El Salvador reiterated its policy of granting asylum to political refugees, provided they refrained from political activities.[309] Because of this stand, relations between Nicaragua and El Salvador remained poor until early 1957. They improved then only because Nicaragua's relations with Honduras had become worse.

In the midst of the general unsettled conditions in Central America, the age-old boundary dispute between Nicaragua and Honduras flared up. The dispute seemed unrelated to the revolutionary movements or exile activities in the region, although following the ouster of Julio Lozano Díaz in October 1956 Honduras had been making strides toward a more democratic government. In April 1957 Honduras charged that its territory had been invaded by Nicaragua and appealed to the Council of the Organization of American States, which invoked the Rio Treaty on 2 May. Once again, the council constituted itself as the provisional Organ of Consultation and sent an Investigating Committee to the scene. It quickly arranged a cease-fire. Under the auspices of an ad hoc committee of the OAS Council, acting provisionally as the Organ of Consultation, the two parties signed an agreement on 21 June 1957, under which they agreed to submit their dispute to the International Court of Justice. This was subsequently done, although it took a year to prepare the matter for submission to the ICJ, and the council did not cancel its call for a meeting of consultation until 27 June 1958.[310] The only references to general Caribbean politics during this dispute were charges by each party that the other had provoked it to divert attention from domestic political problems, and Honduras accused the Dominican Republic of assisting Nicaragua with airplanes, pilots, and equipment.[311] Meanwhile, as Somoza's heirs had feared, Nicaraguan exile groups tried to capitalize upon Nicaragua's internal and international distresses.

There were a number of false alarms and the exhibition of much nervousness on the part of President Luis Somoza before any actual invasion attempt was made. On 4 November 1957 Nicaragua announced that it had frustrated a subversive plot and had arrested a number of civilian and military leaders; it insisted also that Nicaraguan exiles in Honduras were gathering near the frontier.[312] On 6 February 1958 Luis Somoza expressed the perennial fear that a revolution was planned for 21 February, the anniversary of the death of Sandino, and charged specifically that the Dominican Miguel Angel Ramírez and the Nicaraguans Alejandro Cárdenas and Virgilio Vega Fornos planned to use Costa Rica and Honduras as "springboards" for invasions.[313] These apprehensions were calmed somewhat by the visit to Managua of Costa Rican President-elect Mario Echandi, a foe of Figueres, on 8 and 9 March. The rumors of an exile buildup in Honduras persisted, however, although the new president of Honduras, Ramón Villeda Morales, gave Nicaragua permission to fly reconnaissance missions over the border area near Cifuentes, including the area in dispute. Villeda Morales added that his government would adhere to the policy of "nonintervention in the internal affairs of [its] neighbors."[314] Villeda Morales was a leader of the Democratic Left and his top aides included former legionnaires Miguel Francisco Morazán and Francisco ("El Indio") Sánchez, but his situation was too precarious for foreign adventures. Paradoxically, then, although anti-Somoza exiles enjoyed a freedom never experienced before in Honduras, their activities were not in the best interests of their host.

Nicaraguan intelligence had not been too far-off, therefore, for toward the end of April Nicaraguan exiles tried to launch a two-pronged invasion from Honduras and Costa Rica. For over a year Colonel Manuel Gómez Flores had been gathering men and supplies near

Cifuentes, Honduras, and Chester Lacayo had been making similar preparations in San José.[315] The plan, which almost succeeded, was one of
the strangest yet attempted by any of the exile groups. It originated in
Miami, Florida, with the theft of a C-46 transport plane belonging to
Nicaraguan Air Lines (LANICA). The plane was seized on 25 April
1958 by Captain Víctor Manuel Rivas Gómez and Lieutenant Alí
Salomón and flown to Los Horcones, Honduras, near the Nicaraguan
frontier, where Gómez Flores awaited with approximately fifty
men.[316] They quickly loaded the aircraft with arms and equipment,
reportedly worth a half-million dollars, and then scrambled on board.
At the very last minute, however, Honduran officials learned of what
was happening and acted to prevent the takeoff of the C-46. Apparently, the idle boasting of one of the rebel leaders, Mauricio Castellón
Alonso, tipped off Honduran authorities and caused the plan to fail. [317]
The Honduran government interned the would-be invaders and took
steps to deport them to Guatemala, "farther away from revolutionary
temptation."[318] The group in Costa Rica had no better luck.

In early May Chester Lacayo and sixteen followers were arrested by
Costa Rican border guards at the frontier town of Los Chiles. They
were seized with fourteen trunks filled with arms and ammunition,
which they had brought from San José aboard a regularly scheduled
Costa Rican Air Lines (LACSA) flight.[319] Lacayo did not reveal the
details of his movement, but he probably intended to infiltrate by way
of Lake Nicaragua, the same route used by Pablo Leal and his followers
in April 1954. However, at virtually the same time, Lacayo was named,
along with Carlos Pasos, Pedro Joaquín Chamorro, and the Cuban
Eufemio Fernández, as a member of a plot to assassinate Anastasio
Somoza Debayle.[320] The accused parties denied emphatically the existence of such a scheme, and Chamorro was able to show that he was in
Washington, attending a meeting of the Inter-American Press Association, at the time the alleged plot was prepared.[321] Clearly, the Nicaraguan exiles were among the most persistent freebooters of the Caribbean region. Even an old *sandinista* general, Ramón Raudales, tried to
invade Nicaragua from Honduras in October 1958, only to be killed by
Nicaraguan National Guardsmen.

The methods and movements of the Caribbean exiles had taken
numerous forms during the 1950s. From the patient work of influenc-
ing international public opinion against the dictators to the vigorous
activity of organizing armed bands of men, the diaspora had demon-

strated its ingenuity and vitality and had often been at the center of the decade's most serious crises. It had maintained the promise of change and had made the dictators appear not so permanent. The parties of the Democratic Left in exile, in particular, had helped create the image of the dictators as evil and had survived as a viable alternative themselves. Despite all that has been said so far about this process, however, the story is incomplete. The Democratic Left in exile had relied very heavily upon certain internationally organized groups concerned with the issues of human rights, labor, and the press. These groups, based mainly in the United States, contributed immeasurably to the success of the diaspora against the dictators of the Caribbean.

5 | *Friends and Allies*

The Inter-American Association
for Democracy and Freedom

THE INTER-AMERICAN ASSOCIATION for Democracy and Freedom was one of the closest allies and best friends the Democratic Left in exile had. It was founded in Havana in 1950 as a nongovernmental organization dedicated to opposing all forms of dictatorship and to championing the political and civil liberties of the peoples of the Western Hemisphere. Although its founders had no such intention, circumstances forced it to function primarily in the United States through its U.S. committee. Under the devoted leadership of its secretary general, Miss Frances Grant, the IADF evoked sympathy for democratic leaders and loathing for dictators. It had a small but influential membership which endeavored to inform U.S. political leaders and the general public of the transgressions of Latin American dictators, particularly in the area of human rights.

The IADF was the modest product of essentially two ideals shared by a number of Latin and North American political figures. One idea envisioned the establishment of an international or extragovernmental machinery or agency to protect individuals from the abuses of their own governments. The other stressed the need for a bloc of democratic states to apply direct pressure against dictatorial regimes.

The Peruvian Víctor Raúl Haya de la Torre articulated the first concept in 1941. He advocated the creation of an American committee for the defense of democracy, with local committees in each state to receive complaints concerning "violations of the democratic process and civil liberties."[1] Similarly, in 1947, Haya proposed that the American states draw up a continental bill of rights and pledge to condemn any state which might violate the guarantees of its citizens.[2]

The second idea, that of a democratic alliance, reflected the thinking of Rómulo Betancourt. He desired a formal commitment from democratic governments to adopt a policy of opposition to dictatorial governments. This policy included nonrecognition of nonpopular regimes, denunciation before international organizations of violations of individual freedoms, and refusal to cooperate with dictators in any kind of economic, military, or technical activity.[3] Betancourt noted that the Falangists and Communists were organized internationally, but that the democratic and national revolutionary forces of Latin America lacked any kind of coordinating body.[4]

A number of other hemispheric leaders, particularly in the Caribbean area, responded favorably to both of these ideas. José Figueres advocated "sane intervention" as more humane than "indifference toward the burning house of a neighbor," and he affirmed that "respect for the dignity of man" was superior to frontiers.[5] He felt that "all America" was committed ethically and by treaty to secure democratic governments in every country of the hemisphere.[6] Similarly, trade union leaders meeting in Havana in September 1949 favored the creation of a human rights tribunal and passed a resolution calling for an inter-American conference "devoted to the defense of peace and democracy."[7] Earlier the same year, Cuban President Carlos Prío Socarrás had taken the initial steps toward the formation of an antidictatorial bloc.[8] However, the overthrow of Acción Democrática in Venezuela affected the balance of power in the Caribbean and ended serious consideration of a formal alliance of democratic states. The alternative was an organization which could express the democratic viewpoint and advocate its cause in the hemisphere.

The Inter-American Association for Democracy and Freedom was created in a two-day conference in Havana, 12-14 May 1950. Some two hundred individuals from twenty countries attended the sessions. These included the hemisphere's outstanding democratic leaders, among them: Eduardo Frei, Chile; Germán Arciniegas and Eduardo Santos, Colombia; Daniel Cossío Villegas and José Iturriaga, Mexico; Luis Alberto Sánchez, Peru; and Eduardo Rodríguez Larreta, Uruguay. Among those from the Caribbean area were: José Figueres, Gonzalo Facio, and Vicente Sáenz, Costa Rica; Raúl Roa and Aureliano Sánchez Arango,

Cuba; Juan Bosch, Angel Miolán, Buenaventura Sánchez, and Amadeo Soler, the Dominican Republic; Guillermo Toriello, Guatemala; and Rómulo Betancourt, Andrés Eloy Blanco, Valmore Rodríguez, Raúl Leoni, and Gonzalo Barrios, Venezuela. The group from the United States was large and represented a variety of liberal and democratic organizations. It included Roger Baldwin and Frances Grant for the International League for the Rights of Man (ILRM); authors Pearl Buck and Waldo Frank; Walter White for the National Association for the Advancement of Colored People (NAACP); labor leaders Serafino Romualdi (AFL), Ernest Schwartz (CIO), and O. A. Knight (Oil Workers' International); Charles M. LaFollette, James Loeb, and Arthur M. Schlesinger, Jr., for the Americans for Democratic Action (ADA); educators and activists Robert Alexander, Chester Bowles, Jesús de Galíndez, Clarence Senior, and Norman Thomas; and U.S. Congressmen Clifford Case (New Jersey), Charles Howell (New Jersey), Chet Holifield (California), and Clinton McKinnon (California).[9] Mrs. Eleanor Roosevelt was listed as a sponsor, but she did not attend.[10]

The conference met in a time of adversity and slipping fortunes for many of its participants. AD was still recovering from its overthrow, the attempt to invade the Dominican Republic the preceding summer had been a fiasco, and all filibustering activity by Caribbean exiles and governments was under the scrutiny of the Organization of American States. The sessions were held in the chamber of the Cuban House of Representatives, but President Prío denied that Cuba was officially sponsoring the conference, probably because Argentina, Colombia, and Venezuela had threatened to break off relations if he gave the appearance of backing it.[11] While the dictators denounced the conference as a "Kremlin plot," the Communists described it as a "puppet of the State Department."[12]

Nonetheless, from the sessions emerged a permanent organization for the defense of democracy, made up of "the democratic forces of the continent." The resolution founding the IADF stated the urgent need for unity among "genuinely democratic individuals and organizations."[13] Emilio Frugoni, the Socialist leader of Uruguay, was elected president of the association, and he made his headquarters in Montevideo. The post of secretary general went to Frances Grant, who set up her office in New York. In closing the conference, Betancourt stressed its significance in bringing together "men of democratic thought" whether in power or in exile.[14]

Founded in adversity, the IADF did not have an easy time in the decade of the fifties. Miss Grant undertook to form the U.S. committee of the IADF and in January 1951 started publication of the monthly (though not always) bulletin *Hemispherica*. The Latin American head-quarters did not do as well. In October 1951, owing to political condi- tions in Uruguay, but particularly because of Juan Perón's forays against Argentine exiles in Montevideo, it was expedient to close down the presidential office. Thereafter, the office of the secretary general in New York served as the "Caretaker Office" for the presidential head-quarters.[15] Miss Grant's office, in fact, became the IADF. Although the membership of the U.S. committee was distinguished, the staff was minute. All the work was voluntary; the officers took care of their own expenses, and the administrative budget was no more than $7,500 a year.[16] In many respects, it was a "labor of love" for Miss Grant and was often a one-woman operation. As Germán Arciniegas declared in 1954, "she has been the one person to whom we, the Latin Americans, have always come in New York, whenever we had to initiate any struggle in favor of our people, oppressed by dictatorships."[17] Much was accomplished through her contacts with Latin American demo-crats, particularly those in exile. In the United States she was sustained by the collaboration of Robert Alexander, Roger Baldwin, Serafino Romualdi, Clarence Senior, Adolf A. Berle, Herbert Matthews, and Norman Thomas.

On several occasions during the next decade the IADF considered holding a second inter-American conference. It came close once, but the United States inadvertently torpedoed it. In February 1956 Figueres had planned a visit to Muñoz Marín in Puerto Rico, where Betancourt was also residing. Accordingly, Miss Grant and Serafino Romualdi arranged to travel to Puerto Rico in order to meet with these leaders and plan a conference. The meeting was cancelled, however, because, at the insistence of Assistant Secretary of State Henry F. Holland, Betancourt left the island during the time of Figueres' visit.[18] The work was left, therefore, to Miss Grant and the U.S. committee, but they persevered. The success of the IADF may be measured by the nature of the attacks made upon it by Rafael Trujillo, whose propa-gandists described it as "a small, obscure group [with] tremendous power."[19]

One of the activities of the IADF was to intercede with the United Nations and other international agencies on behalf of victims of dictatorial regimes. These intercessions were made particularly with reference to the situation in Venezuela under Pérez Jiménez, and, indeed, it was evident that Acción Democrática supplied the association with pertinent data. In 1952, for example, the IADF, in cooperation with the International League for the Rights of Man, presented UN Secretary General Trygve Lie with a lengthy document outlining political persecutions in Latin America.[20] The portion dealing with Venezuela, which listed the names of political prisoners, jails, and concentration camps, duplicated the information collected by AD and published the same year in *The Black Book*.

In 1953 the IADF was among those appealing for the release from prison of the dying Alberto Carnevali.[21] The appeal was made to the assistant secretary of state for inter-American affairs, John Moors Cabot. Later the same year, with the approach of the Caracas Conference, the IADF issued a "Call to the Free Men of the Americas" to affix their signatures to a petition demanding the release of "no less than four thousand political prisoners . . . being held in the jails of Venezuela."[22] When, in January, before the Caracas Conference, Pérez Jiménez announced the release of four hundred political prisoners and claimed that they represented sixty percent of all those held, the IADF challenged the dictator's figures. It affirmed that there were thousands, not hundreds, remaining in prison and said that it possessed "an authenticated list of political prisoners." It again called for "moral pressure" to secure their release before the Caracas Conference.[23]

In this regard, Miss Grant and the members of the U.S. committee of the IADF called upon Assistant Secretary Cabot before his departure for Caracas in order to present him with a memorandum on Latin American policy. In it they reiterated their plea for the release of political prisoners in Venezuela. The integrity of the conference was threatened, they insisted, because the host country denied its citizens essential freedoms and filled its jails with political prisoners. Moreover, they criticized U.S. policy as friendly to dictators. They urged the United States to refuse aid to any government which violated the conventions on human rights agreed upon at Chapultepec and Bogotá. Miss Grant and her colleagues also appealed for assistance to governments "trying to carry out social reforms through democratic procedures" (*viz.*, Bolivia and Costa Rica) and endorsed the recommendations of Dr. Milton Eisenhower for extensive economic assistance to Latin America.[24] Nineteen fifty-four was, alas, too early for these changes.

Another example of the close cooperation between the IADF and Acción Democrática occurred in October 1956. At that time, it will be recalled, the Venezuelan government had announced the discovery of a plot to assassinate President Marcos Pérez Jiménez. Betancourt, in turn, had described the charges as a maneuver to force his expulsion from Puerto Rico and as a pretense for further persecutions inside Venezuela. He was concerned about the lives of many of those arrested by the Seguridad Nacional and added that he himself was marked for assassination. A major portion of the October 1956 issue of *Venezuela Democrática* was devoted to the exoneration of Betancourt and quoted numerous statements on his behalf by democratic leaders of Latin America. On 3 October Frances Grant for the IADF and Roger Baldwin for the International League for the Rights of Man prepared a detailed statement of the affair and presented a formal protest to UN Secretary General Dag Hammarskjöld. The protest denounced Pérez Jiménez for "wholesale violations of human rights," including illegal imprisonment, torture, and murder. It asked the secretary general to intercede with Pérez Jiménez for the release of political prisoners, specifically those rounded up in connection with the alleged plot and particularly industrialist Mario Pérez Pisanty.[25] Miss Grant and Mr. Baldwin also requested the UN to investigate the situation of all political prisoners in Venezuela and to enjoin the dictatorship to stop its "intimidation and persecution of the exiled leaders of the opposition parties."[26] Specific mention was made of the harassment of Betancourt. These intercessions were designed, of course, to expose the Latin American dictatorships and, at the same time, to arouse public opinion.

As noted, the IADF was critical of U.S. policy toward Latin America. In addition to direct pressure against the State Department and public officials in the hope of promoting a change, the IADF undertook to inform and educate the North American public. According to Miss Grant, the association "organized literally hundreds of meetings, seminars, round-table discussions, mass public meetings, luncheons, and dinners."[27] Significant among these the IADF sponsored public addresses and lectures by leading Latin American democrats. In April 1951 the IADF invited José Figueres to the United States and arranged talks for him in Washington, New York, Boston, Chicago, and Stanford, and on various college and university campuses.[28] In September 1956 Ramón Villeda Morales, the Honduran leader then in exile, was the IADF's guest in the United States for two weeks. His visit was timed to precede elections in Honduras, and the IADF affirmed that his warning of the consequences of a rigged election contributed to the overthrow of the dictator Julio Lozano Díaz the following month.[29]

The IADF took particular pride in the visits of Rómulo Betancourt. In January 1957, marking the publication of his book, *Venezuela: Política y Petróleo,* Betancourt was honored at a luncheon at the Carnegie International Center in New York. The speakers included O. A. Knight, vice-president, AFL-CIO; Andrés Townsend, Peruvian Aprista leader; and Claude Bowers, former U.S. ambassador to Chile and Spain. Knight spoke for free labor and demanded that the Venezuelan government permit all exiles to return home and restore "trade union freedom and other civil liberties."[30] Betancourt, for his part, expressed confidence in the ultimate liberation of Venezuela and acknowledged the help that Acción Democrática had received from "the liberal democratic sectors of the United States and especially [from] the powerful and influential labor movement."[31] A year later the IADF had the pleasure of hosting a farewell dinner for Betancourt before his return to Venezuela following the fall of Pérez Jiménez. On this occasion, Betancourt reviewed the cycle of democratic government and military dictatorship in Latin America. Addressing himself to the countries that had just overcome tyranny, he declared that the survival of democracy depended upon the full cooperation of all political parties and organized civilian groups. However, as "the most effective antidote against the risk of recurring dictatorship," he revived the old dream—an inter-American court of human rights.[32]

Matching the Betancourt dinners in elegance and distinction were the annual functions at which the IADF honored an outstanding personality or organization for "Services to Inter-American Democracy." These luncheons or dinners dramatized specific aspects of the struggle for democracy and human rights in the Americas and provided wide dissemination for the statements of democratic leaders. José Figueres was the first to receive the award and citation for "his courage [by which] he awakened the conscience of his fellow Americans . . . to a new defense of dignity and liberty for the American peoples."[33] In 1953 the award was made to the *New York Times* and to Herbert L. Matthews, of its editorial board, for "their enlightened services to the cause of inter-American understanding and human rights in the Americas." The *New York Times* was described as one of the very few American publications showing "a serious sense of responsibility in its reporting of Latin American events."[34] The republic of Colombia was cited in 1954 for its stand on behalf of the right of asylum in the case of Haya de la Torre.

On 8 October 1955, José Mora, Uruguayan ambassador to the United States and the chairman of the Council of the OAS, received the award for his action during the Costa Rican-Nicaraguan crisis earlier the same year. Professor Robert Alexander spoke on this occasion and noted that Ambassador Mora had in effect carried out the policy long-advocated by his countryman Eduardo Rodríguez Larreta, who, he observed, had been "ahead of his time."[35] In the aftermath of the overthrow of Gustavo Rojas Pinilla in Colombia in 1957, the IADF honored Eduardo Santos, a former president of Colombia and the publisher of *El Tiempo* of Bogotá. In accepting the award, Santos declared that during the Rojas dictatorship, "organized labor, the Inter-American Press Association, and the Inter-American Association for Freedom and Democracy were always articulate when the rights of Free Labor were in peril, when freedom of the press was curtailed, or when human rights were jeopardized."[36] Finally, in 1958, the IADF presented its award to a North American, former Assistant Secretary of State Adolf A. Berle, Jr., who, the citation read, had proven himself "a staunch champion of Democracy and Human liberties." Miss Grant thanked Berle for the "immeasurable" help he had given the IADF along its way.[37] In response, Berle paid tribute to the IADF: "[It] is not great, powerful, rich. It consists of a few people with faith in the inter-American world, in the Latin American peoples, and in democracy. It also has the best information about Latin America currently available."[38]

The IADF made this information available in a number of ways. Its bulletin, *Hemispherica,* was a constant measure of political conditions in Latin America and served as a fever chart for the ills of Latin America. In it Miss Grant synthesized her voluminous correspondence with Latin America's Democratic Left, particularly leaders in exile. Robert Alexander's column, "On the Labor Front," appeared in each issue and reported the activities of labor organizations in the hemisphere. *Hemispherica* was described as a monthly bulletin but appeared irregularly and during 1952 was not published at all.

The IADF also arranged many programs, seminars, and lectures. For example, on 7 April 1956 it sponsored an institute on "Our Stake in Latin American Democracy" at the Carnegie International Center. Miss

Grant and members of the U.S. committee, plus Víctor Andrade (Bolivian ambassador to the United States) and Padre Benjamín Núñez (then the Costa Rican ambassador to the UN) appeared on the program.[39] This activity became permanent in September 1958, when the IADF instituted a fifteen-week course on "Latin America in Crisis." The course, consisting of fifteen two-hour meetings, was presented in cooperation with the New York Board of Education as an In-Service Course for Teachers.[40] Though hardly routine, the IADF's work of interceding, protesting, agitating, publicizing and educating was accentuated by extraordinary events such as the Galíndez case.

The disappearance of Jesús de Galíndez became a rallying point for the IADF. Galíndez had attended the founding conference of the IADF and was a member of the U.S. committee. The March-April 1956 issue of *Hemispherica* was dedicated to his memory, and the IADF without reservation accused Trujillo of murdering him. The association, along with the ILRM, *Iberica* Publishing Company, the Post-War World Council, the Dominican Revolutionary party (PRD), the Workers' Defense League, the Council of Spanish American Societies, and the *Adirondack Daily Enterprise* offered a reward of $10,000 for information leading to the arrest and conviction of the killer or killers of Galíndez. Moreover, the IADF undertook to collect $2,500 in order to publish Galíndez' dissertation, *The Era of Trujillo*.[41] At the same time, Miss Grant, Baldwin, Thomas, Romualdi, Sol Levitas (publisher of *The New Leader*), Louise Crane (publisher of *Iberica*), Francine Dunlavy (president of the Pan American Women's Association), and author Wenzéll Brown addressed a letter to the *New York Times* in which they charged that the Dominican Republic was responsible for the disappearance of Galíndez. They noted that three of the most sinister political crimes in the history of New York had been "committed against opponents of the Trujillo regime." They concluded with the demand that the U.S. Department of Justice investigate the Galíndez case.[42]

As the police investigation of the Galíndez case bogged down, and as Trujillo defended himself by slandering his victim, the IADF and individual members of the U.S. committee campaigned hard against both apathy and calumny. Three months after the disappearance of Galíndez, the IADF sponsored a memorial service for him in New York and, through its contacts in the hemisphere, inspired similar services in Buenos Aires and Puerto Rico. The assembly in New York resolved to ask the Congress of the United States to investigate the Galíndez affair, and the group in Puerto Rico sent a resolution to President Eisenhower urging him to exert every effort to solve the crime.[43] When Trujillo tried to say that Galíndez was not a victim of foul play but had actually fled with money entrusted to him as treasurer of the Basque government-in-exile, Norman Thomas came to Galíndez' defense. Thomas wrote to the *New York Times* that Galíndez kept careful records and was "scrupulously honest." Moreover, he recalled that Galíndez was "enthusiastically" looking forward to receiving his Ph.D. degree from Columbia University in June and to the publication of his dissertation.[44] Thomas subsequently criticized the handling of the Galíndez case by the Federal Bureau of Investigation and the New York Police Department and expressed the view that Attorney General Herbert Brownell had given him "the runaround."[45]

When the Galíndez case became the Galíndez-Murphy case, the IADF no longer had to struggle alone. The sensational aspects of the affair blackened the name of Trujillo and greatly facilitated the anti-dictatorial struggle, despite the Dominican dictator's friends. When Representative Charles O. Porter demanded a congressional investigation of the murders of Galíndez and Murphy, a number of his colleagues criticized him for attacking a "friendly nation" vital to "hemispheric defense," and some undertook to praise Trujillo.[46] The IADF deplored these "fawning statesmen" and asked, "what . . . impels such sycophancy to a tawdry and bloody tyrant?"[47] Porter, of course, secured the congressional investigation, and, as has been seen, the Department of Justice also entered the case. The IADF threw its full support behind Porter and invited him to be the guest speaker at a memorial program on 12 March 1957, marking the first anniversary of the disappearance of Galíndez.[48] Later, Porter and the IADF's Alexander coauthored a book, *The Struggle for Democracy in Latin America.* Porter became a popular figure among Latin American democrats, and the kind of welcome he received in Caracas in July 1958 was in sharp contrast to that given Vice-President Nixon there two months earlier.[49]

In the meantime, the IADF continued to press the advantage and did not give Trujillo any respite. Trujillo's hiring of Morris Ernst to conduct a private investigation of the Galíndez disappearance was treated with scorn, and *Hemispherica* reported in detail the operations in Mexico and Central America of Policarpo Soler and Johnny Abbes García.

On the second anniversary of Galíndez' disappearance, the IADF was among fifty groups honoring his memory in ceremonies in the Community Church Auditorium in New York. Tancredo Martínez, himself the intended victim of Trujillo the preceding September, came from Mexico to speak, at the special invitation of Miss Grant. At this meeting, those in attendance approved a lengthy resolution urging the continuation of the Galíndez investigation, the identification and prosecution of unregistered agents of the Dominican Republic in the United States, action against Dominican diplomatic representatives who might abuse their immunity, the termination of military assistance to Trujillo, and an investigation by the OAS of the status of human rights in the Dominican Republic. The resolution also "deplored" the acceptance by American officials and congressmen of decorations from Trujillo and chastised American businessmen who did business with the "ruthless dictator."[50]

Only a few months later, the publication of the Ernst Report evoked a strong dissent from the IADF. The report affirmed not only that Trujillo was innocent of any crime but suggested that Galíndez was still alive and in hiding somewhere in Latin America. The IADF considered both assertions absurd. The IADF declared that Trujillo had murdered Galíndez, and it cited "at least six" other cases in which opponents of Trujillo had been eliminated "under exactly similar circumstances." It felt that the fates of Bencosme, Requena, Báez, and Galíndez were too similar to be coincidence. Concerning the idea that Galíndez was alive, the IADF observed that he was too well-known in the hemisphere, particularly among exile groups, to go undetected anywhere.[51] Perhaps the most succinct comment concerning the Ernst Report was made by Eduardo Santos. Speaking at the IADF award dinner for Berle on 5 June 1958, the winner of the previous year's award called the Ernst Report "the second assassination of Galíndez."[52] Shortly afterward, the Justice Department released Murphy's flight logbook, which virtually described the crime hour-by-hour and reduced the Ernst Report to rubbish. There was little question that the Galíndez affair had discredited Rafael Trujillo.

While the IADF fought specific causes, it also tried to secure the acceptance of two general concepts in the area of human rights. One was an "inter-American passport for political exiles from American dictatorships," and the other was an "inter-American court of human rights."

In September 1957, following a three-month tour of Latin America,

Miss Grant reported that there were "about 500,000 political exiles from Latin American dictatorships wandering about the Western Hemisphere."[53] She was deeply moved by the plight of these "stateless Americans," whose condition she considered "humiliating and inhuman."[54] Lacking legal documents, she stated, the political refugee often could not find employment, nor could he travel, and was deprived of basic civil rights.[55] In order to alleviate this circumstance, Miss Grant, in the name of the IADF, appealed to the UN to grant to political exiles a United Nations passport.[56] She restated the case in 1958, but a year later, under what seemed to be improving circumstances, she turned to the Organization of American States and demanded the creation of an inter-American passport similar to the Nansen passport once granted stateless persons by the League of Nations.[57] The OAS did not respond.

The idea of an inter-American court of human rights was, of course, long-standing. A human rights convention was discussed at the Bogotá Conference in 1948, and this discussion provided the background for the UN Declaration of Human Rights.[58] As noted, the idea was a factor in the founding of the IADF itself. At the IADF farewell dinner for Betancourt in January 1958, the guest of honor gave high priority to the concept. Later, Acción Democrática set as a major foreign policy goal an inter-American court "to which private citizens of Latin America [could] have recourse in seeking to defend themselves against violations of basic rights and freedoms."[59] The IADF, of which the AD leadership was an integral part, supported the idea fully. Beginning its tenth year in 1959, the IADF urged the democratic governments of America to act within the OAS to establish such a court.[60] Again, the appeal was in vain, and, as before, the IADF alone continued to fill the void.

The first ten years of the work of the IADF had been difficult, mainly because dictatorships dominated the Latin American scene. For the same reason, however, the need that it filled was all the greater. In many instances, it was the lone advocate of the Democratic Left in exile for justice. Because of its extensive contacts with the Latin American Democratic Left and because it was part of the North American intellectual and liberal community, it acted as a nerve center receiving impulses and taking appropriate action. It operated almost exclusively in the United States, where it exerted pressure upon the American government, influenced and aroused public opinion, and had direct access to the major international organizations in New York and Washington. Such activity was important, not only because it exposed the nature of the dictatorial regimes but because a number of North American politicians looked upon the Democratic Left in exile with suspicion and hostility. The attitude and opinion of the powerful United States was an important consideration in the antidictatorial struggle. On the other hand, the activities of Miss Grant and the U.S. committee of the IADF helped prevent a total estrangement between the United States and the democratic leaders of Latin America. This was demonstrated in a personal tribute to Miss Grant by the AD exiles in Mexico on 29 August 1957. Seated next to Rómulo Gallegos, she heard herself described as "the best of the North American liberal tradition and thought."[61] The activities of the IADF, as noted, tended to involve questions of human rights. Not exclusive of these concerns, but having special interests and competence, organized labor also served as an ally of the Democratic Left in exile. Often working in close harmony with the IADF, the free labor movement contributed significantly to the antidictatorial struggle.

The Free Trade Union Movement

Free labor by definition was opposed to all forms of totalitarianism. Hence, its collaboration with the democratic forces of the Caribbean was natural. In fact, the free trade union movement, as represented in the United States by the American Federation of Labor (AFL), sought the assistance of the Democratic Left and trade unions first. At the end of World War II, the only hemispherewide labor organization was Vicente Lombardo Toledano's Communist-sponsored Latin American Confederation of Workers (CTAL). Free labor considered CTAL a failure and charged that it had subordinated the aims of the working class to the interests of the Soviet Union.[62] Consequently, in January 1946 the AFL appointed Serafino Romualdi to handle Latin American labor affairs and assigned him the task of promoting an inter-American free labor organization. Thus began the remarkable career of Romualdi, who served as labor's "ambassador" in Latin America and who was labor's counterpart to Frances Grant. Romualdi's first task took two years to complete and during that time he received indispensable support from Rómulo Betancourt and Víctor Raúl Haya de la Torre.[63]

Romualdi's success was marked by the founding of the Inter-American Confederation of Workers, CIT (Confederación Interamericana de Trabajadores), in its First Congress in Lima, Peru, in January 1948. The new organization was sponsored by the labor confederations of Chile and Peru and the AFL of the United States, with strong support from the trade union organizations of Costa Rica, Cuba, and Venezuela.[64] Communist unions were barred, as was the *Peronista* General Confederation of Labor of Argentina. The Inter-American Confederation of Workers (CIT) dedicated itself to the defense and extension of trade union rights and pledged to oppose all totalitarian threats to the labor movement in particular and to the American political system in general. Bernardo Ibáñez of Chile was elected president, and the vice-presidents included George Meany of the United States, Arturo Sabroso of Peru, Francisco Aguirre of Cuba, and Luis Alberto Monge of Costa Rica. Romualdi was elected secretary of international relations. The headquarters was to be in Lima, but political conditions in Peru dictated its transfer to Santiago, Chile. In September 1949 the headquarters was moved again, this time to Havana, which brought the CIT and its successor, the Inter-American Regional Organization of Workers, ORIT (Organización Regional Interamericana de Trabajadores), directly into Caribbean affairs.

Although the founders of the CIT, particularly in the AFL, thought its main tasks should be organization and the development of trade union techniques, almost immediately its full time and energy were absorbed in the antidictatorial struggle. In October 1948 Manuel Odría seized power in Peru; the Peruvian Confederation of Workers (CTP) was outlawed and CIT Vice-President Arturo Sabroso and hundreds of other labor leaders were imprisoned. Two months later, the overthrow of Rómulo Gallegos resulted in similar repression of trade unions in Venezuela. In exile in Havana, the secretary general of the Venezuelan Confederation of Workers (CTV), Augusto Malavé Villalba, sought help. Free labor was now in the fight.

In the task of defending trade union rights and human liberties, the CIT was in a better position than the IADF. Its trade union affiliates, especially those in the United States, were powerful, and a number of them enjoyed consultative status in the United Nations. Moreover, labor possessed a kind of international court of human rights. The International Labor Organization (ILO), with its unique tripartite system of representation, under which a member state's delegation was made up of government, employer, and worker representatives, enabled labor to act in the international sphere independent of the official policy of a state or group of states. Although the government and employer delegates could outvote those of labor, the latter could bring to the attention of the world complaints against working conditions in any country; few international organizations possessed the supranational powers of the ILO. It was significant, then, that at the annual ILO conference in June 1948, the CIT acquired consultative status and its president, Bernardo Ibáñez, was elected to the governing body. Operating from this base, the CIT undertook to denounce the antilabor policies of Peru and Venezuela before the Fourth ILO Regional Conference of American States in Montevideo in April 1949.[65]

The CIT was unable to achieve all its goals at the Montevideo conference, but it demonstrated its ability to force national governments to respond to its pressure. Although Peru and Venezuela had refrained from sending workers' delegates in order to avoid trouble with the credentials committee,[66] Ibáñez and Romualdi prepared a resolution which condemned the two countries for their violations of trade union rights and urged the ILO to investigate these charges. However, the United States was displeased with the resolution. It seemed willing to work for certain practical results (e.g., restrain the dictators) but not at the expense of "hemispheric solidarity." At that very moment, it was trying to persuade Uruguay to withdraw a resolution in the UN demanding an inquiry of alleged violations of human rights in Venezuela, by trying to arrange assurances that AD prisoners would be released. The U.S. governmental delegate, Ellis Briggs, therefore, pointing out that the resolution would be defeated, induced Romualdi to drop the condemnation of Peru and Venezuela and merely to cite the charges against them, with a request for an inquiry.[67] Briggs then lined up the support of the governmental delegates, and the modified resolution passed. At the same time, the Venezuelan government invited the ILO to send a mission to study labor conditions in Venezuela. While this appeared to save face for Venezuela, the result was the mission of Jef Rens (Supra, pp. 124-125), which, it will be recalled, led to painful embarrassment for the Venezuelan junta.

By the time of its Second Congress, it was evident that the main preoccupation of the CIT was the fight against dictatorial governments. Meeting in Havana in September 1949, the CIT gave its approval to a lengthy report entitled the "Crisis of Democracy in America," which scored the military dictatorships of Peru and Venezuela and condemned the tyrants of the Dominican Republic and Nicaragua.[68] Trujillo was described as a "menace to peace in the Caribbean."[69] The congress, obviously inspired by the ideas of Betancourt, passed a resolution which called upon democratic governments to withhold recognition from military dictatorships, to deny economic and technical assistance to them, and to denounce before the ILO, the OAS, and the UN Human Rights Commission the violations of fundamental rights on the part of dictators.[70] The resolution also recommended the study of a possible labor boycott of goods and products going to or coming from Peru, Venezuela, and the Dominican Republic. The CIT also approved a proposal for the creation of a human rights tribunal and endorsed the idea for an inter-American conference of democratic groups. This was in support of Cuban President Prío, who had addressed the sessions, and it assured free labor's participation in the founding conference of the IADF the following May.

The Second Congress also marked significant steps in the evolution of the free trade union movement. The CIT itself underwent a reorganization. The office of president was retained as a protocolary function, and the post of general secretary was created to assume the executive function. Cuban labor leader Francisco Aguirre was elected general secretary, and the headquarters of the CIT was transferred to Havana. It may be noted also that Malavé Villalba, the Venezuelan labor leader in exile, was elected recording secretary. The move to Havana was made to facilitate participation of the CIT in the establishment of a new international trade union organization.[71] Just as the CIT was created to compete with the Latin American Confederation of Workers (CTAL), the International Confederation of Free Trade Unions (ICFTU)[72] was founded in London in December 1949 to combat the Communist-controlled World Federation of Trade Unions (WFTU). The CIT resolved to send a delegation to the London conference and to recommend to its affiliates that they join the international organization. The CIT realized that affiliation with a worldwide organization would give greater efficacy to its actions and it was prepared, in fact, to become the regional branch of such an organization. Sensing, therefore, that the Second Congress was probably its last, the CIT drafted a "Declaration of Principles" to guide its successor. It reiterated its democratic character and its independence from any form of state control and totalitarian practice and it declared that it was opposed to communism, colonialism, and dictatorship.[73]

Although 1950 was a year of transition for the CIT, inter-American free labor continued the antidictatorial struggle. The executive committee of the CIT met in Havana in January and set into motion the steps necessary to transform the CIT into the inter-American regional organization of the ICFTU. The executive committee and the secretariat served as a "bridge" between the old and the new.[74] There was strong sentiment to make as few changes as necessary, even to keep the name, but since a number of non-CIT groups were involved, including the Canadian Confederation of Labor (CCL) and the Congress of Industrial Organizations (CIO), this hope was not realized.[75] In the meantime, in March, the CIT addressed a letter to the British Trades Union Congress (TUC) and requested it to exert pressure on the British government to stop the sale of arms to Latin American dictators. It noted that the U.S. government had suspended arms sales to these dictators but that the British government had just sold destroyers and aircraft to Trujillo and aircraft and machine guns to the Venezuelan military junta.[76] Free labor, of course, played an important role in the founding of the IADF in May. Aguirre, Ibáñez, and Romualdi served on the organizing committee for the conference, and George P. Delaney, Charles Zimmerman, and Romualdi of the AFL, and Ernest Schwartz of the CIO were members of the U.S. delegation. Romualdi and Schwartz became members of the original U.S. committee of the IADF. In June the AFL's Delaney blocked the seating of the Venezuelan worker delegate at the annual ILO conference in Geneva.[77] Two months later, the ILO published the report of the Rens Mission, which severely criticized the Venezuelan government for its antilabor policies. By this time, the CIT had now completed much of the preliminary work for the founding congress of the new regional organization and in agreement with the ICFTU scheduled it for 8-12 January 1951 in Mexico City.

The CIT was replaced by the Inter-American Regional Organization of Workers, commonly known by the Spanish abbreviated form ORIT (Organización Regional Interamericana de Trabajadores). The new organization was essentially the same as the old, although inter-American free labor had traded its autonomy for the broader scope and greater strength provided by the International Confederation of Free Trade Unions. The headquarters remained in Havana, and Aguirre was elected regional secretary (the equivalent of general secretary; in fact, the title was restored in 1952). Other former CIT officers were retained: Arturo Sabroso of Peru was elected president; Ibáñez and Meany were elected to the executive committee; and Romualdi was appointed assistant secretary for international relations and education. Exiles Malavé Villalba of Venezuela and Arturo Jáuregui of Peru were appointed organizers. New names included John L. Lewis of the United Mine Workers and Jacob Potofsky of the CIO, who were elected to the executive committee, and Schwartz of the CIO, who was appointed assistant secretary for research and social and economic affairs.[78] The aims and purposes of the ORIT reaffirmed those of the CIT, namely, "the defense of the interests and rights of its affiliates and of the working classes in general" and the "permanent struggle against all forms of dictatorship and totalitarianism."[79] The anti-Communist nature of the ORIT was underscored in numerous pronouncements, particularly in the address by J. H. Oldenbroek, the secretary general of the ICFTU.

The congress specifically condemned the antitrade union policies of Rafael Trujillo. A year earlier, Dominican "trade union" delegates had tried to crash the constituent congress of the ICFTU and had been expelled. Trujillo did not send any representatives to Mexico City, but the ORIT resolved to demand that the Dominican government fulfill its international commitments with reference to trade union freedom, human rights, and individual and social guarantees. It resolved also to request the executive committee to send a workers' committee to study the status of labor in the Dominican Republic.[80] Subsequently, the ORIT undertook such a mission, but Trujillo would not allow it to enter his land. In the meantime, the ORIT established close relations with Dominican leaders in exile, particularly with Angel Miolán, who established in Havana in 1952 the Dominican Democratic Workers Committee in Exile, CODDE (Comité Obrero Democrático Dominicano en Exilio).[81] The First Congress of the ORIT also called upon all nations of the hemisphere to permit the return of exiled trade union leaders and to hold free elections.[82]

The founding of the ORIT did not solve all the organizational problems of inter-American free labor. In fact, it compounded some. However, it still provided an effective vehicle for opposition against the dictators of the Caribbean, and in time its internal structure was improved.

The attack upon Venezuela was particularly heavy. With Betancourt and Malavé Villalba in exile in Havana, the ORIT secretariat received a steady flow of reports charging the Caracas junta with the arbitrary arrest and mistreatment of trade union leaders. So effective was the AD-CTV campaign through the ORIT that Venezuelan-Cuban relations in general deteriorated.[83] The information supplied by Betancourt was also forwarded to the ICFTU, which presented a complaint before the UN Commission on Human Rights.[84] On 1 March 1951 Romualdi for the AFL, Schwartz for the CIO, and Anthony Boyle for the United Mine Workers (UMW) called upon the Venezuelan ambassador in Washington, Dr. Antonio Martín Araujo. They expressed to him their concern about the imprisonment of trade union leaders in Venezuela without formal charges and asked him to transmit to the Venezuelan junta their anxiety with reference to organized labor in Venezuela.[85] According to Betancourt, these pressures forced the Venezuelan junta to permit the holding of the traditional May Day parade that year. Although the police broke up the parade and demonstration before any speeches were made, some workers managed to display a banner which proclaimed simply, "*Viva la* ORIT."[86]

In January 1952 the accumulated charges against Venezuela for violations of trade union rights were drawn up in a lengthy report by Matthew Woll, vice-president of the AFL, and Jacob Potofsky, president of the Amalgamated Clothing Workers of America, CIO, and chairman of the CIO Latin American Committee. Acting on behalf of the ICFTU, Woll and Potofsky on 15 January presented their report to the UN Economic and Social Council, where the ICFTU enjoyed consultative status.[87] Woll and Potofsky charged specifically that "three thousand Venezuelan workers had been jailed without due process of law and that all Venezuelan unions had been deprived of their funds and membership records."[88] The ORIT published the report under the title "The Trade Union Movement of Venezuela, Victim of the Military Dictatorship," and on 7 February the ICFTU and the International League for the Rights of Man requested UN Secretary General Trygve Lie to investigate these charges. At the same time, the ICFTU called upon the International Labor Organization (ILO) also to investigate the persecution of trade unions in Venezuela.[89] As a result, the ILO sent another mission to Venezuela under Adrianus Vermeulen, a Dutch trade union official and member of the ILO Committee on Freedom of Association. However, Vermeulen's proposals were not acted upon and, in fact, were overtaken by the events surrounding the Venezuelan elections in 1952. Betancourt was not satisfied with the Vermeulen mission either; he felt it treated the Venezuelan dictatorship leniently.[90]

In the international trade union movement, as in other areas, the spread of dictatorial governments in Latin America in 1952 compounded the difficulties of the Democratic Left in exile. Again, the situation in Venezuela presented the most serious challenge. Reacting to the charges made against it, on 5 April the Venezuelan junta convened a "National Convention of Independent Trade Unions" to replace the dissolved Venezuelan Confederation of Workers (CTV). Notwithstanding the fact that the clandestine AD published intercepted government telegrams exposing the junta's sponsorship of the movement, the convention claimed to represent Venezuelan labor and proceeded to elect workers' delegates to the Fifth ILO Regional Conference of American States, set for Rio de Janeiro, 17-30 April 1952.[91] At the Rio Conference Romualdi led the fight to prevent the seating of the Venezuelan workers' delegates, but this time he was unsuccessful. The Venezuelans were admitted after pledging to fight for the restoration of trade union rights in Venezuela, including the release of imprisoned trade union leaders and the reestablishment of the CTV.[92] Romualdi was greatly disappointed over the fact that both Aguirre and Oldenbroek had advocated the seating of the Venezuelans on the basis of these pledges and that subsequently both showed interest in the possible membership of the new Venezuelan trade union movement (the so-called Movimiento Sindical Independiente de Trabajadores, or MOSIT) in the ORIT-ICFTU. Although the failure of MOSIT to redeem the pledges made at Rio de Janeiro in April, and the events surrounding the fraudulent election of Pérez Jiménez at the end of November, contributed to remove this threat, Romualdi was not satisfied with the ORIT-ICFTU policy concerning dictators.

The debate over the seating of the Venezuelan workers' delegates caused Romualdi to seek changes in the leadership and structure of the ORIT-ICFTU. He complained that Aguirre and Oldenbroek were preoccupied with organization and growth and that they equated success in the trade union movement with the number of affiliates. He noted that they did not regard the ideological question as overriding; they seemed to think that even in a dictatorship trade union rights might be promoted by a trade union with international affiliation. Concessions might hopefully be secured and the worker protected through a cautious policy which avoided antagonizing the regime in question.[93] Similarly, Romualdi detected a growing impatience toward exile labor groups on the part of the ILO, which seemed disposed to regard exile activities as political and even counterproductive.[94] This attitude was noticeable at the annual ILO conference in Geneva in June 1952, where the Venezuelan workers' delegates were admitted without any challenge. Furthermore, the ORIT itself was now located in a country under a dictator. Batista had seized power in Cuba in March. Finally, although Romualdi expressed personal regard for Aguirre, he felt that the secretary was neglecting his office because of the numerous other activities in which he was involved. Aguirre was the president of his own union, an officer in the Cuban labor confederation (CTC), and also a member of the Cuban Congress. For all these reasons, Romualdi and Schwartz managed to move up the Second ORIT Congress, originally scheduled for 1954, to December 1952.[95]

The Second ORIT Congress was a triumph for the exile cause. The headquarters of the ORIT was transferred to Mexico City, where again exile groups could exert direct influence, and a twenty-seven-year old Costa Rican trade union leader, Luis Alberto Monge, was elected general secretary (the old title was restored). According to Romualdi, Monge did not measure the strength of the ORIT by the number of affiliates but by its effectiveness in fighting dictators.[96] As an indication that it meant to follow through with this policy, the ORIT passed a number of resolutions which condemned the dictatorial regimes of Peru, Venezuela, the Dominican Republic, and Argentina and which deplored the fact that other governments, "under euphemistic pretexts," were supplying arms and money to the dictators.[97] From this point on, through the fifties, the ORIT policy stressed opposition to militarism and particularly to U.S. military assistance programs. The Second Congress resolved that the way to combat communism was not by furnishing arms but by attacking "poverty, poor health, ignorance, feudal exploitation, etc."[98] The degree to which the exile cause and the antidictatorial struggle was enhanced by the Second Congress was demonstrated by direct action on behalf of exiled trade unionists.

The Congress instructed the executive committee to create a special body to deal with the problems of exiled workers. The original charge was to take steps to protect such exiles and to organize an employment bureau in cooperation with respective national trade union confederations.[99] However, this resolution led to the formation in Mexico City in May 1954 of the Committee of Latin American Democratic Trade Unionists in Exile, CESDAL (Comité de Exilados Sindicalistas Democráticos de América Latina), which was something quite different. It became the action arm of the ORIT and led the trade union struggle against dictators and rallied public opinion.[100] The ORIT provided the committee with funds for an intensive campaign against dictatorships and even channeled money to the underground in Venezuela.[101] The ICFTU under Oldenbroek did not acquiesce fully to these policy changes, but the commitment of inter-American labor to the antidictatorial struggle was undeniable. Moreover, the secretariat was reorganized by the Second Congress, so that the assistant secretaries (Romualdi, Schwartz, and Alfonso Sánchez Madariaga of Mexico) exercised greater power.[102] Ostensibly, this change was made to prevent any repetition of the inertia which had existed under Aguirre, but it also increased the influence of Romualdi, whose personal friendship and political collaboration with Betancourt during these years was profound.

Free labor, as other democratic elements, regarded the mid-fifties in the Caribbean as the period of lowest fortune. The ORIT asserted that the three years following the Second Congress "would have been tragic" without its pressures, leadership, propaganda, and denunciations before international opinion.[103] The ORIT was conspicuous in the attack upon Caracas as the site for the Tenth Inter-American Conference. It sent a circular message to the American foreign ministries protesting Caracas as long as the jails were filled with political and trade union prisoners and as long as Venezuelans were denied their basic liberties.[104] According to Romualdi, the threat to boycott the conference was in the first instance a tactic to secure a pledge from Venezuela to release political prisoners.[105] In September 1953 Romualdi reiterated the position of the ORIT in an address before the annual AFL Convention in St. Louis, Missouri. The next month, he, Monge, Schwartz, Ignacio González Tellechea (the ORIT assistant general secretary), and Paul Reed (UMW) called upon Assistant Secretary of State John Moors Cabot to present the ORIT's objection to the Caracas site.[106] While the ORIT was involved in the outcry against the location of the Tenth Inter-American Conference, it also took a position with reference to the primary issue of the conference, i.e., the Arbenz regime of Guatemala.

The overthrow of the Arbenz government presented free labor with some hard choices, but despite its anti-Communist stance it denounced the intervention of the Latin American dictators. On 25 June 1954 the ORIT declared that it supported fully the economic and social reforms of the Guatemalan Revolution and in the same manner opposed the "imperialistic interests" of the United Fruit Company.[107] It went on

to explain that it held this position notwithstanding the control exercised by "Communist elements" over the Guatemalan labor movement.
It repudiated the efforts of the United Fruit Company "to control the
destiny of Guatemala" and, at the same time, condemned the attempts
by the Communists to claim credit for Guatemala's revolutionary programs. It also denied, however, the "moral authority" of the Latin
American dictators to set themselves up as the "standard-bearers in the
struggle against Communist infiltration." It observed, in fact, that their
removal would be the best thing for peace and democracy. The ORIT
also suggested that the United States seek the counsel of North American free labor rather than that of the United Fruit Company and that
it ignore the "anti-Communist ranting of dictators."[108] Some elements
suggested that the ORIT was under the thumb of the AFL and was
therefore a "tool of Yankee imperialism,"[109] but this statement concerning Guatemala was obviously not atuned to U.S. policy at the time.

Later in 1954, the voice of free labor was either heeded by the
United States or at least more in harmony with its policies. In August
Romualdi for the AFL and Victor Reuther and Daniel Benedict for the
CIO undertook to alert U.S. labor to the situation developing between
Costa Rica and Nicaragua. They prepared a statement in which they
deplored Somoza's threats against Costa Rica, because, they explained,
Costa Rican labor was "the only truly democratic labor movement
functioning in Central America."[110] The situation improved momen-
tarily owing to the "goodwill" visit to San José by six U.S. Air Force
C-47 transports. When, however, the Somoza-sponsored invasion of
Costa Rica finally took place in January 1955, the AFL, CIO, and
UMW again issued statements in support of Costa Rica. AFL's Matthew
Woll urged the United States "to spare neither effort, nor energy, nor
resources" to help Costa Rica repeal the aggression. [111] From the side-
lines free labor could be influential, but it could also be effective in a
direct confrontation. What came to be the "Vermeulen affair" represented a classic example of the ability of externally based opposition to
deliver a direct blow against a dictatorship. In this case, free labor left
Venezuelan President Marcos Pérez Jiménez bleeding.

The success which Pérez Jiménez had enjoyed as host of the inter-
American conference encouraged him to invite the International Labor
Organization to hold the Fifth Session of the Industrial Committee of
the Petroleum Industry in Caracas. The Workers' Group of the ILO
governing body opposed the invitation vigorously but was outvoted by

government and employer representatives, and the meeting was set for 25 April to 7 May 1955 in Caracas.[112]

On 4 March Luis Alberto Monge called upon all ORIT affiliates to boycott the conference. This stand was endorsed by the ICFTU. Ten days later, George Meany and Walter Reuther, AFL and CIO presidents respectively, issued a joint statement denouncing the suppression of trade union rights by the government of Pérez Jiménez and announced their decision not to send representatives to the Fifth Session of the Petroleum Committee. The International Federation of Petroleum Workers, the British TUC, and Canadian, Mexican, and Colombian petroleum workers' groups quickly followed suit. Nonetheless, the ILO Petroleum Conference opened in Caracas on 25 April as scheduled.[113]

The inaugural session was unforgettable. Representatives of the free trade union movement were, of course, absent, except for Adrianus Vermeulen, the Dutch trade union leader, who had been assigned officially as the workers' member of the ILO governing body delegation. He had been in Venezuela on behalf of the ILO in 1952 and had made an inoffensive report concerning freedom of association and the need to guarantee due process to imprisoned trade union leaders. This time it was different. He took the platform in the Aula Magna of the Central University and, in the presence of Pérez Jiménez, reviewed the complaints which the governing body had received during the previous six years concerning the trade union practices of the Venezuelan regime. He quoted extensively from the reports of the Rens and Vermeulen missions and affirmed that nothing had been done to correct the violations of trade union rights outlined in those documents. Furthermore, he declared, there were still trade unionists in jail, and he named Pedro B. Pérez Salinas, president of the Venezuelan Confederation of Workers (CTV); Ramón Quijada, president of the National Federation of Campesinos; Luis Hurtado, secretary of the CTV; and Ismael Ordaz, Andrés Hernández, and Hermenegildo Borromé, leaders of the Oil Workers' Federation.[114] Under these circumstances, and in view of the lack of freedom of association in Venezuela, Vermeulen declared that he sympathized with the decision of the ORIT and its affiliates to boycott the conference. He said that he had come because he had to obey the majority vote of the governing body but declared that he felt impelled to appeal to the govenment of Venezuela to release all trade unionists not accused of criminal acts, to bring to trial those trade unionists against whom there were criminal charges, and to take steps to guarantee freedom of association as prescribed by the ILO Convention.[115]

The repercussions were immediate. The Venezuelan governmental delegate rushed to the platform to denounce Vermeulen for intervening in Venezuelan internal affairs, and, according to eyewitnesses, Pérez Jiménez was apoplectic. Within two hours, Vermeulen was seized by the ubiquitous security chief Pedro Estrada and was expelled from the country to Curaçao.[116]

On 27 April, David A. Morse, the director general of the ILO, cabled Pérez Jiménez to protest this action and to insist that freedom of speech be respected at the conference and that Vermeulen be permitted to return to his place in the sessions.[117] Venezuela demanded, in turn, that Vermeulen modify his statement, but the labor leader refused to change "even a comma." As a result, the Petroleum Committee decided to adjourn the conference on 2 May, without considering a single point of its agenda.[118] The Venezuelan dictatorship was unable to salvage anything from this encounter and was reduced to the impotent gesture of withdrawing from the International Labor Organization on 3 May.

A salutary effect of the Vermeulen episode was the release after four years in prison of Pérez Salinas and José González Navarro. Once in exile, these two labor leaders expressed their gratitude to Vermeulen.[119] However, Luis Hurtado did not share their fate. He was never seen again by his family and friends, and it was learned subsequently that he had been murdered and disposed of by the Seguridad Nacional.

Shortly before the Petroleum Committee met in Caracas, the ORIT held its Third Congress in San José, Costa Rica, 13-17 April 1955. The congress was hosted by José Figueres, who, despite Somoza's attack three months earlier, praised the ORIT's policy of opposing dictators. In fact, the antidictatorial theme dominated the congress. One of its most important acts was the approval of a statement entitled "The Democratic Trade Union Movement and the Dictatorships of America." The document was a declaration of war; it indicted the military dictators for denying their people freedom and for conspiring against democratic governments. It declared that free labor had to take the offensive to destroy these dictators, because "the complete economic and social emancipation of the workingman . . . [was unattainable without] the achievement and guarantee of freedom and political democracy."[120] To this end, it urged the ORIT to mobilize the laborers of the hemisphere and to demand that democratic governments cease giving military aid to dictatorships. The statement specifically praised the AFL and CIO for their action in asking the United States to stop supplying arms to dictators.[121] In order to carry out this manifesto, the Third Congress approved a series of twelve resolutions. The ORIT resolved to do the following: to promote absolute solidarity with free trade unions of countries under military or dictatorial regimes in order to preserve their integrity and safeguard their membership; to furnish necessary funds for the antidictatorial struggle to the committee of exiled trade unionists (CESDAL); to demand that the democratic governments of the Organization of American States require all member states to respect the democratic rights of peoples in accordance with the OAS Charter; to work through the ICFTU to expose violations of international commitments in the areas of human rights and freedom of association; to oppose intervention by dictators in the internal affairs of other states; and to initiate a labor boycott in the event of aggression against a democratic state by a totalitarian government.[122]

Following the Third Congress, the ORIT intensified its efforts in the Caribbean. As dictatorial rule waned generally in the second half of the fifties, the ORIT regarded the Caribbean as particularly vulnerable to the trade union offensive.

The attack upon the Pérez Jiménez regime continued without abatement. The ORIT and the CTV-in-exile published jointly a pamphlet entitled "The International Democratic Movement against the Venezuelan Dictatorship," which described the efforts they had made to prevent the holding of the Fifth Session of the ILO Petroleum Committee in Caracas.[123] In the summer of 1955, *Petro,* the official magazine of the International Federation of Petroleum Workers, charged that the Venezuelan regime was "an absolute dictatorship" and assured the "oppressed Venezuelan brothers" that it would continue the fight for their freedom.[124] On 17 October 1955 Oldenbroek sent a circular message to all ICFTU affiliates protesting the plans of UNESCO to hold the conference on the "Cultural Assimilation of the Immigrant" in Caracas that December.[125] Pérez Jiménez continued to try for respectability. Owing to the agitation of trade union organizations, the conference was not held in Caracas and was rescheduled for Mexico City in April 1956. In December 1955 Pérez Salinas, the newly exiled CTV president, served as the representative of the ORIT at the conference in New York which marked the merger of the AFL and CIO. At this important gathering he described the plight of the Latin American worker under the dictatorial regimes.[126]

Early in February 1956 the executive committee of the ORIT met in Miami Beach, Florida. Thomas Kennedy, international vice-president of the United Mine Workers, spoke and condemned Venezuela for having the poorest record "with respect to the denial of liberties of the people and especially the trade union movement."[127] After also hearing Pérez Salinas, now a member of the executive committee, the committee passed a number of resolutions, the most important of which called for the release of imprisoned trade union leaders.[128] The meeting also sent a cable to the Third Meeting of the Inter-American Council of Jurists in Mexico City in support of the action taken by the Venezuelan lawyers in exile, who, it will be recalled, denounced the "antijuridical situation" existing in Venezuela.[129]

This agitation produced specific results. In November 1955 the ILO governing body instructed its Committee of Conciliation and Inquiry to undertake a thorough investigation of the "repeated denunciations" of the Venezuelan government for violations of trade union rights.[130] The following month an exasperated Pérez Jiménez released scores of trade union leaders from prison. Some, such as Luis Tovar and Ramón Quijada, were rearrested and imprisoned after only a few weeks of freedom, but others managed to reach safety in exile, although with virtually no more than the clothing they were wearing.[131]

The ORIT and its affiliates, particularly the AFL-CIO, came forth immediately with contributions to assist this new group of exiles, and this gesture was gratefully acknowledged by the CTV-in-exile in its New Year's message.[132] But no one indulged in past achievements. When the Venezuelan Confederation of Workers (CTV) appealed to international free labor on May Day 1957 for help in securing the release from prison of Tovar, Quijada, and other labor leaders, trade union solidarity was manifested. The ICFTU urged its affiliates to make public remonstrances against the trade union situation in Venezuela.[133] The Confederation of Workers of Ecuador and the United Workers' Bloc of Mexico, among others, sent cables to Pérez Jiménez demanding the release of the imprisoned trade unionists.[134]

In the last year of the rule of Pérez Jiménez, free labor closed in, along with other elements, for the final thrust against the dictatorship. In January 1957 the ORIT sponsored a trip through Latin America by a group of Hungarian refugees and sent along two Venezuelan trade union exiles, Vicente Gamboa Marcano and Alcides Rondón, so that the crimes of Pérez Jiménez and Pedro Estrada would be exposed along with those of Kadar and the Soviets.[135] At its meeting in July, the ICFTU executive committee discussed a plan for a worldwide labor boycott of Venezuelan shipping and products.[136] While studying the feasibility of such a plan, the committee prepared a comprehensive denunciation of the Venezuelan dictatorship, which it immediately presented to UNESCO. The document was a history of the violations of human and trade union rights in Venezuela since 1949. It censured the regime for the dissolution of the CTV and the seizure of its offices, records, and funds and condemned Pérez Jiménez for the arrest, torture, exile, and murder of trade union leaders. Its accusations were specific; it presented the names of imprisoned labor leaders, including Carlos Behrens, Salom Meza Espinoza, and Juan José Delpino, who had then been in jail for six years. The document concluded with a request to UNESCO to rebuke Venezuela for violations of the Universal Declaration of the Rights of Man and to require Venezuela to fulfill its international obligations in accordance with the declaration and the ILO Convention.[137] This action opened the prison doors for Carlos Behrens, vice-president of the National Federation of Campesinos, who went into exile in September 1957.

In September also, following the call of the CTV for free elections in Venezuela, the ORIT and a number of the powerful International Trade Secretariats issued a statement proclaiming solidarity with their Venezuelan brothers.[138] The CTV observed that this pronouncement resulted in an inundation of demands and appeals on the part of trade union organizations for the restoration of freedom and democracy in Venezuela.[139] When Pérez Jiménez finally fell in January 1958, Betancourt acknowledged again his gratitude to free labor for its support during the years of exile.[140] As one of the first acts of the junta ruling provisionally after the overthrow of Pérez Jiménez, Venezuela rejoined the International Labor Organization.

The struggle of free labor against the Pérez Jiménez regime was an example of its antidictatorial crusade in general. The trade union offensive was directed against every dictatorship in the Caribbean. Only with reference to Cuba was there a degree of ambivalence in the ORIT-ICFTU policy. The Cuban Confederation of Workers (CTC) continued to function in Cuba during Batista's rule. Although the ORIT declared specifically in October 1957 that its opposition to dictatorships "never excluded" Batista,[141] it remained affiliated with the CTC, which, it noted, had to exercise "a great deal of tact and diplomacy."[142] As will be seen, this tolerance caused a severe crisis for the ORIT when Fidel Castro ascended to power in Cuba. With reference to Rafael Trujillo, however, the ORIT-ICFTU made its position perfectly clear.

Free labor repeatedly denounced the trade union situation in the Dominican Republic and proclaimed its solidarity with the Dominican exiles. In July 1956 Angel Miolán and Nicolás Silfa traveled to Brussels to appeal to the executive committee of the ICFTU for a labor boycott of the Dominican Republic.[143] The ICFTU agreed to consider such a possibility in consultation with its regional labor organizations and passed a number of resolutions attacking the Trujillo regime. It declared that the right to strike was denied Dominican workers and requested its affiliates and the International Trade Secretariats "to protest against the policy of terror, crime, and persecution pursued by the Trujillo regime, as well as against its intrigues abroad and its murders of the enemies of the regime." The ICFTU secretary general was instructed to present these complaints to the ILO and to the UN Human Rights Commission.[144] President George Meany of the AFL-CIO, a month earlier, declined an invitation to visit the Dominican Republic. He pointed out that in 1951 and in 1952 the ICFTU and the ILO respectively had agreed to send study missions to the Dominican Republic, but that at the last minute the invitations were withdrawn. He added that complaints against the Dominican government for the suppression of civil and trade union rights were "not new," and that an investigation by an international body was "highly desirable." However, he did not "see the point" in an invitation to him while "the other two [were] still pending."[145] Meany turned down a second invitation with greater scorn and urged the State Department to "exclude the Dominican government from its good neighbor policy."[146]

As a result of these pressures, Trujillo permitted the ICFTU to send two missions to the Dominican Republic. At the end of 1957, the ICFTU director of organization visited the Dominican Republic, and shortly thereafter Daniel Benedict of the AFL-CIO and Raúl Valdivia of the Federation of Sugar Workers of Cuba arrived in the country. The ICFTU charged that "both missions took note of the true situation of slavery and impotence of the Dominican people under the Trujillo regime."[147] Benedict and Valdivia reported specifically that there was no freedom of association under Trujillo, that collective bargaining did not exist, and that forced labor was practiced on certain sisal plantations and in some rice fields.[148]

The ORIT-ICFTU remained the constant enemy of Trujillo until his death in 1961. In addition to the repeated denunciations of the regime before the ILO and some UN bodies, the free trade union movement sought the expulsion of the Dominican Republic from the OAS and explored other ways of fighting Trujillo, including a labor boycott. [149]

The Fourth Congress of the ORIT, held in Bogotá in December 1958, reflected the changing political situation in Latin America and the Caribbean. In the three years since the previous congress, dictatorial regimes had fallen in Argentina, Peru, Colombia, Honduras, and Venezuela, and Anastasio Somoza of Nicaragua had been assassinated. Although the congress condemned the continuing dictatorships in Cuba, the Dominican Republic, and Paraguay, and expressed its concern over the situation then developing in Haiti, generally it turned its attention to economic matters. For the first time since its founding, the ORIT emphasized the so-called "bread-and-butter" issues: the right to organize and bargain collectively, the eight-hour day and the forty-hour week, and guarantees for working women. It also raised the broader aspects of economic and social progress as a means of improving the workers' conditions: agrarian reform, diversification, industrialization, an inter-American development bank, a Latin American common market, etc.[150] Although the struggle against dictatorship was not over, by the end of 1958 free labor, as the other groups involved in the Caribbean struggle, had completed a phase in its activity. Romualdi believed that the urgency of the political situation had passed and that the ORIT could devote more of its energy and resources to the "organizational and educational aspects" of its program.[151]

In looking back upon this phase, free labor could recall solid achievements in the antidictatorial struggle in the Caribbean. In its campaign for trade union freedom and human rights, it had mobilized some of the most important international organizations and had caused the dictators severe embarrassment, weakening their political positions significantly. In addition, it had secured the release of trade union and political leaders from the dictators' jails. There had been differences of opinion within the free trade union movement concerning its appropriate role in opposing dictatorial rule, but thanks largely to Romualdi, Monge, and Schwartz the objections to "mixing in politics" were overcome. After December 1952, particularly, the collaboration between the ORIT and the Democratic Left in exile became intimate. The ORIT not only coordinated its efforts with the exile groups but provided funds for the support of exile activities in general and employed a number of the exiled trade union leaders on its staff. Although free labor supported the Democratic Left in exile in opposing all violations of human rights and civil liberties, the policies of the dictators with reference to freedom of the press provided yet another opportunity for the exiles to gain a new ally.

The Inter-American Press Association

The Democratic Left in exile sought the support of the press in order to expose conditions in the Caribbean and to rally public opinion to its side. However, the press was not corporate but consisted of many individual newspapers with distinct political viewpoints. Certain newspapers were sympathetic to the exile groups, but others were suspicious of them and some were openly hostile. Obviously, the relations with the press were not as satisfactory as those with the IADF or free labor and relied more upon individual contacts. With reference to the general principle of freedom of the press, however, opinion was more definite, and the Inter-American Press Association (IAPA), or Sociedad Interamericana de Prensa (SIP), was organized to serve as a guardian.

From the standpoint of the exiles, the IAPA had limitations. Virtually new, as a result of a thorough reorganization in 1950, its purpose was to promote a uniformally free press in the Americas, but, again, it represented the full spectrum of political attitudes. Its membership was institutional too, so that it reflected the views of newspaper owners and publishers rather than those of working journalists. It was not a craft guild. In its defense of freedom of the press, the IAPA was less apt to be committed to a particular political solution and was less interventionist in its policies. During the fifties its membership included newspapers being published where dictators ruled. Ostensibly, these newspapers were privately owned and were not the propaganda organs of any state, the two basic requirements of IAPA membership, but the IAPA did not succeed in purging its ranks completely of collaborators with dictatorships.

Neither did the exiles find within the IAPA a champion for their cause of the sort of Frances Grant or Serafino Romualdi. The closest that the IAPA came to such a crusader was with the chairman of its Committee on Freedom of the Press, Jules Dubois. Although Dubois clashed on several occasions with dictators Somoza and Trujillo, he was not identified with the Democratic Left and lacked empathy with the exile leadership. Outspoken and free-wheeling, he represented the conservative *Chicago Tribune* and was aggressively anti-Communist. Juan José Arévalo, on the one hand, attacked him as the "advance agent of the millionaires,"[152] whereas, on the other, Trujillo severely condemned his activities.[153] Nonetheless, the reports of the Dubois committee were no comfort to the dictators of the Caribbean.

Within this situation, the role which the IAPA played in the struggle for democracy in the Caribbean was important. The IAPA opposed the dictators on the issue of freedom of the press specifically and fought in behalf of human rights generally.

Naturally, the individual members of the IAPA exercised the power of the press, but the association itself possessed a number of weapons. Mary A. Gardner, in a monographic study of the IAPA, described these as "tools of pressure." Among them she included "public statements," such as editorials and addresses by IAPA representatives, but particularly the Report of the Freedom of the Press Committee presented at the annual meeting.[154] The IAPA also made use of "envoys" for on-the-spot investigations of press conditions; Dubois was a constant traveler.[155] "Awards" were another form of pressure. The IAPA-Mergenthaler Award for distinguished service in the struggle for a free press could be used to dramatize particular situations. In one case, the award was made to an Argentine editor, David Michel Torino, following his imprisonment by Juan Perón.[156] The IAPA set up a "Freedom of the Press Tribunal" in 1950 to investigate violations of press freedom, but apparently it did not function well and was abandoned.[157] In 1952 the IAPA reached an agreement known as the "Panama Doctrine" with the Inter-American Association of Broadcasters by which the two groups pledged to act in concert against attacks upon either the press or radio. "Freedom of the Press Day," every 7 June, provided an opportunity to call public attention to certain situations. Finally, the IAPA worked in "liaison with other press associations," such as the American Society of Newspaper Editors (ASNE), and, in fact, encouraged the formation of a number of such national and local press groups in Latin America.[158]

The Ninth Annual Meeting in Mexico City in October 1953 marked the IAPA's effective beginning of the antidictatorial struggle. Up to this point, it had been troubled by organizational and financial problems.

Dubois presented a report which surveyed press conditions in Latin America country-by-country. With reference to the Carribean states, it concluded that freedom of the press was "curtailed" in Venezuela, El Salvador, and the Dominican Republic. Venezuela was criticized for its three-day news blackout of the 1952 "elections" and for maintaining a policy of censoring all news dispatches.[159] Owing to the enactment of a restrictive press law, Nicaragua also was added to the list of countries in which freedom of expression was limited.[160] In fact, the IAPA's campaign against the Somoza regime developed into one of its most active and effective.

The IAPA's intense interest in the Nicaraguan situation stemmed from the fact that two of Somoza's bitterest enemies were publishers of Managua dailies, Pedro Joaquín Chamorro of *La Prensa* and Hernán Robleto of *Flecha*. Moreover, Chamorro was himself a member of the Freedom of the Press Committee. It will be recalled that both were implicated in the April 1954 attempt against Somoza and that Chamorro was arrested, while Robleto took asylum in the Costa Rican Embassy. The IAPA's president for 1953-54, Miguel Lanz Duret of Mexico, traveled to Managua personally and secured Robleto's safe-conduct from Somoza.[161]

Dubois also visited Nicaragua numerous times during the crisis. In December 1954 he obtained a pledge from Somoza to lift the state of seige and thus abolish the press censorship in effect since April.[162] He returned to Managua in March 1955 and again in June, finally securing Chamorro's release from prison.[163] Somoza displayed additional willingness to accommodate the IAPA. In April 1956 he declared his intention to revise the press law criticized by the IAPA, the "Zurita Law," which required editors and journalists as a group to be especially responsible for what they said and wrote. Somoza even invited James G. Stahlman, IAPA president for 1955-56, to help draft a new law. Stahlman rejected the invitation, saying that the press did not want special treatment but simply the normal guarantees due all citizens with reference to freedom of expression and freedom of the press.[164]

The assassination of Somoza in September 1956 precipitated a new crisis between the IAPA and Nicaragua. Pedro Joaquín Chamorro was arrested again. Chamorro denied that he was involved in the assassination but asserted that he was tortured in an effort to force him to make a confession and even to implicate Jules Dubois.[165] Once before the IAPA had rescued Chamorro from prison, perhaps saved his life, so at the end of March 1957 Daniel Morales, editor of *Mañana* of Mexico, arrived in Managua to intervene on his behalf.[166] Found guilty of complicity in Somoza's assassination, Chamorro was banished to San Carlos del Río to await sentencing, from where he easily crossed the San Juan River to exile in Costa Rica in April. The IAPA immediately requested President Figueres to grant him asylum.[167]

Chamorro was present at the IAPA's Thirteenth Meeting in October 1957 in Washington, where the Freedom of the Press Committee presented a vigorous denunciation of Nicaragua for restrictions upon freedom of expression. President Luis Somoza, the son of the slain dictator, in an avowed effort to improve Nicaragua's image, sent representatives to the meeting to explain the position of his government and admitted that there were defects in the Zurita Law.[168] In fact, Luis promised to seek repeal of the measure and on 13 December, by action of the Nicaraguan Chamber of Deputies, he fulfilled his pledge. John T. O'Rourke, the IAPA's president for 1957-58, expressed the association's "satisfaction."[169] Even though the Nicaraguan government was undergoing a transition, this action was a clear example of the effectiveness of external pressure upon a dictatorial regime.

Acción Democrática, of course, was aware of the kind of pressure the IAPA could exert. As noted, in 1953 the Freedom of the Press Committee denounced Venezuela as a major transgressor against press freedom; then in April 1955 the IAPA protested the seizure by the Venezuelan government of the Mexican monthly *Humanismo*. This journal, *Bohemia* (Cuba), and *Cuadernos Americanos* (Mexico) were not permitted to pass through Venezuelan customs, and it was "a crime punishable with jail or deportation to possess a copy of any of these publications."[170]

A group of exiled Venezuelan journalists in Mexico, among them Ricardo Montilla, Ildegar Pérez Segnini, and José M. Siso Martínez, sent a telegram on 31 October 1955 to the IAPA Meeting in New Orleans (the eleventh annual meeting) and listed their complaints against the Venezuelan government. They charged that many newspapers had been closed, that those still publishing were censored, and that journalists had been imprisoned, tortured, and exiled. They also cited the martyrdom in exile of journalists Andrés Eloy Blanco, Valmore Rodríguez, and Luis Troconis Guerrero.[171] In response, the IAPA called for the lifting of press restrictions in Venezuela and for the return of exiled journalists. Also, in addition to forwarding appeals to the U.S. State

Department, it considered the possibility of requesting private companies to refuse to sell newsprint and equipment to dictators.[172]

The IAPA's opposition to the Caribbean dictators, particularly Pérez Jiménez, picked up great momentum in 1956 during the presidency of James G. Stahlman of *The Nashville Banner* (Tennessee). In April, at the IAPA Board of Directors meeting in Hamilton, Bermuda, Stahlman declared, "Venezuela may abound in riches, but as for free expression it is totally bankrupt."[173] At the same time, he received an appeal from AD exiles, among them César Gil Gómez of the Venezuelan Association of Journalists, AVP (Asociación Venezolana de Periodistas), for the release of imprisoned journalists Rigoberto Henríquez Vera and Luis Vera Gómez.[174] While the causal relationship was probably more general than specific, Henríquez Vera was released from prison in June. In the same month, Acción Democrática asked the IAPA to investigate charges that Pérez Jiménez was trying to purchase the New York Spanish-language paper *El Diario de Nueva York*. AD asserted that Pérez Jiménez already owned the *Diario las Américas* of Miami. [175] Stahlman opened the Twelfth Annual Meeting in October 1956 with the call for the expulsion from the association of any member who may have "debased our honorable profession or betrayed the high principles of the IAPA by groveling obeisance and sycophantic service to a dictator, or by other conduct unbecoming free men."[176] Simón Alberto Consalvi, the former secretary general of the Venezuelan Association of Journalists, who had been released from prison at the same time as Henríquez Vera, also addressed the conference and pointed out that he was the thirty-seventh Venezuelan journalist to be sent into exile. He complimented Jules Dubois for his report on press conditions in Venezuela and noted that there were no representatives of Caracas newspapers attending the conference. If they came, he affirmed, they would have to ask for the release of imprisoned journalists, "and in Caracas," he concluded, "to demand another's freedom results in the loss of your own."[177]

The report of the Committee on Freedom of the Press to the Twelfth Meeting, to which Consalvi made reference, was the sharpest yet with reference to Venezuela. The committee stated that according to the information which it had received no country matched Venezuela in press censorship and suppression of thought. It admitted, however, that it had been unable to verify these reports and recommended, therefore, that the IAPA take steps to ascertain the situation of imprisoned journalists in Venezuela and ask the Venezuelan government to bring them to trial promptly and with full guarantees.[178] This recommendation was carried out by Stahlman's successor for 1956-57, Guillermo Martínez Márquez, who wrote to Pérez Jiménez and asked him to grant "full public justice" to the Venezuelan press.[179] Pérez Jiménez reacted by cooperating with Trujillo in the publication of a paid announcement in the New York *Herald Tribune,* which attacked the IAPA for presuming to judge the policies of sovereign states. The dictators defended the closing of "subversive" newspapers and charged that the IAPA engaged in acts of intervention.[180]

This maneuver did not deter the IAPA. When its Board of Directors met in San José in April 1957, Venezuelan journalists and AD party members in exile in Costa Rica submitted a lengthy memorandum. As a result of this action, the board resolved to appoint a special subcommittee to investigate press conditions in Venezuela and to report to the next annual meeting.[181] It also approved resolutions requesting Pérez Jiménez either to release imprisoned journalists or to bring them to trial, to lift press censorship, and to permit the return of exiled journalists.[182] On the occasion of Freedom of the Press Day in June 1957, Siso Martínez and other Venezuelan journalists in exile in Mexico sent a communiqué to the Mexican Association of Journalists. While extending their best wishes to their Mexican colleagues, they pointed out that they could not hold such an event in their own country and appealed to the Mexicans for their support in the restoration of freedom of the press in Venezuela.[183]

In accordance with the resolution of its board, the IAPA received a special report on Venezuela at its annual meeting in 1957. The statement confirmed the charges of press censorship against the Venezuelan government and declared that it had been applied "rigidly" since 1949. It affirmed that government releases were the sole source of political news, and it criticized the Venezuelan government for banning the foreign magazines, *Humanismo, Bohemia,* and *Time.*[184] Ominously, the report warned Pérez Jiménez and his fellow dictators in Paraguay and the Dominican Republic that "press censorship could result in their downfall."[185] Following the fall of Pérez Jiménez, and after being freed from jail, Miguel Angel Capriles, publisher of *La Esfera* and *Ultimas Noticias* of Caracas, cabled his appreciation to the IAPA for its advocacy of the free press of Venezuela.[186]

In its campaign for freedom of the press the IAPA also clashed violently with Rafael Trujillo. The Dominican Republic had been criticized for press censorship in the 1953 report of the Freedom of the Press Committee, but the real trouble began in 1955 with the case of Germán Ornes, editor and publisher of *El Caribe*. Up to that time, Ornes had collaborated with Trujillo and had defended him in the annual meetings of the IAPA, but following the meeting in New Orleans in 1955 he elected to remain in the United States. He explained that he had fallen from grace owing to an error in his newspaper which had substituted the phrase "tomb of Trujillo" for "bust of Trujillo." The Dominican Republic, for its part, said Ornes had fled because of financial irregularities.[187] When Trujillo confiscated *El Caribe*, the IAPA supported Ornes and recognized him as the rightful owner of the paper and as its "authorized representative."[188]

As usual, Trujillo's response to such opposition was personal. He attacked Dubois in the captive *El Caribe* as a "turbulent soldier of fortune."[189] At the IAPA's meeting in Havana in 1956, Ramón Marrero Aristy, editor of *La Nación* of Ciudad Trujillo, challenged Dubois to a duel. In early 1957 Dubois was denied a visa to the Dominican Republic because, according to the Dominican Foreign Ministry, he was "a professional Soviet agitator,"[190] and in September he was barred from the Dominican Republic again as an "undesirable adventurer."[191] In the meantime, the IAPA Board of Directors recommended the expulsion of *La Nación* from the association; it was carried out at the Thirteenth Meeting. The action was protested by Marrero Aristy, who charged that Dubois had instituted "a hate campaign against his country."[192]

In expelling *La Nación*, the IAPA had delivered a blow to one of the most ruthless dictators in Caribbean history. Even when the situation in the Caribbean improved after 1958, the IAPA continued to condemn the absence of freedom of expression in the Dominican Republic. And when Trujillo was assassinated in 1961, the IAPA interceded to enable Germán Ornes to recover his newspaper.

Two of the fiercest campaigns conducted by the IAPA have been overlooked here because they are outside the scope of this study (i.e., the actions against the seizure of *La Prensa* of Buenos Aires by Juan Perón and the closing of *El Tiempo* of Bogotá by Gustavo Rojas Pinilla). But the effectiveness of the IAPA in the antidictatorial struggle appears nevertheless manifest.

In discussing the role of the free press in the antidictatorial struggle, it may be noted that on several occasions the exile groups singled out the *New York Times* for particular praise. During an address over Havana radio in October 1951, Betancourt declared, "we are not alone," and he cited a "violent editorial against the dictatorship" in the 16 October issue of the *New York Times.*[193]   As noted, the 1953 Citation of the IADF was awarded to the *New York Times* "for its contribution to Democracy and Freedom in the Americas." *Venezuela Democrática,* in its issue of October 1955, paid tribute to the *New York Times* for its editorials criticizing U.S. policy toward Latin American dictators. It cited, among other things, the *Times'* opposition to the granting of the U.S. Legion of Merit award to Pérez Jiménez and to the supplying of arms to dictators.[194] The *New York Times'* coverage of the Galíndez case caused a pro-Trujillo group to picket the Times Tower in 1956, and its stories about the 26 of July Movement of Fidel Castro contributed to the defeat of Batista. Following the fall of Rojas Pinilla, Eduardo Santos, former president of Colombia and the publisher of *El Tiempo*, wrote to the *New York Times* and expressed the feelings of exiles generally: "Please all of you accept fervent thanks for the splendid and very noble support given to Colombia in her struggle against tyranny."[195] In a struggle where the need to influence public opinion was vital, the Caribbean exiles acknowledged the powerful support of the *New York Times.*

The IAPA, the Inter-American Association for Democracy and Freedom, and the international free trade union movement contributed to the eventual decline of the dictators of the Caribbean. Individually, they were no match for the military dictatorships, but when one puts together their combined struggle over a period of almost ten years the achievements are impressive. The accumulated weight of their opposition undermined the authority of the dictators and forced them to make concessions. When the totality of their activity is added to that of the exile groups, it is clear that Caribbean politics were in a ferment, despite the domination by authoritarian regimes. Moreover, these organizations helped sustain the exile movements during the difficult years, and they influenced the policy and attitudes of certain governments, particularly the United States. When some parties of the Democratic Left began returning to their respective homelands toward the end of the fifties, the IADF, ORIT, and IAPA remained for the most part understanding friends and allies. Such support proved necessary, because the Democratic Left found final victory elusive.

6 | *The Days of Man*

Toward a New Coalition

THE OVERTHROW of Marcos Pérez Jiménez on 23 January 1958 once again placed Venezuela in the democratic camp, but it did not signify its immediate reentry into the antidictatorial struggle. A provisional junta under Rear Admiral Wolfgang Larrazábal governed the nation while it recovered from ten years of dictatorial rule and prepared for the restoration of popular government. Acción Democrática used the time to reorganize and adjust. Its leaders remained committed to the idea of the defeat of all dictatorships but obviously had to establish their domestic base before undertaking any foreign adventures. On the other hand, AD and other parties of the Democratic Left were soon confronted with a new series of challenges which made imperative the formation of a new democratic bloc.

In many respects, the coalition of the streets which had threatened to engulf the dictatorship of Pérez Jiménez in fire and blood represented a revolutionary mood stronger than the mere desire to unseat a tyrant. However, it lost the initiative to the armed forces, which intervened to send the dictator from the country and undertook to provide a peaceful alternative. In the same way, the youthful leaders of the clandestine AD relinquished their positions on the National Executive Committee (CEN) and accepted the leadership of the returning "Old Guard." The fact that the last secretary general of the underground, Simón Sáez Mérida, raised this point later indicated the latent feelings of "those who had been there."[1] The violent spirit erupted briefly after the tyrant's fall with the revenge killings of Seguridad Nacional agents and the looting of the SN headquarters and again in May during the visit of U.S. Vice-President Richard Nixon to Caracas.

Responding to those who were for a revolution, Acción Democrática referred to its philosophy and experience and pointed out the existing political realities. AD was committed to basic economic and social reform but felt deeply that democracy itself must first be secured. On 5 February 1958, before leaving New York, Betancourt told the Inter-American Association for Democracy and Freedom that "only a united welded front of civilians will be able to prevent the danger of a new totalitarian experience."[2] To achieve this, he urged an end to partisan strife and "unworthy disruptive conflicts." Upon his arrival in Venezuela a few days later, Betancourt asked those who came to welcome him not to be moved by vengeance or impatience but to observe the "political truce" and to reorganize and regroup calmly. When the time comes to resume the public debate, he told them, let it begin without "hatred, virulent insult, or impudence."[3] In this regard, AD had already pledged to cooperate with the other political parties, even to the extent of seeking a coalition candidate for the presidency. Just before leaving the United States, Betancourt also reassured American investors. "It does not follow," he affirmed, "that dictators give better security and have more regard to interests of investors than democracies."[4]

It was also a fact of political life that the armed forces were intact. Not only had the armed forces leaders stopped the momentum of the revolution but Larrazábal himself had emerged as a popular hero. AD pledged its loyalty to the Junta of Government and acknowledged the essential patriotism of the armed forces. Betancourt denied that there was any "irreparable breach" between the uniformed and civilian Venezuelan and sought to allay the military's suspicion of him and his party.[5] In seeking this accomodation in Venezuelan society, AD had not abandoned its principles; it only recognized the need to move cautiously, reflecting almost ten years of frustration in exile. However, this circumstance emphasized the gap between the old men of exile and the young men of the 23 of January. It also made all the more attractive the revolutionary voice of Fidel Castro a year later.

Although circumstances forced AD to emphasize domestic affairs, it could not stay out of Caribbean politics entirely. The overthrow of Pérez Jiménez was in itself a psychological boost to the democratic camp. In his farewell to the IADF on 5 February, Betancourt spoke of "an American responsibility . . . to eradicate . . . the cancer of dictatorship," and he proposed specifically the amending of the Charter of the Organization of American States so that only democratically elected governments might belong.[6] The Cuban rebels were especially heartened by the overthrow of Pérez Jiménez and reportedly planned a "Caracas-style" general strike in order to oust Batista. The anti-Batista forces also hoped to secure arms and supplies in Venezuela, and in February Cuban exiles began "flocking" to Caracas.[7] There, at the insistence of Betancourt, the breach among the Cuban revolutionary and exile groups was repaired. On 20 July, representatives of Fidel Castro, Carlos Prío Socarrás, and the Ortodoxos signed the "Pact of Caracas," under the terms of which they agreed, first, to try to organize a general strike; second, to cooperate in the establishment of a provisional government following the fall of Batista; and, third, to hold general elections as soon as possible thereafter.[8] From Caracas also, two radio stations, Radio Continente and Radio Rumbos, began transmitting Castro's speeches for reception in Havana.[9] As hopes ran high during 1958, leaders of the Democratic Left thought increasingly about the future.

In February a manifesto calling for a "New Order" for Latin America was issued by Colombian author and educator Germán Arciniegas. It urged the nations of Latin America "to rally to the principles of individual liberty, self-determination through representative governments, and economic justice."[10] The statement was signed by fifty-seven outstanding public figures, including five former presidents of Latin American countries.

These sentiments acquired substance with the founding in Costa Rica of the International Institute of Political and Social Sciences. Ironically, at the very time that Acción Democrática returned to Venezuela, in Costa Rica José Figueres completed his term of office, and his party's candidate lost the 2 February presidential election.[11] Figueres was not lost to the democratic movement, however, and he helped found the institute "to educate new leaders for the hemispheric fight for social democracy." During 1958, over one-hundred young men studied there under a faculty which included Figueres, Benjamín Núñez, Daniel Oduber, and Luis Alberto Monge.[12]

In mid-1958 the institute began publication of a political journal, *Combate,* which revealed the developing democratic coalition. The Board of Editors was comprised of Figueres, Betancourt, Víctor Raúl Haya de la Torre, and Eduardo Santos, and the managing editor was

Luis Alberto Monge (in 1960 Norman Thomas joined the Board of Editors). During its first year of publication, contributors to *Combate* included Haya, Betancourt, Juan Bosch, Benjamín Núñez, Mario Méndez Montenegro (Guatemala), Emilio Borge González (Nicaragua), and U.S. Senator Hubert Humphrey. The authors generally expressed the goals and strategy of the democratic movement, attacked the dictatorships of the Caribbean, or criticized U.S. policy toward Latin America. The institute and *Combate* were initial steps in the formation of the new coalition of parties of the Democratic Left.

In the meantime, Acción Democrática grew in strength and confidence and began to pay increasing attention to the international sphere. In May 1958, a plenum of leaders began meetings to make preparations for a national convention in August, the first party convention in a decade. These sessions undertook the task of reorganization and the preparation of "theses" to define the party's program and doctrine on vital questions, including party organization, petroleum, labor, agriculture, and education.[13] In effect, these were planks for the party platform. With reference to international affairs, AD admitted that one of its serious errors before 1948 was the failure to promote "a political entente of hemispheric democratic forces." It had learned in exile, it stated, that the fight for democracy was indeed a hemispheric problem and that there was a "deep American conscience ready to manifest itself in active cooperation against dictators and in favor of democratic causes."[14] AD added that it owed "a heavy debt of gratitude" to the democratic forces of the continent. This indebtedness guided the drafting of the international plank of the party platform, which was approved in principle at the National Convention, 10-16 August 1958.

As might be expected, AD repudiated "despotic regimes." It proclaimed its intention to seek "cultural and political understanding with the other nations of Latin America in order to defend democratic institutions and secure effective respect for the rights of man."[15] Specifically, AD stated its intention to negotiate treaties with other democratic nations "to assure the permanence of democratic institutions and values." It pledged to adhere to the principles of democracy and international coexistence, "which constitute the norms of the United Nations and its specialized agencies." And it vowed to fight to transform the OAS from "its present inoperative and bureaucratic mechanism" into "a living, militant organism" dedicated to the preservation of freedom, the eradication of poverty and ignorance, and the stimulation of backward economies.[16] Finally, AD reiterated the call for an inter-American agency to receive the complaints of private citizens against violations of basic democratic rights. The opportunity to activate this program arrived sooner than anticipated.[17]

The Venezuelan political parties had agreed to support a single candidate for the presidency, but they were unable to unite behind one man. The failure to find a unity candidate resulted in individual party candidacies: Rafael Caldera for the Christian Democrats (COPEI), Larrazábal for the Democratic Republican Union (URD), and Betancourt for Acción Democrática (AD). Rather reluctantly, AD put forth its candidacy on 11 October, not quite two months before the election was held. But aside from the individual candidacies, the so-called "spirit of 23 January" was maintained. The parties met at Punto Fijo on 31 October and agreed to respect the outcome of the election and to adhere to the democratic process. They reached a consensus on a basic governmental program and pledged continued consultation. In fact, the winning candidate was committed to a "government of national unity," whereby all parties were to be represented in the cabinet.[18]

Rómulo Betancourt was elected president of Venezuela on 7 December 1958. His victory stemmed largely from AD's strength in the interior. In Caracas, where the revolutionary spirit prevailed, Larrazábal was the overwhelming choice, and mobs rioted when the election returns came in.[19] Through no fault of its own, AD's program for economic and social reform had been interrupted for ten years, and now, to some elements, including the youth of AD, it seemed inadequate. The coming to power of Fidel Castro in Cuba a few weeks later complicated the problem further. Betancourt, however, was determined to solve the problems of Venezuela through democratic institutions and to provide leadership against the totalitarian forces in the Americas.

The opportunity to exert such leadership came with Betancourt's inauguration as president on 13 February 1959. In addition to the official delegations, Betancourt personally invited the outstanding democrats of the hemisphere, many with whom he had collaborated during exile.[20] In their presence, Betancourt recalled Venezuela's resistance against the dictatorship and named with deep emotion those who had fallen in the struggle. It was a particularly proud moment for him to be able to turn to José Figueres and express Venezuela's gratitude for the refusal of Costa Rica to attend the Tenth Inter-American Conference in Caracas. In the spirit of that action, Betancourt called for a quarantine of dictatorial governments and for their expulsion from the OAS. He declared that such regimes "offended the dignity of America" and that only freely elected governments should be members of the OAS.[21]

The assembled democratic leaders responded by drawing up the "Declaration of Caracas." They remained after the inaugural ceremonies to discuss and sign the document on 15 February. In it they declared their faith in democracy as the highest form of political organization and as the most effective system for the attainment of social well-being. "We reaffirm," they stated, "our repudiation of every form of dictatorial or totalitarian rule," and they specifically condemned "as inadmissible within the hemispheric community" the existing governments of the Dominican Republic, Nicaragua, and Paraguay.[22] They called upon the democratic governments of the OAS to exclude from their ranks dictatorial regimes and to admit only popular governments respectful of human rights. They supported other forms of Latin American unity and integration, such as a Common Market and "the close ties of their peoples through the democratic parties, worker and peasant organizations, and student and cultural institutions."[23] At the same time, they extended the hand of friendship to the United States and expressed the view that a "united, free, and strong Latin America" could attain "equitable and fruitful relations" with the nation of the north.[24]

Although not present, Haya de la Torre, the dean of Latin America's Democratic Left, endorsed the manifesto. In vigorous language he scored all forms of totalitarianism: "It is our legitimate right to combat them, to overthrow them, and to aid in their extermination." He added that no plea relying upon the principle of nonintervention could justify the toleration of "cruel and cynical" regimes.[25] Quickly, the signatories, particularly those from the Caribbean and specifically those of Cuba and Venezuela, became known as the "Caracas Group."

Despite this designation, Betancourt's leadership over the movement was by then tenuous. Already in Havana the cry, "Trujillo next, Trujillo next," had been raised.[26] Fidel Castro publicly encouraged refugees from dictatorships to come to Cuba and said he would give them "every assistance."[27] On 25 January 1959 Castro visited Caracas and declared that if the OAS did not expel the tyrants of the Dominican Republic, Nicaragua, and Paraguay from its membership, Cuba would withdraw from the organization.[28] Although he promised to restrain them,

Castro declared that there were thousands of men on the island of Cuba ready to deliver the tyrants to justice. At the same time, he warned that Trujillo would have to deal with both Cuba and Venezuela if he threatened either one of them.[29] Betancourt's reception of Castro on this occasion was cool. However, the presence of Raúl Roa at the inauguration of Betancourt and his adherence to the Caracas Declaration created an appearance of unity, which made the dictators of the Caribbean extremely nervous in the months to come.

President Luis Somoza of Nicaragua in particular seemed apprehensive. He was certain that plans were being made for an invasion of Nicaragua.[30] Hoping to avert this threat, Luis Somoza affirmed that he had liberalized his government and that it was as moderate as any in the Caribbean. He felt it was unjust that he could not shake the "dynasty" label and said, making reference to the two power groups in the Caribbean, the "liberal" of Fidel Castro and Betancourt and the "other" of Trujillo, "I consider my government as belonging to the first group."[31] Unable to ingratiate himself with the "liberal" group and faced with evidence of continued plotting against his regime, Luis Somoza became disillusioned and toward the end of May 1959 began to tighten his grip once again. Gentleness was being mistaken for weakness, he said, "my father often warned me that you cannot feed too much meat to a young baby and now I know what he meant."[32]

Trujillo's nervousness took more predictable forms. It was unsettling for Trujillo to play host to one refugee dictator after another, which he did, to Perón, Pérez Jiménez, and Batista, but he counterattacked by vilifying the democratic leaders. His principal weapon was the smoke screen of anticommunism, especially designed to gain sympathy in the United States. In Ciudad Trujillo he sponsored the Caribbean Anti-Communist Research and Intelligence Bureau, which began in April 1958 to publish a monthly, pocket-sized report in English entitled CARIB. Using selected newspaper clippings, articles, and miscellaneous sources, CARIB endeavored to prove that all the trouble in the Caribbean since World War II could be attributed to "no more than a hundred individuals" comprising a "Caribbean International." The list included the names of every democratic leader worthy of mention, sprinkled indiscriminately with those of actual Communists.

At about the same time, Trujillo retained the services of John A. Clements Associates, a New York public relations firm. Among its activities was a *Report on Venezuela,* which, after tracing the career of

Betancourt, concluded that "it can be stated with emphasis that Rómulo is a Communist."[33] The *Report* also attacked Betancourt's allies. In discussing the founders of the Inter-American Association for Democracy and Freedom, including, of course, Frances Grant, Serafino Romualdi, Roger Baldwin, Norman Thomas, Walter White, Eleanor Roosevelt ("about whose extensive Communist-fronting it is unnecessary to detail"), Eduardo Frei, Juan Bosch, Raúl Leoni, Raúl Roa, and Jesús de Galíndez, *Report on Venezuela* proclaimed that they were, "with few exceptions veteran leftists, including Communists, pro-Communists, fellow-travelers, Socialists, and left-wing liberals. The records of the personnel of the IADF," it concluded, "are sufficient evidence to stamp the organization as an extreme left-wing group."[34] Concerning Herbert L. Matthews, whom the IADF had honored for services to Latin American democracy, the *Report* declared that Matthews had "made a career of slanting the news in favor of every left-wing political adventurer in Latin America and against the so-called dictators of that area."[35] Of José Figueres, who appeared before a committee of the U.S. House of Representatives in June 1958 to discuss the causes of the Nixon riots, the *Report* wrote, "One of the most virulent and, at the same time, cleverest attacks on official U.S. policy and on American foreign investment was launched recently by the self-proclaimed liberal, self-proclaimed ardent friend of the United States, José 'Pepe' Figueres, former president of Costa Rica, whose words and acts seem somehow to follow the Party line."[36] It also charged that under the leadership of Figueres' friend and collaborator, Luis Alberto Monge, "the ORIT unions became heavily infiltrated by the Communists."[37] As noted by Miss Grant, the "nauseating attacks" continued as long as Trujillo put up the money for them.[38]

Trujillo continued to make propaganda, but his opposition was more deeply divided than he was prepared to admit. Although it was freely stated that Betancourt and Castro had agreed in Caracas in January and February to overthrow the dictators of the Caribbean,[39] neither leader was sure of the other, and each viewed the Latin American revolution differently. The situation was similar to that of the coalition of the Western powers and the Soviet Union against Nazi Germany in World War II. These contradictions within the antidictatorial movement came to the surface during the visit of Figueres to Cuba in March 1959.

In appreciation for his assistance to the Cuban Revolution, José Figueres was the guest of Fidel Castro for almost a week beginning 19

March. Figueres expected the visit to be a personal triumph, but he hoped also to bring Castro more definitely into the orbit of the parties of the Democratic Left and to secure his support for a planned invasion of Nicaragua. Figueres was disappointed on all counts. On 21 March, speaking in the Workers' Palace before the Cuban Workers' Confederation (CTC) and over radio and television, Figueres declared that although Latin America, particularly Cuba, had grievances against the United States, these were family matters and should not affect the solidarity of the hemisphere in the Cold War. "Cuba and all Latin America," he said, "should be on the side of the United States and the other democracies."[40] Before Figueres could finish, David Salvador, the secretary general of the CTC, seized the microphone and exclaimed, "We cannot be with the Americans who today are oppressing us!" [41] When Figueres was finally permitted to finish, Castro rose to speak and expressed regrets that his old friend "had been influenced by the campaigns in the international press attacking the Cuban revolution." He asked, "why should Cuba be with either side?" and answered, "Cuba should be neutral."[42]

The public humiliation of Figueres dramatized the gulf between the old democratic leaders and the new revolutionaries. On 3 April, with Figueres having left Cuba, Castro referred to him harshly as "a bad friend, a bad democrat, and a bad revolutionist."[43] Even in Venezuela, with surprising speed, the leaders of the AD Youth echoed these sentiments. They denounced Figueres and also Serafino Romualdi, the Inter-American Regional Organization of Workers (ORIT), and Luis Muñoz Marín. The shocked leaders of AD's National Executive Committee publicly repudiated these statements and reiterated their deep gratitude to the men and organizations which, they affirmed, had done so much for the cause of Venezuelan freedom.[44] In New York, where Figueres traveled next as the guest of Norman Thomas and the Institute for International Labor Research, the Costa Rican leader minimized his difficulties with Castro. He remarked, "If he is for democratic principles, we will stick by him." But Figueres warned of the danger of Communist infiltration into Latin American revolutionary movements.[45]

In this spirit, another effort was made to achieve unity and to maintain the initiative of the parties of the Democratic Left. At the end of May 1959, representatives of the Peruvian American Popular Revolutionary Alliance (APRA), Acción Democrática, and Figueres' Liberación Nacional met in San José, Costa Rica, to draft tentative plans for action against the dictators of the Caribbean. Talks were also held with the Revolutionary party of Guatemala and the Liberal party of Honduras; but Cuba was not included, because, it was explained, its political orientation regarding Communist infiltration was not sufficiently clear. However, leaders of Liberación Nacional expressed the belief that Cuba belonged in the antidictatorial bloc and, while they considered Castro's attack upon Figueres unjustified, they were inclined to excuse it, "because of the excitement of the times and other mitigating circumstances."[46]

The effort to include Castro in the coalition of the Democratic Left was unsuccessful. This is not to say that Castro refused the assistance of democratic groups in his antidictatorial ventures, nor that he played no part in those launched outside of Cuba. In the intense revolutionary activitiy which developed during the invasion of 1959, the forces opposing Trujillo and the Somozas sometimes worked together, sometimes independently, but always with the awareness that basically they were rivals.

The Barbudos

Fidel Castro's take-over in Cuba excited revolutionary activity in the Caribbean. The parties of the Democratic Left had been slowly developing their antidictatorial coalition, but Castro's glamour and unorthodoxy attracted exile leaders and adventurers who wanted action and quick success. The inaugural address of Provisional President Manuel Urrutia on 3 January was an unrestrained attack upon the Caribbean's dictators and served as a siren call to the revolutionaries of the area. Ruby Hart Phillips, who had covered Cayo Confites for the *New York Times* over a decade earlier, reported that the Caribbean Legion was back and that she saw "familiar faces" in Havana.[47] Alberto Bayo, Eufemio Fernández, and Miguel Angel Ramírez were among those who had returned and had resumed revolutionary activities.

Despite the enthusiasm of the exile groups, the Castro regime had no intention of losing control of the situation. It carefully selected the leaders with whom it was willing to work, and Ernesto "Che" Guevara was placed in charge of all operations.[48] Those groups which refused to conform were denied support, and those which still tried to slip away

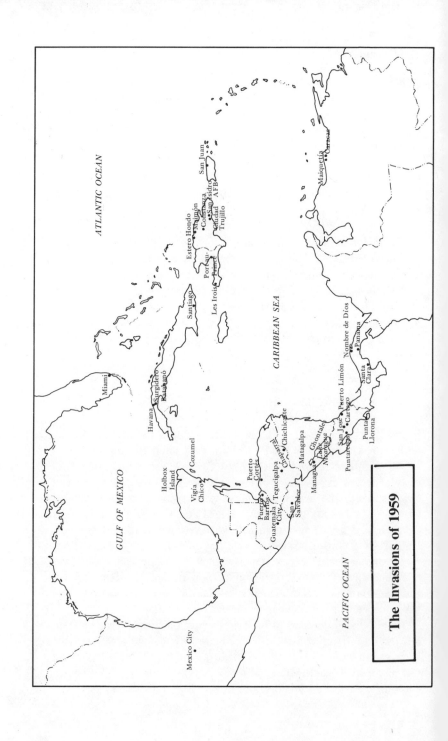

The Invasions of 1959

ATLANTIC OCEAN

San Juan

Constanza
San Isidro
Ciudad AFB
Trujillo

Estero Hondo
Maimón
Puerto Plata
Les Irois

Santiago

CARIBBEAN SEA

Maiquetía
Caracas

Havana
Surgidero
Batabanó

Nombre de Díos
Panama

Miami

Cozumel

Puerto Limón
Santa
Cartago Clara

Holbox
Island
Vigía
Chico

San José Puntarenas
Puerto
Cortés
Chontales Puntarenas Llorona
Puerto Tegucigalpa
Barrios Chalatenango
Guatemala Chichicaste
City Matagalpa
San Managua
Salvador Nicaragua

Mexico City

PACIFIC OCEAN

The Invasions of 1959

were prevented from embarking.[49] As early as 25 March it was reported that Cuba was involved in planning invasions of Haiti, Panama, Nicaragua, and the Dominican Republic.[50]

The earliest public notice of exile activity in Cuba involved a group of Haitians. Louis Dejoie, an exile leader in New York, traveled to Havana at the end of January. There, after conferring with leaders of the revolutionary government, he formed the Haitian Revolutionary Front in collaboration with two other Haitian exile leaders, Clement Jumelle and Daniel Fignole. They called for the overthrow of the government of François Duvalier and began broadcasting in French from Havana twice weekly. By the end of February, it was reported that several thousand Haitians had gathered in Cuba.[51] Castro, however, showed little enthusiasm for the Haitian revolutionaries, and U.S. officials suspected that his "real purpose" was to use Haiti as a base of operations against Trujillo.[52] A decision by the United States to "try to shore up" the Duvalier regime helped allay the threat momentarily. It was, in fact, postponed until August, when, after much frustration and apparently against the wishes of the Cuban government, a small band of twenty-five to thirty men, mostly Cubans, landed on the south coast of Haiti near the village of Irois. They were quickly hunted down and killed, but the affair was quite on the periphery of the events which had been taking place during the preceding months.

The first of the Castro-sponsored invasions was that of Panama on 25 April. The invasion made no sense in the scheme of Caribbean politics. The government of Ernesto de la Guardia was far from perfect, but it in no respect resembled the tyranny of Trujillo or Somoza. No leader of the Democratic Left was involved, and only by projecting the future course of the Cuban Revolution might one find an explanation for Castro's behavior. As Tad Szulc suggested, Castro "showed his hand perhaps too soon in the game."[53]

The invasion itself was an absolute failure. The details of the operation were worked out in Havana with representatives of Roberto Arias, a Panamanian politician whose main achievement until then had been his marriage to the English ballerina Margot Fonteyn. Arias' first cousin, Rúben Miró, the same Miró who had been acquitted of the 1955 murder of President José Antonio Remón, reportedly led the Panama group in Cuba.[54] On 15 April the Panamanian government received reports about the planned expedition and informed the Cuban government, which in turn assured Panama that it would take adequate measures to prevent any such movement. Nonetheless, on 19 April, approximately ninety-two armed men, almost all Cubans, sailed from Surgidero Batabanó, Cuba, under the command of Panamanian Enrique Morales Brid. They supposedly were going to the aid of a group of young Panamanians who had gone into the mountains of Veraguas Province in early April. Roberto Arias himself also led a landing of ten men on 20 April on Panama's Pacific coast near Santa Clara. In the latter action, one Cuban was killed, and Arias hastily took asylum in the Brazilian embassy in Panama City. By the time the main party reached Panama, the internal movement had been suppressed, and the Panamanian National Guard quickly surrounded the expeditionaries in the north coast village of Nombre de Dios. The leader of the expedition, Morales Brid, drowned in the heavy surf at the time of the disembarkation.[55]

The main task now was to arrange the surrender of the Cubans without bloodshed. The Cuban government professed innocence, but with Panama's approval sent two officers, Captain Armando Torres and Lieutenant Fernando Ruiz, to parley with the invaders and to induce them to terminate the action. On 28 April Torres and Ruiz spoke with the new commander of the expedition, César Vega, also an officer of the Cuban Revolutionary Army. The group showed a willingness to surrender if it could retain its equipment and arms and return immediately to Cuba, but Panama rejected the terms.[56] Panama was prepared to be gracious, but it could not overlook the affront to its sovereignty and insisted that the invading force turn over its arms and surrender unconditionally. In the meantime, Panama had taken the matter to the Council of the OAS on 27 April. Its ambassador, Ricardo A. Arias Espinosa, described the events in his country and requested the invoking of the Rio Treaty. He specifically avoided naming any state as the aggressor. The following day, the council resolved to invoke the Treaty of Reciprocal Assistance and acting provisionally as the Organ of Consultation speedily appointed an Investigating Committee to make an on-the-spot study and to report. The Cuban ambassador, Raúl Roa, also spoke at the session. He regretted the events in Panama but reiterated that the Cuban government was not in any way involved and affirmed that Cuba would cooperate fully with the OAS action.[57] The Investigating Committee arrived in Panama early on 29 April and quickly settled the affair.

The Investigating Committee arranged for the Cubans to surrender peacefully and set up air and sea patrols to prevent any additional landings in Panama. On 30 April the committee dropped leaflets over Nombre de Dios explaining its mission and sent in by helicopter two of its military advisors accompanied by an officer of the Panamanian National Guard and the Cuban captain Torres. César Vega returned with them immediately to Albrook Air Force Base in the Canal Zone, where he met with the committee and heard its terms. He said his men had no desire to proceed, because they had been deceived by the Panamanians concerning conditions in Panama and because of the action of the OAS and the wishes of Fidel Castro. On 1 May the Cubans deposited their arms in the post office of Nombre de Dios, and the Panamanian National Guard moved into the village. The expeditionaries were interned in the Cárcel Modelo in Panama City and eventually were permitted to return home to face the contrived wrath of Castro. There had been a report that two vessels, the *Burma* and the *Madaleva,* had left Cuba with reenforcements on 28 April, but if so they were dissuaded by the air and sea patrols organized by the OAS on 1 May. Only three days later, the Investigating Committee returned to Washington to prepare its report, and the following month the Council of the OAS cancelled the call for a meeting of foreign ministers.[58]

The Panama episode made Castro appear more a nuisance than a menace, but even before the OAS officially terminated the affair additional armed invasions had occurred. Chronologically, Nicaragua was next. By this time, style dictated that all invaders wear beards, even though the term *"barbudo"* ("bearded one") was popularly associated with Cuban revolutionaries. "Barbudo" was used in the same sense, with the same accuracy, and aroused the same emotions as the term "Caribbean Legion" earlier. Some of those who invaded Nicaragua on 31 May and 1 June wore beards, but the movement was not directed by Castro and, in fact, was in competition with plans he had.

The invasion of Nicaragua was organized by Dr. Enrique Lacayo Farfán, leader of the Independent Liberal party (Partido Liberal Independiente) and head of a coalition of anti-Somoza groups originally designated as the National Opposition Union, UNO (Unión Nacional de Oposición), but later renamed the Nicaraguan Revolutionary Movement, MRN (Movimiento Revolucionario Nicaragüense).[59] The MRN was based in Costa Rica and had the full support of Liberación Nacional and other parties of the Democratic Left.[60] Despite the fact that Figueres' party was out of power, it controlled the largest bloc of votes in the Legislative Assembly and opposed President Echandi's avowed policy of neutrality.[61] Liberación Nacional provided the Nicaraguans with a training camp at Punta Llorona, a remote area far to the south on the Peninsula of Osa, where training was under the direction of veteran legionnaire Freddy Fernández, a naturalized Costa Rican of Dominican birth.[62] According to Fernández, Figueres contributed "arms, munitions, and advice," and Venezuela supplied money.[63]

Lacayo Farfán had also sought the assistance of Fidel Castro but was unable to obtain it. In order to get that support, the leaders of the MRN explained, it would have been necessary to reach an agreement with another group of Nicaraguan exiles whose ideology was "diametrically opposed to their own."[64] According to Ignacio Briones Torres, this group was made up of Nicaraguan Communists, who had set up a "Revolutionary Junta" in Havana in January 1959 under Guillermo Urbina Vásquez, Armando Amador, and Isabel Palacios. Since the matter of assistance to Nicaraguan exiles was entrusted to "Che" Guevara, Lacayo Farfán could secure no help unless he accepted the collaboration, indeed the leadership, of Urbina Vásquez.[65] One of the aims of Figueres' visit to Cuba in March was to try to mediate this dispute, but he was unsuccessful.

Another group of Nicaraguans under Chester Lacayo also tried to organize in Cuba, but when told by Raúl Castro to join Urbina's group under the military command of Lieutenant Rafael Somarriba or face internment, they fled to Holbox Island off Yucatán.[66] This group then left Holbox in mid-June, stopped off next at Vigía Chico, Mexico, where they terrorized that tiny fishing village for almost two weeks, and finally landed in Honduras "by mistake" only to be immediately captured.[67] When he was released from prison, Chester Lacayo declared that he was still dedicated to the overthrow of the Somozas, "if we can beat el Che and the Communists to the job."[68] According to Pedro Joaquín Chamorro, this same concern, that is, the possibility of a Castro-sponsored invasion of Nicaragua, caused the National Revolutionary Movement (MRN) to launch its attack on 31 May, perhaps prematurely.[69]

A total of one hundred ten Nicaraguan rebels were airlifted from Punta Llorona in two flights on 31 May and 1 June, respectively. They flew in a C-46 Curtis "Commando" belonging to Costa Rican National Airlines (Aerolíneas Nacionales de Costa Rica) and piloted by an employee of the airline, Nicaraguan exile Víctor Manuel Rivas Gómez. The first group was landed in Chontales Department at Los Mollejones, east of Lake Nicaragua, and the second group disembarked at Olama, northeast of Managua, in the department of Matagalpa. The plane was damaged on the second landing and, caught on the ground, was destroyed by aircraft of the Nicaraguan National Guard. The first reports stated that the C-46 had been hijacked for the operation, but the manager of Aerolíneas Nacionales, Manuel Enrique Guerra V., was in fact deeply implicated in the affair.[70]

In Nicaragua, the invaders under Pedro Joaquín Chamorro took to rough country and, avoiding clashes with the National Guard, awaited developments. They found themselves, however, bottled up in very difficult terrain, with superior forces under the command of Anastasio Somoza, Jr., waiting for them to come out. Meanwhile, the nation remained generally calm, and an anticipated general strike in support of the movement did not come off. There were still approximately 160 men at Punta Llorona, but they had not yet completed their training and could not be moved easily now because of strict measures of surveillance imposed by the Echandi government.[71] Echandi's policy of neutrality was again severely castigated in the Legislative Assembly, and there was even talk of impeachment and rumors of a coup.[72] At the same time, Rafael Somarriba had reached Honduras from Cuba with some seventy men, taking up a position near the Nicaraguan frontier in the mountains of Chichicaste and Chaparral. Somarriba, however, made no move to help Chamorro and seemed also to be awaiting developments.[73]

Desperate efforts were made to rescue the flagging rebellion. Figueres, who had been in New York when the invasion occurred, flew on 5 June to Caracas. There he conferred with Betancourt and with Nicaraguan exile leaders.[74] Three days later, he returned to San José in order to meet with Lacayo Farfán. "I wish to God," Figueres said, "they [the rebels] could win."[75] Even as word came that the invaders were surrendering, Nicaragua charged on 10 June that Venezuela had sent two planeloads of arms to Costa Rica to aid the rebellion. The arms allegedly were flown to the finca of Marcial Aguiluz, another veteran of the Caribbean Legion who was at the same time a Honduran national and a deputy in the Costa Rican Legislative Assembly.[76] Almost simultaneously, Aguiluz and Manuel Enrique Guerra V. traveled to Havana, reportedly as a result of conversations between Lacayo Farfán and the Cuban delegate to the conference of the Coffee Growers'

Federation of America, FEDECAME (Federación Cafetalera de América), then meeting in San José.[77] If Castro intended to help, he was too late. The movement collapsed on 11 June. Through the intermediary of a Catholic priest, Chamorro and the other expeditionaries, among them Freddy Fernández, Luis Cardenal, and Reynaldo Téfel Vélez, surrundered to the National Guard. They had not fired a shot.

Although action by the Organization of American States was not necessary to restore the peace in this case, and the OAS showed little desire to become involved, Nicaragua brought the matter before the council. On 2 June it directed a note to the president of the council informing him that Nicaragua had been the victim of an airborne invasion originating in Costa Rica. The following day, in extraordinary session, the council considered the note and listened to remarks by Nicaraguan Ambassador Guillermo Sevilla Sacasa, who requested the convoking of the Organ of Consultation. He reported the details of the invasion which had occurred and asserted that, in addition, three invasion ships were also approaching Nicaragua's Caribbean coast.[78]

Despite the opposition of both Cuba and Venezuela, which considered the matter an internal affair, the council voted on 4 June to convoke the Organ of Consultation and, pending the fixing of a time and place for a meeting of foreign ministers, constituted itself as the Provisional Organ of Consultation. A committee was appointed to collect data and to advise the council, but it was not instructed to undertake an immediate on-the-spot investigation and it proceeded in a dilatory fashion.

There was not much sentiment to move quickly in this case. Hemispheric opinion was strongly on the side of Lacayo Farfán; the national assemblies of Costa Rica, El Salvador, and Venezuela had already voted their solidarity with the rebels, and others were expected to do the same.[79] In the Costa Rican Legislative Assembly, deputies told the OAS to keep out of the affair and accused the United States of supplying arms to dictators on the "pretense" of hemispheric defense.[80] The U.S. ambassador to the OAS, John C. Dreier, who had hardly unpacked his bag after the Panama affair, subsequently wrote that there was "no desire to use the power of the OAS to prevent a revolution that appeared to have democratic objectives."[81] No one had foreseen, he elaborated, that the Rio Treaty "would be used to protect an authoritarian government from a popular uprising just because such an uprising, by force of circumstances, had to start in a neighboring country."[82] The committee, therefore, remained in Washington until 14 June in order to give the rebellion an opportunity to succeed or fail on its own. When it finally arrived in Tegucigalpa, its first stop, it issued a carefully worded communiqué on 15 June explaining that its sole mission was to collect information for the guidance of the OAS Council. Even so, a group of students demonstrated before the committee's hotel to protest its activities.[83]

This protest also made clear the dilemma of Villeda Morales. The Honduran president informed the committee of the measures he had taken to preserve strict neutrality and to adhere to existing international commitments, but he alluded to the fact that Honduran public opinion, especially within his own Liberal party, was sympathetic to the Nicaraguan rebels. The committee suggested, nonetheless, that tensions would be reduced further if Honduras were to ratify the Treaty on Territorial Asylum, negotiated with Nicaragua in February 1959, particularly in view of reports concerning the activities of Somarriba in the frontier zone.[84] Subsequent to the departure of the committee, the Honduran army moved against Somarriba, but apparently too vigorously. The incident, which occurred on 27 June, became known as "the massacre of El Chaparral," because sixteen of the insurgents were shot, allegedly after they had raised their hands in surrender.[85] Even the return of twenty-eight of the rebels to Cuba on 3 July failed to remove the resentment between Villeda's party chieftains and the Honduran army. This was probably behind an attempt by Colonel Armando Velásquez Cerrato to overthrow Villeda on 12 July, the colonel's second try that year.[86]

In the meantime, the OAS committee carried out its assignment. It arrived in Managua on 16 June and met with Nicaraguan officials, including President Luis Somoza, who provided full documentation concerning the invasion. The committee was particularly interested in interviewing the captured rebels. It found them in good health and receiving good treatment, even Pedro Joaquín Chamorro, about whom there was cause for concern. The next afternoon, the committee departed for San José.

During the committee's stay in San José, a strange and revealing postscript to the Nicaraguan invasion took place. On 16 June the Costa Rican government discovered the remaining force at Punta Llorona. Although the rumors flew fast that a group of "barbudos cubanos" had been sighted, the encampment consisted mainly of Nicaraguans under

Colonel Manuel Gómez, with approximately a dozen Costa Ricans led by Frank Marshall.[87] President Echandi dispatched land and sea patrols to the area, but, in possession of reports which implicated National Deputies (Congressmen) Marshall and Aguiluz and leaders of Liberación Nacional, he did not want any bloodshed.[88] In order to resolve his dilemma, Echandi appointed a Junta de Notables, i.e., a committee of leading citizens. They drafted surrender terms for the would-be expeditionaries which would permit the foreigners to leave the country and the Costa Ricans to return to their homes unpunished.[89] Aguiluz was sent to Punta Llorona to arrange the surrender on 18 June, but, although he insisted that an agreement had been reached, when the government troops arrived to intern the force, they found the camp abandoned.[90] In addition, before Aguiluz returned to San José, national detectives had seen him land at his finca "La Lindora" and unload a quantity of arms taken from Punta Llorona.[91]

At Punta Llorona the Costa Rican authorities found a well-equipped and organized camp, which they declared could accommodate five hundred to one thousand men. The rebels had left behind a large amount of Argentine and Dominican arms, two radio transmitters, an electric generator, and large stores of food. A lone barbudo was captured, a young Costa Rican, Manuel Monge Jiménez, who said the few "ticos" (Costa Ricans) had escaped into the mountains with Marshall but he "believed" the others had left by boat.[92] Marshall himself turned up in Puntarenas with his small band on 20 June and claimed that the force had consisted of 170 men, composed of twelve Costa Ricans, four Dominicans, and the remainder Nicaraguans. He denied there were any Cubans.[93] Three other rebels, two Nicaraguans and a Dominican, were captured in the area in dense jungle near a United Fruit Company plantation. They related that they had been at Punta Llorona for forty-two days before being discovered, with their invasion preparations not yet complete. They also asserted that Manuel Gómez and the foreign troops had fled by boat.[94] Although the whereabouts of the main body was not reported, escape in a large vessel seemed unlikely because of the Costa Rican patrols. Apparently they were helped to return quietly to San José or to leave the country, without the embarrassment of internment or deportation proceedings.[95]

The OAS representatives had observed much of this activity. It gave them an opportunity to appreciate the sincerity of Echandi's policy of neutrality, as well as the difficulty in adhering to it. The committee also had an opportunity to interview Lacayo Farfán and noted his complete freedom of action and the strong support he enjoyed in Costa Rica, particularly from Liberación Nacional. Before the committee left Costa Rica for Washington on 20 June, it issued a communiqué in which it praised the government of Mario Echandi for its adherence to the principle of nonintervention, its effort to maintain neutrality, and its humanitarianism on behalf of the principles of asylum.[96] The committee rendered its report to the OAS Council on 26 June, and a month later, with the Nicaraguan case having resolved itself, the council voted its appreciation to its fact finders and canceled its call for a meeting of foreign ministers.[97]

This action, however, was a mere technicality, because already the OAS Council had convoked a foreign ministers meeting stemming from events in another quarter of the Caribbean. While the Nicaraguan affair was still pending, air and sea attacks launched from Cuba had taken place against the Dominican Republic on 14 and 19 June, respectively. Despite Trujillo's warning to the "aggressors" to stay away from the Dominican Republic, unless they "wanted to see their beards and brains flying about like butterflies,"[98] the attack upon Trujillo was inevitable. None of the antidictatorial leaders of the Caribbean concealed his absolute abhorrence of the Dominican regime. It was Castro, however, who most demonstrated his willingness to take direct action. He had invited exile groups to Cuba and promised them aid, scoring Trujillo as a "menace to the hemisphere" and deriding the OAS as a "useless organization."[99] The most important Dominican exiles had gone to Caracas in 1958, but when Castro visited there in January 1959 after coming to power, he conferred with the leaders of a newly formed organization called the Dominican Patriotic Union, UPD (Unión Patriótica Dominicana), and apparently agreed to support a military movement.[100]

The UPD was a coalition of leaders who had been active in the exile movement for a long time. They were neither distinguished nor notorious and included such opportunists as Juan Isidro Jiménez Grullón. The UPD moved its headquarters to Havana, although for purposes of fund raising and recruiting it also had representatives in Caracas, Mexico City, New York, Miami, and San Juan. The principal leaders in New York were Alfonso Canto and Juan Díaz. Missing from the coalition were Juan Bosch, Angel Miolán, and other leaders of the Dominican Revolutionary party (PRD), as well as Horacio Julio Ornes and his Revolutionary Vanguard (VRD). Miolán told Robert Alexander in Caracas in February 1959 that the UPD was Communist-infiltrated and that Horacio Ornes, who had met with its leaders during a visit to Caracas, had been advised by Acción Democrática to work with the PRD.[101]

In accordance with the general political situation of the anti-dictatorial bloc, the role of the parties of the Democratic Left in this movement was ambiguous. Although Trujillo's later charges, based upon "confessions" of captured invaders, were probably extreme, Betancourt and Figueres evidently rendered some assistance. Castro could not ignore the formidable military power of Trujillo, whereas the democratic leaders could not afford to have Castro overthrow Trujillo alone. During the spring, therefore, a somewhat broader coalition emerged known as the Dominican Liberation Movement. However, it set up its headquarters in Havana, and the Dominican Patriotic Union (UPD) remained intact and in charge of military affairs. The PRD still maintained its independence, but the activity of some of its partisans and the cooperation of its allies in Venezuela and Costa Rica provided it with political leverage in the event the movement succeeded.

Raúl Castro, as commander of Cuba's Revolutionary Army, provided much of the logistical support, while Che Guevara continued to act as a kind of political commissar. According to stories by Homer Bigart of the *New York Times* and Keith Wheeler of *Life,* a number of Puerto Rican youths were recruited by the UPD in New York and then sent to Cuba to train for the invasion of the Dominican Republic.[102] CARIB published a so-called Invasion Report containing an interview with a captured rebel, Gonzalo Almonte Pacheco, who allegedly affirmed that he had been recruited by the UPD in Caracas and, with forty others, had been flown from Maiquetía to Havana on 2 March 1959.[103] Miguel Angel Ramírez was named as chief strategist for the Dominican operation, and Alberto Bayo supposedly trained the men in guerrilla tactics.[104] Enrique Jiménez Moya, a Dominican veteran of Cayo Confites, was the commander of the invasion force.

In all, two hundred twenty-four men trained for the attack. Most of them were Dominicans, but there were a number of Cubans and Venezuelans, perhaps as many as twenty each, and a handful of other nationalities, including two North Americans.[105] According to John Bartlow Martin, sixteen of the Dominicans were Communists. Trujillo charged that both Betancourt and Figueres donated money and arms. The invasion plan called for two assaults: the first by air at Constanza in the Central Mountains, and the second by sea on the north coast.

The invasions turned out to be nightmares. On 14 June fifty-six men landed at Constanza in a C-46 supplied by Venezuela. After a brief clash, the invaders fled into the mountains but were pursued and either killed or captured. The unfortunate captives were taken to San Isidro Air Force Base, near Ciudad Trujillo, where they were slain, but only after sport had been made of some of them.[106] Trujillo was further amused when a radio transmitter located in Caracas, but pretending to be a Dominican rebel station, sent out the taped voice of Jiménez Moya, who was already dead.[107] One survivor, Cuban army major Delio Gómez Ochoa, was spared because of his propaganda value. He was paraded before the television cameras and microphones of "La Voz Dominicana," where he declared that the invaders had been duped; they had been told, he said, that the *campesinos* were badly treated and would join the rebellion and that the air force was "on our side." He accused Castro, Betancourt, Figueres, and Muñoz Marín of sending the expedition to certain disaster. "Without their help, the invasion would not have been possible," he stated.[108] In November 1959 Gómez Ochoa was heard again, charging that Raúl Castro and Che Guevara had placed the Cuban army "at the service of the Communist party." He also asserted that he had seen Dr. Marcelino Madrid, a Venezuelan physician, deliver $100,000 to Jiménez Moya.[109] Following this, Gómez Ochoa disappeared.[110]

Six days after the initial invasion, two yachts loaded with a total of one hundred sixty-eight men landed on the Dominican north coast at Maimón and Estero Hondo. They were escorted to near their destination by frigates of the Cuban navy, but failed to maintain radio silence and alerted Trujillo of their approach. Before they landed on the respective beaches, the invasion ships became infernos under the rocket attacks of Dominican Air Force planes. The few invaders who made it to shore were annihilated by army units.[111] All one hundred sixty-eight men were killed, but at least they were spared the barbarities of San Isidro or "La Cuarenta" (Trujillo's torture chamber). Quickly, "captured documents" were published: a "code book" bearing such names as Fidel Castro, Rómulo Betancourt, José Figueres, Luis Augusto Dubuc, Rondón Lovera, Ernesto Guevara, and Camilo Cienfuegos; and a "campaign diary" in which was written, "the internal front is also ripe and the people will close ranks with us. This is definitely assured us by Fidel Castro, Rómulo Betancourt, Muñoz Marín, and José Figueres."[112] Indeed, in the aftermath of the invasions the Trujillo regime became convinced that it had uncovered a substantial underground, and in December 1959 and January 1960 hundreds of Dominicans were herded into jails and torture chambers and many were killed.[113]

The tragedy of these events was compounded by the case of Captain Juan de Dios Ventura Simó. He was a Dominican Air Force officer who had fled to Puerto Rico in his jet fighter in April 1959. He next joined the invaders and was with them when they landed at Constanza. On 21 June, however, "Lieutenant Colonel" Ventura Simó was acclaimed a national hero; according to the press releases, he had only pretended to defect in order to infiltrate the invading force and deliver it to Trujillo. Robert Crassweller affirms that Ventura Simó actually was a defector but had agreed to this charade after his capture at Constanza in order to save his life. At any rate, later, according to the press releases, Ventura Simó died in a plane crash at sea.[114]

The failure of these invasions did not ease the tensions in the Caribbean. In fact, on 26 June Cuba broke diplomatic relations with the Dominican Republic. The Venezuelan government had already ruptured relations with the Dominicans on 12 June.[115] While stories circulated that a three thousand-man invasion force, with the support of twenty-five Venezuelan aircraft, was gathered in Cuba, Trujillo took U.S. newsmen on a three-hour tour to display his military might.[116]

With a Caribbean war a possibility, the Dominican Republic requested the Council of the OAS on 2 July to invoke the Rio Treaty. The Dominican Republic accused Cuba and Venezuela of complicity in the June invasions and of planning new aggressions against it.

Once again, the OAS was caught in the contradiction of its two elemental principles: nonintervention and the effective exercise of representative democracy. Betancourt denounced the Dominican Republic as unworthy of membership in the OAS and denied the legitimacy of its petition. If the OAS resolved to create a committee to investigate Trujillo's charges, he declared, he would not permit it "to set foot in Venezuela."[117] Cuba also indicated that, under the circumstances, an OAS committee would be unwelcome. Faced with this situation, there was considerable diplomatic maneuvering. The United States wanted to put a stop to further armed invasions in the Caribbean but also wished to avoid the appearance that it was acting in favor of the Trujillo dictatorship. As a result, on 10 July Brazil, Chile, Peru, and the United States proposed the convoking of a foreign ministers meeting under articles 39 and 40 of the OAS Charter, which permitted a consultative meeting for the consideration of "problems of an urgent nature and of common interest to the American States." The Dominican Republic, obviously persuaded backstage, facilitated this move by withdrawing its request for the invoking of the Rio Treaty, but Cuba and Venezuela forced a vote to delay action on the four-nation proposal. In this way, they hoped to dissociate completely the call for a foreign ministers meeting from the original request formulated by the Dominican Republic.[118]

On 13 July the Council of the OAS resolved to convoke the Fifth Meeting of Consultation of Ministers of Foreign Affairs, to be held in Santiago, Chile, 12-18 August 1959. The meeting was originally called to discuss the question of unrest in the Caribbean, but at the request of Cuba, Ecuador, Uruguay, and Venezuela the council agreed to include the problems of the exercise of representative democracy and respect for human rights.

The Santiago Conference

The Fifth Meeting of Consultation in Chile was as Marley's ghost. All the old sins and omissions were paraded by. The issues were the same as in 1949, but a decade of futility, expediency, and apathy had intervened, and now there was Fidel Castro. There was something perverse about the boast of the Eisenhower administration in 1959 that during its tenure almost all of Latin America's dictators had fallen.

Even so, the conference marked the end of an era. The phase of Caribbean political activity in which democratic leaders collaborated for the forceful overthrow of dictators was ended. With the rise of Castro and the concern on the part of the United States of Communist infiltration in Latin American revolutionary movements, the Democratic Left recognized the perils of further armed expeditions. It saw the need to find other means and measures for combating dictatorships which would not endanger the democratic revolution nor alienate the United States. The conference, however, failed to produce a viable alternative. As Ambassador Dreier himself noted, "the conflict between the promotion of democracy and nonintervention was met, discussed, and left unresolved."[119]

At the conference, the nations divided into three loose groupings. There were the dictatorships: the Dominican Republic, Haiti, Nicaragua, and Paraguay. Next were the "moderates," among them Argen-

tina, Brazil, Chile, Peru, and the United States, who sympathized with
the need to guarantee representative democracy and the respect for
human rights but adhered to the principle of nonintervention and
wished to avoid the denunciation of specific regimes. Within the moderate bloc, certain states, such as Brazil and Peru, perceived that economic ills were basic to the political problems and hoped to interest the
United States in a program of economic development. Finally, there
were the "dissenters," who maintained that the toleration of dictators
was too high a price to pay for solidarity and that collective action in
defense of democracy was not intervention. They wanted specific defi-
nitions of what constituted the exercise of representative democracy
and respect for human rights and, in the event these standards were
violated, to impose sanctions upon the offending states.[120] Venezuela
and Cuba, the most outspoken in the latter group, demanded the out-
right denunciation of the Dominican Republic and other dictatorships.
During the Conference, Betancourt sent a cable pointing out that,
according to the OAS Charter, membership in the organization was
restricted to "freely elected governments respectful of human rights."
He insisted upon the establishment of a rigorous quarantine of the
despotic governments.[121] In many respects, Cuba constituted a fourth
group by itself. In Havana, Castro referred to the Santiago Conference
as "a farce."[122]

For the United States, the Santiago Conference provided particular evidence of past shortcomings. During the previous decade, the most powerful state in the Caribbean had pursued the least imaginative policy. What
was worse, Salvador de Madariaga observed, it lost its "moral authority,"
which, he held, was essential for victory in the Cold War.[123] Yet, in the
name of Cold War exigencies, the "main objective" of U.S. Latin American policy was "to maintain maximum tranquility in the area."[124] Its
adherence to the principle of nonintervention was, in essence, an excuse
for not doing anything about the Latin American dictators. The Nixon
riots awakened some to the dangers of this policy, and President Eisenhower sent his brother, Milton Eisenhower, on a fact-finding mission to
Central America in July 1958. At the same time, however, the United
States missed an opportunity to recover lost ground. President Jusc-
elino Kubitschek of Brazil proposed the so-called "Operation Pan
American" (OPA) urging the United States to help Latin America
achieve an economic and social revolution. The OPA envisioned a
massive program of economic development, but the United States failed

to do then adequately, when the time was ripe, what it had to do three years later, when its "moral authority" had further depreciated.[125]

At Santiago the United States remained in the background. It did not offer a single draft resolution and preferred to see others in the moderate bloc exercise leadership. Secretary of State Christian Herter provided some direction, however, in his address to the opening session on 12 August. Some change and freshness in approach were noticeable in Herter's remarks, although the old ambivalence was still there. He insisted that to weaken the principle of nonintervention in the name of the promotion of democracy was "counterproductive," because, he affirmed, the tensions of the previous six months had not encouraged democracy but had set it back. According to Herter, the unrest in the Caribbean resulted in more repressions by dictators, weakened new democracies and rendered them vulnerable to rightist coups, diverted resources from necessary economic and social programs into military expenditures, and provided opportunities for international communism. He recognized, however, that the "lack of democratic fulfillment" was a contributing factor to the Caribbean unrest and suggested economic progress as a means of achieving political stability. Herter also showed sympathy for the Venezuelan position by referring to the possible creation of a commission within the OAS, "to gather views of the American governments and people, to clarify the nature of representative democracy, and to chart a course which the OAS could follow in evoking the maximum cooperation of governments for the effective achievement of democratic principles."[126]

The statements of many of the other foreign ministers were less polite. In fact, the exchanges between the Cubans and Dominicans degenerated into shouting matches. The Dominican foreign minister, Porfirio Herrera Báez, repeated his government's charges against Cuba and Venezuela and, in order to demonstrate that the June invasions were Communist-inspired, asserted that the invaders had in their possession a number of Communist books and pamphlets.[127] Not to be outdone, Cuban Foreign Minister Raúl Roa charged that the Dominican Republic was cooperating with "war criminals" in Miami and Ciudad Trujillo for counterrevolutionary purposes. He added that recent counterrevolutionary invaders captured in Cuba had also carried books, which, he said, included *Mein Kampf,* by Adolf Hitler.[128] It appeared that the invaders could be identified by their reading matter.

Almost in the midst of this debate, a bizarre event took place in

Cuba. Counterrevolutionary forces based in the Dominican Republic were lured to Cuba and captured on 14 August. Major William A. Morgan, a soldier of furtune who had joined the Cuban rebellion against Batista, played the role of double agent. Feigning disillusionment with Castro, he planned an uprising and invasion with agents of Trujillo and Johnny Abbes García. After lengthy planning and the expenditure of a great deal of money, Morgan radioed that he was prepared to begin the uprising and asked for reenforcements of men and arms. When the plane carrying them landed in Cuba, it was seized by the Revolutionary Army and Fidel Castro personally.[129] In the confusion of the Morgan affair, however, a band of bearded Cubans stole away to try to invade Haiti. Thus, while Roa enjoyed the embarrassment of the Dominican delegation at the conference, he experienced some of his own in the presence of Haitian Foreign Minister Louis Mars. Nonetheless, the conferees continued their labors.

The work of the conference concentrated upon the three themes: nonintervention, exercise of democracy and respect for human rights, and economic underdevelopment and political unrest. The principal concern of the United States was to prevent further fighting in the Caribbean, but it now recognized the greater complexities of the issue and made concessions. This was evident in Resolution IV, the most significant act of the conference. It instructed the Inter-American Peace Committee to make a study of the questions which had led to the convoking of the Santiago Conference. It empowered the committee to look into these matters at the request of any government, or, more importantly, upon its own initiative, although, obviously, it could not visit any country without its consent. While this resolution had the earmarks of a delaying action, the various aspects of the proposed study were detailed and they demonstrated real progress against the once heavy bias in favor of nonintervention. In addition to a study of the methods and procedures for preventing externally based revolutionary activity, the committee was told, first, to examine the relationship between violations of human rights and the absence of functioning democracy, on the one hand, and political tensions which affect hemispheric peace, on the other, and, second, the relationship between economic underdevelopment and political instability.[130] These studies and others ordered were to be presented at the Eleventh Inter-American Conference, which, as it turned out, never met.

One should not overlook the fact, however, that some states, such as

Mexico and Argentina, regarded the principle of nonintervention as sacred. Whereas the United States might favor action against a Communist regime, or even against a Trujillo if prerequisite for steps against a Communist regime, Mexico and Argentina were consistent in their defense of nonintervention. Hence, during the conference both countries sponsored resolutions designed to safeguard this principle. A Uruguayan resolution also called for strict observance of nonintervention.

The country which took the lead in favor of human rights and representative democracy was Venezuela. It proposed a treaty to establish procedures for determining the exercise of democracy and to fix sanctions against violator states, but all it obtained was a diluted resolution recommending a draft convention on the effective exercise of representative democracy.[131] Venezuela did better in the area of human rights. Supported by Chile, Colombia, El Salvador, Ecuador, Peru, and Uruguay, Venezuela secured Resolution VIII, which requested the Inter-American Council of Jurists to prepare draft conventions dealing with human rights and the creation of an inter-American court of human rights. The resolution also created an inter-American commission for the protection of human rights to function under the direction of the OAS Council.[132] These actions were also to be considered at the Eleventh Conference.

In the economic sphere, Argentina, Brazil, Chile, Ecuador, and Peru were the most active, although Cuba also presented a draft resolution on "economic underdevelopment and political instability." The "moderates" were anxious to find means "to accelerate and intensify 'Operation Pan American,' " with Cuba itself maintaining that a low level of economic development was the major factor in the rise of dictatorial regimes. The discussions produced a resolution entitled "Economic Underdevelopment and the Preservation of Democracy," headed by a lengthy preamble which affirmed that the survival of democracy depended upon the solution of grave economic and social ills. The resolution asserted the right of the individual to better health, education, opportunity, and social security and declared that the state was responsible for the promotion of economic and social well-being. Believing, however, that the prevailing economic and social problems exceeded the resources and power of individual states, it foresaw their solution only through inter-American cooperation. It was apparent at Santiago that the issue of democracy versus dictatorship was fast losing ground to the requirements of economic and social revolution.

Although the need to act was clearly stated, the operative clause of the resolution was a disappointment. While the Eleventh Conference seemed imminent there was perhaps some excuse for delay, but the resolution merely requested the states to encourage the OAS Council and appropriate organs to accelerate and facilitate measures already proposed by the so-called "Committee of Twenty-One" (Operation Pan American) for the establishment of "new bases for economic cooperation among the American nations."[133] The resolution was meaningless as long as the United States was unwilling to make a major commitment to Latin American economic development.

Brazil, the leader among the nations seeking an economic solution, also presented the "Declaration of Santiago de Chile," which was approved as Resolution I. The declaration was an enunciation of the "principles and attributes of the democratic system in the hemisphere" which might serve as a standard for judging political regimes in the Americas and hopefully promote the elimination of despotism. [134] According to the declaration, governments must be freely elected and the exercise of power ought to be limited by a fixed tenure. Also, the rule of law must be assured by the separation of powers and through safeguards imposed by competent organs of the state. Democracy does not function, the statement contended, without freedom of press and expression and a system of civil liberties and respect for human rights through effective judicial measures.[135] Despite these standards, the Dominican Republic signed the Final Act of the Conference.

Numerous other states put forth proposals touching upon the basic themes. A Bolivian resolution was approved calling upon governments to reduce military spending in order to release funds for general economic and social progress. And a Nicaraguan plan for the appointment of observers for presidential elections was referred to the Council of the OAS.

The Santiago Conference was a strange meeting. It considered issues which should have been acted upon ten years earlier and ignored new issues produced by the delay. The conference had said that "democracy could not be imposed on countries by force,"[136] but, according to José Figueres, it had actually prescribed another political truce in the Caribbean, because Castro had betrayed the antidictatorial movement by opening it to Communist infiltration.[137] Yet, the conference showed a willingness on the part of the American states (especially the United States) to criticize harshly and officially the conduct of the

Caribbean's dictators. The position of Rafael Trujillo, in particular, had deteriorated, although it would soon be apparent that he was to be sacrificed, essentially, in order to get at Castro.[138] But nothing emerged from the conference of a positive nature for remedying basic economic and social ills, now clearly the test for the survival of any governmental form. This situation was especially poignant for the Democratic Left, because it fell heir to conditions created by those it had fought. Although not completely safe from Trujillo or internal reaction, the Democratic Left faced the challenge of new revolutionaries who doubted the efficacy of democratic institutions for promoting real economic and social change.

"La Lucha Sin Fin"

After devoting their political careers to the struggle against reactionary forces, the leaders of the Democratic Left found their revolutionary credentials challenged. In contrast to Fidel Castro, they seemed to move too slowly and to be willing to compromise too readily. Whereas in Cuba young people were making a revolution, in Venezuela the university youth of Acción Democrática were advised by Betancourt to study and work and avoid excessive political activity.[139] The Democratic Left endeavored to prepare for the future while making the best of the realities of the present, but to the youth such conduct seemed a betrayal.

In Venezuela the estrangement of youth and the Democratic Left became especially acute. Almost from the beginning of Castro's accession to power, many of the AD youth were swept up by the vigor of his anti-imperialist, antifeudal pronouncements. Led by Domingo Alberto Rangel, Simón Sáez Mérida, Gumersindo Rodríguez, and Américo Martín, these young leaders, or so-called *"muchachos"* (boys), were disillusioned with the Old Guard of the party. They argued, however, that their dissent was ideological not generational, that the older leaders were submissive in their dealings with the military and the foreign oil companies and were neglecting the needs of the masses. They declared that democracy should seek its support in the people and that by serving their needs would find sufficient defense against counterrevolutionary forces. As noted, they criticized Betancourt's friendship with Figueres and Muñoz Marín and warned that the measures adopted at the Santiago Conference, while admirable for opposing the tyranny of Trujillo, should not provide a pretext for attacking Cuba.[140]

The fight was kept within the party for a little over a year following Betancourt's inauguration. The AD leadership had learned in 1945-48 the high price of extremism and believed that history and a sense of the possible, not the loss of revolutionary ardor, dictated a responsible, even cautious, policy. The Old Guard was able to contain the "muchachos"; the young radicals alone lacked sufficient strength to be elected to any important party office and their influence was confined to the party's Youth Bureau. At AD's Tenth Annual Convention in September 1959, Raúl Leoni was elected party president over the strenuous opposition of the "muchachos," who were at the same time severely censured for their factionalism.[141] Shortly afterward, a "muchacho," writing under a pseudonym, affirmed that although the youth overthrew Pérez Jiménez, they had been pushed aside and forgotten by "those who came from outside."[142] This attitude was a strong factor in the resentment of Rangel and Sáez Mérida, who were further influenced by the events in Cuba. Increasingly, the "muchachos" referred to 23 January 1958 as an insurrection, not a *golpe,* and to themselves as the Revolutionary Left.

AD responded to this interpretation by reviewing the history of the party's struggle, emphasizing particularly the role of its martyrs. Carlos Canache Mata, himself a youthful party leader, reminded the "muchachos" that "those who came from outside" had not been on any "pleasure cruise," but had been expelled from the country after "months or years" in the resistance and had continued the fight in exile in order to achieve "the hour of liberty."[143] Without the inspiration of the founders of the party, he said, without the "painful martyrdom" of Valmore Rodríguez in his jail cell in 1949, without the "stoic sacrifice" of Alberto Carnevali, without the "wave of anger" which followed the murder of Leonardo Ruiz Pineda, without the "courageous example" of Cástor Nieves Ríos, without the "legendary" resistance of Salom Meza in the torture chamber, without the assassination of "that new Sucre," Antonio Pinto Salinas, without the "untiring and wise direction from exile" of Rómulo Gallegos and Rómulo Betancourt, "without all that, the 23 of January 1958 would have been just another day and not the day on which shone the sun of liberation."[144] This invoking of its heroes and the full trajectory of its resistance became a regular feature of AD propaganda. AD tried to draw upon a proud record not only to respond to the "muchachos" but also to build a modern, ideological party.

The struggle with the "muchachos," however, became more serious as the separation between Acción Democrática and Castro became greater. Many of the viewpoints of the "muchachos," particularly the avowed impatience with representative democracy, were reflections of those of Castro. Hence, as accusations of communism were made against Castro, so were they made against AD's young radicals. Likewise, as Castroism was looked upon as subversive, so was the loyalty of the "muchachos" questioned. Castro and Betancourt had all but severed relations by November 1959, particularly after Venezuela "urged" Cuba to cancel a scheduled visit to Caracas of Raúl Castro and Che Guevara. Venezuela reportedly explained that their presence might cause demonstrations which "the Communists here would use to their own ends," but Castro indignantly recalled his ambassador.[145] In that same November, the Cuban Confederation of Workers (CTC) withdrew from the ORIT, which it attacked as "an agency of American imperialism."[146] As has been seen, the ambivalence of the ORIT with reference to Batista, largely because of the policy of its affiliate, the CTC, was a source of embarrassment. Still, the friendship and cooperation between the ORIT and the Democratic Left was a matter of record, so that Castro's action, in effect, showed his scorn for both of them.

Conspiracies of the Right also contributed to the crisis between Betancourt and the "muchachos." In July and September 1959, and again in January 1960, the Venezuelan government uncovered and suppressed counterrevolutionary plots. The "muchachos," undoubtedly inspired by Castro's revolutionary tribunals, charged that Betancourt treated the conspirators too leniently. "We do not say that the appropriate way of handling them is 'up against the wall,'" asserted Sáez Mérida, "but we do propose that stern punishment be imposed resolutely and energetically."[147] In January 1960, when the Betancourt government uncovered a plot against it, which involved some officers of the armed forces,[148] President Betancourt addressed the nation and declared that all guilty individuals, regardless of rank, would be punished in accordance with the laws. At the same time, and with obvious reference to the "muchachos," he warned that he would prosecute all persons who made false accusations concerning the involvement of members of the armed forces in the conspiracy.[149]

He then denounced the "muchachos" directly, thus airing publicly the split within Acción Democrática. Betancourt referred to them as "hotheads," who had accused the government of "inflexibility" and of being unconcerned with the urgent problems of the people, such as unemployment and the cost of living. Betancourt scoffed at the charge that his government "passed out a sweet, ineffective nirvana to solve the nation's problems." He referred to its efforts to stimulate production as "the only real means of reducing the cost of living." To meet unemployment, he cited his government's program of public works, inducements to permanent sources of work, and collaboration with the private sector. The nation, he said, was fighting "backwardness, poverty, and cultural insufficiency." He recognized the difficulties, he said, but his goals were "full employment" and the achievement of a "modern industrialized state." He affirmed that Venezuela needed foreign capital but gave assurances that the resources of the nation, "under a responsible and concerned regime were being placed at the service of the people."[150]

From that point on, the "muchachos" faced expulsion from the party. The climax came in March 1960, first, as a result of two articles by Américo Martín, and, second, over the conduct of Domingo Alberto Rangel. Martín wrote an article critical of the Peruvian APRA in which he cited the differences between its old guard and young radicals; a few days later, in defiance of a party ban against such writing, he again attacked Figueres and Muñoz Marín. Rangel defied party discipline by publicly attacking AD's position concerning contract negotiations between the oil workers' union and the foreign petroleum companies. [151] When the young leaders were ordered to appear before AD's National Disciplinary Tribunal, they chose instead to resign. On 12 April 1960, joined by other dissident members of the National Youth Bureau, including Sáez Mérida and Eduardo González, they formed AD de Izquierda (Leftist AD). Upon withdrawing, they denied that they were Communists but complained that AD had done nothing to defend them from such charges and indeed had tacitly approved the allegations. "We do not have the problem which faces the government," Sáez Mérida declared, "lack of definition. We are leftists and nothing more. The government does not know if it is rightist or leftist. But it favors the right."[152] Shortly afterward, the former AD youth renamed their organization the Movement of the Revolutionary Left, MIR (Movimiento de Izquierda Revolucionaria). And by the end of 1960, they were fighting the Betancourt government in the streets.

The alienation of AD youth from the party was a tragic result of the stolen opportunity of the fifties. One may question the wisdom of forcing the exit of the dissident youth from Acción Democrática, particularly since democracy has functioned best under a system of a few parties embracing varying, even antagonistic, viewpoints and interests. However, according to John Martz, there was "no apparent way" for AD to contain "the energies of the muchachos and their followers. . . . Broad as AD was, it had little to offer such men as Rangel and others."[153] The question of who started the violence was more controversial. On the one hand, when the "muchachos" pulled out of AD, they declared that the disciplinary action against them was for ideological reasons, not because they had violated any party statute, and they called for an extraordinary national convention to determine the validity of the measures taken by the AD party leadership.[154] It has been affirmed that the young radicals "preferred the ballot to the bullet" and that their subsequent resort to "illegal means" was the result of persecution by the Betancourt government.[155] On the other hand, the obeisance of the "muchachos" to Fidel Castro, when the latter was clearly a threat to the constitutional government of Venezuela, could not be overlooked by Rómulo Betancourt. In April 1960 the "muchachos" demanded the "most active solidarity with the Cuban Revolution." "We have not sought," they added, "a carbon copy of the Cuban process, but the incorporation of some of its teachings and the firm resolve to defend it, because it constitutes day-by-day the best hope of the Latin American national revolution. Our country ought to have a defined policy of cordial relations and belligerent solidarity with Cuba."[156] It was this international content that explained the stern reaction of Betancourt to the MIR. Betancourt was no tyrant—he was a democratically elected president with a genuine program for economic and social reform—but he was a seasoned fighter and was determined to fulfill his mandate.

These problems of Acción Democrática were typical of the Democratic Left in general, to wit: Castro, youthful dissent, and the changed nature of the antidictatorial struggle. These common problems promoted a new unity, no longer distracted by the futile task of accommodating Castro. The first manifestation of this firmer unity was an undertaking encompassing all three problems.

From 25 through 29 November 1959, representatives of the parties of the Democratic Left of the Caribbean and of Peru met on Figueres' finca "La Lucha Sin Fin." Those present included: Ramiro Prialé and Ricardo Temoche of APRA; Luis Beltrán Prieto of AD; Figueres, Daniel Oduber, Luis Alberto Monge, and Padre Benjamín Núñez of Liberación Nacional; Aureliano Sánchez Arango and Emilio A. Rivero of the National Democratic Front, Triple A, of Cuba; Mario Méndez Montenegro and Francisco Villamar of the Revolutionary Party of Guatemala; Francisco ("el Indio") Sánchez Reyes of the Liberal party of Honduras; Rodolfo Abaunza of the Nicaraguan Revolutionary Movement; César Pereira of the Panamanian Democratic Groups; and Harry Kantor and Sacha Volman of the Institute of International Labor Research of New York.[157]

They came together to found the Inter-American Institute of Political Education (later renamed the Inter-American School of Democratic Education). It was an extension of the Institute of Political and Social Sciences already functioning in Costa Rica, but the scope and participation were broader. The parties agreed to contribute to the operation of the school and to send their promising young leaders to study. The representatives noted that for forty years the Communists had been concerned with the training of leaders, but that until then the democratic parties of the hemisphere had no leadership program at the international level.[158]

The goals of the institute were ideological and practical. The democratic parties recognized the need to train young leaders in organization and political action, but they also wanted to define their ideology "in the light of principles, lessons, experiences, and positive achievements of democracy in the service of the people." The institute provided, of course, a basis for comradeship, which would hopefully promote future solidarity among the parties. It was designed to be, at the same time, a research center which, drawing upon broad contacts and resources, would facilitate the study of individual and common problems. In a similar manner, the school was to serve as an exchange and information center for parties of the Democratic Left. Finally, the institute was created for the preparation of leaders "for the fight for hemispheric unity, within a democratic inter-Americanism free of imperialism." [159]

In principle, the school was scheduled to hold three, ten-week sessions annually on its site just outside of San José. However, from the time of the inauguration of its program on 3 October 1960 until May 1965, it conducted only eight sessions, enrolling a total of three hundred twenty-one young men from twenty countries and representing forty distinct political parties or civic institutions.[160] Later, disclosures that funds supplied by the U.S. Central Intelligence Agency had been channelled to the institute were, of course, damaging, although the school received the money from apparently legitimate sources, with no conditions attached. At the time of this writing, the institute continues to operate. It may be noted also that in 1962 the AFL-CIO established the American Institute for Free Labor Development (AIFLD) in Washington, D.C., and Front Royal, Virginia, for labor leadership training in the Americas.

In 1960 the Democratic Left made two additional efforts to reaffirm its unity and common purpose. The Second Inter-American Conference for Democracy and Freedom was held in Maracay, Venezuela, 22 to 26 April 1960, and the First Conference of the Popular Parties of Latin America met in Lima, Peru, 1 to 4 August 1960.

The Maracay Conference contrasted sharply with the founding meeting of the Inter-American Association for Democracy and Freedom (IADF) in Havana ten years earlier, when dictatorial regimes dominated Latin America. Many of the two hundred delegates had been in exile in 1950 but now held high political office. Despite the fact that the opening of the conference was delayed by an abortive uprising under General Jesús María Castro León, the conference did not display the former enthusiasm for the antidictatorial fight.[161] The delegates endorsed the stand of Venezuela at the Santiago Conference, that is, the expulsion of nonpopular regimes from the OAS and the imposition of diplomatic and economic sanctions, but they were more concerned with the problem of maintaining hard won political freedom, particularly through the solution of economic and social problems. There were, of course, strong stands taken on behalf of human rights, and, in an effort to establish the moral position of democratic leadership, the delegates approved strong measures against illegal enrichment in office. This included the confiscation of properties and assets of former officials (deposed dictators) found guilty of peculation.

There were few references to the Cuban Revolution during the conference, but it, in fact, dictated the mood of the sessions. Many delegates, anxious to prove their revolutionary passion, took, in essence, a defensive stance by strongly criticizing the United States and affirming their independence from North American control. Behind many of the speeches, discussions, and background papers, however, was the fear that the United States would fail the democratic leadership in the struggle against poverty and underdevelopment, as it had failed it in the struggle against dictatorship. No one appreciated this apprehension better than Miss Frances Grant, who, nonetheless, received a mandate to continue the fight.[162]

The Lima Conference was an important step toward formal, interparty collaboration. In attendance were two parties from the Caribbean area and three from South America: AD of Venezuela, Liberación Nacional of Costa Rica, APRA of Peru, the National Revolutionary Movement of Bolivia, MNR (Movimiento Nacional Revolucionario), and the Febrerista party of Paraguay (Revolucionario Febrerista). The conference called for the establishment of an interparty congress and set down common principles and goals in its "Declaration of Lima."

The "popular parties" specifically reiterated their belief in the democratic political system and their determination to give it an economic and social content. The parties desired economic, political, and cultural integration by means of a "federation of peoples" and hemispherewide coordination of effort. Generally, the purpose of such integration was to strengthen the bargaining position of Latin America vis-á-vis the United States. Running through the declaration was the theme that the industrialized states were responsible for and, indeed, perpetuated the economic backwardness of Latin America. Undoubtedly forced into a more militant position because of the popularity of the anti-U.S. policy of Castro, the parties of the Democratic Left exhibited deep frustration over the political and economic policies of the United States. On the other hand, the declaration rejected Soviet imperialism and Communist penetration of Latin America.[163]

The Declaration of Lima called for a "new democratic interAmericanism" as the basis for eliminating all forms of imperialism and for establishing "just relations" between Latin America and the United States. In order to accomplish this, it summoned the Latin American peoples and democratic governments to a struggle against the remaining dictatorships and demanded that the United States cooperate with these efforts by denying "all forms of assistance" to tyrannical regimes. Economic affairs, including integration, planning, and international cooperation, dominated all aspects of the declaration. The Democratic Left had not given up the hope for U.S. economic assistance but demanded at least some means of adjusting prices between the basic commodities which Latin America exported and the capital goods which it imported.[164]

The conference approved three additional resolutions. One called for a boycott of tyrannical regimes, particularly a labor boycott under the leadership of trade union organizations of democratic countries. Another was a specific denunciation of the Trujillo regime. In June Trujillo had attempted to assassinate Betancourt,[165] and the democratic leaders demanded the imposition of absolute diplomatic and economic sanctions, in accordance with Article VIII of the Río Treaty. The third resolution tried to define the position of the Democratic Left with reference to the Cuban Revolution. It applauded the overthrow of Batista and the economic and social reforms of the revolutionary government. Moreover, it recognized the right of Cuba to establish its own form of government, in accordance with the principle of self-determination. However, it warned that the Cuban Revolution must not be a source of division among the popular movements of the hemisphere and declared that "the Cuban revolutionary process, as every American revolutionary process, must be guided by the system of representative democracy, since popular sovereignty is the basis and norm of national sovereignty."[166]

The Lima Conference was a reaffirmation of the Caracas Declaration and the "La Lucha" conference and expanded the operation of the Inter-American Institute of Political Education. It was an effort to emphasize the revolutionary content of the Democratic Left in response to growing impatience for the solution of economic and social problems. The Democratic Left clung to its belief in political democracy and exhibited a willingness to cooperate with the United States; two concepts which would be increasingly difficult to maintain in view of its own bitter experience over the previous fifteen years. Indeed, the Democratic Left enjoyed only modest success in the next decade.

It was not the intention of this study to discuss events after 1959. As has been explained, the nature of the antidictatorial struggle in the Caribbean changed after the Santiago Conference, and the decade of the sixties presented entirely new challenges to the Democratic Left. Some overlap, however, was unavoidable. For example, when Fidel Castro invaded Cuba in December 1956, he did not seem any different than the other antidictatorial leaders of the fifties. On the other hand, the Lima Conference in August 1960 was the realization of the idea for an entente of democratic parties, which could be traced to the discussions between Betancourt and Carlos Prío Socarrás in Havana in

1949. One could not overlook either the pathos in the triumph of the
Democratic Left. Given the magnitude of the problems, it did not
expect to have an easy time following the defeat of the dictators, but
the concurrent rise of Fidel Castro threatened to overwhelm it completely. Certainly, the activism of youth in the sixties found its inspiration in the Cuban Revolution. If one wished to tie up loose ends, there
might be an argument for treating the condemnation and sanctioning of
Trujillo at the Sixth Meeting of Consultation in San José in August
1960, or for tracing events to the time of his assassination in May 1961;
but even as this is written the problem of dictatorship in the Caribbean
persists. Some thread undoubtedly links the Bay of Pigs with Cayo
Confites and the other filibustering expeditions of the forties and
fifties. Ultimately, the determination of the amount of overlap has been
personal, guided by a sense of the historical period and by the availabil-
ity of documents and the degree of perspective.

The period 1945-59, however, has unity. During this period a unique
generation of men from a number of Caribbean countries collaborated
for the realization of the democratic ideal. They were thrown together
in exile, because they stood for fundamental change in societies not
ready to accept or tolerate them. In exile their common purpose united
them, and they maintained a political opposition not permitted to exist
in their respective homelands. The purpose of this book was principally
to chronicle that opposition. It was concerned with who fought, how
they fought, and where and why they fought. A function of history
may simply be the preservation of the record, and the function of the
historian to present it honestly and clearly. But, in view of the inconclusive results of the antidictatorial struggle, the relating of the tale may
serve another purpose.

In many respects, the antidictatorial struggle was the contribution of
one generation of the Democratic Left. It seems important to transmit
the story of that struggle to succeeding generations, so that they may
appreciate fully their place in time. The generation of Betancourt,
Figueres, and Muñoz Marín ultimately broke the power of the dictators,
not merely by overcoming them physically but by helping to create the
atmosphere which made them obsolete. However, because of the length
and difficulty of the struggle, this generation of leaders was unable to
seize the opportunity which their opposition had made. The tragedy of
their victory was that it took so long to achieve, that they had ex-
pended so much of their energy in the struggle, and that the delay had

created new problems for which their solutions seemed inadequate. Only belatedly did they undertake efforts to encourage new leaders to continue the struggle of the Democratic Left. They had triumphed by the end of the fifties, the important question was whether or not they could transmit their ideals to a new group of leaders.

> The days of man are but as grass; for he flourisheth
> as a flower of the field.
> For as soon as the wind goeth over it, it is gone;
> and the place thereof shall know it no more.

Psalm 103

Notes

Introduction

1. Interview with José Figueres, 16 December 1966.
2. U.S., Congress, Senate, Committee on Foreign Relations, *United States-Latin American Relations,* 86th Cong., 2d sess., 1960, Senate Doc. 125, p. 10.
3. Ibid., pp. 10-11.
4. *Rómulo Betancourt: pensamiento y acción* (Mexico, D.F., 1951), pp. 214-18.
5. Ibid., p. 216.
6. Robert J. Alexander, *Prophets of the Revolution: Profiles of Latin American Leaders* (New York: The Macmillan Company, 1962), pp. 79-80.
7. Ibid., p. 83.
8. Ibid., pp. 85-89. See also Harry Kantor, "*Aprismo:* Peru's Indigenous Political Theory," *The Dynamics of Change in Latin American Politics,* ed. John D. Martz (Englewood Cliffs, N.J.: Prentice-Hall Inc., 1965), pp. 88-91. The weakness of the *Aprista* program has been its lack of a strategy for achieving power. There have been numerous times since 1930 when APRA might have won a free election in Peru but was not permitted to present its candidacy.

Chapter 1

1. Ricardo Montilla, *La Generación del 28 en la Historia de Venezuela,* Publicación del Gobierno del Estado Guárico (Caracas: Imprenta Nacional, 1964), p. 14. The latter part was an allusion to the regime's practice of using convicts (political prisoners) to construct roads in the interior.
2. *Rómulo Betancourt, interpretación de su doctrina popular y democrática,* editado por SUMA, librería y editorial (Caracas, 1958), p. 86.
3. Ibid.   4. Ibid., pp. 21-22.   5. Ibid., pp. 22-23.
6. Montilla, *Generación,* p. 16.
7. John D. Martz, *Acción Democrática. Evolution of a Modern Political Party in Venezuela* (Princeton: Princeton University Press, 1966), pp. 120-21.
8. *Betancourt, su doctrina,* p. 147.
9. Interview with Ricardo Montilla, 17 June 1965.
10. *Betancourt, su doctrina,* p. 122.
11. Montilla, *Generación,* p. 16..   12. Ibid.

13. Martz, *Acción Democrática,* p. 122.
14. *Betancourt: pensamiento y acción* (Mexico, D.F., 1951), p. 217.
15. Ibid., p. 218.   16. *Betancourt, su doctrina,* p. 71.
17. Ibid., pp. 135-36.   18. Ibid., p. 147.   19. Ibid., p. 91.   20. Ibid., p. 124.
21. Martz, *Acción Democrática,* pp. 28-29.
22. Ibid., p. 29.   23. Ibid., pp. 31-33.
24. *Betancourt, su doctrina,* pp. 125-26.
25. Martz, *Acción Democrática,* pp. 34-35.
26. Interview with Montilla. Also see Martz, *Acción Democrática,* pp. 123-24.
27. Martz, *Acción Democrática,* p. 40.
28. *Betancourt, su doctrina,* pp. 33, 127.
29. Ibid., pp. 130-31.   30. Ibid., p. 131   31. Ibid., pp. 55, 128.
32. Ibid., p. 55.   33. Ibid., p. 127.   34. Ibid., p. 58.   35. Ibid., p. 62.
36. Ibid., p. 131.   37. Ibid., p. 132.   38. Ibid., p. 107.
39. Robert J. Alexander, interview with Rómulo Betancourt, 11 September 1955, the manuscripts of Robert J. Alexander. Cited hereinafter as Alexander MSS.
40. Russell H. Fitzgibbon, *Cuba and the United States, 1900-1935* (Menasha, Wisconsin: George Banta Publishing Company, 1935), p. 191.
41. The unhappy events of the Machado years were reported at the time by *New York Times* correspondent J. D. Phillips, and later recounted in a book by his wife, Ruby Hart Phillips, *Cuban Sideshow* (Havana, 1935). Mrs. Phillips became the *Times* Havana correspondent following the death of her husband in 1936. Also see, Carleton Beals, *The Crime of Cuba* (Philadelphia: J. B. Lippincott Company, 1933).
42. Ruby Hart Phillips, *Cuba: Island of Paradox* (New York: McDowell, Obolensky, 1959), p. 47. Mrs. Phillips scoffed at the idea of geometric progression and claimed that the ABC was made up of no more than two thousand persons. Carleton Beals also described the ABC cell structure, but somewhat differently. See Beals, *Crime,* p. 310.
43. Beals, *Crime,* pp. 314-15.
44. Quoted in Luis E. Aguilar, ed. *Marxism in Latin America* (New York: Alfred A. Knopf, 1968), p. 113.
45. Sumner Welles, *The Time for Decision* (New York: Harper and Brothers Publishers, 1944), p. 198.
46. Federico G. Gil, "Antecedents of the Cuban Revolution," *Reform and Revolution. Readings in Latin American Politics,* ed. Arpad von Lazar and Robert R. Kaufman (Boston: Allyn and Bacon, Inc., 1969), p. 296.
47. Wyatt MacGaffey and Clifford R. Barnett, *Twentieth Century Cuba* (Garden City, New York: Doubleday and Company, 1965), pp. 128-33 and p. 151.
48. *New York Times,* 8 September 1944, p. 21.
49. Robert J. Alexander, *Prophets of the Revolution: Profiles of Latin American Leaders* (New York: The Macmillan Company, 1962), pp. 144-45.
50. James L. Busey, *Notes on Costa Rican Democracy,* University of Colorado Studies, Series in Political Science, no. 2 (Boulder, Colorado: University of Colorado Press, 1962), p. 64.
51. León Pacheco, "Evolución del pensamiento democrático de Costa Rica," *Combate* 3, no. 15 (March-April 1961): 41.
52. Busey, *Notes,* p. 26.
53. Interviews with José Figueres, 16 December 1966, and Father Benjamín

302 Notes to pp. 41 to 52

Núñez, 4 January 1969. The author has visited "La Lucha" and its fábrica,
which even today is a remarkable island of industrial activity in a remote
agricultural zone.

54. Arturo Castro Esquivel, *José Figueres Ferrer. El hombre y su obra* (San José,
Costa Rica: Imprenta Tormo, 1955), pp. 24-35. In 1959 Mora charged that
Figueres was expelled at the insistence of the U.S. Embassy, because he had
allegedly revealed information about secret antisubmarine bases under construction on Costa Rica's Caribbean coast. *Diario de Costa Rica,* 16 April
1959, p. 17.

55. Ibid., p. 44. Figueres also studied the cultivation of henequén, which he
perceived to have qualities superior to cabuya and he introduced its cultivation at "La Lucha."

56. *Betancourt: pensamiento,* p. 241. When Figueres founded his party in 1952,
he acknowledged a debt to Haya de la Torre and referred to his movement as
"a minor disciple" of AD.

57. Castro E., *Figueres,* pp. 52-55.

58. Thomas Mathews, *Luis Muñoz Marín* (New York: American R.D.M. Corporation, 1967), p. 52.

59. Alexander, *Prophets,* p. 191.

60. Thomas Aitken, Jr., *Luis Muñoz Marín: Poet in the Fortress* (New York: The
New American Library, 1965), p. 157.

61. Alexander, *Prophets,* p. 191.

62. The author concurs with the thesis of Professor Ronald Schneider, who concluded that Guatemala's "lack of preparation" in self-government and failure
to develop a viable democratic alternative made it vulnerable to Communist
infiltration after the revolution of 1944. See Ronald M. Schneider, *Communism in Guatemala, 1944-1954* (New York: Frederick A. Praeger, 1959).

63. Schneider, *Communism,* p. 8.

64. Amy Elizabeth Jensen, *Guatemala. A Historical Survey* (New York: Exposition Press, 1955), p. 134.

65. Mario Rosenthal, *Guatemala. The Story of an Emergent Latin American
Democracy* (New York: Twayne Publishers, Inc., 1962), pp. 193, 201.

66. Ibid., pp. 202-14; Schneider, *Communism,* pp. 11-12.

67. Schneider, *Communism,* pp. 12-14.   68. Ibid., p. 18.

69. Juan José Arévalo, *Istmania; o, la unidad revolucionaria de Centroamérica*
(Buenos Aires: Editorial Indoamérica, 1954), pp. 18-19.

70. There is an extensive bibliography concerning Rafael Trujillo, but the best
general work in English is Robert D. Crassweller, *Trujillo: The Life and Times
of a Caribbean Dictator* (New York: The Macmillan Company, 1966). In
Spanish, one should not overlook Jesús de Galíndez, *La Era de Trujillo*
(Santiago de Chile: Editorial Pácifico, 1956).

71. Mario Rodríguez, *Central America* (Englewood Cliffs, N.J.: Prentice-Hall,
Inc., 1965), p. 136.

72. Ibid., p. 135; also see, John D. Martz, *Central America: The Crisis and the
Challenge* (Chapel Hill: University of North Carolina Press, 1959), pp.
128-29.

73. Martz, *Central America,* p. 120.

74. Neill Macaulay, *The Sandino Affair* (Chicago: Quadrangle Books, 1967), p.
237.

75. See Ibid., p. 247, and "Notes to Chapter Eleven," n. 28, p. 306.

76. Ibid., pp. 105, 113.

77. Macaulay affirms that "Sandino lacked insight as a social revolutionary rather

than resources for bringing the guerrilla struggle to a victorious conclusion. Before Sandino's death in 1934 guerrilla warfare had become the instrument of social revolutionaries more astute than the Nicaraguan rebel." *Sandino*, p. 266.

78. *Betancourt: pensamiento,* pp. 143-44.
79. Aitken, *Muñoz,* pp. 157-58.
80. Martz, *Central America,* p. 3.
81. Castro E., *Figueres,* p. 53.
82. Quoted in Schneider, *Communism,* p. 11.
83. J. Lloyd Mecham. *A Survey of United States-Latin American Relations* (Boston: Houghton Mifflin Company, 1965), p. 172.
84. Ibid., pp. 172-73.
85. Rómulo Betancourt, *Venezuela: política y petróleo* (Mexico: Fondo de Cultura Económica, 1956), pp. 463-64.
86. Quoted in Mecham, *Survey,* p. 173.
87. *Betancourt, su doctrina,* p. 107.
88. *Venezuela y Guatemala. Discursos con motivo de la visita del Presidente Betancourt a Guatemala, 26 de julio de 1946* (Guatemala: Tipografía Nacional de Guatemala, 1946), pp. 17-18.
89. Betancourt, *Venezuela,* p. 463.
90. *New York Times,* 31 January, 2 February, and 4 February 1947.
91. Ibid., 20 June 1947, p. 4.
92. Mecham, *Survey,* p. 174.
93. José Vicente Pepper, *I Accuse Braden* (Ciudad Trujillo: Editora Montalvo, 1947).
94. In July 1947 Braden received Guatemala's highest decoration, the Order of the Quetzal. It was withdrawn six years later, when Braden declared in an address at Dartmouth College that the Guatemalan government was a Communist regime.
95. *Bohemia* (Havana) 41, no. 34 (1949): 58. The exile leaders affirmed that they turned to military action only after exhausting every peaceful means for promoting political change.

Chapter 2

1. Enrique V. Corominas, *In the Caribbean Political Areas,* trans. L. Charles Foresti (New York: University Press of Cambridge, Inc., 1954), p. 127.
2. Ruby Hart Phillips, *Cuba: Island of Paradox* (New York: McDowell, Obolensky, 1959), p. 244.
3. Horacio Ornes, *Desembarco en Luperón. Episodio de la lucha por la democracia en la República Dominicana* (Mexico: Ediciones Humanismo, 1956), pp. 29-30.
4. Interview with Genovevo Pérez Dámera, 9 August 1967.
5. See the *New York Times,* 2 November 1946, p. 5; 3 February 1947, p. 5.
6. Robert D. Crassweller, *Trujillo: The Life and Times of a Caribbean Dictator* (New York: The Macmillan Company, 1966), p. 236.
7. *Bohemia* (Havana) 41, no. 26 (1949): 70.
8. Ibid., 41, no. 34 (1949): 58.   9. Ibid.   10. Ibid., 41, no. 26 (1949): 69-70.   11. Ibid., 41, no. 34 (1949): 58.
12. Alberto Bayo, *Tempestad en el Caribe* (Mexico, 1950), p. 196.
13. Rosendo Argüello, Jr., *By Whom We Were Betrayed . . . and How* (facts of

publication missing), p. 56. The publication of the Argüello book was probably paid for by Rafael Trujillo, who wanted to conceal his sponsorship.
14. Bayo, *Tempestad,* p. 123.
15. Unión Panamericana, Departamento de Asuntos Jurídicos, *Aplicaciones del Tratado Interamericano de Asistencia Recíproca, 1948-1960* (Washington, D.C., 1960), p. 106.
16. *Bohemia* 41, no. 34 (1949): 59.
17. William Krehm, *Democracia y tiranías en el Caribe* (Buenos Aires: Editorial Parnaso, 1957), p. 182.
18. Bayo, *Tempestad,* p. 208. The Union was vehemently antidictatorial and equated the struggle against dictators with the struggle for Central American union.
19. *CARIB,* Report No. 4 (May 1958), pp. 32-33.
20. Argüello, *By Whom,* p. 32.
21. Ibid., pp. 32-33.
22. Argüello, *By Whom,* p. 14; Arturo Castro Esquivel, *José Figueres Ferrer. El hombre y su obra* (San José, Costa Rica: Imprenta Tormo, 1955), p. 45.
23. Argüello, *By Whom,* p. 14.   24. Ibid.
25. Interview with Figueres.
26. Castro E., *Figueres,* pp. 62-63; Argüello, *By Whom,* p. 19.
27. Argüello, *By Whom,* p. 20. Dr. Zepeda had been one of Augusto Sandino's chief advisors.
28. Ibid., p. 23.   29. Ibid., p. 24; Castro E., *Figueres,* pp. 110-11.
30. *New York Times,* 12 February 1947, p. 8.
31. *CARIB,* Report No. 4 (May 1958), p. 48.
32. *New York Times,* 4 October 1947, p. 8.
33. At Luperón, the Dominican Republic, on 20 June 1949.
34. *Bohemia* 41, no. 26 (1949): 70.
35. Interview with Figueres.
36. *New York Times,* 26 November 1947, p. 26.
37. Unión Panamericana, *Aplicaciones,* pp. 101, 103.
38. Ibid., pp. 100-01.   39. Ibid., p. 101; *Bohemia* 41, no. 26 (1949); 70.
40. *Bohemia* 41, no. 26 (1949): 70.
41. U.S. Foreign Broadcast Information Service, *Daily Report: Foreign Radio Broadcasts,* 9 December 1947, p. D2 (hereinafter cited as FBIS).
42. *New York Times,* 22 September 1947, p. 7; *Noticias de Hoy* (Havana), 24 September 1947, p. 1.
43. *Bohemia* 41, no. 26 (1949): 70; Unión Panamericana, *Aplicaciones,* p. 101.
44. Unión Panamericana, *Aplicaciones,* p. 102.
45. Corominas, *Caribbean,* p. 78.
46. *El Mundo* (Havana), 2 October 1947, p. 12, and 3 October 1947, p. 1. Future President Prío was then the minister of labor.
47. Interview with Figueres.
48. Crassweller,*Trujillo,* p. 236.
49. Horacio Ornes, *Desembarco,* p. 28.
50. *New York Times,* 27 July 1947, p. 19, and 24 August 1947, p. 42.
51. Corominas, *Caribbean,* p. 56.   52. Ibid., p. 125.
53. Germán E. Ornes, *Trujillo: Little Caesar of the Caribbean* (New York: Thomas Nelson and Sons, 1958), p. 107.
54. Unión Panamericana, *Aplicaciones,* p. 102.
55. *New York Times,* 27 July 1947, p. 19.
56. Phillips, *Cuba,* p. 242.

57. *New York Times*, 30 July 1947, p. 7, and 31 July 1947, p. 3.
58. Corominas, *Caribbean*, p. 58.
59. *Bohemia*, 10 October 1948, p. 125.
60. *New York Times*, 6 August 1947, p. 9.
61. Corominas, *Caribbean*, p. 32; Unión Panamericana, *Aplicaciones*, p. 102.
62. Corominas, *Caribbean*, p. 32.
63. *New York Times*, 19 August 1947, p. 12. 64. Ibid.
65. *New York Times*, 21 August 1947, p. 16: Virgilio Díaz Ordóñez, *La Era de Trujillo. 25 años de Historia Dominicana*, vol. 2, *La política exterior de Trujillo* (Ciudad Trujillo [Santo Domingo]: Impresora Dominicana, 1955), p. 127.
66. Díaz Ordóñez, *Trujillo*, 2: 127.
67. Corominas, *Caribbean*, p. 37. 68. Ibid. 69. Ibid., p. 78. 70. Ibid.
71. *New York Times*, 20 August 1947, p. 2.
72. *Bohemia* 41, no. 26 (1949): 70.
73. *El Mundo* (Havana), 4 October 1947, p. 12. 74. Ibid.
75. John Bartlow Martin, *Overtaken by Events. The Dominican Crisis from the Fall of Trujillo to the Civil War* (New York: Doubleday and Company, Inc., 1966), pp. 46-47.
76. *El Mundo* 4 October 1947, p. 12; *New York Times*, 30 September 1947, p. 1.
77. Corominas, *Caribbean*, p. 57.
78. Martin, *Overtaken*, p. 317. 79. Ibid.
80. *New York Times*, 22 September 1947, p. 7.
81. Ibid., 30 September 1947, p. 1.
82. *Bohemia* 41, no. 26 (1949): 70.
83. *El Mundo*, 3 October 1947, p. 1. Rodríguez was still in Havana, and Eufemio Fernández had allegedly gone to Venezuela for more aircraft.
84. Ibid., 4 October 1947, p. 12. 85. Ibid., 2 October 1947, p. 12.
86. Ibid., 5 October 1947, p. 1.
87. *New York Times*, 6 October 1947, p. 2.
88. *Bohemia*, 41, no. 26 (1949): 70.
89. Phillips, *Cuba*, p. 242.
90. Corominas, *Caribbean*, p. 58; Díaz Ordóñez, *Trujillo*, 2: 128; *New York Times*, 18 January 1948, pt. VI, p. 35. In this connection, when Manolo Castro was killed in a Havana gun-fight on 22 February 1948, the Dominican Republic asserted that the young revolutionary was "mowed down" by his own comrades because his indiscretions had resulted in "disastrous publicity" for the Cayo Confites expedition. See, *CARIB*, Report No. 4 (May 1958), p. 57.
91. Crassweller, *Trujillo*, p. 239.
92. Horacio Ornes, *Desembarco*, p. 28.
93. *Bohemia*, 10 October 1948, p. 129.
94. Ibid., 41, no. 26 (1949): 70. 95. Ibid., 42, no. 2 (1950): 70.
96. *Washington Post*, 22 September 1947, p. 1.
97. *New York Times*, 30 September 1947, p. 1.
98. *Bohemia* 41, no. 35 (1949), Suplemento, p. 1.
99. Ibid. 100. Ibid.; Unión Panamericana, *Aplicaciones*, p. 106.
101. Interview with Genevevo Pérez Dámera, 9 August 1967.
102. Unión Panamericana, *Aplicaciones*, p. 102.
103 *New York Times*, 2 October 1947, p. 22.
104. Unión Panamericana, *Aplicaciones*, p. 103; Corominas, *Caribbean*, p. 32.
105. Díaz Ordóñez, *Trujillo*, 2: 128.

106. Ibid., pp. 135-36; Corominas, *Caribbean,* p. 29. The Committee on Pacific Settlement had been created at the Havana Consultative Meeting in 1940 but had remained inoperative until its restoration in July 1948 specifically to hear the Dominican complaint.
107. Corominas, *Caribbean,* p. 44.
108. *Bohemia* 41, no. 34 (1949): 59.
109. Castro E., *Figueres,* pp. 71-72, 109-10.
110. *New York Times,* 24 July 1947, p. 1.
111. Castro E., *Figueres,* p. 88. 112. Ibid., p. 70.
113. Argüello, *By Whom,* p. 28.
114. Ibid., p. 32. 115. Ibid., p. 33. 116. Ibid., pp. 33-36
117. See Martz, *Central America,* p. 256; FBIS, 21 January 1955.
118. Interview with Figueres.
119. *Bohemia* 41, no. 34 (1949): 58.
120. *CARIB,* Report No. 7 (July 1958), p. 34. There is little evidence of Venezuelan involvement in this particular phase of the Caribbean conflict, but Sánchez Arango played the same role in Caribbean intrigue under Prío as José Alemán had performed under Grau.
121. *New York Times,* 2 March 1948, p. 15.
122. Ibid., 9 March 1948, p. 9; Castro E., *Figueres,* pp. 101-02.
123. *New York Times,* 11 March 1948, p. 11.
124. Castro E., *Figueres,* p. 196.
125. Interview with Figueres.
126. *Bohemia* 41, no. 34 (1949): 81.
127. Castro E., *Figueres,* p. 114.
128. *Bohemia* 41, no. 34 (1949): 58. 129. Ibid., p. 59. 130. Ibid., pp. 59, 80.
131. Argüello, *By Whom,* pp. 38-39.
132. Phillips, *Cuba,* pp. 242-43.
133. *Bohemia* 41, no. 26 (1949): 67.
134. Castro E., *Figueres,* pp. 106, 116.
135. *Bohemia* 41, no. 34 (1949): 80-81; *New York Times,* 23 March 1948, p. 17.
136. *Bohemia* 41, no. 34 (1949): 81.
137. *New York Times,* 17 March 1948, p. 6.
138. Ibid., 22 March 1948, p. 14, and 23 March 1948, p. 17.
139. Ibid., 6 April 1948, p. 13   140. Ibid., 17 March 1948, p. 6
141. Ibid., 4 April 1948, p. 9
142. Ibid., 26 March 1948, p. 9. 143. Ibid., 1 April 1948, p. 2. 144. Ibid.
145. Castro E., *Figueres,* p. 121; Argüello, *By Whom,* pp. 44-45; *Bohemia* 41, no. 34 (1949): 81.
146. Argüello, *By Whom,* p. 47   147. Ibid.
148. Interview with Figueres.
149. Interview with Padre Benjamín Núñez, 3-4 January 1969; *New York Times,* 14, 15, 17, 19, and 20 April 1948.
150. Interview with Padre Núñez.
151. Ibid. This agreement caused future embarrassment for Figueres. His political opponents spoke darkly about the "Pact of Ochomogo" and maintained that Figueres had made a deal with the Communists. Padre Núñez explained that Mora needed a statement in order to convince the Politburo to stop fighting and that explicitly on his own he gave what he considered innocuous pledges in order to prevent further bloodshed.

152. FBIS, 22 April 1948, p. O1.
153. *New York Times,* 20 April 1948, p. 1, and 21 April 1948, p. 12.
154. Castro E., *Figueres,* pp. 125-27, 151-52.
155. Ibid., pp. 135-40, 151.   156. Ibid., p. 155.
157. *New York Times,* 3 May 1948, p. 6.
158. Ibid., 10 May 1948, p. 17.
159. Argüello, *By Whom,* p. 61.
160. *Bohemia* 41, no. 26 (1949): 67.
161. Phillips, *Cuba,* p. 244; interview with Figueres.
162. *Bohemia* 41, no. 26 (1949): 67.   163. Ibid.
164. Horacio Ornes, *Desembarco,* p. 30.
165. *New York Times,* 24 May 1948, p. 9.
166. Bayo, *Tempestad,* p. 73.   167. Ibid., pp. 39, 50.
168. Ibid., p. 87.   169. Ibid., p. 77.   170. Ibid., p. 83.   171. Ibid.
172. Ibid., p. 85.
173. Argüello, *By Whom,* pp. 99-100.
174. Bayo, *Tempestad,* p. 93.   175. Ibid., pp. 114-15.
176. Argüello, *By Whom,* pp. 80-81, 110-11.
177. Bayo, *Tempestad,* p. 90.   178. Ibid., pp. 92-93.   179. Ibid., p. 90.
180. Ibid., p. 133.   181. Ibid.; Argüello, *By Whom,* pp. 66-67, 70.
182. Argüello, *By Whom,* p. 67.   183. Ibid., p. 71.
184. Castro E., *Figueres,* pp. 271-73.
185. Bayo, *Tempestad,* p. 98.
186. Ibid., p. 96.   187. Ibid., p. 88.   188. Ibid., pp. 114, 154; Argüello, *By Whom,* p. 111.
189. Argüello, *By Whom,* p. 111.
190. *New York Times,* 29 May 1948, p. 13, and 28 August 1948, p. 28. At the end of May, several unidentified individuals fired machineguns from a passing car at the Nicaraguan legation in San José, and in August, Dr. Pedro Joaquín Ríos, a Nicaraguan deputy visiting in San José, was assaulted by Nicaraguan exiles and had to be hospitalized.
191. FBIS, 23 December 1948, p. F1.
192. *New York Times,* 16 October 1948, p. 5.
193. Ibid., 2 November 1948, p. 22; Horacio Ornes, *Desembarco,* p. 30.
194. *New York Times,* 17 October 1948, p. 6.
195. Ibid., 2 November 1948, p. 22.
196. FBIS, 31 January 1949, p. D5.
197. Argüello, *By Whom,* p. 101.   198. Ibid., pp. 102-03.
199. Bayo, *Tempestad,* pp. 135-36.
200. Unión Panamericana, *Aplicaciones,* p. 25.
201. Argüello, *By Whom,* p. 103.
202. Unión Panamericana, *Aplicaciones,* p. 19.
203. Ibid., p. 21.   204. Ibid., pp. 23-25.   205. Ibid., p. 26.   206. Ibid., pp. 26-27.
207. Argüello, *By Whom,* p. 108.
208. FBIS, 15 February 1949, p. G1.
209. Unión Panamericana, *Aplicaciones,* p. 39.   210. Ibid., pp. 44-46.
211. Jules Dubois, *Operation America: The Communist Conspiracy in Latin America* (New York: Walker and Company, 1963), pp. 244-45.
212. *New York Times,* 20 December 1948, p. 22.
213. Bayo, *Tempestad,* p. 105.   214. Ibid., p. 157.

215. FBIS, 14 February 1949, p. D2
216. Ibid., 15 February 1949, p. D2.   217. Ibid., 25 February 1949, pp. D1-D2.
218. Ibid., 15 March 1949, pp. D2-D3. The broadcast gave the names of Octavio Caldera, Alberto Vallardes Cortez, and Alfonso Castillo Ybarra.
219. Ibid., 6 April 1949, p. D5.
220. Unión Panamericana, *Aplicaciones*, p. 104.
221. FBIS, 23 April 1952, p. D1.
222. *Bohemia* 41, no. 26 (1949): 67.
223. Horacio Ornes, *Desembarco*, p. 137; Corominas, *Caribbean*, p. 61.
224. FBIS, 30 June 1949, p. D4.
225. *Bohemia* 41, no. 26 (1949): 68. Rumors also circulated at one time or another during early 1949 that the Caribbean Legion was planning invasions of Honduras and Venezuela.
226. *Bohemia* 41, no. 26 (1949): 67.
227. Ibid., p. 68   228. Ibid.; FBIS, 24 December 1948, p. D1.
229. Horacio Ornes, *Desembarco*, p. 31.
230. *Bohemia* 41, no. 26 (1949): 68. Alberto Bayo affirmed that "hundreds" underwent training. He added that he himself had been asked to go to Havana, from whence he was to sail with a group of reenforcements. At the time of the invasion, the Liberation Army had two vessels, the *Patricia* and the *Alicia*, anchored in Cuban waters. See Bayo, *Tempestad*, pp. 177-78, 188; and Unión Panamericana, *Aplicaciones*, pp. 106-07.
231. Horacio Ornes, *Desembarco*, p. 31; *Bohemia* 41, no. 26 (1949): 68; 41, no. 34 (1949): 89-90.
232. Horacio Ornes, *Desembarco*, p. 30; *Bohemia* 41, no. 26 (1949): 68.
233. Bayo, *Tempestad*, pp. 165-66. Bayo insisted that Román Durán had given him such assurances.
234. Ibid., p. 168.   235. Ibid., p. 169.
236. *New York Times*, 23 June 1949, p. 3.
237. Bayo, *Tempestad*, p. 170.
238. Ibid., pp. 166-67; Corominas, *Caribbean*, pp. 63-65.
239. Corominas, *Caribbean*, p. 64.
240. Unión Panamericana, *Aplicaciones*, pp. 104-05.
241. Bayo, *Tempestad*, p. 171.   242. Ibid., p. 201.
243. *Bohemia* 41, no. 34 (1949): 59.
244. Unión Panamericana, *Aplicaciones*, p. 104.
245. *Bohemia* 41, no. 34 (1949): 89.   246. Ibid.
247. *Bohemia* 41, no. 34 (1949): 90; Bayo, *Tempestad*, p. 171. The pilots were Mexicans Pablo Herrera and Arturo Camacho.
248. Bayo, *Tempestad*, p. 171. The C-47 carried Mexican registry XA-HOS.
249. The crew was made up of Mexicans José María del Castillo Altamirano, Mario Treviño Baxter, José Cardona, and Julián Valderrama Ibarra.
250. Bayo, *Tempestad*, pp. 178, 197.
251. *Bohemia* 41, no. 34 (1949): 90.
252. Horacio Ornes, *Desembarco*, pp. 153-54;   253. Ibid., p. 154.
254. Unión Panamericana, *Aplicaciones*, p. 105.
255. Bayo, *Tempestad*, p. 172.
256. *Bohemia* 41, no. 34 (1949): 90.
257. Horacio Ornes, *Desembarco*, p. 154.
258. Bayo, *Tempestad*, p. 190.
259. Horacio Ornes, *Desembarco*, p. 35.

260. Ibid., p. 37.   261. Ibid., pp. 32-33.   262. Ibid., p. 48.
263. Ibid., p. 46.   264. Ibid., p. 56.   265. Ibid., pp. 58-59.
266. Ibid., p. 128; *New York Times,* 28 June 1949, p. 11.
267. Horacio Ornes, *Desembarco,* p. 115.   268. Ibid., pp. 88-94.
269. FBIS, 30 June 1949, pp. D3-D4.
270. Horacio Ornes, *Desembarco,* p. 144.
271. Ibid., p. 112; Corominas, *Caribbean,* p. 66.
272. Horacio Ornes, *Desembarco,* pp. 112-13.
273. Corominas, *Caribbean,* p. 66.
274. Bayo, *Tempestad,* pp. 191-92.
275. Horacio Ornes, *Desembarco,* p. 175.
276. FBIS, 30 June 1949, p. D1.
277. Germán Ornes, *Trujillo,* p. 127.
278. Horacio Ornes, *Desembarco,* pp. 156-57.
279. Ibid., p. 158; Corominas, *Caribbean,* p. 72.
280. *CARIB,* Report no. 7 (July 1958), p. 30.
281. Horacio Ornes, *Desembarco,* pp. 90, 119.
282. Unión Panamericana, *Aplicaciones,* p. 106.
283. Ronald M. Schneider, *Communism in Guatemala, 1944-1954* (New York: Frederick A. Praeger, 1959), p. 30; *CARIB,* No. 7, p. 35.
284. *CARIB,* no. 7 (July 1958), p. 35.
285. Schneider, *Communism,* p. 30.
286. *CARIB,* no. 7 (July 1958), pp. 30-31.
287. *Bohemia* 41, no. 33 (1949): 69.
288. Unión Panamericana, *Aplicaciones,* p. 106.
289. *Bohemia* 41, no. 33 (1949): 68-69.   290. Ibid., p. 69.
291. Corominas, *Caribbean,* pp. 137-38.   292. Ibid., p. 53.   293. Ibid., p. 71.
294. Ibid., pp. 74-75.   295. Ibid., pp. 75-84.   296. Ibid., pp. 84-89.
297. Ibid., pp. 90-91.   298. Ibid., pp. 92-93.
299. *New York Times,* 21 August 1949, pt. IV, p. 6.
300. Ibid., 26 August 1949, p. 18.
301. U.S. Department of State, *Peace in the Americas,* Department of State Publication 3964 (Washington, D.C.: U.S. Government Printing Office, 1950), pp. 5-7.
302. Ibid.   303. Ibid., p. 27.
304. Ibid.; *New York Times,* 20 September 1949, p. 1.
305. Department of State, Publication 3964, p. 27.
306. *Bohemia* 41, no. 33 (1949): 68.
307. Unión Panamericana, *Aplicaciones,* p. 108.
308. Ibid.; *New York Times,* 30 November 1949, p. 11.
309. Unión Panamericana, *Aplicaciones,* p. 108.   310. Ibid.
311. *New York Times,* 8 December 1949, p. 41.
312. Unión Panamericana, *Aplicaciones,* p. 109.
313. Díaz Ordóñez, *Trujillo,* 2: 133.
314. *New York Times,* 15 December 1949, p. 1.
315. Ibid., 1 January 1950, p. 10.   316. Ibid., 14 December 1949, p. 21.
317. FBIS, 24 December 1948, p. D1.
318. *Bohemia* 41, no. 34 (1949): 90.
319. FBIS, 11 February 1949, p. D3.
320. Corominas, *Caribbean,* p. 49.
321. Unión Panamericana, *Aplicaciones,* p. 96.
322. Ibid.   323. Ibid., p. 98.

324. Ibid., p. 69; see also, Crassweller, *Trujillo,* pp. 246-47.
325. Unión Panamericana, *Aplicaciones,* p. 75.   326. Ibid., pp. 81-88.
327. Edward A. Jamison, *Keeping Peace in the Caribbean Area,* U.S. Department of State Publication 3918 (Washington, D.C.: U.S. Government Printing Office, 1950), p. 21.
328. Unión Panamericana, *Aplicaciones,* p. 100. Much of the sting of this rebuke disappeared when President Estimé was deposed by a military coup on 10 May 1950. Trujillo's relations with Estimé's successor, Colonel Paul Magloire, were more cordial.
329. Ibid., pp. 103-04.   330. Ibid., pp. 109-10.   331. Ibid., p. 110.
332. Ibid.   333. Ibid., p. 111.   334. Ibid.
335. Ibid., pp. 113-15.   336. Ibid., p. 115.   337. Ibid., p. 116.
338. Ibid., pp. 116-18. The report on the effective exercise of representative democracy was never completed.

Chapter 3

1. Valmore Rodríguez, *Bayonetas sobre Venezuela* (Mexico, 1950), p. 97.
2. José Rivas Rivas, ed. *Historia Gráfica de Venezuela,* vol. 2, *El mundo y la época de Pérez Jiménez: Una historia contada en recortes de periódicos* (Caracas: Pensamiento Vivo, C. A., 1961), pp. 48-15. This is a valuable volume, which consists of clippings from Caracas newspapers during the rule of the Military Junta and Pérez Jiménez, 1948-58. The volume is divided into years, so that the pagination indicates first the specific year, then the actual page within the section.
3. Ibid., 2: 48-15 (*El Nacional,* 11 December 1948), and 49-10 (*El Universal,* 28 January 1949).
4. Comité Ejecutivo Nacional del Partido Acción Democrática, *Venezuela bajo el signo del terror, 1948-1952. El libro negro de la dictadura* (Santiago de Chile: Publicaciones Valmore Rodríguez, [1953]), pp. 51-52. Hereinafter cited as *Libro negro.*
5. *New York Times,* 11 December 1948, p. 6.
6. Rómulo Betancourt, *Venezuela: política y petróleo* (Mexico: Fondo de Cultura Económica, 1956), p. 469.
7. *Rómulo Betancourt: pensamiento y acción* (Mexico, D.F., 1951), p. 63.
8. José Rodríguez, *Quién derrocó a Gallegos?* (Caracas: C. A. Tipografía Garrido, 1961), pp. 131-32.
9. Ibid., p. 154.   10. Ibid., p. 212
11. Betancourt, *Venezuela,* pp. 470-71.
12. *Betancourt: pensamiento,* p. 186.
13. Betancourt, *Venezuela,* p. 478.
14. *Betancourt: pensamiento,* p. 285.   15. Ibid.
16. Ibid., pp. 71-72.   17. Ibid., p. 284.   18. Ibid., pp. 368-69.
19. Ibid., pp. 78-79.
20. Serafino Romualdi, *Presidents and Peons. Recollections of a Labor Ambassador in Latin America* (New York: Funk and Wagnalls, 1967), p. 461.
21. *Libro negro,* p. 27.   22. Ibid., pp. 13, 149.   23. Ibid., pp. 53-54.
24. Ibid., p. 26; see also, John D. Martz, *Acción Democrática. Evolution of a Modern Political Party in Venezuela* (Princeton: Princeton University Press, 1966), pp. 119-46.
25. *Libro negro,* pp. 26-27.   26. Ibid., p. 27.

27. Ibid., p. 26; Martz, *Acción Democrática*, p. 137.
28. José Vicente Abreu, *Se llama S.N.*, 2d ed. (Caracas: José Augustín Catalá, Editor, 1964), pp. 27-28.
29. Interview with Ricardo Montilla, 17 June 1965.
30. Valmore Rodríguez, *Bayonetas*, pp. 114, 122.
31. José Rodríguez, *Quién*, p. 214.   32. Ibid., pp. 214-15.
33. Interview with Rigoberto Henríquez Vera, former secretary-general of the clandestine AD, 16 June 1965; Martz, *Acción Democrática*, p. 135.
34. Interview with Henríquez Vera.
35. Martz, *Acción Democrática*, pp. 134-35.   36. Ibid., p. 136.
37. Interview with Henríquez Vera; Robert J. Alexander, *Prophets of the Revolution: Profiles of Latin American Leaders* (New York: The Macmillan Company, 1962), p. 136; *Bohemia* 41, no. 30 (1949): 9.
38. The information in the preceding paragraph was given to the author by Henríquez Vera.
39. Interview with Henríquez Vera; Edilberto Moreno, *Vida y lección de Antonio Pinto Salinas* (Mérida, Venezuela: Talleres Gráficos Universitarios, 1964), p. 82.
40. Martz, *Acción Democrática*, p. 136.
41. *A.D.* (Caracas), 23 October 1964. 42. *Bohemia* 41, no. 30 (1949): 9.   43. Ibid.   44. Ibid.
45. *Libro negro*, p. 149.   46. Ibid.   47. Ibid., p. 150.
48. Ibid., p. 151; Eulogy by Luis Beltrán Prieto Figueroa at graveside in Costa Rica on 23 December 1951, reprinted in *El Nacional* (Caracas), 27 November 1958, p. 10.
49. *Libro negro*, pp. 144-45.
50. *Bohemia* 41, no. 30 (1949): 10.   51. Ibid.   52. Ibid.
53. Betancourt, *Venezuela*, p. 523.
54. Rivas, *Historia*, 2: 49-7 (*El Universal*, 19 January 1949); *New York Times*, 18 January 1949, p. 14.
55. *Libro negro*, p. 357.   56. Ibid., p. 359.
57. Betancourt, *Venezuela*, p. 524; *New York Times*, 7 May 1949, p. 6.
58. *Libro negro*, p. 360.
59. Betancourt, *Venezuela*, p. 527.
60. *Libro negro*, p. 363.
61. Betancourt, *Venezuela*, p. 527. Betancourt commented that the end result was the infiltration of the labor movement by the Communists. AD, which the dictators labeled as Communist, had virtually eliminated the influence of the Communists in the labor movement, whereas the Military Junta suppressed the democratic leadership and permitted Communist labor leaders freedom to organize.
62. *Libro negro*, p. 363.
63. Ibid., pp. 363-64; Betancourt, *Venezuela*, p. 528.
64. *New York Times*, 22 August 1950, p. 18.
65. Rivas, *Historia*, 2: 49-25 (*Tribuna Popular*, 23 October 1949).
66. *Hispanic World Report* 2, no. 11 (November 1949): 19. (Published as *Hispanic American Report*, beginning January 1950.)
67. Betancourt, *Venezuela*, p. 481.
68. *Betancourt: pensamiento*, pp. 385-86.
69. Betancourt, *Venezuela*, pp. 481-82.
70. *Betancourt: pensamiento*, p. 240.
71. *New York Times*, 26 December 1949, p. 29.

72. *Libro negro,* pp. 141-42.
73. Ibid., p. 142.   74. Ibid., p. 159.   75. Ibid., p. 143.
76. Moreno, *Vida,* pp. 76-77.   77. Ibid., p. 77; *Libro negro,* p. 143.
78. *Libro negro,* p. 143.   79. Ibid., p. 213.
80. *New York Times,* 24 April 1950, p. 8.
81. *Libro negro,* p. 365.
82. Ibid., pp. 210-11, 365-67; Rivas, *Historia,* 2: 50-7.
83. Rivas, *Historia,* 2: 50-12 (*El Nacional,* 14 May 1950).
84. *Betancourt: pensamiento,* p. 318.
85. *Libro negro,* pp. 211-12.
86. *New York Times,* 3 June 1950, p. 5.
87. *Libro negro,* p. 212.   88. Ibid.
89. *New York Times,* 15 May 1950, p. 8; *Bohemia* 42, no. 19 (1950): 68; *Bohemia* 42, no. 21 (1950): 102-07.
90. *Betancourt: pensamiento,* p. 307.   91. Ibid., pp. 311-19.   92. Ibid., p. 388.
93. Rivas, *Historia,* 2: 56-15–56-17 (trial transcript).
94. Ibid., 2: 50-17–50-18; 50-21–50-22.
95. Betancourt, *Venezuela,* pp. 482-83.
96. *Libro negro,* p. 146.   97. Ibid., pp. 146-47.
98. Betancourt, *Venezuela,* p. 485.
99. *Betancourt: pensamiento,* p. 380.   100. Ibid., p. 387.
101. Betancourt, *Venezuela,* p. 485.   102. Ibid., p. 510.   103. Ibid.
104. *New York Times,* 14 November 1950, p. 1.
105. Ibid., 1 February 1951, p. 8.
106. Ibid., 4 March 1951, pt. IV, p. 8 (letter dated 22 February 1951).
107. *Libro negro,* pp. 126-27.
108. Betancourt, *Venezuela,* p. 860.
109. *Hemispherica* 1, no. 2 (February 1951): 2.
110. *Libro negro,* pp. 297-302.   111. Ibid., p. 306.   112. Ibid., p. 303.
113. Rivas, *Historia,* 2:51-18 (*El Nacional,* 7 October 1951).
114. *Betancourt: pensamiento,* p. 227.
115. *New York Times,* 3 March 1951, p. 5.
116. Betancourt: *Venezuela,* pp. 848-49.
117. Rivas, *Historia,* 2: 51-10 (*El Nacional,* 10 May 1951).
118. *Betancourt: pensamiento,* p. 225; *Hemispherica* 1, no. 6 (July-August 1951): 2.
119. *Betancourt: pensamiento,* p. 225.
120. Betancourt, *Venezuela,* pp. 541-42.
121. *Betancourt: pensamiento,* p. 228.
122. *Libro negro,* p. 214.
123. Rivas, *Historia,* 2: 51-21 (*El Nacional,* 14 October 1951).
124. *Betancourt: pensamiento,* pp. 231, 233.
125. *New York Times,* 21 October 1951, pt. IV, p. 8 (letter dated 17 October 1951).
126. Abreu, *Se llama,* pp. 94-95.
127. *Libro negro,* pp. 307-08.
128. Rivas, *Historia,* 2: 51-23 (*El Nacional,* 31 October 1951).
129. *Libro negro,* p. 317.
130. Betancourt, *Venezuela,* p. 517.
131. Rivas, *Historia,* 2: 52-5 (*El Nacional,* 31 January 1952); *Libro negro,* p. 317.
132. *Libro negro,* p. 319.

133. Rivas, *Historia*, 2: 52-6 (*Ultimas Noticias*, 23 February 1952).
134. Betancourt, *Venezuela*, pp. 489, 850.
135. *Libro negro*, pp. 216-26; Abreu, *Se llama*, pp. 324-27.
136. Antonio Pinto Salinas, quoted in Moreno, *Vida*, p. 86.
137. Betancourt, *Venezuela*, pp. 490-91; *Libro negro*, pp. 241-42; Abreu, *Se llama*, p. 231-35.
138. Betancourt, *Venezuela*, pp. 490-91; Abreu, *Se llama*, pp. 231-40.
139. *Libro negro*, p. 252; Abreu, *Se llama*, p. 238.
140. *Libro negro*, pp. 245-53, 259-61.
141. Quoted in Betancourt, *Venezuela*, p. 495.
142. *Libro negro*, p. 243.   143. Ibid., pp. 258-62.
144. Betancourt, *Venezuela*, p. 498.
145. *New York Times*, 31 November 1952, p. 31.
146. Ibid., 27 June 1952, p. 6.
147. Ibid., 30 June 1952, p. 18 (letter dated 25 June 1952).
148. Betancourt, *Venezuela*, p. 497.   149. Ibid.
150. FBIS, 12 March 1952, p. H2.
151. *Hispanic American Report* 5, no. 3 (April 1952): 18. Hereinafter cited as HAR.
152. *New York Times*, 11 March 1952, p. 1. On the day of the coup, the Venezuelan military attaché, Major José Teofilo Velazco, acting on behalf of his government, went to Camp Columbia to congratulate Batista.
153. Ibid., 1 November 1951, p. 8.   154. Ibid., 19 November 1951, p. 3.
155. HAR 4, no. 13 (January 1952): 23-24. The nature of this campaign was described by the Dominican government. It asserted that it possessed a letter in which Betancourt requested two Puerto Rican legislators, Víctor Gutiérrez Franqui and Ernest Ramos Antonini, to sponsor a resolution before their Constituent Assembly similar to those passed by the national legislatures of Ecuador, Cuba, Costa Rica, Guatemala, and Panama, "with the aim of stimulating vigorous civil resistance in Venezuela and to lay an additional basis for possible joint action of various democratic governments." See, FBIS, 20 February 1952, pp. D1-D2.
156. Rivas, *Historia*, 2: 52-9 –52-10 (*El Nacional*, 15 April 1952); Abreu, *Se llama*, pp. 255, 262, 270, 271, 272.
157. Rivas, *Historia*, 2: 52-9.   158. Ibid., p. 52-10.
159. HAR 5, no. 4 (May 1952): 27-28.
160. Abreu, *Se llama*, p. 291.
161. Martz, *Acción Democrática*, p. 139.
162. *New York Times*, 17 May 1952, p. 18 (letter dated 13 May 1952).
163. Ibid., 22 April 1952, p. 9.
164. *Libro negro*, p. 158.
165. Ibid., pp. 71-76, 102-21; Betancourt, *Venezuela*, p. 550.
166. *Libro negro*, p. 81.
167. Ibid., pp. 95-96.   168. Ibid., p. 97.   169. Ibid., p. 80.
170. Ibid., p. 15. A second edition of *The Black Book (Libro Negro)* was published in 1956 and printed in Chile, with the sponsorship of "a distinguished Chilean industrialist."
171. Ibid., p. 25.   172. Ibid., pp. 42-43.   173. Ibid., pp. 30, 38.
174. Ibid., pp. 33-35.   175. Ibid., pp. 45-46.   176. Ibid., pp. 81-101; Betancourt, *Venezuela*, p. 550.
177. *Libro negro*, p. 93. *The Black Book* omitted an argument used by Betancourt in October, to wit, the junta wanted a legal government because Venezuela

was scheduled to host the Tenth International Conference of American States in 1953. See *New York Times,* 16 October 1952 (letter to the editor, 5 October 1952).
178. *Libro negro,* pp. 102-21.
179. Ibid., pp. 103-04.   180. Ibid., pp. 78-81.   181. Ibid., p. 100.
182. *New York Times,* 1 October 1952, p. 13.
183. Betancourt, *Venezuela,* p. 551.   184. Ibid.
185. Martz, *Acción Democrática,* pp. 325-27.
186. Rivas, *Historia,* 2: 52-15 (*El Universal,* 30 September 1952).
187. Ibid.; Abreu, *Se llama,* p. 329. According to later charges, 116 lives were lost in these actions, with over 300 persons wounded and 680 arrested. Betancourt claimed that aircraft strafed the "machete-bearing civilians." See, Betancourt, *Venezuela,* p. 552.
188. *Libro negro,* p. 381.
189. Betancourt, *Venezuela,* p. 854.   190. Ibid., pp. 553, 854.
191. *Libro negro,* picture and caption opposite p. 272 and p. 381; Abreu, *Se llama,* p. 328.
192. Abreu, *Se llama,* pp. 328-29.   193. Ibid., p. 328.
194. *Libro negro,* p. 46; *A.D.,* 23 October 1964, pp. 12-13.
195. Rivas, *Historia,* 2: 52-18 (*El Universal,* 22 October 1952).
196. *A.D.,* 23 October 1964, pp. 12-13.
197. HAR 5, no. 10 (November 1952): 20.
198. Ibid.: *A.D.,* 23 October 1964, pp. 12-13.
199. Martz, *Acción Democrática,* p. 326.
200. The SN gave no sign that it intended to relax its attacks upon AD. On 26 October Dr. Germán González, the owner of the 1952 Chevrolet in which Ruiz Pineda was riding at the time of his death, was tortured and machine-gunned to death in the offices of the SN. Ruiz Pineda's widow, Aurelena, was arrested when she came to claim his body and three months later she and her two small daughters were sent into exile. *Libro negro,* pp. 160, 388.
201. Martz, *Acción Democrática,* pp. 326-27. On 12 January 1953 Betancourt wrote Robert Alexander that AD ordered its militants to vote for the URD "a última hora." Alexander MSS.
202. *Hemispherica* 2, no. 1 (January 1953): 2.
203. Betancourt, *Venezuela,* p. 556; *Libro negro,* p. 388; Martz, *Acción Democrática,* p. 329.
204. *New York Times,* 3 December 1952, p. 1.
205. Rivas, *Historia,* 2: 52-25 (*El Universal,* 1 December 1952); five hours earlier, the *New York Times* had made a telephone call to a "private source" in Caracas and received figures of 450,000 for the URD, and 206,000 for the COPEI, but the call was interrupted before any count was given for the FEI. *New York Times,* 2 December 1952, p. 1.
206. *Libro negro,* p. 388; Betancourt, *Venezuela,* p. 556.
207. *Libro negro,* p. 389; Martz, *Acción Democrática,* p. 328.
208. Betancourt, *Venezuela,* pp. 554, 559; Rivas, *Historia,* 2: 52-31 (*El Universal,* 19 December 1952).
209. Rivas, *Historia,* 2: 52-29—52-30 (*El Nacional,* 17 December 1952); *New York Times,* 18 December 1952, p. 11.
210. Rivas, *Historia,* 2: 52-30.
211. *New York Times,* 1 February 1953, p. 28.
212. *Libro negro,* pp. 390-91.
213. Abreu, *Se llama,* p. 263; letter, Rómulo Betancourt to the author, 3 March 1969.

214. Rivas, *Historia*, 2: 53-54 (*El Nacional*, 6 January 1953). No prominent AD
leaders were taken in the raid, but a number of the men were experienced
members of the underground, including José Atilio Contreras, wanted by the
SN since 1951 for his alleged role in the 12 October uprising of that year;
Andrés López Garay, arrested previously on charges of operating a clandestine radio; and José de Jesús Osuna Rodríguez, once arrested for suspected
ties with Carnevali. The leader of the group, Luciano Ochoa Lucero, managed
to escape at the time, but he was known to the SN, "because of his intense
clandestine activity." See Abreu, *Se llama*, pp. 263, 276, 304, 308, 330.
215. Rivas, *Historia*, 2: 53-9–53-10 (*El Nacional*, 20 January 1953).
216. Ibid.
217. *Hemispherica* 2, no. 2 (February 1953): 3. Among those taken prisoner with
Carnevali were Juan Gualberto Rojas López, a shoemaker, who was the zone
chief of the Santa Teresa, El Valle, and Santa Rosalía parishes of Caracas;
José Antonio Vargas, a labor leader, who had been exiled in December 1949
but had returned to the country clandestinely; Germán Pacheco Blanco, a
schoolteacher, who had once been an AD nominee for Congress from the
state of Miranda; Pantaleón Sánchez Sánchez, a member of the Secretariat of
Organization of the clandestine AD, who had been in charge of convoking the
meeting; and Ramón Alirio García, a student, who was shot during the skirmish and who died of his wounds on 23 January. See Abreu, *Se llama*, pp.
277-330.
218. *Libro negro*, p. 385.
219. *Venezuela Democrática* 1, no. 2 (May 1955): 12. Newspaper published by
the Venezuelan exiles in Mexico. Fifteen issues appeared between April 1955
and September 1957. Hereinafter cited as VD.
220. *Hemispherica* 2: no. 4 (May-July 1953): 5-6.
221. Rivas, *Historia*, 2: 53-23 (*La Esfera*, 22 May 1953).
222. *Libro negro*, p. 385; *New York Times*, 24 May 1953, p. 24.
223. Abreu, *Se llama*, pp. 330-31; VD 1, no. 8 (January-February 1956): 12; José
Rivas Rivas, ed., *Historia Gráfica de Venezuela*, vol. 4, (*El Gobierno de Rómulo Betancourt* (Caracas: Pensamiento Vivo, C.A., 1965), 59-34.
224. Abreu, *Se llama*, p. 299.
225. Ibid., p. 331; Betancourt, *Venezuela*, p. 562.
226. Abreu, *Se llama*, p. 315.   227. Ibid., p. 313.   228. Ibid., p. 281.
229. Ibid., p. 265; Rivas, *Historia*, 2: 53-16–53-17 (*El Universal*, 11 April 1953).
230. Abreu, *Se llama*, pp. 299, 303. Arrested with Anzola were Dr. Alirio Gómez,
a medical doctor who was serving as his driver, and Trino Jiménez Oliveros, a
businessman who was in charge of raising funds for the clandestine struggle.
231. Ibid., p. 331.
232. Moreno, *Vida*, p. 82.   233. Ibid., pp. 82-83.
234. Abreu, *Se llama*, p. 303; *A.D.*, 11 June 1965, p. 3.
235. Moreno, *Vida*, p. 86; Abreu, *Se llama*, pp. 256, 263.
236. *A.D.*, 11 June 1965, p. 3; Abreu, *Se llama*, pp. 256, 263.
237. Interview with Tejera-París.
238. Moreno, *Vida*, p. 87; VD 1, no. 3 (June 1955): 8.
239. Abreu, *Se llama*, p. 331.
240. Interview with Henríquez Vera.
241. *Rómulo Betancourt: interpretación de su doctrina popular y democrática*, ed.
SUMA, librería y editorial (Caracas, 1958), p. 163.
242. Ibid., p. 164.
243. *Libro negro*, p. 402; *New York Times*, 21 December 1953, p. 30.
244. Rivas, *Historia*, 2: 54-3 (*El Universal*, 2 January 1954). AD claimed that

there were at least five thousand political prisoners at that time in Venezuela's jails. See *Hemispherica* 3: no. 1 (January-February 1954): 1.
245. HAR 7, no. 2 (March 1954): 16.
246. Quoted in *New York Times,* 14 December 1953, p. 25.   247. Ibid.
248. Abreu, *Se llama,* p. 272.   249. Ibid., p. 290.   250. Ibid., p. 302.
251. Rivas, *Historia,* 4, Appendix, document two.
252. Abreu, *Se llama,* p. 316. He became the clandestine chief in 1957.
253. HAR 7, no. 3 (April 1954): 22-23.
254. Betancourt, *Venezuela,* p. 748.
255. Abreu, *Se llama,* p. 302.
256. Ibid., p. 302-03. Outside of Caracas, the AD underground was most active in the east, in Maturín and Puerto la Cruz.
257. Betancourt, *Venezuela,* pp. 572-73.
258. *VD* 1, no. 3 (June 1955): 4.
259. Rivas, *Historia,* 2: 56-13 (*El Nacional,* 10 August 1956).
260. *VD* 2, no. 10 (October 1956): 11.
261. Ibid., 2, no. 11 (January 1957): 16. There is no evidence of political activity on the part of Pérez Pisanty, but he had been a friend of some AD leaders.
262. Ibid., 2, no. 10 (October 1956): 10-11.
263. Ibid., p. 14. Gallegos spoke on the occasion of AD's Fifteenth Anniversary in September 1956.
264. *Ultimas Noticias* (Caracas), 24 August 1958, p. 39.   265. Ibid., p. 38.
266. HAR 7, no. 4 (May 1954): 22; Betancourt, *Venezuela,* pp. 750-51.
267. HAR 7, no. 4 (May 1954): 22.
268. Betancourt, *Venezuela,* pp. 573, 862. Aparently the SN was concerned about Droz Blanco because he was a skilled marksman, who had distinguished himself in international competition in Helsinki, Finland.
269. Ibid.; Abreu, *Se llama,* p. 332. Jesús Alberto Blanco was shot to death by the SN on 6 January 1955 while "attempting to escape." Blanco had been in jail since March 1952 and had even been assigned to Guasina. In December of the same year, the Security Police shot José Mercedes Santeliz allegedly while in the act of committing a robbery. Santeliz was not a common thief but a schoolteacher and an important clandestine leader in eastern Venezuela. He had been arrested in 1954 and had been released after fourteen months in prison.
270. Rivas, *Historia,* 2: 56-5 (*El Nacional,* 4 February 1956).
271. *VD* 1, no. 8 (January-February 1956): 9-10.
272. Ibid., p. 9.   273. Ibid.
274. *New York Times,* 14 September 1955, p. 17.
275. Ibid., 17 March 1956, p. 6.
276. *VD* 1, no. 5 (September 1955): 7.

Chapter 4

1. *Hemispherica* 6, no. 4 (September-October 1957): 2, and 10, no. 1 (January 1961): 1. Miss Grant, one of the founders of the Inter-American Association for Democracy and Freedom (IADF) will be discussed in the following chapter.
2. *Rómulo Betancourt: pensamiento y acción* (Mexico, D.F., 1951), p. 263.
3. Ibid., p. 354.   4. Ibid., pp. 55-56.
5. *VD* 1, no. 5 (September 1955): 4.

6. *New York Times,* 27 November 1955, p. 20.
7. Oscar Falchetti, "Haya de la Torre: Odiseo de Indoamérica," *Combate* 4: no. 24 (September-October 1962): 68.
8. Arturo Castro Esquivel, *José Figueres Ferrer. El hombre y su obra* (San José, Costa Rica: Imprenta Tormo, 1955), p. 44.
9. Harry Kantor, "El programa aprista para Perú y Latinoamérica," *Combate* 1, no. 3 (November-December 1958): 26.
10. *New York Times,* 3 January 1958, p. 6.
11. HAR 7, no. 12 (January 1955): 14.
12. *VD* 2, no. 9 (June 1956): 29.
13. John D. Martz, *Central America: The Crisis and the Challenge* (Chapel Hill: University of North Carolina Press, 1959), p. 29.
14. The author attended this class as a student.
15. Juan Bosch, *The Unfinished Experiment: Democracy in the Dominican Republic* (New York: Frederick A. Praeger, 1965), p. 3; "Instituto de Educación Política," *Combate* 2, no. 8 (January-February 1960): 5-6.
16. *VD* 2, no. 10 (October 1956): 7.   17. Ibid., 2, no. 11 (January 1957): 1.
18. Ibid., 3, no. 14 (August 1957): 3.   19. Ibid., 2, no. 11 (January 1957): 1.
20. HAR 10, no. 7 (August 1957): 366-67.
21. *Hemispherica* 5, no. 6 (October-December 1956): 1; *New York Times,* 20 September 1956, p. 11.
22. *VD* 2, no. 11 (January 1957): 4.
23. Ibid., 3, no. 12 (May 1957): 12.
24. Germán E. Ornes, *Trujillo: Little Caesar of the Caribbean* (New York: Thomas Nelson and Sons, 1958), p. 307.
25. *VD* 1, no. 3 (June 1955): 2.
26. Ibid., 1, no. 6 (October 1955): 8.
27. *New York Times,* 3 July 1956, p. 8.
28. *VD* 1, no. 7 (November-December 1955): 12, and 2, no. 11 (January 1957): 16.
29. Ibid., 2, no. 11 (January 1957): 15.
30. Ibid., 1, no. 6 (October 1955): 6.
31. Anti-Communist Liberation Movement of Venezuela, *Proof of the Communist Domination of Venezuela* (Caracas, 1959), p. 30. Betancourt denied this charge emphatically. See Rómulo Betancourt, *Venezuela: política y petróleo* (Mexico: Fondo de Cultura Económica, 1956), p. 475.
32. *New York Times,* 26 October 1952, p. 39; 4 November 1952, p. 16; and 15 March 1953, p. 70.
33. Ibid., 20 December 1952, p. 15; 2 June 1954, p. 9; and 8 September 1954, p. 1.
34. Ibid., 29 September 1957, p. 24.
35. Germán Ornes, *Trujillo,* pp. 302-03.
36. *Hemispherica* 6, no. 1 (January-February 1957): 6.
37. *VD* 3, no. 12 (May 1957): 4.
38. *New York Times,* 19 February 1967, p. 1.
39. Ibid., 22 February 1967.
40. *Bohemia* 40, no. 41 (1948): 95.
41. Germán Ornes, *Trujillo,* pp. 109, 113; Robert D. Crassweller, *Trujillo: The Life and Times of a Caribbean Dictator* (New York: The Macmillan Company, 1966), pp. 311-12, 330.
42. *Hemispherica* 1, no. 1 (January 1951): 4.
43. Horacio Ornes, *Desembarco en Luperón. Episodio de la lucha por la demo-*

cracia en la República Dominicana (Mexico: Ediciones Humanismo, 1956), p. 27; Crassweller, *Trujillo,* p. 312.
44. *New York Times,* 22 April 1951, p. 17. About two years later, following the overthrow of Prío, Cuban police asserted that Báez had actually been "executed" by Cuban "political terrorists" of the *Acción Revolucionaria Guiteras,* because he was suspected of betraying Dominican exile activities to Trujillo. See HAR 5, no. 8 (September 1952): 18.
45. Ibid.; *Hemispherica* 1, no. 4 (April 1951): 1-2.
46. *New York Times,* 24 August 1951, p. 4.
47. Ibid., 4 October 1952, p. 3.   48. Ibid.
49. FBIS, 7 October 1952, p. D1; HAR 5, no. 10 (November 1952): 17.
50. *New York Times,* 7 October 1952, p. 60.
51. Crassweller, *Trujillo,* p. 193.
52. *Hemispherica* 4, no. 5 (September-November 1955): 6.
53. Ibid.; HAR 8, no. 10 (November 1955): 469.
54. Crassweller, *Trujillo,* p. 343.
55. *VD* 1, no. 7 (November-December 1955): 3.
56. HAR 8, no. 11 (December 1955): 515.
57. See HAR 9, no. 2 (March 1956): 6; 9, no. 8 (September 1956): 380-81; 9, no. 11 (December 1956): 528-29; and 10, no. 3 (April 1957): 185; also see *New York Times,* 28 February 1956, p. 12; 13 August 1956, p. 2; 7 October 1956, p. 6; 29 October 1956, p. 6; and 28 November 1956, p. 8.
58. *Hemispherica* 6, no. 4 (September-October 1957): 5.
59. *New York Times,* 1 December 1956, p. 1; HAR 10, no. 1 (February 1957): 17; Crassweller, *Trujillo,* p. 344.
60. In the author's opinion, the essential details of the Galíndez affair are accurately summarized in Crassweller, *Trujillo,* pp. 311-28.
61. *New York Times,* 20 September 1956, p. 27. Robert Alexander maintains, however, that Trujillo ordered the liquidation of Galíndez, because Galíndez had written an article which questioned the legitimacy of Trujillo's son, "Ramfis." Professor Alexander states that the Galíndez dissertation was quite dull and that Trujillo was aware of the small number of people who read a doctoral dissertation.
62. Germán Ornes, *Trujillo,* p. 320.
63. Arturo Espaillat, *Trujillo: The Last Caesar* (Chicago: Henry Regnery Company, 1964).
64. *New York Times,* 21 March 1956, p. 29, and 29 March 1956, p. 26.
65. Ibid., 7 June 1956, p. 5.
66. Crassweller, *Trujillo,* pp. 314-16.
67. HAR 10, no. 5 (June 1957): 251-52.
68. *New York Times,* 14 May 1957, p. 14.
69. HAR 10, no. 11 (December 1957): 599-600.
70. Ibid., and 10, no. 12 (January 1958): 664-65.
71. Ibid., 10, no. 12 (January 1958): 664-65.   72. Ibid.
73. Ibid., 11, no. 6 (June 1958): 319-20.   74. Ibid.
75. *VD* 2, no. 11 (January 1957): 2, and 3, no. 15 (September 1957): 16.
76. *Hemispherica* 6, no. 4 (September-October 1957): 5.
77. Ibid., 7, no. 2 (March-April 1958): 2.
78. Ibid., 6, no. 4 (September-October 1957): 5; HAR 10, no. 5 (June 1957): 239.
79. Ibid.; *New York Times,* 13 November 1957, p. 23.
80. *Hemispherica* 7, no. 2 (March-April 1958): 1-2.

81. Crassweller,*Trujillo*, p. 330.
82. *New York Times,* 6 December 1957, p. 18. Escobar lived just long enough to identify his assailants, who in turn confessed and implicated Abbes Garcia. See *Hemispherica* 7, no. 1 (January-February 1958): 7.
83. HAR 10, no. 12 (January 1958): 649.
84. Crassweller, *Trujillo*, p. 336.
85. *New York Times,* 10 August 1958, p. 27.   86. Ibid.
87. *Rómulo Betancourt: interpretación de su doctrina popular democrática* (Caracas: SUMA, 1958), p. 39.
88. FBIS, 26 June 1952, p. H1.
89. Benjamín Núñez. "La función social de la religión," *Combate* 1, no. 4 (January-February 1959): 36.
90. Ibid., p. 35.   91. Ibid., p. 36.
92. HAR 9, no. 12 (January 1957): 584.
93. Ibid., 10, no. 5 (June 1957): 251-52.
94. *New York Times,* 2 December 1959, p. 16.
95. HAR 11, no. 3 (March 1958): 148.
96. *CARIB,* Report No. 5 (June 1958), pp. 53-54.
97. HAR 10, no. 11 (December 1957): 590.
98. VD 1, no. 7 (November-December 1955): 3.
99. Crassweller, *Trujillo*, p. 264; *New York Times,* 28 June 1950, p. 16.
100. *New York Times,* 6 January 1953, p. 19.
101. FBIS, 3 February 1953, p. I1.
102. *New York Times,* 12 May 1955, p. 11.
103. Betancourt, *Venezuela,* pp. 847, 848; VD 2, no. 10 (October 1956): 10.
104. FBIS, 23 June 1954, p. E4. Although unmarked, the aircraft was identified as Venezuelan by the crew of a Dutch (KLM) airliner. The pornographic leaflets contained obscene drawings and captions. Of course, not only was Figueres sheltering Betancourt and rendering assistance to AD exiles, but he had boycotted the Caracas Conference.
105. Betancourt, *Venezuela,* pp. 568-69.
106. VD 2, no. 10 (October 1956): 10.
107. Ibid., pp. 1, 10. One of the SN agents supposedly carrying out this scheme was Braulio Barreto, who had been arrested in Barranquilla, Colombia, in June 1954 in connection with the murder of Lieutenant León Droz Blanco.
108. Betancourt maintained that the plan was to force him to move to a place where it would be more convenient to murder him. See VD 2, no. 10 (October 1956): 4.
109. José Rivas Rivas, ed., *Historia Gráfica de Venezuela,* vol. 2, *El mundo y la época de Pérez Jiménez: Una historia contada en recortes de periódicos* (Caracas: Pensamiento Vivo, C.A., 1961), p. 56-14 (*El Nacional,* 10 August 1956).
110. VD 2, no. 10 (October 1956): 10.
111. Ibid.
112. *New York Times,* 17 August 1953, p. 3.
113. FBIS, 3 March 1955, p. H1.
114. *New York Times,* 26 June 1956, p. 6.
115. Ibid., 5 January 1958, p. 19.
116. HAR 11, no. 2 (February 1958): 88, and 11, no. 7 (July 1958): 377.
117. Quoted in *New York Times,* 8 September 1954, p. 1.
118. Ibid., 5 June 1956, p. 22.
119. HAR 11, no. 9 (September 1958): 496.

120. *VD* 3, no. 15 (September 1957): 8-9. Messages of congratulations were received from Prío and Tancredo Martínez.
121. Ibid., 1, no. 6 (October 1955): 1 and 2, no. 11 (January 1957): 16.
122. Ibid., 1, no. 6 (October 1955): 1.
123. Ibid., p. 4. This statement was made in a eulogy to Juan Regalado, a labor leader and long-time militant, who died in exile in Costa Rica in 1955, after five years in prison in Venezuela. His name was added to the list of martyrs.
124. Betancourt, *Venezuela,* p. 843.
125. Ibid., p. 535; ORIT-CIOSL, *15 años de sindicalismo libre interamericano, enero 1948-enero 1963,* 2d ed. (Mexico, 1963), p. 122.
126. *VD* 1, no. 6 (October 1955): 5, and 1, no. 7 (November-December 1955): 4; Betancourt, *Venezuela,* p. 853. The conference, "The Cultural Assimilation of the Immigrant," was eventually transferred to Mexico City in April 1956.
127. *VD* 2, no. 9 (June 1956): 12.   128. Ibid., p. 4.
129. Ibid., 2, no. 10 (October 1956): 3.
130. Ibid., pp. 15-16. The letter was signed by Salvador Azuela, Juan Hernández Luna, Raúl Roa, Luis Alberto Sánchez, José Luis Romero, and Edelberto Torres.
131. Ibid., p. 4.   132. Ibid., 1, no. 8 (January-February 1956): 1.
133. Ibid., 2, no. 10 (October 1956): 15-16.
134. Ibid., 2, no. 11 (January 1957): 3, 6. The IAPA was an important agency of international pressure and its relationship with the exile movement will receive closer scrutiny.
135. Ibid., 3, no. 12 (May 1957): 11.   136. Ibid., 3, no. 14 (August 1957): 2.
137. Ibid., 2, no. 9 (June 1956): 5.   138. Ibid., p. 2.
139. Betancourt, *Venezuela,* p. 576.   140. Ibid., pp.593-94.
141. Ibid., p. 642.   142. Ibid., p. 632.   143. Ibid., p. 650.   144. Ibid., p. 656.
145. *New York Times,* 21 January 1957, p. 33.
146. *VD* 1, no. 7 (November-December 1955): 12-11. Kamleshwar Das, acting on behalf of the UN Secretariat, notified the students that their protest would be considered at the Twelfth Session of the Human Rights Commission.
147. Ibid., 2, no. 11 (January 1957): 16.
148. Ibid., 3, no. 12 (May 1957): 5.
149. Ibid., 1, no. 5 (September 1955): 8.
150. Ibid., p. 3.   151. Ibid., p. 8.
152. Ibid., 1, no. 8 (January-February 1956): 3. The exiles were subsequently released on good behavior.
153. Ibid., 3, no. 14 (August 1957): 9.
154. Ibid., 1, no. 5 (September 1955): 7.
155. John D. Martz, *Acción Democrática. Evolution of a Modern Political Party in Venezuela* (Princeton: Princeton University Press, 1966), p. 144. The Communists were excluded.
156. *Ultimas Noticias* (Caracas), 24 August 1958, p. 38. The committee also noted the assassination of Anastasio Somoza and the invasion of Cuba by Fidel Castro.
157. Ibid.
158. Quoted in a letter, Rómulo Betancourt to the author, 3 March 1969. See also, *Hemispherica* 6, no. 1 (January-February 1957): 3.
159. *VD* 3, no. 13 (June 1957): 8.   160. Ibid., p. 4.
161. Ibid., 3, no. 14 (August 1957): 1, 6.   162. Ibid.
163. Ibid., 3, no. 15 (September 1957): 14.

164. Enrique Tejera París traveled secretly to Venezuela with a copy of the agreement concealed in his shoe in order to secure the signature of Rafael Caldera. Interview with Tejera París.
165. *VD* 3, no. 15 (September 1957): 15.
166. Ibid., p. 7.   167. Ibid., p. 15.
168. *Ultimas Noticias* (Caracas), 24 August 1958, p. 38.
169. Ibid.   170. Ibid.   171. Ibid.
172. HAR 5, no. 7 (August 1952). Among the approximately one hundred guests were the president of the United States, the governors of the then forty-eight states, North American officials, and "distinguished Latin American intellectuals and politicians."
173. *New York Times,* 23 April 1957, p. 18.
174. Antonio Santiago Ruiz, "La acción revolucionaria del Partido Auténtico," *Combate* 2, no. 9 (March-April 1960): 39.
175. Ibid.
176. Ibid.; Ruby Hart Phillips, *Cuba: Island of Paradox,* (New York: McDowell, Obolensky, 1959), pp. 313-14. Prío furnished a yacht and arms for this expedition.
177. *New York Times,* 19 September 1957, p. 18.
178. HAR 6, no. 6 (July 1953): 17.
179. Phillips, *Cuba,* p. 276.
180. HAR 10, no. 10 (November 1957): 528-29.
181. Wyatt MacGaffey and Clifford R. Barnett, *Twentieth Century Cuba* (New York: Anchor Books, 1965), p. 29.
182. Phillips, *Cuba,* p. 276.
183. *New York Times,* 24 July 1958, p. 8; HAR 11, no. 8 (August 1958): 435.
184. Germán Ornes, *Trujillo,* p. 302.
185. Bosch, *Experiment,* p. 12.
186. Germán Ornes, *Trujillo,* pp. 306-07.   187. Ibid., p. 307.
188. HAR 9, no. 10 (November 1956): 478.
189. John B. Martin, *Overtaken by Events. The Dominican Crisis from the Fall of Trujillo to the Civil War* (New York: Doubleday and Company, Inc., 1966), pp. 74, 129-30.
190. In 1959 Díaz was listed as a leader of the Dominican Patriotic Union (*Unión Patriótica Dominicana*) and charged with recruiting young Dominicans and Puerto Ricans in New York for an invasion of the Dominican Republic. See The Caribbean Anti-Communist Research and Intelligence Bureau, *Invasion Report: Constanza, Maimón, Estero Hondo. Communist Aggression Against The Dominican Republic* (Ciudad Trujillo, 1959), pp. 131-32.
191. *New York Times,* 28 February 1947, p. 11, and 4 August 1947, p. 3; Germán Ornes, *Trujillo,* p. 308.
192. *New York Times,* 12 January 1953, p. 7.
193. HAR 6, no. 2 (March 1953): 15.   194. Ibid.
195. Ibid., 7, no. 8 (September 1954).
196. *New York Times,* 21 December 1955, p. 52.
197. *Hemispherica* 5, no. 3 (May-July 1956): 1.   198. Ibid.
199. Ibid., 6, no. 2 (March-April 1957): 4.
200. *New York Times,* 6 May 1956, p. 16.   201. Ibid., 30 October 1958, p. 8.
202. Ibid., 7 August 1956, p. 9.   203. Ibid., 20 August 1957, p. 10.
204. Betancourt, *Venezuela,* p. 849.
205. *VD* 1, no. 1 (April 1955): 7.   206. Ibid.
207. Betancourt, *Venezuela,* p. 849.

208. *VD* 1, no. 5 (September 1955): 7, and 2, no. 11 (January 1957): 9.

209. Ronald M. Schneider, *Communism in Guatemala, 1944-1954* (New York: Frederick A. Praeger, 1959), p. 282.

210. Ibid., pp. 141-43. CTAL and its parent World Federation of Trade Unions (WFTU) were the Communist hemispheric and international counterparts of the ORIT and ICFTU, respectively.

211. *CARIB*, Report No. 8 (July 1958), p. 32.

212. U.S. Department of State, *Intervention of International Communism in Guatemala*, Department of State Publication 5556 (Washington, 1954), pp. 46-47. Despite the school closing, the Salvadoran Communists remained influential. Guerra Méndez became a member of the Political Committee of the Guatemalan Labor party, PGT (Partido Guatemalteco del Trabajo), which was Guatemala's Communist party, and he served as secretary of organization of the General Confederation of Guatemalan Workers, CGTG (Confederación General de Trabajadores de Guatemala); Mármol Chicas also was active in the PGT and CGTG; and Abel Cuenca was a very influential politician and held a position in the Guatemalan Institute of Social Security. See also, Schneider, *Communism*, p. 209.

213. State Department, No. 5556, p. 71; Schneider, *Communism*, p. 205.

214. State Department, No. 5556, p. 80; Schneider, *Communism*, p. 260.

215. FBIS, 6 February 1952, p. H1, and 19 June 1952, p. H3.

216. Ibid., 18 April 1952, p. H1, and 19 June 1952, p. H3.

217. State Department, No. 5556, p. 87; Schneider, *Communism*, p. 281.

218. Schneider, *Communism*, p. 281.

219. State Department, No. 5556, p. 40; *New York Times*, 23 February 1954, p. 4.

220. State Department, No. 5556, p. 88.

221. *New York Times*, 2 May 1953, p. 4.

222. State Department, No. 5556, pp. 78-80; Schneider, *Communism*, pp. 253-58.

223. *New York Times*, 8 April 1953, p. 21; HAR 6, no. 4 (May 1953): 12-13.

224. *New York Times*, 31 January 1954, p. 13; HAR 7, no. 1 (February 1954): 11-12.

225. The debate between Guatemalan Foreign Minister Guillermo Toriello and U.S. Secretary of State John Foster Dulles over United States intentions in calling for measures to combat communism in the Western Hemisphere.

226. *Diario de Costa Rica* (San José), 19 May 1954, p. 1

227. Daniel James, *Red Design for the Americas: Guatemalan Prelude* (New York: The John Day Company, 1954), p. 224; Martz, *Central America*, p. 59.

228. Martz, *Central America*, pp. 131-34.   229. Ibid., p. 131.

230. Ibid., p. 132; Schneider, *Communism*, p. 298.

231. Martz, *Central America*, p. 135; Schneider, *Communism*, p. 299.

232. *New York Times*, 25 May 1954, p. 1.

233. Martz, *Central America*, pp. 59-61.

234. U.S. Congress, House, *Report of the Subcommittee to Investigate Communist Aggression in Latin America to the Select Committee on Communist Aggression*, 83rd Cong., 2d sess., 1954, p. 15. Hereinafter cited as *Hillings Report*.

235. *CARIB*, Report No. 8 (July 1958), pp. 18-20.

236. John A. Clements Associates, *Report on Venezuela* (New York: John A. Clements Associates [1959]), p. 102.

237. Ibid., p. 103.

238. Ibid., p. 105; *Hillings Report*, pp. 13-14.

239. Interview with Figueres; see also Oduber and Monge, *Combate* 2, no. 9 (March-April 1960): 19.

240. *La Prensa* (Managua), 13 May 1954.
241. Ibid., 23 April 1954, and 13 May 1954.
242. State Department, No. 5556, p. 88.
243. *Diario de Costa Rica,* 15 May 1954.
244. *La Prensa,* 13 May 1954.
245. The officers of the new party were: Leal, president; Arturo Velásquez, vice-president; Adolfo Ortega Díaz, secretary general; Ibarra Mayorga, secretary for propaganda; Alberto Gámez, recording secretary; and Manuel Gómez, General Alejandro Cárdenas, and Dr. Carlos Agüero, committeemen. *Diario de Costa Rica,* 19 May 1954.
246. Ibid.   247. Ibid., 15 May 1954.
248. Ibid.   249. Ibid.; *La Prensa,* 13 May 1954.
250. The sixteen Nicaraguans were: Manuel Gómez, José María Tercero, Luis F. Gabuardi, Juan José Ruíz, Amadeo Baena, Juan Martínez Reyes, Virgilio Vega Fornos, Miguel Ramírez Reyes, Ernesto Peralta, Carlos Prado Corroto, Francisco Caldera, Antonio Velásquez Bolaños, Luis Armando Morales Palacios, Gustavo Adolfo Zavala, Rafael Praslin, and Francisco Guadamuz. The remaining five and their nationalities were: Ribas Montes and Eduardo Granillo, Honduran; Octaviano Morazán, Guatemalan; Edgar Gutiérrez, Costa Rican; and Amadeo Soler, Dominican. *Diario de Costa Rica,* 19 May 1954.
251. Ibid.; *La Prensa,* 9 April 1954, and 13 May 1954.
252. *La Prensa,* 28 April 1954, and 24 September 24 1954.
253. Ibid., 23 April 1954, and 24 September 1954.
254. *Hillings Report,* p. 13; *New York Times,* 5 April 1954, p. 17.
255. *La Prensa,* 24 September 1954.
256. Ibid., 25 April 1954.
257. Ibid., 18 September 1954, and 30 September 1954. The remaining survivors were the Nicaraguans Amadeo Baena, Luis Armando Morales Palacios, and Carlos Prado Corroto. The author is unable to account for Virgilio Vega Fornos, who was listed as an expeditionary, but who was alive in Costa Rica in 1956.
258. *La Prensa,* 9 April 1954; Pedro Joaquín Chamorro, *Estirpe sangrienta: los Somoza* (Buenos Aires: Editorial Triángulo, 1959), p. 119. Two other names appeared on the casualty lists, Manrique Umaña and Carlos Ulises Gómez, but they had not been listed among Leal's original force.
259. Emilio Borge González, "Nicaragua por dentro," *Combate* 1, no. 5 (March-April 1959), p. 39; Chamorro, *Los Somoza,* pp. 65-66, pp. 108-09, 119.
260. *La Prensa,* 9 April 1954.
261. Chamorro, *Los Somoza,* p. 107.   262. Ibid., pp. 51, 87.
263. *La Prensa,* 5 June 1957. On 2 June 1957 *El Centroamericano* of León had published a small notice indicating that the alleged attempt to escape and consequent death of Ribas Montes had occurred the preceding (October! Later the same month, authorities gave only vague answers about the whereabouts of Morales Palacios; his mother was told that he had left Nicaragua in August 1956, but she had not heard from him and claimed (or hoped) he was still in prison. See ibid., 4 and 30 June 1957.
264. *La Prensa,* 25 and 28 April 1954. Others who took asylum were: Ibarra Mayorga, Solórzano Thompson, and Fernando Agüero; and some of those arrested were: Humberto and Roberto Chamorro, Domingo Aguilar, Fernando Solórzano Chamorro, José Dolores Masís, and Emilio Alvárez Montalván.
265. Ibid., 24 September 1954.   266. Ibid., 12 February 1955.
267. *Diario de Costa Rica,* 19 May 1954; FBIS, 20 May 1954, pp. E1-E2; *CARIB,*

Report No. 8 (July 1958), pp. 32-35. The Nicaraguans to be expelled included: Federico Solórzano Montiel, General Cárdenas, Antonio Orúe Reyes, Edmundo Vargas Vásquez, Carlos Agüero, Roberto Hurtado, Alberto Gámez, General Adán Vélez, Adolfo Ortega Díaz, and Arturo Velásquez Alemán.
268. *La Prensa,* 25 July 1954.
269. Betancourt, *Venezuela,* p. 568; Rivas, *Historia,* 2: 53-38–53-39 (*El Universal,* 21 October 1953.
270. FBIS, 3 February 1954, p. D1, and 8 February 1954, p. D1; *New York Times,* 5 February 1954, p. 9.
271. *New York Times,* 9 April 1954, p. 3.
272. Serafino Romualdi, *Presidents and Peons: Recollections of a Labor Ambassador in Latin America* (New York: Funk and Wagnalls, 1967), pp. 464-65.
273. FBIS, 21 April 1954, p. E1.
274. *New York Times,* 5 July 1954, p. 3.
275. Betancourt, *Venezuela,* p. 860.
276. FBIS, 13 July 1954, pp. E1-E2, and 16 September 1954, p. E1.
277. *New York Times,* 23 January 1955, p. 1.
278. FBIS, 1 September 1954, p. E1.
279. Romualdi, *Presidents,* p. 465.
280. FBIS, 5 October 1954, p. E1.
281. Unión Panamericana, Departamento de Asuntos Jurídicos. *Aplicaciones del Tratado Interamericano de Asistencia Recíproca, 1948-1960* (Washington, D.C., 1960), p. 164. Two days after the invasion, three rebel aircraft were observed at La Cruz: a C-47 and two AT-6s (World War II trainers).
282. FBIS, 12 January 1955, pp. N2-N3.
283. Unión Panamericana, *Aplicaciones,* pp. 145-46.
284. Ibid., pp. 148-49.   285. Ibid., p. 151.   286. Ibid., pp. 152-53.
287. Ibid., p. 155.   288. Ibid., pp. 156-57.   289. Ibid., p. 158.
290. Interview with Figueres.
291. Unión Panamericana, *Aplicaciones,* pp. 154-56.
292. *New York Times,* 13 January 1955, p. 1.
293. Unión Panamericana, *Aplicaciones,* p. 159.
294. Ibid., pp. 160-63.   295. Ibid., pp. 173-74.   296. Ibid., pp. 187-94.
297. Interview with Figueres.
298. *New York Times,* 25 April 1955, p. 13.
299. Ibid., 27 January 1955, p. 9, and 30 April 1955, p. 18.
300. Ibid., 25 April 1955, p. 13.
301. Chamorro, *Los Somoza,* pp. 125-26.
302. Borge González, *Combate* 1, no. 5 (March-April 1959): 39.
303. *VD* 2, no. 10 (October 1956): 16.
304. Ibid., 3, no. 15 (September 1957): 16.
305. Chamorro, *Los Somoza,* pp. 20, 83-84. The following were arrested with Chamorro: Francisco Fixione, Enrique Lacayo Farfán, Enoc Aguado, and Emilio Borge González. See, ibid., p. 160, and Borge González, *Combate* 1, no. 5 (March-April 1959): 40.
306. *New York Times,* 27 September 1956, p. 13; Martz, *Central America,* p. 203. Sevilla Sacasa made the following lsit of exiles whom he particularly wanted placed under surveillance: Manuel Gómez Flores, Hernán Robleto, Juan José Meza, Adolfo Zanura, and Alberto Gámez, all residing in Mexico; Adolfo Díaz (the former president of Nicaragua), Ernesto Solórzano Thompson, and Virgilio Vega Fornos, who were living in Costa Rica; and Toribio Tijerino (General Chamorro's secretary), who was then in El Salvador. See *New York Times,* 28 September 1956, p. 10.

307. *New York Times,* 20 January 1957, p. 8.   308. Ibid.   309. Ibid.
310. Details of this affair may be found in Unión Panamericana, *Aplicaciones,* pp. 219-92.
311. Ibid., pp. 236, 244-46. Honduras subsequently modified this complaint when the Dominican Republic reacted angrily and recalled its ambassador from Tegucigalpa.
312. HAR 10, no. 11 (December 1957): 587-88.
313. Ibid., 11, no. 2 (February 1958): 79-80.
314. Ibid., 11, no. 4 (April 1958): 197.
315. Ibid., 11, no. 5 (May 1958): 252; *New York Times,* 10 May 1958, p. 10.
316. HAR 11, no. 4 (April 1958): 198-99; *New York Times,* 26 April 1958, p. 10.
317. HAR 11, no. 4 (April 1958): 198-99, and 11, no. 5 (May 1958): 252. Gómez Flores later described Castellón as an "indiscreet exhibitionist."
318. Ibid., 11, no. 4 (April 1958): 197.
319. *New York Times,* 10 May 1958, p. 10.
320. HAR 11, no. 5 (May 1958): 252.   321. Ibid.

Chapter 5

1. Robert J. Alexander, *Prophets of the Revolution: Profiles of Latin American Leaders* (New York: The Macmillan Company, 1962), p. 96.
2. *New York Times,* 16 March 1947, p. 12.
3. *Rómulo Betancourt: pensamiento y acción* (Mexico, 1951), pp. 187-92.
4. Ibid., pp. 132-33.
5. Arturo Castro E., *José Figueres Ferrer. El hombre y su obra* (San José, Costa Rica: Imprenta Tormo, 1955), p. 247.
6. Ibid., p. 248.
7. *New York Times,* 11 September 1949, p. 39.
8. Ibid., 29 January 1949, p. 5.
9. *Bohemia* 42, no. 19 (1950): 68, and 42, no. 21 (1950): 102-07.
10. John A. Clements Associates, *Report on Venezuela* (New York: John A. Clements Associates [1959]), p. 133.
11. *New York Times,* 14 May 1950, p. 33.
12. *Betancourt: pensamiento,* p. 254.
13. Inter-American Association for Democracy and Freedom, *Report of the Second Inter-American Conference for Democracy and Freedom* (New York, 1961), pp. 42-43.
14. *Betancourt: pensamiento,* p. 244.
15. IADF, *Report,* p. 46.   16. Ibid., p. 76.
17. *Hemispherica* 3, no. 3 (June-July 1954): 3.
18. Serafino Romualdi, *Presidents and Peons: Recollections of a Labor Ambassador in Latin America* (New York: Funk and Wagnalls, 1967), p. 477. In deference to the wishes of Betancourt this incident was not publicized, but Figueres lodged an official complaint through his ambassador in Washington. Figueres also wrote to Professor Alexander to express his dismay, as follows: "At times the Department of State does not seem to understand that the democrats of the hemisphere form in fact a brotherhood. They believe that we are isolated. They do not see the bonds which unite us, over and above nationality, with roots in the sentiments of the people." Letter from Figueres to Robert Alexander, 1 March 1956, Alexander MSS.
19. *CARIB,* Report No. 8 (July 1958), p. 42.
20. IADF, *Report,* p. 54; *New York Times,* 14 February 1952, p. 7.

21. *Hemispherica* 2, no. 4 (May-July 1953): 5.
22. Ibid., 2, no. 6 (November-December 1953): 1.
23. Ibid., 3, no. 1 (January-February 1954): 1, 3.   24. Ibid., pp. 1-2.
25. Ibid., 5, no. 6 (October-December 1956): 3. As already discussed, Pérez Pisanty died while being held by the Seguridad Nacional.
26. Ibid.; *VD* 2, no. 10 (October 1956): 1.
27. IADF, *Report*, p. 69.
28. *Hemispherica* 1, no. 4 (April 1951): 2-3. Figueres generally stated the need for unity among democratic organizations of the Americas and for the awakening of North American interest in Latin America.
29. Ibid., 5, no. 6 (October-December 1956): 1.
30. Ibid., 6, no. 1 (January-February 1957): 3.   31. Ibid.
32. Ibid., 7, no. 1 (January-February 1958): 3.
33. Ibid., 1, no. 4 (April 1951): 2.
34. Ibid., 2, no. 4 (May-July 1953): 3-4.
35. Ibid., 4, no. 5 (September-November 1955): 2.
36. Ibid., 6, no. 3 (May-July 1957): 3.
37. Ibid., 7, no. 4 (June-July 1958): 2.
38. Ibid., p. 3. Other recipients on the IADF Award were Luis Muñoz Marín in 1954 and Alberto Gainza Paz of Argentina in 1955.
39. Ibid., 5, no. 2 (March-April 1956): 2, 4.
40. Ibid., 7, no. 5 (August-September 1958): 3. An interesting list of topics was prepared, which, with Miss Grant in charge, were presented by an impressive array of guest lecturers. The course was so successful that it was repeated annually.
41. Ibid., 5, no. 2 (March-April 1956): 1-3.
42. *New York Times,* 29 March 1956, p. 26.
43. *Hemispherica* 5, no. 3 (May-July 1956): 1, 4.
44. *New York Times,* 31 July 1956, p. 22.
45. Ibid., 13 September 1956, p. 33.   46. Ibid., 1 March 1957, p. 8.
47. *Hemispherica* 6, no. 2 (March-April 1957): 1.   48. Ibid., p. 4.
49. *New York Times,* 7 July 1958, p. 1.
50. *Hemispherica* 7, no. 2 (March-April 1958): 2.
51. Ibid., 7, no. 4 (June-July 1958): 7.   52. Ibid., p. 1.
53. *New York Times,* 29 September 1957, p. 13.
54. *Hemispherica* 6, no. 4 (September-October 1957): 2.   55. Ibid.
56. Ibid., 6, no. 5 (November-December 1957): 5.
57. Ibid., 8, no. 1 (January 1959): 3.
58. Ibid., 7, no. 5 (August-September 1958): 1.
59. John D. Martz *Acción Democrática. Evolution of a Modern Political Party in Venezuela,* Princeton:(Princeton University Press, 1966), p. 229.
60. *Hemispherica* 8, no. 1 (January 1959): 1.
61. *VD* 3, no. 14 (August 1957): 8.
62. ORIT-CIOSL, *15 años de sindicalismo libre interamericano, enero 1948 – enero 1963,* 2nd ed. (Mexico, 1963), p. 8.
63. Romualdi, *Presidents,* p. 42.
64. The following labor confederations were the most active in the founding Congress of the CIT: Confederación de Trabajadores de Chile (CTCh); Confederación de Trabajadores del Perú (CTP); the American Federation of Labor (AFL); Confederación Costarricense de Trabajadores "Rerum Novarum" (CCT); Confederación de Trabajadores de Cuba (CTC); and Confederación de Trabajadores de Venezuela (CTV).

65. Romualdi, *Presidents*, p. 91.
66. *New York Times*, 25 April 1949, p. 5.
67. Romualdi, *Presidents*, pp. 92-93; *New York Times*, 7 May 1949, p. 6.
68. *New York Times*, 10 September 1949, p. 6.
69. Ibid., 12 September 1949, p. 5.
70. ORIT-CIOSL, *15 años*, pp. 111-12.
71. Romualdi, *Presidents*, p. 94.
72. In Spanish, Confederación Internacional de Organizaciones Sindicales Libres (CIOSL).
73. ORIT-CIOSL, *15 años*. pp. 17-18.
74. Ibid., pp. 19-20.
75. Romualdi, *Presidents*, p. 95.
76. ORIT-CIOSL, *15 años*, pp. 112-13.
77. Rómulo Betancourt, *Venezuela: política y petróleo* (Mexico: Fondo de Cultura Económica, 1956), p. 530; Romualdi, *Presidents*, pp. 446, 452-53.
78. Romualdi, *Presidents*, pp. 119-20.
79. ORIT-CIOSL, *La lucha permanente del movimiento sindical libre contra las dictaduras criollas* (Mexico, 1960), p. 3.
80. ORIT-CIOSL, *15 años*, p. 123.
81. Interview of Robert Alexander with Angel Miolán, 20 March 1952, Alexander MSS.
82. ORIT-CIOSL, *15 años*, p. 25.
83. HAR 4, no. 13 (January 1952): 23-24.
84. Romualdi, *Presidents*, p. 449.   85. Ibid.
86. Betancourt, *Venezuela*, p. 531; see also Romualdi, *Presidents*, p. 455. Apparently, these events deeply moved Martín Araujo; in May of the following year, in the wake of the closing of the Central University and in the midst of the clamor over Guasina, the ambassador quietly resigned and went to Spain to live.
87. Betancourt, *Venezuela*, p. 712.
88. *New York Times*, 9 February 1952, p. 4.
89. HAR 5, no. 2 (March 1952): 22.
90. Interview by Robert Alexander with Betancourt, 1 September 1955, Alexander MSS.
91. Betancourt, *Venezuela*, pp. 532, 852; see also Romualdi, *Presidents*, p. 455.
92. Romualdi, *Presidents*, p. 456.
93. Ibid., pp. 456-57, 127.   94. Ibid., pp. 456-57.
95. Ibid., pp. 123-24.   96. Ibid., p. 127.
97. ORIT-CIOSL, *15 años*, pp. 28-29, 113-14.
98. Ibid., p. 31.   99. Ibid., p. 114.   100. Ibid., pp. 34, 114.
101. ORIT-ICFTU, *The Permanent Struggle of the Free Trade Union Movement Against Latin American Dictatorships* (Mexico City, 1960), p. 9; Romualdi, *Presidents*, p. 130.
102. Romualdi, *Presidents*, p. 127.
103. ORIT-CIOSL, *15 años*, p. 32.   104. Ibid., pp. 121-22.
105. Romualdi, *Presidents*, p. 461.
106. *Hemispherica* 2, no. 6 (November-December 1953): 4. It will be recalled that in December 1953 the U.S. Committee of the IADF, of which Romualdi and Schwartz were members, also presented a protest to Cabot.
107. ORIT-ICFTU, *Struggle*, pp. 22-23.   108. Ibid.
109. George Morris, *CIA and American Labor. The Subversion of the AFL-CIO's Foreign Policy* (New York: International Publishers, 1967), p. 91.

110. *New York Times,* 1 August 1954, p. 24.
111. Romualdi, *Presidents,* p. 269. The U.S. sale of four F-51 fighter planes to Costa Rica accomplished just this purpose.
112. ORIT-ICFTU, *Struggle,* p. 25; see also Romualdi, *Presidents,* pp. 466-68.
113. Betancourt, *Venezuela,* p. 535 *VD* 1, no. 1 (April 1955): 4-5.
114. ORIT-ICFTU, *Struggle,* pp. 25-28.   115. Ibid., pp. 28-29.
116. Betancourt, *Venezuela,* pp. 536-37.
117. ORIT-ICFTU, *Struggle,* pp. 30-31.
118. Betancourt, *Venezuela,* p. 537. It seems likely that Vermeulen did not act on his own, because at two separate points in his address he declared that he was speaking on behalf of the Workers' Group of the Governing Body. In an interview on 1 September 1955, Betancourt told Professor Robert Alexander that Vermeulen's action surprised him. Alexander MSS.
119. *VD* 1, no. 2 (May 1955): 9.
120. ORIT-ICFTU, *Struggle,* p. 8; see also ORIT-CIOSL, *15 años,* pp. 37-41.
121. ORIT-ICFTU, *Struggle,* p. 9.
122. Ibid., pp. 9-10. Luis Alberto Monge was reelected general secretary for another three years, but he was immediately granted a leave, and Arturo Jáuregui was named acting general secretary. Romualdi and Schwartz continued as assistant secretaries.
123. *VD* 1, no. 4 (July-August 1955): 5.   124. Ibid., p. 8.
125. Reproduced in *VD* 1, no. 6 (October 1955): 5.
126. Ibid., 1, no. 7 (November-December 1955): 1, 9.
127. Quoted in *Hemispherica* 5, no. 1 (January-February 1956): 6.
128. *VD* 1, no. 8 (January-February 1956): 2.
129. Supra, p. 182.
130. *VD* 2, no. 11 (January 1957): 5, 9-10.
131. Ibid., pp. 4, 10.   132. Ibid.   133. Ibid., 3, no. 13 (June 1957): 4.
134. Ibid., pp. 4, 11.   135. Ibid., 2, no. 11 (January 1957): 4.
136. Ibid., 3, no. 13 (June 1957): 4.   137. Ibid., 3, no. 14 (August 1957): 8-7.
138. The International Trade Secretariats involved included the Postal, Telegraph, and Telephone International, the International Transport Workers' Federation, and the International Union of Food and Allied Workers' Associations.
139. *VD* 3, no. 15 (September 1957): 4, 6.
140. *Hemispherica* 6, no. 1 (January-February 1957): 3.
141. ORIT-ICFTU, *Struggle,* p. 34.   142. Ibid.
143. Interview by Robert Alexander with Angel Miolán, 15 February 1959, Alexander MSS.
144. ORIT-CIOSL, *15 años,* p. 126; *New York Times,* 8 July 1956, p. 7.
145. *Hemispherica* 5, no. 3 (May-July 1956): 5.
146. Ibid., 5, no. 5 (August-September 1956): 6.
147. ORIT–ICFTU, *Struggle,* p. 21.
148. HAR 11, no. 4 (April 1958): 207; see also *Hemispherica* 7, no. 3 (May 1958): 4.
149. ORIT-ICFTU, *Struggle,* p. 20.
150. ORIT-CIOSL, *15 años,* pp. 45-48.
151. Romualdi, *Presidents,* p. 134.
152. Juan José Arévalo, *Anti-Kommunism in Latin America. An X-ray of the Process Leading to a New Colonialism,* trans. Carleton Beals (New York: Lyle Stuart, Inc., 1963), p. 190.
153. HAR 10, no. 3 (April 1957): 190.
154. Mary A. Gardner, *The Inter-American Press Association: Its Fight for Free-*

dom of the Press, 1926-1960, Latin American Monographs, No. 6, Institute of Latin American Studies, The University of Texas (Austin: The University of Texas Press, 1967), p. 76.

155. Ibid. 156. Ibid., p. 78. 157. Ibid., p. 86. 158. Ibid., p. 92.

159. *Hemispherica* 2, no. 5 (August-October 1953): 5. Because an exiled Peruvian newsman declared at the meetings that Rafael Trujillo was a "filthy dictator," Germán Ornes, representing *El Caribe* of Ciudad Trujillo, picked up the twelve-page report and beat him with it. See, HAR 6, no. 10 (November 1953): 11.

160. HAR 6, no. 9 (October 1953): 14.

161. Gardner, *Association*, p. 76; FBIS, 8 October 1954, p. E1. Lanz Duret climbed through a window of the Costa Rican embassy in order to interview Robleto.

162. *New York Times*, 4 December 1954, p. 3.

163. HAR 8, no. 5 (June 1955): 211.

164. Ibid., 9, no. 5 (June 1956): 231.

165. Chamorro, *Los Somoza*, p. 259. 166. Ibid., p. 257.

167. HAR 10, no. 3 (April 1957): 182.

168. Ibid., 10, no. 10 (November 1957): 524-25.

169. Ibid., 10, no. 12 (January 1958): 655.

170. Betancourt, *Venezuela*, p. 511.

171. *VD* 1, no. 6 (October 1955): 7.

172. HAR 8, no. 10 (November 1955): 449-51.

173. *VD* 2, no. 9 (June 1956) 5; Betancourt, *Venezuela*, p. 511.

174. *VD* 2, no. 9 (June 1956): 5.

175. Ibid., p. 4. Stanley Ross, the editor of *El Diario de Nueva York*, was subsequently ousted by the IAPA on charges that he had offered "to sell his pen to Rafael Trujillo." See, Gardner, *Association*, pp. 30-31.

176. Quoted in *New York Times*, 30 October 1956, p. 8.

177. *VD* 2, no. 11 (January 1957): 6. 178. Ibid., p. 3.

179. HAR 9, no. 11 (December 1956): 535.

180. *VD* 2, no. 11 (January 1957): 3.

181. Ibid., 3, no. 12 (May 1957): 12-11. 182. Ibid., p. 11.

183. Ibid., 3, no. 13 (June 1957): 12-11.

184. HAR 10, no. 10 (November 1957): 538.

185. *New York Times*, 18 October 1957, p. 11. It was, in fact, a young journalist, Fabricio Ojeda, who organized the demonstrations which led to the overthrow of Pérez Jiménez in January 1958.

186. Gardner, *Association*, p. 108.

187. *New York Times*, 30 December 1955, p. 10.

188. Ibid., 17 January 1956, p. 7.

189. Quoted in HAR 9, no. 10 (November 1956): 480.

190. Ibid., 10, no. 3 (April 1957): 190.

191. *New York Times*, 19 September 1957, p. 14.

192. HAR 10, no. 10 (November 1957): 534-35. Marrero Aristy himself died in the Dominican Republic in 1959 under circumstances which suggested that he had been the victim of a political murder. See Robert D. Crassweller, *Trujillo: The Life and Times of a Caribbean Dictator* (New York: The Macmillan Company, 1966), pp. 398-400.

193. *Betancourt: pensamiento*, pp. 358-59.

194. *VD* 1, no. 6 (October 1955): 8 and 7.

195. Ibid., 3, no. 12 (May 1957): 30.

Chapter 6

1. José Rivas Rivas, ed., *Historia Gráfica de Venezuela*, vol. 4, *El gobierno de Rómulo Betancourt* (Caracas: Pensamiento Vivo, C.A., 1965), p. 60-21.
2. *Hemispherica* 7, no. 1 (January-February 1958): 2.
3. *Rómulo Betancourt: posición y doctrina*, ed. Editorial Cordillera (Caracas: Editorial Cordillera, 1959), p. 40.
4. Quoted in *New York Times*, 2 February 1958, pt. III, p. 1.
5. *Betancourt: posición*, p. 38.
6. *Hemispherica* 7, no. 1 (January-February 1958): 2.
7. HAR 11, no. 2 (February 1958): 88.
8. *New York Times*, 24 July 1958, p. 8.
9. HAR 11, no. 7 (July 1958): 377.
10. *New York Times*, 20 February 1958, p. 51.
11. Figueres was philosophical about the outcome: "I consider our defeat as a contribution, in a way, to democracy in Latin America. It is not customary for a party in power to lose an election." See, HAR 11, no. 2 (February 1958): 81.
12. *Hemispherica* 8, no. 2 (February 1959): 2.
13. Acción Democrática, *Doctrina y Programa*, Publicación de la Secretaría Nacional de Propaganda (Caracas, 1962); see also John D. Martz, *Acción Democrática. Evolution of a Modern Political Party in Venezuela* (Princeton: Princeton University Press, 1966), pp. 227-52.
14. AD, *Doctrina y Programa*, pp. 62-63.   15. Ibid., p. 236.   16. Ibid.
17. Honduran President Ramón Villeda Morales enunciated a similar "Continental Policy." Among the related ideas in his plan, he proposed to "strengthen democracy by collective defense" among freely elected governments and, while respecting the principle of nonintervention, "to create a climate of effective inter-American democracy, to the end of eradicating despotic governments." See, *Hemispherica* 7, no. 5 (August-September 1958): 2.
18. See Martz, *Acción Democrática*, pp. 104, 331; Jesús A. Paz Galarraga, "Acción Política del Gobierno Democrático," Address before the Popular University, "Alberto Carnevali," Caracas, 1963, p. 1. (Mimeographed.)
19. *New York Times*, 9 December 1958, p. 1.
20. *Hemispherica* 8, no. 3 (March-April 1959): 1.
21. Rómulo Betancourt, *Tres años de gobierno democrático, 1959-1962* (Caracas: Imprenta Nacional, 1962), 1: 21.
22. "La 'Declaración de Caracas,' " *Combate* 1, no. 4 (January-February 1959): 2.
23. Ibid.
24. Ibid. The signers of the declaration included Eduardo Frei Montalva and Salvador Allende of Chile; Eduardo Rodríguez Larreta of Uruguay; Jesús Silva Herzog of Mexico; Raúl Roa, Aureliano Sánchez Arango, and Levi Marrero Artiles of Cuba; Luis Alberto Monge, José Figueres, Francisco Orlich, and Alberto Cañas of Costa Rica; Juan Angel Núñez Aguilar of Honduras; Jaime Posada of Colombia; Alfredo Pareja of Ecuador; Andrés Townsend, Ramiro Prialé, and Arturo Sabroso of Peru; and Raúl Leoni, Humberto Cuenca, Luis Beltrán Prieto Figueroa, César Rondón Lovera, Domingo Alberto Rangel, and Gonzalo Barrios of Venezuela.
25. Víctor Raúl Haya de la Torre, "La declaración democrática de Caracas," *Combate* 1, no. 5 (March-April 1959): 30.
26. Robert D. Crassweller, *Trujillo: The Life and Times of a Caribbean Dictator* (New York: The Macmillan Company, 1966), p. 346.

27. *New York Times,* 21 February 1959, p. 8.
28. Rivas, *Historia,* vol. 4, Appendix, Document No. 1.   29. Ibid.
30. In February, Luis Somoza was accused of trying to overthrow Honduran President Villeda Morales. He denied the charge and asserted that it was a pretense to justify attacks upon his government and eventually to carry out an invasion of Nicaragua. See *New York Times,* 15 February 1959, p. 4.
31. Ibid., 20 February 1959, p. 8.   32. Ibid., 1 June 1959, p. 11.
33. John A. Clements Associates, *Report on Venezuela* (New York: John A. Clements Associates [1959]), p. 183.
34. Ibid.,pp. 157-58.   35. Ibid., p. 167.   36. Ibid., p. 80.   37. Ibid., p. 81.
38. *Hemispherica* 8, no. 1 (January 1959): 2.
39. *New York Times,* 13 March 1959, p. 8.
40. *New York Times,* 23 March 1959, p. 1.
41. Ibid.   42. Ibid.   43. Ibid., 4 April 1959, p. 1.
44. *El Nacional* (Caracas), 4 April 1959.
45. *New York Times,* 29 April 1959, p. 6.   46. Ibid., 27 May 1959, p. 1.
47. Ibid., 1 March 1959, p. 1, and 18 March 1959, p. 7.
48. Ibid., 28 July 1959, p. 2, and 23 August 1959, p. 33; Ignacio Briones Torres, "Angustia y esperanza de Nicaragua," *Combate* 3, no. 17 (July-August 1961): 44-50.
49. *New York Times,* 15 March 1959, p. 32, and 18 March 1959, p. 7.
50. Ibid., 25 March 1959, p. 13.   51. Ibid., 1 March 1959, p. 1.
52. Ibid., 28 February 28 1959, p. 1.
53. Tad Szulc, *The Winds of Revolution. Latin America Today–And Tomorrow* (New York: Frederick A. Praeger, 1963), p. 122.
54. *New York Times,* 20 April 1959, p. 1.
55. Unión Panamericana, Departamento de Asuntos Jurídicos, *Aplicaciones del Tratado Interamericano de Asistencia Recíproca, 1948-1960* (Washington, D.C., 1960), pp. 295-96, 307-8.
56. Ibid., pp. 307-08.
57. Ibid., pp. 301-02. It seems appropriate to recall here Roa's violent attack upon Adlai Stevenson in the UN at the time of the Bay of Pigs invasion.
58. Ibid., pp. 307-15.
59. *Diario de Costa Rica,* 2 June 1959, p. 18, and 3 June 1959, p. 9. The coalition was made up of Nicaragua's traditional parties: the Conservative, Liberal, and Independent Liberal; and three minor parties: Social Christian (Social-Cristiano), National Renovation (Renovación Nacional), and Republican Mobilization (Movilización Republicana). It included the same leaders who had been trying to unseat the Somozas for years: Carlos Pasos, Pedro Joaquín Chamorro, Luis Cardenal, Adán Selva, Emilio Borge González, and Reynaldo Téfel Vélez.
60. *New York Times,* 8 June 1969, p. 11; Unión Panamericana, *Aplicaciones,* p. 355.
61. In early March 1959, the National Assembly voted to censure President Echandi for meeting with Luis Somoza in a "cordial atmosphere." See *New York Times,* 11 March 1959, p. 5.
62. Unión Panamericana, *Aplicaciones,* p. 352.
63. *Diario de Costa Rica,* 14 June 1959, p. 1.
64. Unión Panamericana, *Aplicaciones,* p. 352.
65. Briones Torres, *Combate* 3, no. 17 (July-August 1961): 44-50.
66. *New York Times,* 20 April 1959, p. 1, and 23 August 1959, p. 33.

67. Ibid., 12 July 1959, p. 18, and 23 August 1959, p. 33.
68. Ibid., 23 August, 1959, p. 33.
69. Jules Dubois, *Operation America: The Communist Conspiracy in Latin America* (New York: Walker and Company, 1963), p. 242.
70. Unión Panamericana, *Aplicaciones,* pp. 352, 356. Suspecting that something was up, the Costa Rican government met with owners and managers of all airlines on 29 May and instructed them for the time being to use only pilots whom they trusted completely.
71. Ibid., p. 356; *Diario de Costa Rica,* 24 June 1959, p. 1.
72. *New York Times,* 10 June 1959, p. 15.
73. Unión Panamericana, *Aplicaciones,* p. 354; Briones Torres, *Combate* 3, no. 17 (July-August 1961): 47.
74. *Diario de Costa Rica,* 5, 6, and 9 June 1959; *New York Times,* 12 June 1959, p. 8.
75. *New York Times,* 12 June 1959, p. 8.
76. *Diario de Costa Rica,* 10 June 1959, p. 15; *La Prensa* (Managua), 10 June 1959, p. 1.
77. *Diario de Costa Rica,* 12 June 1959, p. 12, and 13 June 1959, p. 3.
78. Unión Panamericana, *Aplicaciones,* pp. 341-45. The source of the latter allegation was Johnny Abbes García, who claimed that the Dominican Military Intelligence Service had intercepted a message to Lacayo Farfán which related that three vessels loaded with armed reenforcements had departed from Batabanó, Cuba, for Nicaragua. See *Diario de Costa Rica,* 4 June 1959, p. 16.
79. *New York Times,* 8 June 1959, p. 11.
80. Ibid., 10 June 1959, p. 15.
81. John C. Dreier, *The Organization of American States and the Hemisphere Crisis* (New York: Harper and Row, 1962), p. 68.
82. Ibid., p. 69.
83. Unión Panamericana, *Aplicaciones,* pp. 349, 379-80.
84. Ibid., p. 354. In February 1959 Nicaragua and the Dominican Republic were suspected of aiding Honduran Colonel Armando Velásquez Cerrato in an attempt to overthrow Villeda Morales. The coup failed, and under the auspices of the OAS Honduras and Nicaragua signed a pact agreeing to control the activities of exile groups and to prevent the use of their territory for the preparation of subversive movements. The OAS felt that the failure of Honduras to ratify the treaty undermined the chances for peace in Central America.
85. *Diario de Costa Rica,* 28 June 1959, p. 7; *New York Times,* 12 July 1959, p. 20.
86. *New York Times,* 4, 12, and 13 July 1959.
87. *Diario de Costa Rica,* 19, 20, and 24 June 1959.
88. Ibid., 16 June 1959, p. 1.
89. Unión Panamericana, *Aplicaciones,* p. 357.
90. *Diario de Costa Rica,* 20 June 1959, p. 1.
91. Ibid., 21 June 1959, pp. 20, 25. The *Aerolíneas Nacionales* manager, Manuel Enrique Guerra V., was at the finca when the arms were delivered.
92. Ibid., 20 June 1959, p. 5.   93. Ibid., 21 June 1959, p. 10.
94. Ibid., 24 June 1959, pp. 1, 15.
95. See Unión Panamericana, *Aplicaciones,* p. 357.   96. Ibid., p. 381.
97. See Ibid., p. 353. The only loose end of the affair was the committee's inability to prove or disprove Nicaragua's charge that three ships with armed invaders had sailed from Cuba for Nicaragua.

98. *New York Times,* 12 March 1959, p. 15.
99. Ibid., 21 February 1959, p. 8
100. Rivas, *Historia,* 4: 59-7; interview by Robert Alexander with Angel Miolán, 15 February 1959, Alexander MSS. Castro conferred with the following: Francisco Castellanos, Francisco Canto, and José Horacio Rodríguez.
101. Interview by Alexander with Miolán, 15 February 1959, Alexander MSS.
102. *New York Times,* 9 August 1959, p. 1; *Life,* 17 August 1959.
103. The Caribbean Anti-Communist Research and Intelligence Bureau, *Invasion Report: Constanza, Maimón, Estero Hondo. Communist Aggression Against The Dominican Republic* (Ciudad Trujillo, 1959), p. 113. The *Invasion Report* asserted that the recruits were virtual prisoners and were subjected to Communist indoctrinating sessions.
104. Ibid., pp. 113-27, 220-22.
105. Ibid., p. 103; John B. Martin, *Overtaken by Events. The Dominican Crisis from the Fall of Trujillo to the Civil War* (New York: Doubleday and Company, Inc., 1966), p. 50.
106. Martin, *Overtaken,* p. 50; Crassweller, *Trujillo,* pp. 365-66.
107. *Invasion Report,* p. 76.   108. Ibid., p. 108.
109. *New York Times,* 6 November 1959, p. 9.
110. Szulc, *Winds,* p. 124.
111. Crassweller, *Trujillo,* p. 348.
112. *Invasion Report,* pp. 163, 177.
113. Martin, *Overtaken,* p. 51; Crassweller, *Trujillo,* pp. 371-72.
114. Crassweller, *Trujillo,* pp. 348-49.
115. Venezuela had contemplated this action for some time but had delayed out of concern for the safety of thirteen Dominicans who had taken refuge in its Ciudad Trujillo embassy in February 1959. There was also evidence that the Venezuelan embassy had been in contact with the Dominican underground.
116. *New York Times,* 29 June 1959, p. 8, and 11 July 1959, p. 1.
117. Rivas, *Historia,* 4: 59-37.
118. Unión Panamericana, *Aplicaciones,* pp. 387-90.
119. Dreier, *Organization,* p. 101.
120. See *Hemispherica* 8, no. 6 (September 1959): 1.
121. OEA, *Quinta Reunión de Consulta de Ministros de Relaciones Exteriores,* Santiago, Chile, 1959, documento 34.
122. *New York Times,* 15 August 1959, p. 1.
123. Salvador de Madariaga, *Latin America Between the Eagle and the Bear* (London: Hollis and Carter, 1962), p. 72.
124. Dreier, *Organization,* p. 75.
125. Szulc, *Winds,* pp. 115-16.
126. Organization of American States, *Ministers of Foreign Affairs, Fifth Meeting,* Santiago, Chile, 1959 (OEA/ser. F/II.5 Eng.), document 36, pp. 5-6.
127. OEA, *Quinta Reunión,* document 21, p. 14. Herrera Báez listed the following books as examples: *Historical Materialism, How to Be a Good Communist, The Work of the Party Among the Masses, Categories of Dialectical Materialism,* and *The Coming of the Revolution in Russia.*
128. Ibid., document 39. Roa also listed, *What is Fascism?,* by Benito Mussolini, and *Democratic Caesarism,* by Laureano Vallenilla Lanz.
129. Crassweller, *Trujillo,* pp. 349-52.
130. Unión Panamericana, *Quinta Reunión de Consulta de Ministros de Relaciones Exteriores, Santiago de Chile, Acta Final* (Washington, D.C., 1960), p. 8.

131. OAS, *Fifth Meeting,* document 18. This was in addition to the proposed study of the matter by the Peace Committee.

132. Organización de Estados Americanos, Séptima Reunión, San José, Costa Rica, 1960, *Documentos,* "Defensa y preservación de la democracia en América," memorandum preparado por la Secretaría General, PAU, pp. 12-13. (Mimeographed.) The Council of Jurists met in Santiago immediately after the Consultative Meeting and drew up treaty proposals for the creation and functioning of an inter-American court of human rights and for the functioning of the Human Rights Commission.

133. Unión Panamericana, *Quinta Reunión . . . Acta Final,* pp. 13-14.

134. Ibid., p. 5.   135. Ibid.

136. *New York Times,* 19 August 1959, p. 1, and 21 August 1959, p. 2.

137. Interview with Figueres.

138. Crassweller, *Trujillo,* p. 420; Dreier, *Organization,* pp. 97-98; Madariaga, *Latin America,* p. 127.

139. Martz, *Acción Democrática,* p. 296.

140. Rivas, *Historia,* 4: 62-21.

141. Martz, *Acción Democrática,* p. 180.

142. Quoted by Carlos Canache Mata, "La juventud de AD," *A.D.,* 23 November 1959.

143. Ibid.,   144. Ibid.

145. *New York Times,* 8 November 1958, p. 34.

146. Ibid., 23 November 1959, p. 1.

147. Rivas, *Historia,* 4: 60-21.

148. On 19 January 1960 Venezuelan authorities arrested the leader of the conspiracy, Carlos Savelli Maldonado, and seized documents outlining extensive plans for sabotage, terrorism, and assassination to be carried out by local terrorists, *perezjimenistas,* and Dominican agents. See ibid., p. 60-10.

149. Ibid.   150. Ibid., p. 60-11.

151. See Martz, *Acción Democrática,* pp. 180-81.

152. Rivas, *Historia,* 4: 60-21.

153. Martz, *Acción Democrática,* p. 182.

154. Rivas, *Historia,* 4, "Documento de los jóvenes de A.D. a la Dirección Nacional y a la militancia del partido," Appendix, document no. 5.

155. James Petras, "Revolution and Guerrilla Movements in Latin America: Venezuela, Guatemala, Colombia, and Peru," *Latin America: Reform or Revolution?,* ed. James Petras and Maurice Zeitlin (Greenwich, Connecticut: Fawcett Publications, Inc., 1968), pp. 339-40.

156. Rivas, *Historia,* 4, Appendix, document no. 5.

157. Rafael Pantoja, "El Instituto Internacional de Educación Política," *Combate* 3, no. 14 (January-February 1961): 59.

158. Escuela Interamericana de Educación Democrática, *Información General* (San José, Costa Rica, 1965), p. 9.

159. Ibid., pp. 10-11.

160. Ibid., p. 12. The author visited the school in March 1966.

161. General Castro León was aided by Rafael Trujillo in his attempt to overthrow Betancourt on 20 April. See Rivas, *Historia,* 4, 60-27.

162. *Hemispherica* 9, no. 3 (Summer 1960): 1-5.

163. "Declaración de Lima," *Latinoamérica más allá de sus fronteras,* Ediciones *Combate* (San José, Costa Rica, 1960), pp. 109-112.

164. Ibid.

165. On 24 June, Venezuela's Army Day, agents of Rafael Trujillo concealed an

explosive charge in an automobile parked along the traditional parade route. As Betancourt's presidential limousine passed by, the charge was detonated by a radio signal. Betancourt emerged from the flaming wreckage with severely burned hands, a military aide seated at his side was killed instantly. See Rivas, *Historia,* 4, 60-35–60-53, and Unión Panamericana, *Aplicaciones del Tratado Interamericano de Asistencia Recíproca: Suplemento, 1960-1961* (Washington, D.C., 1962), p. 24 passim.
166. "Declaración de Lima," pp. 113-15.

Bibliography

SOURCES

Public Documents

Acción Democrática. *Posición y Doctrina.* Publicación de la Secretaría Nacional de Propaganda. Caracas, 1962.

Comité Ejecutivo Nacional del Partido Acción Democrática. *Venezuela bajo el signo del terror, 1948-1952. El libro negro de la dictadura.* Santiago de Chile: Publicaciones Valmore Rodríguez [1953].

Dominican Republic. Ministry for Home Affairs. *White Book of Communism in the Dominican Republic.* Ciudad Trujillo [Santo Domingo], 1958.

Inter-American Association for Democracy and Freedom. *Report of the Second Inter-American Conference for Democracy and Freedom.* New York, 1961.

Jamison, Edward A. *Keeping Peace in the Caribbean Area.* U.S. Department of State Publication 3918. Washington, D.C., 1950.

Organization of American States. *Ministers of Foreign Affairs, Fifth Meeting.* Santiago, Chile, 1959. Documents 1-89. OEA/ser. F/II.5 Eng. (Mimeographed.)

Organización de Estados Americanos. *Quinta Reunión de Consulta de Ministros de Relaciones Exteriores.* Santiago, Chile, 1959. OEA/ser. F/II.5 (Mimeographed.)

ORIT-CIOSL. *15 años de sindicalismo libre interamericano, enero 1948-enero 1963.* 2d ed. Mexico, 1963.

ORIT-CIOSL. *La lucha permanente del movimiento sindical libre contra las dictaduras criollas.* Mexico, 1960.

ORIT-CIOSL. *The Permanent Struggle of the Free Trade Union Movement Against Latin American Dictatorships.* Mexico, 1960.

Unión Panamericana, Departamento de Asuntos Jurídicos. *Aplicaciones del Tratado Interamericano de Asistencia Recíproca, 1948-1960.* Washington, D.C., 1960.

Unión Panamericana, Departamento de Asuntos Jurídicos. *Quinta Reunión de Consulta de Ministros de Relaciones Exteriores, Santiago de Chile, Acta Final.* Washington, D.C., 1960.

U.S. Department of State. *American Foreign Policy, 1950-1955: Basic Documents.* 2 vols. Publication 6446. General Foreign Policy Series 117. Released July 1957.

U.S. Department of State. *American Foreign Policy: Current Documents, 1956.* Publication 6811. Released August 1959.

U.S. Department of State. *American Foreign Policy: Current Documents, 1957.* Publication 7101. Released February 1961.

U.S. Department of State. *A Case History of Communist Penetration: Guatemala.* Publication 6465. Washington, D.C., 1957.

U.S. Department of State. *Intervention of International Communism in Guatemala.* Publication 5556. Washington, D.C., 1954.

U.S. Department of State. *Peace in the Americas.* Publication 3964. Washington, D.C., 1950.

U.S. Foreign Broadcast Information Service. *Daily Report: Foreign Radio Broadcasts.* Vols. 1-351. January 1947-July 1955.

U.S. House of Representatives. *Report of the Subcommittee to Investigate Communist Aggression in Latin America to the Select Committee on Communist Aggression.* 83rd Cong., 2d sess., 1954. (Hillings Report.)

U.S. Senate, Committee on Foreign Relations. *United States-Latin American Relations.* Document No. 125, 86th Cong., 2d sess., 1960.

Venezuela y Guatemala. Discursos con motivo de la visita del Presidente Betancourt a Guatemala, 26 de julio de 1946. Guatemala: Tipografía Nacional de Guatemala, 1946.

Books

Abreu, José Vicente. *Se llama S.N.* 2d ed. Caracas: José Agustín Catalá, Editor, 1964.

Anti-Communist Liberation Movement of Venezuela. *Proof of the Communist Domination of Venezuela.* Caracas, 1959.

Arévalo, Juan José. *Anti-Kommunism in Latin America. An X-Ray of the Process Leading to a New Colonialism.* Translated by Carleton Beals. New York: Lyle Stuart, Inc., 1963.

Arévalo, Juan José. *Istmania; o, la unidad revolucionaria de Centroamérica.* Buenos Aires: Editorial Indoamérica, 1954.

Arévalo, Juan José. *The Shark and the Sardines.* Translated by June Cobb and Raúl Osegueda. New York: Lyle Stuart, Inc., 1961.

Argüello, Jr., Rosendo. *By Whom We Were Betrayed . . . And How.* (Facts of publication missing.)

Batista, Fulgencio. *The Growth and Decline of the Cuban Republic.* Translated by Blas M. Rocafort. New York: The Devin-Adair Company, 1964.

Bayo, Alberto. *Tempestad en el Caribe.* Mexico, 1950.

Betancourt, Rómulo. *Tres años de gobierno democrático, 1959-1962.* 3 vols. Caracas: Imprenta Nacional, 1962.

Betancourt, Rómulo. *Venezuela: política y petróleo.* Mexico. Fondo de Cultura Económica, 1956.

Bosch, Juan. *Trujillo: causas de una tiranía sin ejemplo.* Caracas: Librería "Las Novedades," 1959.

Bosch, Juan. *The Unfinished Experiment: Democracy in the Dominican Republic.* New York: Frederick A. Praeger, 1965.

The Caribbean Anti-Communist Research and Intelligence Bureau [CARIB]. *Invasion Report: Constanza, Maimón, Estero Hondo. Communist Aggression Against The Dominican Republic.* Ciudad Trujillo, 1959.

Castro Esquivel, Arturo. *José Figueres Ferrer. El hombre y su obra.* San José, Costa Rica: Imprenta Tormo, 1955.

Chamorro, Pedro Joaquín, *Estirpe sangrienta: los Somoza.* Buenos Aires: Editorial Triángulo, 1959.

Clements, Associates, John A. *Report on Venezuela.* New York: John A. Clements Associates [1959].

Corominas, Enrique V. *En las áreas políticas del Caribe.* Buenos Aires: Editorial "El Ateneo," 1952.

Corominas, Enrique V. *In the Caribbean Political Areas.* Translated by L. Charles Foresti. New York: University Press of Cambridge, Inc., 1954.

Damiron, Rafael. *Resumen. A los enemigos de Trujillo.* Ciudad Trujillo: Editora Montalvo, 1947.

Díaz Ordóñez, Virgilio. *La política exterior de Trujillo.* Vol. 2, *La Era de Trujillo. 25 años de Historia Dominicana.* Ciudad Trujillo: Impresora Dominicana, 1955.

Escuela Interamericana de Educación Democrática. *Información general.* San José, Costa Rica, 1965.

Espaillat, Arturo. *Trujillo: The Last Caesar.* Chicago: Henry Regnery Company, 1964.

Figueres, José. *Cartas a un ciudadano.* San José, Costa Rica: Imprenta Nacional, 1965.

Latinoamerica más allá de sus fronteras. Ediciones *Combate.* San José, Costa Rica, 1960.

Llovera, Analuisa. *Entre dos fuegos. Crisis de los derechos humanos en América.* Mexico: Ediciones Humanismo, 1957.

Montilla, Ricardo. *La Generación del 28 en la Historia de Venezuela.* Caracas: Imprenta Nacional, 1964.

Moreno, Edilberto. *Vida y lección de Antonio Pinto Salinas.* Mérida, Venezuela: Talleres Gráficos Universitarios, 1964.

Ornes, Germán E. *Trujillo: Little Caesar of the Caribbean.* New York: Thomas Nelson and Sons, 1958.

Ornes, Horacio. *Desembarco en Luperón. Episodio de la lucha por la democracia en la República Dominicana.* Mexico: Ediciones Humanismo, 1956.

Pepper, José Vicente. *I Accuse Braden.* Ciudad Trujillo: Editora Montalvo, 1947.

Rivas Rivas, José, ed. *Historia Gráfica de Venezuela.* Vol. 2, *El mundo y la época de Pérez Jiménez: Una historia contada en recortes de periódicos.* Vol. 4, *El gobierno de Rómulo Betancourt.* Caracas: Pensamiento Vivo, C.A., 1961 (vol. 2), 1965 (vol. 4).

Rodríguez, José. *Quién derrocó a Gallegos?* Caracas: Tipografía Garrido, 1961.

Rodríguez, Valmore. *Bayonetas sobre Venezuela.* Mexico, 1950.

Romualdi, Serafino. *Presidents and Peons: Recollections of a Labor Ambassador in Latin America* New York: Funk and Wagnalls, 1967.

Rómulo Betancourt: interpretación de su doctrina popular y democrática. Editado por SUMA, librería y editorial. Caracas, 1958

Rómulo Betancourt: pensamiento y acción. Recopilado y editado por miembros de Acción Democrática en el exilio. Mexico, 1951.

Rómulo Betancourt: posición y doctrina. Edited by Editorial Cordillera. Caracas: Editorial Cordillera, 1959.

Welles, Sumner. *The Time for Decision.* New York: Harper and Brothers Publishers, 1944.

Articles and Periodicals

A.D. Organo Central del Partido Acción Democrática. Caracas, Venezuela. 1962-1965.

Bohemia (Havana). 1948-1952.

Borge González, Emilio. "Nicaragua por dentro." *Combate* 1, no. 5 (March-April 1959): 33-42.

Briones Torres, Ignacio. "Angustia y esperanza de Nicaragua." *Combate* 3, no. 17 (July-August 1961): 44-50.

CARIB (Ciudad Trujillo [Santo Domingo]). Fourteen Issues (Reports). April 1958-October 1958.

"La 'Declaración de Caracas.' " *Combate* 1, no. 4 (January-February 1959): 2.

Falchetti, Oscar. "Haya de la Torre: Odiseo de Indoamérica." *Combate* 4, no. 24 (September-October 1962): 59-71.

Haya de la Torre, Víctor Raúl. "La declaración democrática de Caracas." *Combate* 1, no. 5 (March-April 1959): 29-32.

Hemispherica. Bulletin of the U.S. Committee of the Inter-American Association for Democracy and Freedom. 1951-1960.

Hispanic American Report. Stanford University: Hispanic American Studies. 1948-1958.

"Instituto de Educación Política." *Combate* 2, no. 8 (January-February 1960): 5-6.

Núñez, Benjamín. "La función social de la religión." *Combate* 1, no. 4 (January-February 1959): 32-41.

Oduber, Daniel, and Monge, Luis Alberto. "Dictaduras, imperialismo y democracia." *Combate* 2, no. 9 (March-April 1960): 12-20.

Pacheco, León. "Evolución del pensamiento democrático de Costa Rica," *Combate* 3, no. 15 (March-April 1961): 31-43.

Pantoja, Rafael. "El Instituto Internacional de Educación Política." *Combate* 3, no. 14 (January-February 1961): 59-61.

Ruíz, Antonio Santiago. "La acción revolucionaria del Partido Auténtico." *Combate* 2, no. 9 (March-April 1960): 36-40.

Venezuela Democrática. Editado por Venezolanos Desterrados. Fifteen issues. Mexico, April 1955-September 1957.

Villanueva del Campo, Armando. "Partidos democrático-revolucionarios en Indoamérica." *Combate* 3, no. 18 (September-October 1961): 13-18.

Newspapers

Diario de Costa Rica (San José). 1954-1959.
El Mundo (Havana). September-October 1947.
El Nacional (Caracas).
New York Times. 1944-1959.
Noticias de Hoy (Havana). September 1947.
La Prensa (Managua). 1954-1959,
Ultimas Noticias (Caracas). 1958.

Other Sources

Alexander, Robert J. Manuscripts. Consisting of papers, letters, and transcribed interviews from the personal files of Professor Robert J. Alexander. Department of Economics, Rutgers, The State University, New Brunswick, New Jersey.

Ameringer, Charles D. Personal interview with Simón Alberto Consalvi. Caracas, Venezuela, 14 June 1965.

Ameringer, Charles D. Personal interview with José Figueres. San José, Costa Rica, 16 December 1966.

Ameringer, Charles D. Personal interview with Miss Frances Grant. New York, 20 September 1966.

Ameringer, Charles D. Personal interview with Rigoberto Henríquez Vera. Caracas, Venezuela, 16 June 1965.

Ameringer, Charles D. Personal interview with Ricardo Montilla. Caracas, Venezuela, 17 June 1965.

Ameringer, Charles D. Personal interview with Raúl Nass. Washington, D.C., 21 February 1969.

Ameringer, Charles D. Personal interview with Father Benjamín Núñez. San José and La Lucha, Costa Rica, 3-4 January 1969.

Ameringer, Charles D. Personal interview with General Genevevo Pérez Dámera. Miami, Florida, 9 August 1967.

Ameringer, Charles D. Personal interview with Enrique Tejera-París. University Park, Pennsylvania, 19 April 1965.

Ameringer, Charles D. Personal interview with Norman Thomas. New York, 20 September 1966.

Paz Galarraga, Jesús A. "Acción política del gobierno democrático." Address before the Popular Unviersity, "Alberto Carnevali." Caracas, 1963. (Mimeographed.)

Secondary Works

Aguilar, Luis E., ed. *Marxism in Latin America.* New York: Alfred A. Knopf, 1968.

Aitken, Thomas, Jr. *Luis Muñoz Marín: Poet in the Fortress.* New York: The New American Library, 1965.

Alba, Víctor, *Populism and National Awareness in Latin America.* Occasional Publications no. 6. Center of Latin American Studies. The University of Kansas. Lawrence, Kansas, June 1966.

Alexander, Robert J. *Prophets of the Revolution: Profiles of Latin American Leaders.* New York: The Macmillan Company, 1962.

Alexander, Robert J. *The Venezuelan Democratic Revolution. A Profile of the Regime of Rómulo Betancourt.* New Brunswick: Rutgers University Press, 1964.

Beals, Carleton. *The Crime of Cuba.* Philadelphia: J. B. Lippincott Company, 1933.

Crassweller, Robert D. *Trujillo: The Life and Times of a Caribbean Dictator.* New York: The Macmillan Company, 1966.

Dreier, John C. *The Organization of American States and the Hemisphere Crisis.* New York: Harper and Row, 1962.

Dubois, Jules. *Operation America: The Communist Conspiracy in Latin America.* New York: Walker and Company, 1963.

Eisenhower, Milton S. *The Wine is Bitter. The United States and Latin America.* New York: Doubleday and Company, Inc., 1963.

Fitzgibbon, Russell H. *Cuba and the United States, 1900-1935.* Menasha, Wisconsin: George Banta Publishing Company, 1935.

Gardner, Mary A. *The Inter-American Press Association: Its Fight for Freedom of the Press, 1926-1960.* Latin American Monographs, no. 6. Institute of Latin American Studies. The University of Texas. Austin: University of Texas Press, 1967.

Gil, Federico G. "Antecedents of the Cuban Revolution." *Reform and Revolution. Readings in Latin American Politics.* Edited by Arpad von Lazar and Robert R. Kaufman. Boston: Allyn and Bacon, Inc., 1969.

James, Daniel. *Red Design for the Americas: Guatemalan Prelude.* New York: The John Day Company, 1954.

Jensen, Amy Elizabeth. *Guatemala. A Historical Survey.* New York: Exposition Press, 1955.

Kantor, Harry. "The Development of Acción Democrática de Venezuela." *Journal of Inter-American Studies* 1, no. 2 (1959): 237-55.

Kantor, Harry. "El Programa Aprista para Perú y Latinoamérica." *Combate* 1, no. 3 (November-December 1958): 19-27.

Krehm, William. *Democracia y tiranías en el Caribe.* Buenos Aires: Editorial Parnaso, 1957.

"Latin America's Nationalistic Revolutions." *The Annals* of the American Academy of Political and Social Science, 334 (March 1961). Complete issue.

Lipset, Seymour Martin, and Solari, Aldo, eds. *Elites in Latin America.* New York: Oxford University Press, 1967.

Macaulay, Neill. *The Sandino Affair.* Chicago: Quadrangle Books, 1967.

MacGaffey, Wyatt, and Barnett, Clifford R. *Twentieth Century Cuba.* Garden City, New York: Doubleday and Company, 1965.

Madariaga, Salvador de. *Latin America Between The Eagle and The Bear.* London: Hollis and Carter, 1962.

Martin, John Bartlow. *Overtaken By Events. The Dominican Crisis from the Fall of Trujillo to the Civil War.* New York: Doubleday and Company, Inc., 1966.

Martz, John D. *Acción Democrática. Evolution of a Modern Political Party in Venezuela.* Princeton: Princeton University Press, 1966.

Martz, John D. *Central America: The Crisis and the Challenge.* Chapel Hill: University of North Carolina Press, 1959.

Martz, John D., ed. *The Dynamics of Change in Latin America.* Englewood Cliffs, New Jersey: Prentice-Hall, Inc., 1965.

Mathews, Thomas. *Luis Muñoz Marín.* New York: American R.D.M. Corporation, 1967.

Mecham, J. Lloyd. *A Survey of United States-Latin American Relations.* Boston: Houghton-Mifflin Company, 1965.

Mecham, J. Lloyd. *The United States and Inter-American Security, 1889-1960.* Austin: University of Texas Press, 1961.

Morris, George. *CIA and American Labor. The Subversion of the AFL-CIO's Foreign Policy.* New York: International Publishers, 1967.

Petras, James, and Zeitlin, Maurice, eds. *Latin America: Reform or Revolution?* Greenwich, Connecticut: Fawcett Publications, Inc., 1968.

Phillips, Ruby Hart. *Cuba: Island of Paradox.* New York: McDowell, Obolensky, 1959.

Rodríguez, Mario. *Central America.* Englewood Cliffs, New Jersey: Prentice-Hall, Inc., 1965.

Rosenthal, Mario. *Guatemala. The Story of an Emergent Latin American Democracy.* New York: Twayne Publishers, Inc., 1962.

Schneider, Ronald M. *Communism in Guatemala, 1944-1954.* New York: Frederick A. Praeger, 1959.

Serxner, Stanley J. *Acción Democrática of Venezuela. Its Origin and Development.* The Latin American Monograph Series, no. 9. The University of Florida. Gainesville: University of Florida Press, 1959.

342   *Bibliography*

Silvert, Kalman H. *The Conflict Society: Reaction and Revolution in Latin America.* New Orleans: The Hauser Press, 1961.
Szulc, Tad. *The Winds of Revolution. Latin America Today—And Tomorrow.* New York: Frederick A. Praeger, 1963.
Wilgus, A. Curtis, ed. *The Caribbean: Its Political Problems.* Gainesville: University of Florida Press, 1956.

Index